For Tracie,

With appreciation for your helpfulness in helping me through "the end" of the book and best wishes to a wonderful young woman with many talents.

Andy.

Ellen

QUALITY CHILD CARE

QUALITY CHILD CARE

A Comprehensive Guide
for Administrators and Teachers

Ellen S. Cromwell

Georgetown Hill Child Care Center, Inc.
Potomac, Maryland

Allyn and Bacon

Boston • London • Toronto • Sydney • Tokyo • Singapore

I dedicate this book to you, the reader,
in whose hands children will place their trust.

Copyright © 1994 by Allyn and Bacon
A Division of Paramount Publishing
160 Gould Street
Needham Heights, Massachusetts 02194

Library of Congress Cataloging-in-Publication Data

Cromwell, Ellen S.
    Quality child care: a comprehensive guide for administrators and
  teachers / Ellen S. Cromwell.
        p.   cm.
    Includes bibliographical references and index.
    ISBN 0-205-15322-4
       1. Day care centers—United States. 2. Child care—United States.
  3. Child development—United States. I. Title.
HV854.C76   1994
362.7'12'068—dc20   93-30883
                                               CIP

Credits

Pages xii, 64, 175, 192, 352, and 378: Poetry from *Everychild's Everyday* by Cindy Herbert and Susan
  Russell. Copyright © 1980 by Learning About Learning. Used by permission of Doubleday, a
  division of Bantam Doubleday Dell Publishing Group, Inc.

Pages 72–74: Insurance information provided by Kathleen O'Brien of the Child Care Law Center
  from their December 1992 publication. Used with permission.

Page 303: Poem from "Weather Conditions" in *4-Way Stop and Other Poems* by Myra Cohn
  Livingston. Copyright © 1976 by Myra Cohn Livingston. Reprinted by permission of Marian
  Reiner for the author.

Pages 342–43: Information about children's literature from Shelton, H., ed., "Books for Children,"
  in *Childhood Education*, 1989, 1990. Reprinted by permission of Helen Shelton and the Association for Childhood Education International (11141 Georgia Avenue, Suite 200, Wheaton, MD).
  Copyright © by the Association.

Printed in the United States of America
10 9 8 7 6 5 4 3 2 1   97 96 95 94 93

About the Author

Ellen Cromwell is the Director/Founder of the Georgetown Hill Child Care Center in Montgomery County, Maryland. The Center has been recognized as a model for quality child care by the State of Maryland. She has worked in the field of early childhood education for twenty-five years as an administrator and a teacher. Through direct experience she has gained knowledge and insight about children in out-of-home environments.

While earning her master's degree in education from The American University, Washington, D.C., Ellen designed a language experience reading model for pre-school children. The project was published in an educational periodical and eventually developed into a book, *Feathers in My Cap: Early Reading Through Experience,* that was published in 1980 by Acropolis Books, Ltd., Washington, D.C.

Ellen has conducted numerous workshops in early childhood education for teachers and parents. She is an active member of the Association for Childhood Education International's Maryland chapter, a member of the National Association for the Education of Young Children, the Maryland Community Association for the Education of Young Children, and is active in community child care organizations. She especially enjoys children's literature and, inspired by the recent arrival of two grandchildren, is currently working on several picture books.

Contents

Foreword

For many years early childhood professionals have studied development of the "whole" child within the family and the community. We have been persistent in making the point that all areas of development—social, emotional, physical, as well as intellectual—are important if a child is to reach her or his full potential. We also have been crusaders for integrative curriculum and developmentally appropriate practice that speaks to the needs of the whole child within the family and the community.

In this book, Ellen Cromwell applies the same principles to the development, administration, and implementation of quality early childhood programs by presenting the "whole" of quality early childhood programs. She has not segregated the history, theory, philosophy, and current public policy of early childhood education from the day-to-day operation and curriculum of an early childhood program. In presenting her "PLAN" curriculum, Ellen demonstrates the integration of theory, philosophy, research, best practice, her own creativity, and her years of experience.

Quality Child Care: A Comprehensive Guide for Administrators and Teachers should be especially helpful to college and university professors, education coordinators, and directors of day care programs who are working with preprofessionals. Often, it is difficult for preprofessionals to see the relationships between history, child development theory, philosophy, and the public policy of early childhood education as they relate to their daily lesson plans. By looking at the history and the current status of early childhood education in this and other countries around the world, this book gives the reader a sense of where early childhood education has been developmentally, and where we are now. Chapter 3, A New Century: A New Beginning, gives readers a glimpse of the not so distant future.

Ellen's integrative approach demonstrates that continuing improvement of quality in early childhood programs is very complex and multifaceted. Today, it is not enough for administrators and teachers to understand just child development, or to be just a curriculum "whiz," if it ever was. Now, more than ever, it is important to know and internalize the "whole" to achieve a quality early childhood program. *Quality Child Care* will help readers begin the journey toward providing quality programs for all young children.

Kim F. Townley, Ph.D.
Associate Professor
Director Early Childhood Laboratory
University of Kentucky

I like to think
In my room alone,
I like to dream
In a tree,
I like to invent on
The kitchen table,
In the backyard,
I like to run free,
I like to ponder,
On the living room couch,
In the big chair with you,
I read,
I like to watch things
Outside my window
Each place in my home
Is a special place
That fits the life
I lead.

—From Everychild's Everyday
by Cindy Herbert and Susan Russell

Preface

The purpose of this book is to provide a useful guide for quality child care environments at preschool and school-age levels for all children from ages one through ten. It is appropriate for use by college and university students, professionals and practitioners in the field, administrators, and by any organization that is advocating for child care at the workplace. Parents also may find the book helpful in selecting and evaluating a child care center and in understanding child development.

Quality Child Care: A Comprehensive Guide for Administrators and Teachers has, in large part, been written out of a concern for children in child care environments. It is based on the premise that current standards for child care alone will not ensure quality or provide children with the requisites for growing up in today's society. If children are to grow up feeling good about themselves and about the world they live in, their early environments must begin to be modeled after home environments, and teachers need to become more like mothers. When that happens, teachers will be able to:

* Work with children from a total child perspective;
* Recognize the importance of nurturing in children's development;
* Help children value and respect themselves and others;
* Train children in practical life skills so that they can develop independence and competency;
* Help children develop good habits for healthy living;
* Help children make thoughtful and appropriate choices;
* Motivate and stimulate the creative potential in children;
* Give children time and space to experience the world through their eyes—in the child's own way;
* Help children cope with problems, stress, and feelings of aloneness;
* Help children feel happy, secure, and loved.

Within this extended family concept, parents and caregivers naturally become partners in raising and caring for children. Each acknowledges the importance of the other in the life of a child. Together, they share in the joys, the memorable moments, and the disappointments that are part of a child's every day.

The rewards will be great. A parent will leave a child in the morning feeling confident that every moment of the day will hold potential for the child. The parent will know the teacher and the teacher will know the parent. Each will recognize the importance of working together on behalf of the child. The child will think of the day care environment as something like home and the caregiver(s) as someone like a real mom. The child will have a sense of connection and continuity between center and home.

This book is divided into six sections: a prospectus on child care, designing a child care center, partners in leadership, child development, a child-centered curriculum, and a child centered-environment. The sections are carefully integrated and interdependent. The book evolves from a child-centered philosophy. Each section provides valuable information and ideas for developing a quality child care center at preschool and school-age levels. From an *administrative perspective,* the reader will become informed about designing and managing a center that is homelike in feeling and attitude yet efficiently run. From an *educational perspective,* the reader will become familiar with relevant principles of child development and learn how to apply them to a child-centered program. From an *environmental perspective,* the reader will become excited about creating an environment that makes children eager to explore and discover. From a *practical perspective,* the reader will become motivated by the wide range of creative activities, teaching methods, and ideas that complement and reinforce the curriculum presented in this book. In most cases, feminine pronouns are used when referring to teachers, administrators, and directors because women have been, and continue to be, the ones working in child care professions.

The child development approach developed in *Quality Child Care* is articulated through a curriculum called *PLAN.* The curriculum is based on the belief that preschool and school-age children in child care environments thrive if they experience an integrated, developmentally appropriate program that includes as primary components: *Play, Learning, the Arts,* and *Nurturing.* The PLAN program reflects current thinking among leading educators in the field, is appropriate to all child care environments, and is developmentally appropriate for children at all age levels. It is premised on a child-centered philosophy of respecting children's natural ability and desire to learn. In a child-centered environment, children experience themselves as positive, caring, and productive members of a group.

The ongoing theme presented here is that children must be given the opportunity to fully experience the stages and needs of childhood without losing their identity or their natural enthusiasm for learning. This can best be accomplished by designing a program that provides a variety of experiences in an unhurried, supportive environment—an environment that allows time for self-exploration and discovery as well as group experiences. An open, supportive environment encourages children to believe in and nurture their talents and resources. Like *The Little Engine That Could,* a combination of self-belief, initiative, encouragement, and friendship helps children climb mountains.

In this context, learning is considered an open-ended, building-block process that is generated by the learner, guided by the teacher, and reinforced by the environment. Time is not an imperative in the PLAN program. Within existing constraints, children are free to complete projects and transition comfortably from one activity to another. Structure is not an imperative in this program. In a positive, challenging environment that is process oriented, teachers do not feel compelled to over-schedule or hurry a child through a day.

In a child-centered environment, children begin to know themselves and believe in themselves. They will:

- Be accepting and caring friends;
- Be supportive and helpful;
- Respect their center, their friends, and themselves;
- Be responsible members of the group;
- Use their time constructively;
- Develop initiative and resourcefulness;
- Cultivate interests and talents;
- See value in work and play;
- Plan, begin, and complete projects naturally as they interact with materials and express ideas;
- Solve problems, make choices, and practice good thinking;
- Practice self-care, independence, and healthy habits;
- Develop healthy values and responsible points of view;
- Express love and kindness toward all living things;
- Be productive and caring members of society.

In a homelike environment that *feels right* and *fits right,* children can experience the potential in *every day.* They experience themselves as initiators and creators and act like positive and caring members of a group. They become active, enthusiastic learners, cultivating the seeds for lifelong learning so that even in the city, a garden will grow and little blue trains will continue to puff along life's way saying, *"I think I can!"*

> *Children must have at least one person who believes*
> *in them. It could be a counselor, a teacher, a preacher,*
> *a friend. It could be you. You never know when a*
> *little love, a little support, will plant a small seed of*
> *hope* (The Measure of Our Success, *1992*).
> —*Marian Wright Edelman, President*
> *Children's Defense Fund*

Acknowledgments

I would like to acknowledge with special appreciation the child development specialists who have reviewed and contributed to the development of this book: Nick Coleman, The University of Georgia, Athens, Georgia; Elizabeth (Bettie) Gehring, Bowling Green State University, Bowling Green, Ohio; Penny Luken, Broward Community College, Coconut Creek, Florida; Roger Neugebauer, Publisher/Editor, *Child Care Information Exchange,* Redmond, Washington; Carolyn Rybicki, Program Director, Child Care Programs of St. Louis, Missouri; and Kim Townley, University of Kentucky, Lexington, Kentucky.

Many thanks to Mylan Jaixen, Editor, and Susan Hutchinson, Editorial Assistant, at Allyn and Bacon for their confidence and encouragement; and to my editor, Marilyn Rash, at Ocean Publication Services for her unfailing support, patience, and helpfulness in bringing this book to completion.

Doubleday gave me permission to use several beautiful verses from *Everychild's Everyday,* written by Cindy Herbert and Susan Russell, from the Learning About Learning Educational Series, 1980. The Montgomery County Department of Health, Child Care Division, Montgomery County, Maryland, gave much appreciated permission to use portions of their informative publication, *Health Guidelines for Child Care Providers,* written by Lisa Kohlman, Sandra Straud, and Kathleen Woods. I also would like to acknowledge the assistance provided by state and local community leaders and the Montgomery County Public School System.

My heartfelt thanks to my staff for their contributions to quality child care and to the Georgetown Hill Child Care Center; to Ken Cobb for his beautiful and sensitive photographs of children at play; to Joyce Berghane for giving me the wonderful photograph that is on the cover of the book; to Nichole Queen and Tracie Czerwinski for their secretarial assistance and belief in this book; to my children—Bill, John, Peter, Kristen; to Mary Batz Cromwell; and especially to my husband Bill for his unfailing encouragement and inspiration throughout this project; and to my grandchildren Kelly and Sam for reminding me once again of the miracles of childhood.

And last, but not least, my thanks to the many children who have touched and continue to touch my life every day.

Now the garden-beds are blooming,
Water-pot in hand we're coming,
All the thirsty plants to sprinkle,
All the buds begin to twinkle,
Scatter now their perfume rare,
They open their petals one by one,
They roll out their cups to the glowing sun,
Rewarding all our tender care.

— From Mother-Play and Nursery Songs
by Friedrich Froebel (1878)

PART I

A PROSPECTUS ON CHILD CARE

The purpose of a nation depends primarily upon the way its children were brought up a generation earlier. The way to improve the nation of tomorrow is to improve the lives of its children today.

— *Robert J. Havighurst*

1

AN HISTORICAL PERSPECTIVE

CHANGING PATTERNS

Children, like plants, need tender care. They need nurturing from caring adults and nourishment from their surrounding environment. They need to experience a world that is large enough to inspire imagination yet small enough to investigate in the palm of a hand. They need quality environments to care for and protect them until they are old enough to plant their own gardens.

Amidst the undercurrents of anxiety surrounding the issue of child care, it is natural to look back in time to nursery rhymes and poetic verses with a sense of nostalgia and loss. In Friedrich Froebel's kindergarten imagery, the young child was nurtured in a gardenlike environment away from the evils of society. The child danced, played, and learned in a wholesome, protected environment. The "garden" was a place to cultivate and awaken children's natural curiosity and manifold talents, a place where children were shielded from a far less innocent adult world. To a modern-day educator, Froebel is likened to a Mother Goose character—perhaps the Pied Piper who was always there to lead children in the right direction. And even when children went astray, there was always a quick remedy or a happy ending to satisfy the enraptured child.

Not so long ago, children lived at home during their formative years under traditional childrearing systems that provided, for most children, a sense of continuity and security. Now many young children spend ten hours a day in child care environments outside of their natural homes. During most of their waking hours, mothers have been replaced by caregivers and brothers and sisters by peers.

While the locus of child care has changed, children's needs have not. The basic needs of nourishment, affection, and security still provide the basis for a healthy childhood. These needs were accessible to yesterday's child—strolling in the park with grandpa, storytime on grown-up laps, decorating for holidays, catching tadpoles in nearby streams, and playing in mud. There was ample time for imagination and uninterrupted play.

Kindergarten used to be a long-awaited milestone for the growing-up child. For most children it was a gentle, positive beginning to school. Play was still the springboard for child development but now it took place under supervised conditions. Children learned to adjust their play patterns to the rules of school, and there were compensations—new games, new friends, new experiences. To the young child, school was almost, but not quite, like home.

The transition from kindergarten to first grade was not without adjustment, at least until 3:00 P.M. when once again the child's world became one of play and freedom. In a natural, unstructured setting, drama was not staged by adults—children invented their own pretend games using the resources available to them. They chose their activities and competed with one another on their own terms. They made the rules and knew the importance of team play. If there were problems, they were solved quickly so as not to interrupt the game. Despite occasional battle scars, the child learned to function and to prosper without a great deal of supervision. As children invented, solved problems, cooperated, and controlled their own play world, they developed useful skills that were preparing them for adulthood.

For most children in home environments, play was balanced with work—household chores, sibling care, and homework. At the end of the day, lessons were spread on a kitchen table marred by time and scarred by pencils. With few interruptions, the work got done. Then too, there was always the smell of dinner to hurry the child along—aromas of childhood that would linger well into adulthood.

These natural childhood experiences are less accessible to today's child. Many little children are on the doorsteps of centers before 7:00 in the morning. Barely walking, they are pushed out of the nest at an early age and expected to fly. In the hustle-bustle of managing time, there is not much thought to the readiness or adjustment process. With a quick signature, children are entrusted to an environment that will become a primary influence in their formative years.

Unfortunately, the environment is not always homelike in appearance or feeling. For a child in group day care, a bed has been replaced by a cot and a bedroom by a resting room with matching cots spaced to accommodate many children in one room. Sleep does not come easily for children in day care centers, perhaps because they are overly stimulated from routines, instructions, and too many distractions. Sitting on cots, rubbing their eyes, young children wait patiently for someone to help them make the transition into afternoon activities. If there are more than twelve children in the room, the wait can be interminably long—but children can adjust, so we are told.

In many child care environments, each day becomes a copy of the day before. There can be no park or store stops when mom and dad are working. There is little opportunity for visiting with friends or relatives after school, no dog to wag its tail in an after-school greeting, and no telephone for after-school companionship. The smells of the kitchen are reduced to instant meals and tables are no longer set for evening companionship. After a long day, parents have little time or energy left to entertain children. Quality time has been replaced by television—an escape from a routinized, uneventful everyday.

Today's method of childrearing is raising questions that suggest deepening concern about the well-being of young children. A young child is surrounded by a number of interrelated circumstances, many of which he or she has little control over. He may be told that mommy is going to work, but he cannot possibly comprehend how this information will affect him. "What will happen to me?" often is acted out by the child's behavior—anxiety, thumb sucking, bed-wetting, temper tantrums, speech disorders.

We are not certain what is happening to children. We only know that there is now an entrenched system of childrearing practices brought about by changing patterns of family life. Until research studies can systematically evaluate this new method of childrearing, we can only speculate about the effects of out-of-home care on children. Meanwhile, parents continue to feel concern about their children. What is my child doing at 10:00 in the morning? at 12:00? Is she a happy child? Has she eaten her lunch? Will she get enough rest and outdoor play? What does she talk about? And the provider? What is her background and training? What qualifies her to care for my child? When does she find respite from the children in her care? How many jobs is she holding down in order to make a living? Questions lead to doubt and to feelings of uneasiness. The sometimes negative image of day care does little to quell the inner voices of anxious parents.

In *The Hurried Child,* David Elkind (1981) expresses the concern educators and parents are feeling about the discomforting conditions that are changing childhood.

The contemporary parent dwells in a pressure cooker of competing demands, transitions, role changes, personal and professional uncertainties, over which he or she exerts slight direction. We seek release from stress whenever we can, and usually the one sure ambit of our control is the home. Here, if nowhere else, we enjoy the fact (or illusion) of playing a determining role. If childrearing necessarily entails stress, then by hurrying children to grow up, or by treating them as adults, we hope to remove a portion of our burden of worry and anxiety and to enlist our children's aid in carrying life's load. We do not mean our children harm in acting thus—on the contrary, as a society we have come to imagine that it is good for young people to mature rapidly. Yet we do our children harm when we hurry them through childhood.[1]

The state of child care in today's society challenges educators and newcomers to the field. A fertile field requires careful attention if it is to yield a good harvest. Until child care is seen as an *integral* part of the American educational experience, it will not give rise to quality, it will not provide children with a strong foundation on which to grow and prosper, and it will not serve the basic needs of the American family.

THE BEGINNINGS OF CHILD CARE

Day Nurseries

Traditionally, childrearing has been seen as the responsibility of parents. Good childrearing practices have been identified with common values that have been passed on from generation to generation. Throughout much of our history, however, parents have not always been able to provide proper care for their children. Since the national government, for the most part, has been unwilling to subsidize child care, efforts to care for children in poverty were begun and promoted not by national policies but by individuals.

At the turn of the century, early reformers were successful in raising consciousness about children in poverty. Rescuing neglected children from urban squalor became a mission of mercy for early reformers like Jane Addams. Settlement houses, such as Hull House, founded in Chicago in 1889, sprang up in industrial areas to help immigrants assimilate into a new world and to provide children with basic care and training that was meant to lift them out of poverty and make them productive citizens.[2] Immigrant families, unfamiliar with the American way of life, found refuge and friendship in these centers. The provision of comprehensive care to children of needy families, in the form of day nurseries, began what is now called the child care movement. Throughout the century, and particularly during the World Wars when women were expected to work, day nurseries were considered integral support systems for families and society.

Contemporary child care should be seen as a full-service system providing families and centers with a network of support and resources to draw upon. All children need access to high-quality child care programs. Families need support and training in caring for their young, in selecting appropriate out-of-home environments, and in finding the resources that enable them to raise their children with a sense of pride and dignity. Community centers can serve families and centers by making resources and activities available at little or no cost. They might have, for example, a lending library of toys, books, records, and parent-education magazines. They also might provide family workshops and counseling in parenting, childrearing, and selecting a child care center.

The German Kindergarten

Friedrich Froebel (1782–1852) is credited with designing a school that reflected the nature of the young child. Froebel organized the first kindergarten in Germany in 1837. Characterized as "children's gardens," these kindergartens were intended to awaken the child's inner spirit through creative activities. Froebel believed that all children were born with a capacity for beauty and knowledge and that from the beginning, they should experience perfect harmony and tranquility. This was best accomplished through playlike experiences that encouraged cooperation and natural expression.[3]

Froebel's activities for children's play were carefully prescribed to arouse interest and investigation. Children engaged in games and constructive activities that were carefully designed to hold attention. He defined ten "gifts" (objects)—the first three consisted of a ball, a cube, and a cylinder. The gifts were designed to awaken perceptions of unity, relations, connections, and diversity in the young child.[4] The precise nature and use of the gifts reflected Froebel's penchant for logical thinking. He designed the gifts with materials such as craftwork or clay in order to foster curiosity and a desire to learn. The curriculum was augmented by pleasureful group activities that also were carefully prescribed by Froebel. Children engaged in group singing, games, and nature study.

A curriculum for young children should reflect their developmental levels and interests. Learning by doing is fundamental to understanding. A program must provide alternating periods for active and quiet play so that children can exercise and rest their bodies and their minds. Children need to become familiar with the gifts of nature. Nature contains a vast reservoir of materials for teaching and learning through hands-on, sensory experiences. In a natural, outdoor environment, children are their happiest and most resourceful. They learn about shapes and textures and living things as they experiment with nature. They discover rainbows, spider webs, and the happenings of early spring. A child care classroom should be designed as an indoor/outdoor environment.

American Kindergartens

The Froebelian kindergarten quickly became implanted on American shores. The first kindergarten program was established in Watertown, Wisconsin, in 1856. Influenced by philosopher John Dewey (1858–1952), American kindergartens gradually resembled small communities organized around democratic living.[5] Rejecting Froebel's prescribed system for learning through play, Dewey believed that play should reveal a child's innate resources—images and interests that are expressed experientially through constructive activities and interests. This was an active, organic approach to learning that encouraged experimentation, reasoning, and problem solving.

In 1923, Patty Smith Hill, an innovative early educator, applied Dewey's child-study movement to an experimental kindergarten curriculum that focused on children's play and expressive activities, such as art and music, as primary channels for learning. Her concept rapidly became a model for early education in the United States. Under Hill's guidance, kindergarten was perceived as a unique experience that was decisively different from formal schooling. In Hill's design, a teacher of young children was perceived more as a guide than as an instructor. The curriculum, referred to as *Conduct Curriculum,* encouraged children toward initiative, independence, good habits, and social cooperation.[6] Children's progress was carefully monitored and evaluated according to Hill's list of desirable habits for young children.

Blocks were an important medium for learning through cooperative play. Varying sizes and shapes of blocks were carefully designed and organized so that children could discover their physical properties. Hands-on learning through play engaged and motivated the young child.

During the decade of the sixties, a traditional child-centered approach to kindergarten was seen by many as denying children a valid, purposeful educational experience—one that would prepare them for academic proficiency in public school. Gradually, a more formal, content-oriented approach to teaching and learning began to dominate kindergarten environments. Readiness skills were considered essential to preprimary learning. Table work, which did little to generate thinking or active learning, was identified with industriousness. Work and play were treated as two separate functions—work (identified with learning) was something children had to do; play (identified with enjoyment) was recreation.

Similarly, a readiness mentality began to filter down to nursery schools that increasingly resembled "little kindergartens." In the process, children's active play needs were pushed aside. Tables and chairs encroached on play space while learning charts monopolized wall space. Like the kindergarten teacher, the nursery school teacher saw herself as an instructor rather than guide, and the child as a member of a group rather than an individual. In recent years, there has been a shift away from a skill-oriented, readiness approach to early childhood education.

Kindergarten education influences both preschool and school-age curriculums. A child care teacher should keep abreast of trends and issues in the field so that the curriculum can reinforce and expand what children are learning.

Today, kindergarten stands at the forefront of educational reform. According to developmentally appropriate guidelines, programs are reflecting child development trends: rocking chairs, gerbils, drama, whole language, critical thinking, problem solving, and value training. Children are singing and reciting poems again. Play and imagination are considered important dimensions of childhood experiences in the play yard and in the classroom. Activity centers increasingly reflect variety in thematic designs and in furnishings. Hands-on experiences that entice children toward discovery are visible in classrooms. Eggs are hatching and flowers are blooming. Paints and magnifying glasses are replacing numbers and letters on classroom shelves. Transitions are fewer allowing more time for exploration. Hands-on activity centers are replacing structured classroom arrangements. Teachers are advised not to interfere with the child's innate unfolding processes. Readiness no longer is defined by age, norms, or achieved levels of skills. Now it is influenced primarily by the quality of an environment and the child's own unique readiness timetable.

Child care programs must therefore reflect these trends. Early learning should be considered a *natural* outgrowth of awareness and active participation. Children in child care centers should have ample time and space to construct with blocks and to play cooperatively. A growing child should be exposed to hands-on experiences that encourage self-awareness and the acquisition of both general and specific knowledge. The child should have the opportunity for group interactions and cooperative learning through teacher-initiated projects and activities. He should participate in the planning and organization of his room, his activities, and his own learning. Children develop habit formation when they learn to respect and care for their environment. Their educational experience should prepare them for developing the tools for lifelong learning. Therefore, value training and training in basic readiness skills also are essential components of a five-year curriculum.

Frank Newman (1991), President of the Education Commission of the States from 1991 to 1992, wrote:

Quite frankly, every school in America—preschool and kindergarten, elementary, secondary, and post-secondary—should be a place where students learn to investigate, discover, and create. And schools should teach the youngest and the oldest students to think critically, solve problems, analyze, synthesize, reflect, and work collaboratively in ways appropriate to their age. Exploring, wondering, examining, creating, questioning, and investigating are natural dispositions in children—all children—and they should be encouraged and regarded as the building blocks for learning—lifelong learning.[7]

Montessori Education

Maria Montessori (1870–1952) opened the first "Children's House" in a slum district of Rome, Italy, in 1907—in theory and in practice, this approach was to revolutionize early education for years to come. The school taught children who lived in the slums manners, good work habits, hygiene, and basic skills all before they were five years of age.[8] The environment was carefully prepared for hands-on experiential learning through sensory exploration (i.e., touching, smelling, listening, tasting, seeing) that required specific tasks and materials for children to master in a sequential order. Montessori's no-fail, "learn-by-doing" approach provided children with a positive self-concept as well as a sense of mastery over their environment.

In Montessori schools, all materials are self-taught so children can see and correct their mistakes as they manipulate objects and perfect skills. In this way, children are allowed to direct and take responsibility for their own learning.[9] The tactility and aesthetic appeal of Montessori materials holds the attention of the young child. Children work at their own pace in mixed age groups. After initial instructions on the proper use of materials, little adult intervention is needed. Many of the tasks are oriented toward practical life skills—polishing shoes, washing tables, learning to button and snap. In traditional Montessori schools, children's play/work is purposeful; they do not typically engage in free and imaginary play. In less orthodox Montessori schools, children are given opportunities for creative, noninstructional play.

Noncompetitive, independent learning is *fundamental* to early development. Children develop confidence when they are not being compared to others or criticized by adults. When children know what is expected and feel in charge of their own learning experience, they need less adult coaching. Children also need to learn organizational skills at an early age. To encourage organization, materials should be selected carefully and arranged so as not to overwhelm the child/learner. The sorting and placement of play items on shelves encourages self-mastery and concept building. An organized environment does not inhibit creativity, it provides a sense of *harmony* that is conducive to exploration and discovery. When materials and equipment are seen by the child as an extension of her- or himself, it is the child who takes responsibility for their care. In the Montessori system, a valid concern is that a child, restricted in the selection and use of materials, is not given ample opportunity to be inventive, or to self-initiate his own learning.

The English Infant/Primary School

In 1910 the McMillan sisters opened a nursery school in the Deptford slums near London laying the foundation for the English system of educating young children. The sisters chose the word *nursery* to represent the love, nurturance, and care that children would receive and the word *school* to acknowledge that children would not only experience love but would learn as well.[10] Like most day nurseries, the school was seen primarily as a caregiving environment for impoverished, neglected children. Once the physical needs of the children were met, educational concerns were addressed. The nursery had a garden that became a veritable learning environment for children. Children learned to identify colors and shapes from flowers, and they learned to count by sorting vegetables. Within a short time, homemade wooden letters and geometric toys became part of a child's interior environment.[11] Through natural, hands-on experiences, children learned basic skills. Children's learning was facilitated by a loving and able staff and a comfortable and inspiring environment.

In contemporary English schools, a friendly, informal atmosphere immediately impresses a visitor. Children play and work in an unhurried, comfortable, and childlike environment. As in Montessori schools, children are not grouped by age. By mixing children in age groups, cooperation and cross-bonding are facilitated.

Teachers are well trained in education and respected as important contributors to children's school and home life. Visiting children at home is an important part of their responsibility. Because early childhood teachers are integral to the education process, they take pride in their work and have little incentive to make career changes. Children, therefore, have the benefit of continuity and stability. In an English infant/primary school:

- Creative activities abound; children enjoy art work, dramatic play, vocational and instrumental music, and original writing.
- Student projects promote socialization, cooperation, and motivation.
- There is an emphasis on trust, self-discipline, and respect.
- The head mistress is an educator and a role model who is revered and respected by teachers and families.
- Every nook and cranny in a classroom is used to promote independence, interaction, and the efficient management of space.
- Teachers have a warm, gentle style that promotes interaction and a friendly atmosphere.
- There is an absence of tracking and testing.
- The schools are community based and bonded to the families they serve.[12]

A child's day must be seen as too precious to waste or to mishandle. A happy child is an *involved* child who identifies positively with the surroundings. He is a child who smiles a lot and who looks forward to coming to his child care center. Feeling secure, he can break hands with mom and say good-bye without undue trauma. Quickly occupied, the child does not need to be coaxed or bribed to behave appropriately. The English system is ideal for all child care environments because of its emphasis on nurturing and active, child-initiated learning. A child always should want to return to his friends at school—he should never feel like he has to! Every child should experience a real garden outside and inside the classroom with lots of flowers to smell, vegetables to eat, worms to watch, and objects to paint.

Head Start

In 1965, Project Head Start was inaugurated as a federally funded preschool program for children from age three years to school entry. At the time, the commonly held theory was that society's inequities caused disadvantaged children to begin school ill-equipped. Therefore, it was the responsibility of society to compensate by providing a "head start" to disadvantaged youngsters. In concept, Head Start resembled the day nursery movement by providing early training and care in all facets of child growth and development.[13] Its comprehensive program encompassed readiness skills, health, nutrition, and social services. Children attended on a part-time basis, and parents were expected to participate in training and in classroom programs. The program was monitored carefully and evaluated, primarily from a cognitive (skill-oriented) perspective. Teachers were educated and specially trained to work with children on a one-to-one basis.

Project Head Start has been singled out by federal policymakers as a key area for continued funding and development in the nineties. In 1991, Congress, joined by President Bush, called for full participation in Head Start by all income-eligible children and set 1994 as the target date to reach this goal.[14]

The Head Start program has the potential to become a model for comprehensive child care. Its attention to all aspects of growth and development and emphasis on teacher training gives the program credibility in the educational community. Teachers and parents must be educated to understand the critical relationship between quality care at early childhood levels and productive adult lives. Every educator must be concerned about the quality of each day for every child in this country.

Bank Street: A Model for Contemporary Child Care

Throughout the century, the Bank Street College of Education in New York City has championed open education. Its child care approach represents a child's world. The center, located in an old, restored building in mid-town New York, offers a homelike environment. Like the English infant school, children are free to play expressively and creatively in an unhurried, comfortable environment. They move from room to room choosing activities that attract or interest them. Hands-on materials, such as blocks, paint, and clay, provide opportunities for self-initiated exploration and discovery. When materials are not limited by boundaries or form, they become permanent tools for continued growth.[15]

In this kind of environment, the primary catalyst for learning is the child. The tools for learning have meaning and interest for the child. Learning is experiential. What a child can see, feel, hear, or touch he can identify with. In the process, an awareness of the interplay between environmental and human factors develops. For example, a child may perceive that a cloudy day endangers a planned outing to a park or that a chilly day requires buttoning up before venturing outdoors. Buttoning up may not be easy for the young child, but in a supportive, unhurried environment, the child will eventually accomplish his needs.

To the visitor, a homelike environment projects a sense of authenticity. Children and staff interact through friendly and supportive communication. The furnishings are comfortable yet unpretentious. Charming and childlike paintings adorn the walls and affirm the uniqueness of childhood. One has the feeling of having been here before—of education being a continuum. Yesterday's child and today's child are both a part of this foundation. Nearby is Central Park—a place to run, to swing, and to play the games that Froebel's teachers once played with children in a distant time and at a distant place.

Direct experiences that generate children's own learning potential are essential at early childhood levels. Communities are filled with unlimited opportunities for learning that can be directly experienced and interpreted in ways that are understandable to a child. A surrounding neighborhood can be a primary resource for teaching and learning. Children love outdoor activities. They love going places and seeing things. Trips to a supermarket, to a construction site, or to a bakery help children connect their center with their community.

Classroom projects should, in part, develop from first-hand experiences. What a child experiences first-hand has more relevancy than what he experiences through teacher-initiated activities. Rather than isolating learning within the boundaries of a classroom, teachers should bring children into their community. Children need to derive meaning through *personal* experience that brings them in touch with their senses, their feelings, their perceptions, and their world. On a community outing, they can learn to read signs, to identify objects, and to develop concepts. They can also make observations and develop ideas.

Oftentimes, adults assume the ordinary is boring, failing to understand that for a child the ordinary is almost always extraordinary. Often it is easier for adults to substitute vicarious experiences for the real thing. To a child, however, art is a real building, math is counting the steps at a zoo or jumping rope, language is how people talk, science is the sound of a cricket or the sight of leaves being whipped up by the wind. For the child, learning is derived, in large part, from *authentic* experiences—those *spontaneous* moments that occur and capture the interest and imagination of the spectator.

SUMMARY

For some time, day care has invoked a negative, custodial image among workers in the field, professionals, and advocates for improvement. It has not been recognized as a serious, worthwhile service that supports and enriches family life. There is confusion about names (child care or day care or day nurseries), about titles (moms and pops, caregivers, providers, teachers), about the purpose of child care (custodial or educational or both), and there is confusion about credentials (what qualifies a person to direct, teach, or assist in child care settings).

We fail to recognize that day care has a proud heritage to identify with and build on. It has models and mentors waiting to be revisited and reshaped for contemporary systems of care. In shaping child care environments for the future, educators must not lose sight of the larger framework that has already been established by leaders in the field over the years.

NOTES

1. David Elkind, *The Hurried Child: Growing Up Too Fast Too Soon* (Reading, MA: Addison-Wesley, 1981), p. 3.

2. Robert L. Church and Michael W. Sedlack, *Education in the United States* (New York: Macmillan, 1976), p. 271–74.

3. Ibid., pp. 317–19.

4. Evelyn Weber, *Ideas Influencing Early Childhood Education* (New York: Teachers College Press, 1984), pp. 39–41.

5. Ibid., p. 88.

6. Church and Sedlack, *Education in the United States*, pp. 335–36.

7. Frank Newman, "School Readiness and State Action," in *Perspectives on Early Childhood Education*, ed. David Elkind (Washington, DC: National Education Association, 1991), pp. 100–101.

8. Carol Seefeldt and Nita Barbour, *Early Childhood Education: An Introduction*, 2d. ed. (New York: Macmillan, 1990), p. 8.

9. David Elkind, *Miseducation: Preschoolers at Risk* (New York: Knopf, 1987), p. 111.

10. Seefeldt and Barbour, *Early Childhood Education*, p. 5.

11. Gail Stout, ed., "Rachel McMillan Nursery School: Deptford, London, England," *Child Care Center* 1(2) (November 1986): 23–26.

12. Veryl M. Short and MaryLouise Burger, "The English Infant/Primary School Revisited," *Childhood Education* 64(2) (December 1987): 75–79.

13. Church and Sedlack, *Education in the United States*, pp. 454–55.

14. *Beyond Rhetoric: A New American Agenda for Children and Families.* (Washington, DC: The National Commission on Children, 1991), p. 190.

15. Dorothy H. Cohen, *The Learning Child* (New York: Schocken Books, 1972), p. 92.

RESOURCES

American Public Health Association (1015 Fifteenth Street, NW, Washington, DC 20005) *Caring for Our Children*, 1992.

Bronfenbrenner, U. "Discovering What Families Can Do," in *Rebuilding the Nest: A New Commitment to the American Family*, ed. D. Blankenhorn, S. Bayme, and J. B. Elshtain. Milwaukee, WI: Family Service American, 1990.

Dimidjian, Victoria Jean. *Early Childhood at Risk: Actions and Advocacy for Young Children.* Washington, DC: National Education Association, 1989.

Hayes, C. D., J. L. Palmer, and M. J. Zaslor, eds. *Who Cares for America's Children? Child Care Policy for the 1990s.* Washington, DC: National Academy Press, 1990.

The National Commission on Children (1111 Eighteenth Street, NW, Suite 810, Washington, DC 20036) *Beyond Rhetoric: A New American Agenda for Children and Families*, 1991.

All of society has a stake in providing high quality services to our nation's youngest citizens. Only when we recognize that all sectors of society have a role and responsibility in supporting the care and education of young children, will we remove the barriers to full quality in early childhood programs.

— Barbara Willer
National Association for the Education
of Young Children (NAEYC)

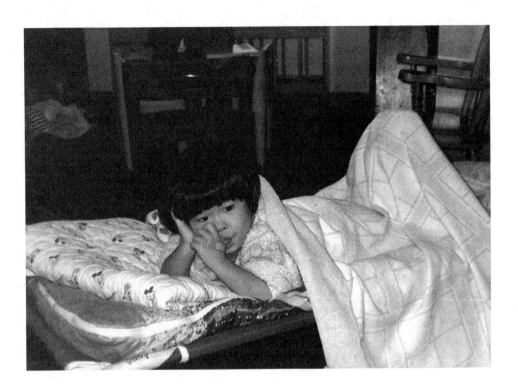

2

A CONTEMPORARY PERSPECTIVE

WHAT IS HAPPENING TO OUR CHILDREN?

Historically, a predominantly middle-class society shaped the direction of education in the United States. Children's school experiences were seen as a complement to tightly knit family structures. Women, for the most part, remained in the home as primary caretakers and this role was unchallenged. Nursery school was a symbol of upward mobility for those willing to trust their children to out-of-home environments for a few hours each day. Neither the state nor the federal government perceived themselves in a custodial role in early training nor did families want the intrusion of government in areas of private domain. Indeed, in the United States, most children did not begin formal schooling until they were six years old. Until recent times, education was primarily a family matter and a family's choice.

National guidelines for early intervention or for funding model programs were not considered within the purview of the national government until the mid-sixties when Project Head Start was inaugurated for disadvantaged children. Traditionally, the proper role of government was not to mandate a single system but to encourage diversity within the system. During times of major social or economic upheaval, such as the depression in the thirties, World War II, and the War on Poverty in the sixties, the government assumed a somewhat more assertive role in funding child-related projects, but for the most part the role of the federal government in caring for children has been limited and noncontinuous. This absence has been felt particularly by early educators and, more recently, by child care experts who do not have a unified system in place to work with. Consequently, early childhood education has developed in a piecemeal, unsystematic fashion that is obstructing progress in upgrading present-day child care standards.

The closest the federal government came to a national day care policy was in 1971 when a Comprehensive Child Development Bill passed both Houses of Congress, only to be vetoed by the president. This was a personal and bitter defeat for its architect, Dr. Edward Zigler, and for its vocal advocates who saw this bill as a framework for action and development. "That was one of the great, great defeats of my life—for me personally and certainly for the country. Just think, that bill provided the embryonic child care system that could have grown up and been fully in place by now."[1]

The absence of federal and state assistance in areas of child care became more marked as women began entering the workplace in growing numbers. Where they existed, state guidelines were formulated by health departments whose primary concern was the health and safety of children. Areas of program development, staff qualifications, and training were given less attention. Dissatisfied with state sluggishness, many counties elected to "run their own show" by implementing more stringent guidelines that addressed children's total needs. Local agencies, such as the 4 C's (Community Coordinated Child Care), became the backbone of the growing trend toward improving child care at grass-roots levels.

Unlike most advanced countries, child care in the United States, has germinated within the private sector on an ad hoc basis. Arrangements and tuition varied from caregiver to caregiver, as did the quality of care. Women who called themselves caregivers were typically well-intentioned but minimally trained and educated. They were relatives (and sometimes reluctant relatives), neighbors, and moms on the block who were comfortable just being babysitters. Gradually, as the movement expanded, children were placed in unfamiliar, unlicensed home care. With little challenge and few demands, unlicensed caregivers enjoyed their autonomy. They didn't have to worry about inspections, upgrading their programs, or training requirements.

During the decade of the eighties, child care became a challenging, nationwide industry. Most of its growth has been in the licensed, group-care sector. Group centers were able to accommodate more children than home centers. To many parents, they were seen as less risky, more stable, and more interesting environments than were home centers. Accelerated growth, however, was not conducive to quality. With limited licensing requirements and few guidelines, group centers tended to adopt minimal standards. The institutionalized image projected by these centers has caused many educators to once again look at home care, especially for young children, as the preferred method of out-of-home childrearing.

Most centers, and particularly the good ones, have waiting lists. The demand for child care services and the shortage of affordable, good centers has created a supply/demand imbalance that has driven up the cost of child care. Economically advantaged parents still can find good centers, but disadvantaged families and single mothers cannot. The lack of affordable child care has forced many families back into unlicensed, home-care environments. The state of child care at the dawning of the twenty-first century is *not* a credit to the educational system of the United States. A depressed, undervalued industry cannot provide quality care to all children.

The Disappearance of Childhood

Increasing concern about childrearing practices and facilities are causing many educators to prophesy the disappearance of childhood; there are many reasons for this, and they cannot all be blamed on day care. Media continues to invade households with all kinds of distorted, unhealthy messages for and about children. Most television shows are inappropriate for viewing by children yet this is how children spend the majority of their time when they are not in school. Moreover, there is reason to believe that in many child care centers, television has become an unhealthy substitute for active learning through real-life, child-active experiences. Educators, such as Professor Neil Postman, have expressed alarm about the corrosive, pervasive influence of media on children's lives:

> I am going to argue that a new media environment, with television at its center, is leading to the rapid disappearance of childhood in North America; that childhood will probably not survive to the end of this century; and that such a state of affairs represents a social disaster of the first order.[2]

Postman's words express the opinion of many experts who view excessive television viewing as inappropriate and damaging to children's early development. Educators are advocating a system of education that begins before birth and continues through adulthood. On May 1, 1991, after two years of intensive investigation, The National Commission on Children unanimously approved a blueprint for change in early childhood education in the United States:

> The seeds of educational success are sown early, in the prenatal period and the first months and years of life. During this time, children develop basic language and reasoning skills. They also acquire social skills, confidence, and a sense of self-worth, and they come to see themselves as important and competent members of their family and of other small communities in their lives. Children who arrive at school incapable of managing the kindergarten routine can quickly lose confidence in their ability to learn. Traditionally, society's responsibility for educating children began when they entered school. Growing knowledge of child development, however, compels us as individuals and as a society to place far greater emphasis on children's early development to ensure that every child is prepared for school.[3]

Most would agree that a great deal of corrective action must be taken at early childhood levels to ensure the proper growth and development of our young. Child care can become a catalyst for change if we recognize and correct its inadequacies. We realize that:

- Despite the availability of child-appropriate guidelines, many centers do not have written programs or a philosophy of teaching and learning.

- Knowledge in child development does not assure its practice in homes and group centers where directors and staff may be untrained or insensitive to the needs of children.
- The cost of quality programs precludes availability for the majority of children and particularly for those who are at risk or disadvantaged.
- Many unlicensed providers, lacking resources and education, have little incentive to upgrade programs.
- Better programs necessitate an increase in tuition costs to parents, many of whom are barely making ends meet.
- Even the most minimally adequate programs are not available to "latchkey" children—children who are unsupervised after school hours.
- There are growing numbers of preschool children who are neglected and mistreated in centers.
- Many parents, for whatever reasons, are not able to provide children with their basic needs.
- Many centers are unwilling to assume the role of parents in the care and training of young children.

Most would agree that standards of excellence must be given time to germinate at the grass-roots level, statistics do not support waiting for quality child care environments, too many good centers are financially imperiled, and too many children on waiting lists may never reap the benefits of quality child care.

We are at a crossroads between understanding and finding the wherewithal to extend and improve existing child care delivery systems at national and state levels. Meanwhile, there are so many children at risk that numbers no longer impress. In its Senate testimony in 1978, The Day Care and Child Development Council of America made the following statement:

> It is not the numbers on computer cards and in neat columns in reports that really describe the dilemma. It is the voice of the mother frantically searching for adequate arrangements, and the vacant look in the eyes of the child who suffers from the lack of developmental care, that give definition to the problem. It is tragic but not unusual that a ten-year-old is kept home from school to stay with the baby; that a well-meaning but untrained neighbor crowds a group of infants and preschoolers into her house for an uneventful and fretful day.[4]

DETERRENTS TO OBTAINING SATISFACTORY CARE

Demand

In recent years, the majority of American women have chosen a new direction for their lives—one that splinters their responsibilities between home and career. For most women, work has become a necessary commitment equal to childrearing. In an excellent monograph entitled *Early Childhood at Risk*, Victoria Jean Dimidjian comments:

Propelled by the converging forces of economic necessity, changing social roles and increasing educational/professional opportunities, young women today assume that combining the responsibilities of work and family life will fall into place easily. But that assumption is sorely challenged, often shattered, as families search for adequate child care. Most turn to some form of in-home care where family monitoring of quality care is to some degree possible and costs are relatively low.[5]

The most rapid increase in the work force may be found among women with children under the age of 6. Between 1970 and 1990, the proportion of mothers with children under age 6 who were working or looking for work outside their homes rose from 32 to 58 percent. "Today, approximately 10.9 million children under the age of 6, including 1.7 million babies under one year and 9.2 million toddlers and preschoolers, have mothers in the labor force."[6] "Mothers of school-age children are even more likely to be working. In 1990, more than 74 percent of women whose youngest child was between the ages of 6 and 13 were working or looking for paid work."[7]

The Pervasiveness of Poverty

In *What Every American Should Be Asking Political Figures in 1988,* The Children's Defense Fund reminds us that children make up the poorest age group in the United States. "One in four of all preschoolers and one in five of all children are poor; among children born into single-parent households, one in two is poor; among children of teenage single mothers, 84.4 percent are poor; and among children with two parents younger than 22, one in three is poor."[8]

Most vulnerable are single-headed families. "Nearly 75 percent of the children growing up in single-parent families experience poverty for some period during their first 10 years compared to 20 percent of those in two-parent families."[9] "The average income of mother-headed families is about 40 percent of the average income of two-parent families. The median earnings of young female householders was $3,005 in 1989, barely 36 percent of the official poverty level for a family of two and substantially below the poverty level for a family of three."[10] Under these circumstances, poor families cannot even afford subsidized child care.

Children born into poverty grow up without the basic foundation, care, and support to prepare them for life. Because a large number of these children are at risk or developmentally dysfunctional, the need for affordable, quality care for every child is intensified.

In an article entitled "Foundations for Success: Early Childhood and Family Education," William B. Keene provides additional insight:

The realities for the nearly four million infants born in the late 1980s and early 1990s are as follows:

- Fifty percent will have mothers entering or reentering the work force before their babies are one-year-old;

- Seventy percent will receive some or much of their care outside their homes by the time they are three years old;
- Twenty-five percent will begin their lives already at risk of personal and educational failure because of the poverty and stress in their families; and
- Those at risk economically will have less opportunity to participate in high-quality early childhood programs, thus widening the chasm between the disadvantaged and those more fortunate.[11]

Problems at the Marketplace

Child care is caught in a web of circumstances that prevent qualitative growth. At the micro level of purchaser and supplier, an increase in quality must be offset by an increase in tuition. Quality affects cost, and therefore affordability. Affordability (what parents will pay for a service) affects how much a child care center can charge.[12] Most parents cannot afford to pay for quality and, for many, quality is not understood. Without information and education, most parents do not know what to look for or what to ask for. Chances are they will enroll their child in the least expensive center available. A director who is attempting to upgrade her service by charging a somewhat higher tuition than parents can afford or are willing to pay when shopping for a center, may eventually be forced out of business by competitors.

The Cost of Child Care

The cost of child care prevents a low- or moderate-income parent from obtaining satisfactory care. The National Child Care Survey (1990) reported the following findings about the cost of care countrywide:

- In 1990, employed mothers with a child younger than age five spent an average of $63 per week, about 10 percent of their weekly family income, on all types of child care for all children in the family.
- Families with annual incomes under $15,000 who paid for child care spent as much as 23 percent of their income on the services.
- Fees tend to vary by the ages of children, program characteristics, the amount of time that a child spends in a center, geographic region, and program auspices. A family in the Northeast, for example, would expect to pay $2.18 per hour for a group center and $2.02 per hour for a regulated family day care home; while a family in the South might pay $1.29 per hour for a group center and $1.32 for a regulated family day care home.
- Services for infants, toddlers and twos, where more staff and fewer children are required, tend to be more costly than services for older preschool-age children.
- Part-time care is more costly per hour than full-time care.
- Publicly funded programs, such as Head Start and public school programs, cost families the least.[13]

A disproportionate number of children are, by necessity, tracked into less-than-adequate child care environments during their formative years because acceptable child care is beyond the reach of most American families. Being shifted from one environment to another, from one adult to another, and from one set of rules to another, children are at risk of losing their sense of identity and importance. . . . *When nobody cares, why should I?*

Lizbeth B. Schorr (Harvard University Working Group on Early Life) spoke for neglected children:

> Despite the evidence of worsening conditions, the services which could buffer disadvantaged children against the impact of their harsh surroundings and strengthen families in their efforts to improve the odds for these children, remain painfully inadequate. Many services have been reduced as a result of budget cuts, but their weaknesses go deeper than budgets. The kind of schools, preschools, day care, health clinics and social services that might help, are, with a few stellar exceptions, simply not reaching those who need them most. So, instead of protecting against the destructive impact of the concentration of devastation, our social institutions often contribute to it.[14]

The Cost to Children

At the most critical stage of development, when character and values are forming, an increasing number of children are being placed in childrearing environments of *questionable quality*. For preschool children growing up under adverse, unhealthy conditions, there is little chance for a promising and productive adulthood.

For school-age children growing up without after-school supervision, there is constant risk. Studies of children who care for themselves reveal that anxious, lonely children tend to overeat and underexercise. They are often underachievers because there is no adult present to supervise their work and study habits. These children find companionship in junk food, the telephone, and soap operas. When they are tired of television, there are corners to hang out on and malls to roam around in. The world of malls, like the world of soap operas, is an escape hatch for dissatisfied, bored children. When children are tired of malls there are other means of entertainment far more destructive than merely "hanging out."

Survival books, self-help training, and telephone monitoring cannot begin to address the debilitating feelings of loneliness. Loneliness is symbolic of the times. It is a creeping shadow that moves slowly but surely over children who feel unaccepted and uncared for.

The Cost to Staff

Improving the compensation system for child care workers is closely interrelated with improving conditions for children. Despite higher levels of training in the field, salaries have not increased significantly during the eighties. This is, in large part, a reflection of an undervalued system of child care that does not accord adequate recognition to its teachers. In 1990, the average annual salary for a preschool teacher (excluding assistant teachers and aides) in child care centers was approximately $11,000 per year while the average hourly wage was $7.49 per hour.[15] Employee benefits, which might contribute to staff satisfaction, are not easily addressed, particularly in centers that fall under the "small employers" category. A job applicant is less than enthusiastic about accepting employment at a center that does not include health insurance, sick leave, vacation leave, tuition benefits for children, or educational benefits for continued training. A study conducted by the Institute for Women's Policy Research (1989) found that "only one-third to one-half of child care workers have any kind of employer-provided health care coverage . . . [and] retirement pensions and life insurance [are] received by perhaps one-fourth of child care employees."[16] When a professionally trained staff is not given adequate compensation and benefits, the turnover rate is high. Once again, it is children who ultimately pay the price for a depressed system of child care.

The Cost to Parents

For most families in the United States child care is only one of many problems. Family life has been eroded by changes at virtually every level of existence and in a short span of time. In some families, children are seen as one more burden tipping an already precariously balanced scale. Child care is provided by a friend or a neighbor who looks after children. It probably is not a quality center. In the absence of a national system that provides equal care and concern for all children, parents can only hope they have made the right choice.

HOW DO WE COMPARE TO OTHER INDUSTRIALIZED NATIONS?

In bold contrast to the scant attention the United States has given child care, most developed nations already have exemplary, comprehensive systems in place for all families. A study team of child care professionals returning from France was struck by the stark contrast in protective policies for children between the two countries.

The group found a coordinated, comprehensive system in France, linking day care, early education and health care—a system that is accessible to virtually every family. The study team found that in countries where preventative health services are integrated with child care programs, infant mortality is low. In France, infant mortality is fourth lowest among the industrial nations while in the United States it is the nineteenth lowest.[17]

The Scandinavian countries have equally impressive child care systems. In Denmark, for example, all family day care homes are locally controlled but conducted according to a set of national guidelines. There is a family day care supervisor assigned to each provider. This person has a caseload of not more than fifty children and must visit each child at least twice a month. In addition, the supervisor must be available for consultation on a regular basis with the home provider and with parents.[18] In Denmark, as in most other countries that legislate for children, senior citizens are included as an integral part of the nurturing process in caring for young children.

The findings of a California-based employee study—conducted during a six-month period in 1988—of 227 day care centers in Atlanta, Boston, Detroit, Phoenix, and Seattle stand in marked contrast.[19] Their findings indicated that:

- Centers across the country are suffering from the effects of low-quality care, largely as a result of high turnover in a field filled with underpaid workers.
- Middle-income parents had their children in worse centers than either low-income or high-income families.
- While some low-income families received government subsidies to send their children to high-quality centers, nonsubsidized, low-income parents actually paid higher fees on average than middle-income parents.
- Nonprofit centers generally provided better care than for-profit centers, on which more middle-income parents relied.
- The low salaries of teachers, averaging $5.35 an hour or $9,363 a year for full-time work with poor benefits, are far less than the pay of other workers with comparable education levels.
- Forty-one percent of child care workers in the survey left their jobs within one year.

The study group concluded that salary levels were the best predictor of quality care. Better salaries correlate with better training, more positive attitudes, higher esteem, more commitment, and, therefore, less staff turnover.

SUMMARY

Traditionally, child care has been seen as outside of the educational mainstream. Out of economic necessity, child care is becoming the focus of debate, deliberation, and controversy. Increasingly, public attention is focusing on issues of availability, affordability, and quality. As elements of quality are defined, the image of child care is gradually shifting from one of custodial care to professional care. Parents and educators are no longer willing to accept "less than the best" for their children. A depressed system must work at becoming an exemplary system—one that earns the right to be described by other countries as a "model system."

NOTES

1. Edward F. Zigler, "Project Day-Care," *Psychology Today* (December 1987): 34.

2. Neil Postman, "The Disappearance of Childhood," *Childhood Education* 61(4) (March/April 1985): 286.

3. *Beyond Rhetoric: A New American Agenda for Children and Families* (Washington, DC: The National Commission on Children, 1991), p. 187.

4. Edward M. Kennedy, "Child Care—A Commitment to Be Honored," in *Day Care Scientific and Social Policy Issues,* eds. Edward F. Zigler and Edmund W. Gordon (Dover, MA: Auburn House, 1982), p. 261.

5. Victoria Jean Dimidjian, *Early Childhood at Risk: Actions and Advocacy For Young Children* (Washington, DC: National Education Association, 1989), p. 13.

6. Bureau of Labor Statistics, "March 1990: Current Population Survey," Table 48; cited in *Beyond Rhetoric,* p. 22.

7. Ibid., Tables 15 and 48, p. 22.

8. Children's Defense Fund, "What Every American Should Be Asking Political Leaders in 1988" (Washington, DC: The Fund, 1988), p. 59. As cited in Dimidjian, *Early Childhood at Risk,* p. 10.

9. D. T. Ellwood, *Poor Support: Poverty in the American Family* (New York: Basic Books, 1989), p. 84 and Figure 4.1.

10. N. Fogg and A. Sum, "Median Earnings of Young/Female Family Householders" (Boston: MA: Northeastern University, Center for Labor Market Studies, 1991).

11. William B. Keene, "Foundations for Success: Early Childhood and Family Education," in *Perspectives on Early Childhood Educa-tion,* ed. David Elkind (Washington, DC: National Education Association, 1991), p. 78.

12. Mary L. Culkin, Suzanne W. Helburn, and John R. Morris, "Current Price Versus Full Cost: An Economic Perspective," in *Reaching the Full Cost of Quality in Early Childhood Programs,* ed. Barbara Willer (Washington, DC: NAEYC, 1990), p. 12.

13. Barbara Willer, Sandra L. Hofferth, Ellen E. Kisker, et al., *The Demand and Supply of Child Care in 1990* (Washington, DC: NAEYC, 1991), pp. 30–31.

14. Lisbeth B. Schorr, "Breaking the Cycle of the Disadvantaged: New Knowledge, New Tools, New Urgency," cited in George Miller, ed., *Giving Children a Chance: The Case for More Effective National Policies* (Washington, DC: The Center for National Policy Press, 1989), p. 169.

15. Barbara Willer, Sandra L. Hofferth, Ellen E. Kisker, Patricia Divine-Hawkins, Elizabeth Farquhar, and Frederick B. Glantz, eds., *The Demand and Supply of Child Care in 1990* (Washington, DC: NAEYC, 1991), p. 35.

16. Heidi I. Hartman and Diana M. Pearce, *High Skill and Low Pay: The Economics of Child Care Work,* prepared for Child Care Action Campaign (Washington, DC: The Institute for Women's Policy Research, January 1989).

17. Hillary R. Clinton, "In France, Day Care Is Every Child's Right," *The New York Times,* 7 April 1990.

18. David A. Corsini, "Family Day Care in Denmark: A Model for the United States?" *Young Children* 46(5) (July 1991): 10.

19. Sandra Evans, "Day-Care Workers' Pay Raises Urged," *The Washington Post,* 20 October 1989.

RESOURCES

Aldous, J. *Family Careers: Developmental Change in Families.* New York: John Wiley, 1978.

Carnegie Council on Adolescent Development. *Turning Points, Preparing American Youth for the 21st Century.* New York: Carnegie Corporation, 1989.

Children's Defense Fund, *A Vision for America's Future: An Agenda for the 1990s.* Washington, DC: The Fund, 1988.

Edelman, Marian Wright. *Families in Peril: An Agenda for Social Change.* Cambridge, MA: Harvard University Press, 1987.

The National Commission on Children, *Speaking of Kids: A National Survey of Children and Parents.* Washington, DC: The National Commission on Children, 1991.

Schorr, L. B. *Within Our Reach: Breaking the Cycle of Disadvantage.* New York: Doubleday, 1988.

U.S. Department of Health and Human Services, Select Panel for the Promotion of Child Health. *Better Health for Our Children: A National Strategy.* Washington, DC: Government Printing Office, 1981.

Weikart, D. *Quality Preschool Programs: A Long-term Social Investment.* U.S. Department of Commerce, Bureau of the Census, Washington, DC: Government Printing Office, 1988.

Zill, N., and C. A. Schoenborn, *Developmental, Learning, and Emotional Problems: Health of Our Nation's Children.* Hyattsville, MD: U.S. Department of Health and Human Services, National Center for Health Statistics, 1990.

Too many of today's children and adolescents will reach adulthood unhealthy, illiterate, unemployable, lacking moral direction and a vision of a secure future. This is a personal tragedy for the young people involved and a staggering loss for the nation as a whole. We must begin today to place children and their families at the top of the national agenda.

— Senator John D. Rockefeller IV, Chairman
National Commission on Children

3

A NEW CENTURY:
A NEW BEGINNING

INVESTING IN CHILDREN

More and more legislators at national and state levels are looking toward corrective action that will extend services to all families and ensure a healthy, nurturing environment for children in the United States. In recent years, there has been an acceleration of federal assistance to child care and a greater sense of partnership between the federal and state governments.

Federal Assistance to Child Care

During the eighties, the largest federal assistance to child care was the child care tax credit; the next largest was Title XX (authorizing 75 percent matching grants to states for social services, including child care); and the third was Project Head Start, focusing on low-income populations.[1] In October 1990, Congress enacted a comprehensive package of child care measures referred to as *P.L. 101–508*. The legislation included a Child Care and Development Block Grant, two expanded tax credit programs, and an increase in Head Start funds.[2]

The Block Grant

The Child Care and Development Block Grant[3] represents the most impressive U.S. legislation to date for children. With the help of federal funding, states will be motivated to reexamine and improve their existing services. They will be encouraged to use additional funds to supplement their own funding programs and to upgrade existing facilities. Although states are not required to match federal funds, they are required to meet basic standards designed to protect children and to improve the quality of care. For example, to be eligible for funding, states are required to strengthen their licensing and regulatory systems, particularly in areas of health and safety, to review and improve training requirements, to upgrade their resource and referral systems, to receive and disburse funds according to specific guidelines, and to extend services to target populations.

The grant allocates $750 million the first year for improving child care afford-ability, supply, and quality. Seventy-five percent of the block grant funds are to be used to defray child care costs for low-income families. To receive assistance, parents must be working or attending a job training or education program. Their children must be under 13 years of age and their family income must be less than 75 percent of a state's median income. Children receiving protective services and those in foster care are also eligible for aid. The remaining 25 percent is to be used for quality improvements in areas that include: resources and referral programs, training, compensation, grants or loans to providers, monitoring and compliance, and more services for both early-childhood and school-age care.

Under a *Grants to States Title IV-A* provision of the Block Grant, a total of $300 million per year for the next five years will be available to states for children at risk. Families who qualify for assistance are those that need child care in order to work and who are not eligible to receive child care assistance under the Family Support Act of 1988. States are required to match funds received.

Dependent Care Tax Credit
This method of subsidizing child care allows a family to claim a percentage of child care costs on their income tax as a credit to offset expenses for child care or the care of other infirm or elderly members of a family. The DCTC is a credit of up to $2,400 for one child and $4,800 for two or more qualified children or individuals.[4]

Earned Income Tax Credit
This law "provides a tax credit for low-income families with children under one year of age and another credit to subsidize health-insurance costs for low-income families with dependent children. Over a five-year period beginning in 1991, subsidies to families with dependent children will increase by more than $18.3 billion."[5]

Project Head Start
Head Start also was given a tremendous boost in 1990 when, under the Augustus F. Hawkins Human Services Reauthorization Act, an additional $400 million was authorized for the first year. The annual funding level for Head Start is authorized to reach $7.6 billion by fiscal year 1994. Funds will be set aside for salary increases and training as well as new programs that meet the full-day, year-round needs of parents.[6]

State Assistance to Child Care

More and more states are recognizing the importance of the early years to child development, realizing that to ensure a healthy beginning, it is necessary to strengthen the infrastructure of child care systems. This task requires coordination and collaboration at state and local levels. Asa G. Hilliard III reminds us of our collective responsibility:

> Is there anyone in our profession who really needs more years of research and experience to discover that a high-quality environment for children is one in which:
>
> - Children are well nourished,
> - Children are healthy,
> - Children are safe,
> - Children have adequate space,
> - Children have ample materials and equipment for learning,
> - Staff are trained in child development and teaching methods,
> - There is good planning and organization, and
> - Strong links to parents are maintained?[7]

Meeting the Challenge

Federal assistance to states in the form of block grants is making day care more accessible to families who would not ordinarily qualify for assistance. Financial assistance has also raised the consciousness of providers and families about the importance of quality programs. Single mothers who fall within a certain income bracket have benefited from voucher arrangements that subsidize child care costs. In recent years, many states have implemented excellent training programs and delivery systems for comprehensive child care. Although the government stipulates who qualifies for assistance, states have been given reasonable discretionary power as to the distribution of funds available for child care.

Resource and Referral Agencies

As the need for a more responsive system of support for families and children continues to grow, communities are responding in kind. Resource and referral (R & R) agencies provide important information about child care services. By consolidating and disseminating information, the child care system can function more efficiently and effectively. Educating consumers on how to select centers inspires healthy competition and better services among child care providers. Many states now have impressive systems for distributing information about child care to parents, providers, and staff. Parents can receive lists of licensed caregivers, guidelines for selecting a center, and sources for financial assistance. They can obtain information about placing special-needs children and about assisting children with personal problems. Many agencies provide lists of professionals who will provide consultation and follow-up services for families in need of this kind of assistance.

These agencies also offer assistance to child care providers, i.e., a job bank for recruiting staff, information about training opportunities, and the names of consultants who are available to set up and/or evaluate new centers for a modest fee. In addition, many agencies keep an updated file of organizations lobbying for legislation or generating ideas for growth and development at local levels.

Providers can benefit by the added publicity that comes from professional recommendations—especially good recommendations. Homes and centers are screened by agencies before they can be referred for placement. Agencies ask questions pertaining to program specifics, such as the type of program offered, the level of training of staff, the policy for a sliding scale or subsidized voucher care, the policy for mainstreaming special-needs children, the availability of transportation, and other unique features of the program. By increasing public awareness, resource and referral agencies provide an invaluable service to communities and to families.

Training

The new Child Care and Development Block Grant will provide an impetus to training programs already in place. National organizations such as The National Association for the Education of Young Children (NAEYC), Head Start, and the National Black Child Development Institute (Washington, DC) are examples of leading organizations that have established standards for teaching in the field. As competition increases in the marketplace, there will be more demand for workshops and career training in child development and administration. Increasingly, experts in the field are accelerating the demand for credentials and equitable compensation. Many communities are forming leadership groups to foster quality environments for children and staff. They are encouraging the business sector, the private sector, and government agencies to increase their commitment and resources to the field.

Licensing

State regulatory agencies are making significant strides in improving child care services. Each state has the power to write and enforce its own regulations; more and more the regulations are beginning to sound alike. Common concerns, such as immunization, nutrition, child abuse, and sanitary measures, are being articulated through laws written to maximize the care and protection of young children.

Enforcement is taken more seriously. In a large center, an inspector may spend a complete day with the director, asking questions, reviewing procedures, and documenting findings. Centers in violation of regulations may be fined, prosecuted, put on a probationary status until violations have been corrected, or, at worst, closed. If offenses are minimal, directors are usually given a short period of time to correct violations and to "sign off." (See Chapter Four, Features of Quality.)

Back to the Future

This statement by the NAEYC is reminiscent of the past—a reminder that the roots of child care, planted a century ago, are finally sprouting: "Our dream is that by the year 2001, all programs for young children will provide high-quality, developmentally appropriate care and education."[8]

Gradually, concerted and aggressive lobbying by leaders, parents, and child care proponents is changing the image and direction of child care. National policy and leadership are responding to the mood and the needs of the time. State agencies are increasingly upgrading and broadening standards that protect, nurture, and educate children. State and local leaders are collaborating and cooperating for better delivery services and stricter, more enforceable guidelines. The career potential in child care services is now commonly recognized. Universities and colleges are establishing child care departments at both undergraduate and graduate levels, adding credibility and status to the movement. No longer willing to accept a custodial image, child care staff are earning the right to be called "teachers."

Every time there is a gathering of people sharing ideas, there is the potential for growth. When professionals and practitioners interact, there are sparks of commonality and congeniality. And, when centers and communities work in tandem to improve child care, the network is strengthened.

Child Care in the Twenty-first Century

In the words of esteemed educator and leader-in-the-field, Dr. Bettye M. Caldwell, the real name of our field should be *educare:* ". . . We cannot educate without protecting, and we would hardly be protecting children if we did not provide them with opportunities for appropriate education."[9]

Tomorrow's Model

A prototype of tomorrow's center might resemble a miniature community concept that educator John Dewey ascribed for progressive schools during the first half of the twentieth century.

. . . In a miniature community, a center and a home are reinforcing and complimentary. Parents and providers cooperate in childrearing so that children experience a sense of continuity between center and home. Learning is considered an integral part of a child's daily experiences—a trip to the grocery store, a walk through a nature center, an original, hand-written story. Children learn from one another through cooperative interaction. They are connected through friendship and common experiences. They are self-sufficient learners; drawing on their own resources to work out problems, seek solutions, and find answers. They engage in productive and challenging activities that allow them to develop an understanding about their immediate and greater world. As often as possible, they enjoy direct experiences that open their minds to the power of learning through investigation and discovery. In a familylike environment, children do not feel threatened or lonely, anxious or afraid. They sense that they are an integral and important part of a continuing social unit.

. . . In a miniature community, child care workers assume greater responsibility for training and caring for children and they are adequately compensated. Training includes teaching children traditional values and good work habits that can be extended into homes and communities. Child care workers perceive child care as a total environment centered on the nature of each child and the needs of a social unit.

There is a strong interface between state regulatory agencies and providers, and between providers and the community. By sharing responsibility and coordinating resources, children's needs and interests are protected and enhanced.

Public schools provide space and care for school-age children—before and after school, during holidays, half-days, and summer months. State and local jurisdictions continue to lobby to make public schools, closed schools, and unused county buildings available for all levels of child care on a priority basis with long-term occupancy options. Unoccupied county and public school facilities and land are made available to child care providers at minimal cost. With the help of state bonds, guaranteed loans, and low-interest loans, centers are constructed on public land.

More and more businesses begin to provide their employees with on-site centers that encourage a family/center partnership. Children are assured continuity during their preschool years and parents benefit from the security of knowing their young children are near by and in good hands.

In tomorrow's model there is a trend toward community coordinated child care centers. Community resources and recreational facilities work in partnership to implement and expand the child care network. Public parks and recreation facilities designate specific blocks of time for child care users. A park that ordinarily opens at 10:00 A.M. opens at 9:00 A.M. to accommodate child care centers. Outdoor and indoor community pools, ice skating rinks, and tennis courts are made available to child care centers at minimal cost. Libraries, museums, art galleries, and other public "attractions" expand their hours, personnel, and resources to accommodate children in child care environments. They are staffed by professionals and volunteers who can relate to children. Throughout communities, special places become children's places—primary resources for their growth and development.

Tomorrow's child care professionals share a common philosophy, working cooperatively toward achieving quality care. Parents become proponents of around-the-clock supervision for their children from birth through the middle-school years when children are making the transition into adulthood. When providers and parents make an aggressive and affirmative commitment to comprehensive child care and to standards of excellence, policymakers can no longer look the other way.

A new image of child care emerges, one of . . .

Happiness and caring,
Hope and sharing,
Trust and giving.
Busy hands and open minds,
Absorbing every moment in time,
Experiencing the joy of living.

SUMMARY

It is the responsibility and privilege of child care leaders and workers to preserve the feeling and message of childhood as a time to wonder, a time to play, and a time to grow so children can remember the way it was and carry happy memories into tomorrow's world. The challenge is to progress beyond the custodial image of child care toward a dynamic role of *shared responsibility* and *common concern.*

Where children are concerned, we all are responsible for their safety and well-being, if for no other reason than it is humane and civilized to care for those who cannot care for themselves. We pick up stray dogs and cats, we feel outrage for animals harmed by greed or used for recreation, we fight to keep trees alive and to clean polluted streams, we are concerned about nutrition and a long life, and we are concerned about the rights of an unborn child. Now we must turn attention and resources to *all* children—to those who have already claimed the right to life. By so doing, we will preserve the meaning of childhood for generations to come and prepare children for a productive, meaningful life.

NOTES

1. M. Whitebrook, C. Howes, and D. Phillips, *Who Cares? Child Care Teachers and the Quality of Care in America,* (Oakland, CA: Child Care Employee Project, 1989), p. 334.

2. National Research Council, *Caring for America's Children* (Washington, DC: National Academy Press, 1991), p. 7.

3. Helen Blank, *The Child Care and Development Block Grant and Child Care Grants to States Under Title IV-A of the Social Security Act* (Washington, DC: The Children's Defense Fund), pp. 35–36.

4. Committee on Ways and Means, "Overview of Entitlement Programs" (Washington, DC: The National Commission on Children, 1991), p. 87. (Cited in *Beyond Rhetoric.*)

5. National Research Council, *Caring for America's Children* (Washington, DC: National Academy Press, 1991), 8.

6. Ibid., p. 41.

7. A. G. Hilliard III, "What Is Quality Child Care?" (Washington, DC: NAEYC, 1985). As cited in Jerome Harris, "The Rhetoric of Early Childhood Education Must Be Replaced by Decisive Action," in *Perspectives on Early Childhood Education,* ed. David Elkind (Washington, DC: National Education Association, 1991), p. 127.

8. National Institute for Early Childhood Professional Development, "A Vision for Early Childhood Professional Development," as cited in *Young Children* 47(1) (November 1991): 35.

9. Betty M. Caldwell, "Early Childhood Education in the 21st Century," *Child Care Information Exchange* 64 (December 1988): 14.

RESOURCES

Antler, J. *Lucy Sprague Mitchell: The Making of a Modern Woman.* New Haven: Yale University Press, 1987.

Coleman, M. *Latchkey Children: Teacher's Taking Action.* Athens, GA: University of Georgia Cooperative Extensive Service, 1984.

Dewey, J. *Democracy and Education.* New York: Macmillan, 1916.

Hill, P. S. "The Function of the Kindergarten Children." *Young Children* 42(5), 1987: 12–20.

Hymes, J. L., Jr. *Early Childhood Education: An Introduction.* Washington, DC: NAEYC, 1975.

Katz, Lilian G., and Sylvia C. Chard, *Engaging Children's Minds: The Project Approach.* Norwood, NJ: Ablex Publishing, 1991.

Shapiro, M. S. *Child's Garden.* University Park, PA: The Pennsylvania State University Press, 1983.

Snyder, A. *Dauntless Women in Childhood Education.* Washington, DC: NAEYC, 1972.

Willer, Barbara, ed. *Reaching the Full Cost of Quality in Early Childhood Programs.* Washington, DC: NAEYC, 1990.

Willer, Barbara, Sandra L. Hofferth, Ellen E. Kisker, et al. *The Demand and Supply of Child Care in 1990.* Washington, DC: NAEYC, 1991.

Families enter a child care facility from the outside. A building creates an image that is meant to attract clientele. Inside a child care center, however, there is another image that is less visible to the public. This image should reflect the real, untouched, untarnished world of childhood; a world of special moments that creates a day for children that is at once unique, special, and memorable; a day unlike any other day.

P A R T II

DESIGNING A CHILD CARE CENTER

No matter what else it does, a good school will seek to build greater enjoyment of people. It will fill each child's school hours with talking to others, thinking together, working with others—with arguing, listening, compromising, laughing. It will provide the experiences a child needs to live, happily and constructively, on a little planet packed with people.

— *James L. Hymes, Jr.*

4

LAYING THE FOUNDATION

CHILD CARE SETTINGS AND CHARACTERISTICS

Child care in the United States is a large and diverse system of home- and group-based centers in multiple settings under many sponsorships. Centers are operated in homes, churches, recreation centers, hospitals, colleges, shopping malls, at the workplace, and in any other location suitable for children. A person entering the field as a director or a teacher will want to consider several options before making a decision. She may prefer to work in a small independently owned center, in a home-care environment, or in a large less personal center that offers benefits such as health care, sick pay, vacation pay, or tuition benefits.

Although centers operate in many settings under various sponsorships, they are generally categorized as group or family day care centers. The *National Child Care Survey* (1990), a collaborative, national research study sponsored by leading organizations and educational institutions, defined out-of-home standard child care arrangements as:

Center Care—Center care takes place in establishments where children are cared for in a group or in a nonresidential setting for all or part of the day. These centers may be nonprofit (sponsored and independent) or for-profit (independent and members of a chain). Nonprofit centers include those sponsored by churches, public schools, community agencies, and the federal Project Head Start program.

Family Day Care—Family day care provides for a small group of children in a caregiver's home. Family day care may be regulated or nonregulated. Nonregulated care refers to care by people who are not licensed or registered.[1]

The pattern of usage tends to shift from family care preferences for children under three years of age to center care for children ages three to twelve years. (See Figure 4–1.)

A companion study (funded by the U.S. Department of Education, Office of Policy and Planning), *A Profile of Child Care Settings* (1990) focusing on the

FIGURE 4–1 Substantial Use of Supplemental Care by Age of Child

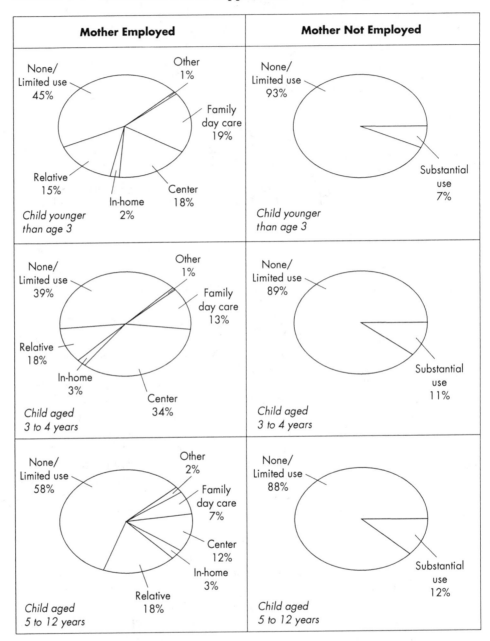

Figures reflect the supplemental child care arrangement used for the most hours per week by the youngest child, excluding school or kindergarten attendance, for those children spending at least 20 hours per week in supplemental care if younger than age 5 or at least 5 hours per week in care if ages 5 to 12.

Source: From *Demand and Supply of Child Care in 1990,* Barbara Willer, et al. Copyright 1991 by The National Association for the Education of Young Children. Reprinted with permission of NAEYC.

FIGURE 4–2   Auspices of Centers

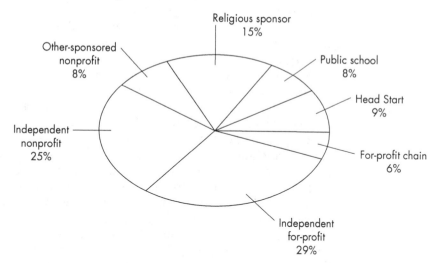

Source: From *Demand and Supply of Child Care in 1990,* Barbara Willer, et al.
Copyright 1991 by The National Association for the Eduction of Young Children.
Reprinted with permission of NAEYC.

characteristics of child care programs, "estimates that there are 80,000 centers serving 4 million preschool children and an additional 1 million school-age children. There are approximately 118,000 regulated family day care providers serving 700,000 children." The National Child Care Survey (1990) "estimates that there are 3.1 million children in nonregulated family day care and any where from 668,000 to 1.2 million nonregulated family day care providers."[2]

The study further reveals that two-thirds (65 percent) of preschool centers are nonprofit organizations, and the remaining one-third (35 percent) operate for-profit. More than half (61 percent) of nonprofit centers are sponsored by another organization—primarily religious organizations, public schools, or Head Start. For-profit programs are more likely to be independent than a part of a local or national chain. Sponsorship tends to reflect regional differences. For example, there are more for-profit centers in the South than in any other region. For-profit centers tend to be located in rural and suburban areas and are least likely to be located in urban areas.[3] (See Figure 4–2.)

LEARNING ABOUT THE FIELD

A First-hand Introduction

The best way to learn about the field is by first-hand experience. Most communities have licensing agencies that can provide written guidelines as well as resource persons to facilitate entry into the field. The primary agencies for licensing child care are generally social welfare agencies and health departments. Another way to obtain information is through resource and referral (R & R) agencies usually listed under county or local government agencies. An R & R agency can provide demographics about facilities and furnish valuable resources for developing a program. Libraries, government offices, and recreation centers can provide pamphlets and resources for parents and providers. By reviewing documents and talking with experts, a person will soon become familiar with the licensing process and the regulations that govern group child care and family care in a given region.

It is not unusual to find considerable differences among licensed facilities in areas of quality, in the background and training of staff, in costs, and in community attitudes toward child care in a given region. Some communities have comprehensive delivery and support systems while others prefer not to extend existing services. In the latter instance, unlicensed home care may be the preferred method of care because it is available and affordable. A director who has set up a licensed center may have to make some necessary adjustments, such as lowering tuition, in order to gain entrance into a community. This may be only a temporary measure until a center becomes established.

Visiting Centers

By visiting centers, a provider will gain valuable insight and information about the kinds and quality of services offered in a community. Talking to a resident director can be very informative. A resident director knows the terrain; she knows what parents are looking for, what they can realistically afford to pay, and what is or is not presently available. She can suggest various plans that guarantee enrollment such as part- and full-time services for preschool and school-age children. The director may even be willing to recommend a newcomer to wait-listed parents. She also may be willing to provide information about recruiting and training staff as well as practical information—where to purchase supplies and equipment, how to construct a staffing pattern and design a classroom, how to find and use community resources. In most instances, child care providers are interested in sharing ideas and in developing close networks within the field.

Visiting with Leaders in the Field

Other community resources available are: libraries, child care consultants, local colleges and universities, public and private agencies, planning experts (who can provide data on population, land availability, zoning, and economic trends), intragovernmental agencies (park and planning, environmental protection, public school, fire, safety and zoning, health coordinators), and accreditation agencies (i.e., The National Academy of Early Childhood Programs, an independent accrediting system sponsored by NAEYC). For further information on accreditation write to the National Academy of Early Childhood Programs (NAEYC), 1834 Connecticut Avenue., N.W., Washington, DC 20009-5786, or telephone NAEYC at 202-232-8777 or 800-424-2460.

A new provider may decide to enlist the services of a consultant to assist in opening a center. The consultant probably has worked in child care for some time and developed a reputation as an expert in the field. She will be familiar with licensing procedures, start-up costs, marketing, advertising, and community resources. Assistance can be provided in interpreting regulations, writing policies and procedures, writing job descriptions, planning a budget, setting up a salary scale, recruiting staff, and designing an environment. Practical guidance at the beginning stages of leadership can prevent costly mistakes.

Conducting a Needs Assessment

A needs assessment is an information-gathering process designed for a specific purpose. If the purpose is to set up a child care center, a prospective director will gather and assess information about existing facilities and day care needs in a community. A preliminary survey will influence decision making, the choice and size of a center, the kind of program to be offered, and the age-levels of children to be served. It also will provide a guideline for setting tuition fees and salaries. Although a needs assessment will not in itself ensure enrollment, it can predict, with reasonable certainty, where the market potential lies. Therefore, it will assist a newcomer in deciding on a program and in marketing a program.

A needs assessment can be conducted by personal interviews, by disseminating questionnaires, and/or by conducting a telephone survey. Possible interview and information resources are: public and private schools, churches, libraries, resource and referral services, community centers, health departments or community service agencies, existing centers, and publications targeted to working women's child care needs.

A Format

When obtaining information about the need and availability of child care, a provider should use a written format that includes: a brief introduction, the purpose of the contact, and specific questions related to the market. A written questionnaire should include assurances of confidentiality, a request for a follow-up phone call, a request for a mailing address, and a stamped, return-address envelope. Questions might include:

- What programs are available in the area?
- What populations are currently being served?
- What do trends reveal (new schools, homes, businesses)?
- What centers are scheduled to open in the next few years?
- What school or county buildings are scheduled for closure?
- What building might have potential for child care services?
- How can existing services be improved?
- How many families receive or need financial assistance?
- What support services are available?
- What after-school programs are available to school-age children?
- What transportation is available?
- What centers are available at the workplace?

- What programs are available to children during the summer months?
- How satisfied are parents with existing arrangements?
- What are the qualities they look for in providers?
- What kinds of activities should be available to school-age children?

After reviewing the data, a provider can evaluate options and select a program that is right for him or her.

SELECTING A LOCATION

Renting Space

After surveying the child care "landscape," a provider will be ready to select a suitable location. Finding a location that is accessible, affordable, appropriate for licensing, and attractively situated is a formidable challenge. Given the volatility and risk-prone nature of the field, the preferred way to obtain space is by renting a building already zoned and licensed for child care. The demand for child care and the shortage of usable space creates competition among applicants. A delay in decision making may cause a provider to lose a prime location. Public schools, churches, and recreational facilities are preferred buildings for child care centers because they meet licensing requirements. Even when a suitable location has been found, it may not pass licensing requirements without substantial modifications. There may not be adequate space for outdoor play. A parking area may not meet specifications for the number of children expected to attend. Indoor space may not be adequate for the number of children expected to attend. Paint and building materials may be hazardous to health. The size and placement of doors, windows, screens, hallways, stairways, and bathrooms are also factors in gaining approval.

In some communities, resistance to a child care facility may become vocal enough to delay a scheduled opening. A child care center may be seen by homeowners as a negative factor in property value assessments. Neighbors also may cite noise levels, traffic increases, or safety as reasons for not having a child care center in a residential community. Community activists or spokespersons can be very persuasive when they organize to stop a project. Before leasing a building or a home in a residential neighborhood, a director may want to interview neighbors and meet with citizens' groups to be certain there is no opposition.

Difficulty in obtaining space is compounded by the day care image that continues to influence landlord/center relationships. Traditionally child care centers have not been preferred tenants and for very good reasons. A full-service (7:00 A.M. to 6:00 P.M.) program is very hard on a facility. Children quickly wear out buildings, landscaping, and generous landlords. They rearrange landscapes, dig up annuals, gather twigs and rocks, dig around bushes, and take stones from driveways. They make trenches and mud puddles, and wear down grassy areas. They bring the outside world inside with muddy shoes, sand, and fingerprints.

Another problem is one of reliability. Traditionally, child care centers have not been seen as stable, viable organizations. They are usually one of the first public services affected by adverse changes in the economy. When family-assistance funds are no longer available, centers must absorb the loss or dismiss a child. When jobs are threatened, parents look for alternative, less costly, means of child care.

Still another problem is one of hidden, unexpected costs that are not covered in leases. A modest rental fee can quickly escalate when landlords begin to look at budget overruns. A center may be required to pay a fair share of mounting utility and maintenance bills. It may be asked to build additional storage space for trikes and outdoor equipment that are currently being stored in hallways. As is often the case, the good intentions that brought a provider and a landlord together may become strained by common problems.

It is not unusual for child care centers to experience several moves before they find a home. A home is a place that has passed the break-in test. It is a place where children and staff can grow—where they can feel comfortable and accepted, make changes, plant flowers, and report broken items without experiencing too many raised eyebrows.

Renting Space in a Religious Facility

Advantages.   Churches and other religious facilities generally make extremely desirable environments for independently owned child care centers. They convey a sense of security, are usually minimally used during the week, and are environmentally pleasing. In addition, churches often are willing to offer amenities that are not always available to centers, such as the use of a social hall for family/center events, the use of a bus and, in some instances, liability insurance. In a church environment that is appropriate for summer use, a center may extend its services to include a summer camp, thereby generating additional revenue.

Disadvantages.   Independent child care centers may not enjoy long-term security in religious institutions. Many churches, recognizing the advantages of sponsoring a church-run child care center, are no longer willing to lease classroom space to independent providers. In fact, nine of the ten organizations with the most child care centers in this country are religious organizations. According to the publisher/editor of the *Child Care Information Exchange,* Roger Neugebauer, these programs constitute ". . . a dominant diverse, vibrant, growing segment of the child care world."[4] Churches have a variety of reasons for opening centers—the opportunity to provide religious education, to better serve a community, to provide church members an opportunity to work or volunteer for a church-sponsored project. In addition, a congregation views child care as a revenue-producing asset that is a week-day complement to other church functions.

When space is available for leasing, nursery schools or small private schools are often viewed as more compatible tenants than day care centers. Such schools do not require use of a building during religious holidays and tend to limit their hours to accommodate church needs. In instances where such schools are extending their services to include extended care, they tend not to offer full-service, full-year programs. Working parents who need year-round coverage are not likely to register in part-time centers. Increasingly parents are confronted with agonizing choices in selecting a center: "Which center will best meet my needs and those of my child?"

Renting Space in Public Schools

Advantages.   Public schools offer many advantages. They have a natural population for a center to draw from, and they are ready candidates for licensing. The presence of professionals in a building tends to lessen parental concerns about child safety. In addition, there are opportunities for center children to participate in cultural events, to buy hot lunches, and to share outdoor equipment with school-age children. Principals often are willing to provide indoor equipment as well: gymnastic mats; jump ropes; balls; tables; chairs; shelves; library items; discards from science, math, and language departments; video equipment; and art supplies.

Child care and public school personnel become good friends. A cook, a custodian, a librarian, a gym teacher, a school nurse, a bus driver, a secretary, and a playground aide frequently interact with a child care staff. Public school teachers, unaccustomed to little children walking through hallways, enjoy the presence of familylike centers in their building. Some may even elect to work in centers before and after school.

Disadvantages.   The physical amenities of being located in a public school may be offset by limited space, frequent room changes, and a short-term annual lease. Rarely will schools commit space for more than one year at a time. As public schools grow in enrollment, centers are forced to reduce space. Under volatile circumstances, centers cannot feel secure about the future. They cannot plan beyond one year, and they cannot offer families the security of long-term care. Insecurity causes them to avoid making costly financial commitments to staff such as fringe benefits or higher salaries.

In public schools that house preschool centers, young children must share bathrooms (if they are not in kindergarten space), and they must contend with crowded hallways and playgrounds. Teachers are compelled to reduce children's noise levels and limit activities to accommodate the school's needs. They may, for example, avoid using musical instruments or large-motor play that generates noise. Children are expected to walk in lines, wait their turn, and speak softly. They learn to contend with public announcements they don't understand, to be awakened for a schoolwide fire drill, and to experience ill-mannered "big kids" who use bad language and sometimes push them around.

Ways to Foster Good Feelings.   To strengthen relationships between a school and a center, a director may want to consider these suggestions:

* Avoid letting dissension fester into an unpleasant relationship.
* Develop an honest, reinforcing relationship with public-school personnel.

- Volunteer to serve on a PTA board as a child care representative.
- Invite a principal and/or members of the staff to serve on a center's Advisory Board.
- Find ways a center and a school can work in tandem on schoolwide or community projects.
- Invite principals and staff to workshops and special events.
- Distribute center newsletters.
- Consult with public-school teachers on children's behavior and progress.
- Reinforce and expand a curriculum in appropriate ways.
- Get to know counselors, librarians, and custodians.
- Model a program through positive interaction and communication.

Renting Space on or Near a Workplace

Advantages.   Leasing a building that is on or near a workplace or business corridor will ensure enrollment. Many employers prefer not to get into the business of child care. Issues of cost and liability tend to discourage on-site facilities. Benefits such as liberal parental-leave policies, flexitime, and work-at-home options are less problematic ways to support employees. Many companies, therefore, are amenable to supporting off-site centers in return for guaranteed space for employees' children. In a reciprocal relationship, a company may offer to renovate a building for child care, assist in the start-up phase by subsidizing the cost of equipment, and market a new center through company channels. In addition to guaranteeing space for children, a provider might ask members of a business community to serve on a board of directors.

A center close to a workplace will naturally draw working parents. Parents not only save time, but they are able to spend quality time with their young child during break times or lunch hours. In this way, they can get to know a center's staff and the children in their child's environment. In some circumstances, these centers will provide sick, after-hour, and emergency care as enrollment incentives. Parents naturally experience less stress, less absenteeism, and greater productivity.

Disadvantages.   There do not appear to be many disadvantages to a center designed for working parents unless parents have to change locations or jobs or unless children outgrow the center. A mother of a two-year-old and a six-year-old may find herself commuting between two centers at some distance from each other. A group center that serves both preschool and school-age children may better meet her needs.

Other Suitable Facilities

By no means, should a provider be limited to traditional settings when selecting a site for a child care center. Swim clubs, warehouses, shopping malls, gymnastic centers, places of business, government buildings, private schools, college campuses, nurseries, nursing homes, and hospital wings can be adapted to serve as child care settings. Suffice it to say, any new venture needs vision as well as practicality. A creative entrepreneur can find a building in urban, suburban, or rural settings that, with a little imagination, an initial investment, and a lot of hard work, can become a beautiful children's center.

Overcoming Barriers

Sometimes an initial setback can become an opportunity. If a director is unable to secure space in the private sector, she may be in a favorable position to lobby for space in a county building. By demonstrating competency and by convincing public officials child care is needed, she may secure a location that heretofore was not available. A written proposal and documentation that supports such a need will facilitate the process. With the demand for child care so great, schools are looking for innovative ways to solve an increasingly burdensome problem. They are recognizing the positive correlation between full-day, quality care and school performance. Moreover, they are increasingly sensitive to parental pressure to provide school-age child care in a child's home school. It is commonly understood that a child who lacks supervision and guidance before and after school hours is a likely prospect for poor academic performance, behavioral difficulties, and eventual school drop-out.

Negotiating a Rental Agreement

Before signing a lease, a director should confer with an attorney, who can help a director to protect an investment. An attorney might be successful in defraying some of the initial start-up costs (such as an advance deposit requirement), in reducing monthly payments, in gaining in-kind services such as janitorial help, and in extending the length of a lease beyond one year. A rental lease generally includes most or all of the following:

- The general terms and duration of the agreement
- The penalty for default on rent
- Insurance requirements
- Utilities and grounds responsibility
- Parking stipulations
- Provisions for trash removal
- Provisions for custodial services
- Space allocations: classrooms, storage rooms, bathrooms, play areas, and auxiliary space—a gym, an all-purpose room, a media center, a library, a health room, computer access, hall lockers, a teacher's lounge
- Contact persons for plumbing or maintenance problems
- Sublet restrictions
- Responsibility for replacing consumables (e.g., light bulbs, screens, paper towels, soap, trash liners)
- Procedures and the cost for renting space beyond designated hours and for renting auxiliary space
- Provisions for bus transportation (a child who participates in an after-school activity may need transportation to a child care center)
- Persons to contact: lessee, lessor

Purchasing Land

Buying land (or a building) is not financially possible for most independent caregivers without sufficient resources to invest. Even with start-up capital, commercial loans are difficult to obtain because child care is a high-risk, volatile industry whose continuance depends on many variables: the reputation of a director, a center's following, the ability to secure insurance, economic contingencies, population trends, and competition in the field. The most likely candidates to qualify for a commercial loan are a husband-and-wife team or a partnership with a proven financial record—individuals who are looking for an investment. Obtaining help from a real estate agent is an important first step because an agent is cognizant of zoning ordinances, land availability, and its accessibility to major arteries or roadways that connect centers to workplaces. At the outset, it is important to look at a site from the perspective of its market potential by answering these questions:

- What programs are nearby?
- What ages are served?
- Are the programs fully enrolled?
- Are there waiting lists?
- What are the population trends in the area?
- What are the business and commercial plans for the surrounding areas?
- What residential projects are being planned?
- What schools are opening or closing?
- What hidden costs might be incurred?
- What else do I need to know: zoning and land-use restrictions, the cost of preparing the site, architectural and engineering fees, licensing and permit fees, legal fees, information about builders, the attitude of a community home-owners' association toward child care, real estate taxes, land value, and/or other uses for the building?

Zoning

Zoning ordinances regulate land use. When choosing a location for a day care center, it is necessary to review the zoning requirements for the site. Each city and town has ordinances that control the use of land. An examination of the zoning requirements will determine whether day care is a permitted use or if it is necessary to obtain a special exception from a local zoning board. In many residential areas, getting zoning approval is a problem for child care providers because centers tend to increase density and traffic and noise levels. For these reasons day care centers are viewed by many as undesirable neighbors. It is not unusual for a family that once depended on a center for child care to petition against its expansion if personal property values are at risk. Complying with zoning requirements can be a tedious and costly process, often requiring legal and technical assistance.

Leasing County Land, Building a Center

Negotiating with a county agency or a school board to lease public land that is not projected for future development may attract some child care investors. Most county-owned land falls under less stringent zoning requirements than residential or commercial property. Without the added cost of purchasing land and with fewer obstacles to gaining permits and licensing approval, a provider may be able to find the capital for a building. A school district may be willing to explore land-leasing arrangements with nonprofit providers or with cooperative sponsors, such as parents, as a means for creating affordable space for a prospective child care center.

A director may initiate a land search by talking to a park and planning expert or a school principal. Once land has been leased, the challenge is putting together enough financial resources to complete the project. A long-term land lease (e.g., fifteen years) will facilitate borrowing money for a building from a commercial lender.

Under a land-lease arrangement, a public or private school will require certain rights of ownership with regard to the upkeep and use of a building and its adjoining property. Activities and hours of operation may be restricted so as not to disturb the neighborhood. A sublet clause may further limit the use of a building. Most school systems or county agencies, however, would be receptive to allowing co-tenant occupants who are both compatible and community-oriented—senior citizens, religious groups, recreation programs, the performing arts, or child care related organizations. By teaming up with such a group, a director may be better able to finance a building.

Raising Capital for a Building

An innovative director may want to consider the following ideas:

1. *Write a proposal for foundation money:* There are over 21,000 foundations in the United States whose purpose is to encourage and support worthwhile causes that are in keeping with the aims and purposes of the foundation. Projects targeted toward enriching community life such as child care definitely are considered worthy. The more focused a proposal is, the more likely it is to attract attention— i.e., combining child care with special needs or intergenerational programs that benefit children and communities, creating an arts and child care model, creating a model infant–toddler program, creating an internship program that provides training opportunities for students at high school and college levels.

2. *Form a limited partnership of investors* in which each partner has some degree of decision-making authority and a continued interest in the financial success of a center.

3. *Form a partnership* with a special needs center, a performing arts group, or a counseling service—a combination that might qualify for grant or foundation money.

4. *Require parents to pay a facilities fee* at the time of registration, but be prepared to make exceptions for those parents who can't afford to participate in the plan. A family might be asked to pay a user fee of $250 to be returned in full when a family leaves the center. A facility fee, interest-bearing account will provide a center with much needed cash flow during the construction phase of a project.

5. *Offer a pre-pay opportunity* to a limited number of families to reduce their tuition significantly (e.g., 10 percent). This plan will reduce monthly revenue, but it will provide the necessary capital to get started.

6. *Write a proposal or solicit help from local politicians* to obtain state money for the construction of a building. After considerable paperwork, lobbying, and effort, a state matching bond or a direct loan may be obtained.

7. *Form a partnership with a public school system* whereby both parties collaborate in building a multi-age center.

8. *Look into county or local loans* for child care providers.

9. *Solicit businesses and organizations* for financial assistance or in-kind services in exchange for guaranteeing slots for their employees.

10. *Plan a gala fundraiser or special event* with a goal in mind; plan ahead, organize carefully, and make it a blockbuster that will set a precedent for future fundraisers.

11. *Solicit in-kind services* from local lumber companies, electrical supply companies, builders, nurseries, fencing companies, and business and community leaders.

12. *Offer friends the opportunity to participate* in a building-related project that gives them recognition and a sense of identification, e.g., buy a brick, plant a tree, contribute something to a room such as a media center or to a playground.

By demonstrating effectiveness in raising capital and gaining support from public and private sources, a director will be in a favorable position to complete or expand a project. A bank will look upon the project as a secure and worthy investment. Local businesses will want to be a part of a center's success when they know there is benefit to a community. They may participate by offering a contribution or by extending in-kind services—a landscaping company may provide trees and fencing; a home security company, protection; and a builder, a paved driveway or storage shed.

Leasing Modulars for On-site Use

A director may find it more advantageous to lease a modular unit(s)—a pre-fab building that is assembled on site—than to construct a freestanding building on county-owned land. A good place to obtain modulars is from public facilities such as schools and libraries who use these buildings as add-ons or as temporary classrooms. If a modular is placed on land contiguous to a school, a director might expect public-school services and support and would not have the burden of ownership. Many modulars, however, are not space-appropriate for all-day early childhood use.

Near-site Alternatives

Some public-school principals prefer to work with a center that is in the neighborhood. They may be willing to provide free transportation to a child care home or group center. By providing support services, a principal is meeting needs while relieving his school of the responsibilities and problems associated with child care. For child care providers who are within the proximity of public schools, this form of assistance is very welcome.

Purchasing an Existing Building

Purchasing and renovating a building or a home for child care use has a great deal of appeal to those people who enjoy a creative challenge. Before embarking on such a venture a careful investigation of the existing facility and its surroundings must be made. The following questions will facilitate decision making:

- What is its proximity to other centers?
- Does the building meet safety and fire codes?
- Are the environs suitable for staff?
- Can the space be adapted to school-age use?
- Does the building meet specifications for physically disabled children: ramps for wheel chairs, support bars in bathrooms, low water fountains?
- What is the general condition of the land and of the building? What modifications will need to be made?
- Has the building or site been inspected and approved for child care use by a fire marshal, a health inspector, a sanitary official, an engineer, a licensing coordinator, and a child care consultant?
- What are the possibilities for expansion?
- Are there zoning ordinances or restrictions?
- How accessible is the property?
- What is it going to take to make this work—what is the cost estimate, where will the funds come from, how long will it take to get zoning or license approval?

SELECTING A PROGRAM

A Profile of Family Care

A provider should visualize herself as a leader and worker in a specific kind of environment—in a smaller home setting or in a larger group setting. One's background, training, personality, financial and family status, and personal goals will assist in this important decision-making process.

In general, a licensed home provider is limited to six children. With minimal space needs, a children's area is set up in a recreation room that has outdoor access and a fenced play area. A licensed group home is somewhat larger and more integrated into a family home. It may serve as many as thirteen children at a time. A provider would be required to hire an assistant during much of the day and to have a formal program for children in her care.

Traditionally a home provider has been likened to a mom—a warm, kind person who soon becomes a member of a family. She enjoys doing what she has always done—taking care of children and sees herself as a caregiver, more custodial than educative in orientation. Under her supervision, children play and amuse themselves much of the time. When companionship is needed, "mom" is there to comfort children with a hug or with something special from the kitchen. An added treat is the presence of "pop" or a visiting relative who knows how to make a child smile.

The custodial image identified with home care is changing, however. An increasing number of young, educated females are opening their homes to child care for quite different reasons: companionship for their own children, a desire to be with their children during the formative years, a need to be purposefully occupied, a desire to feel a sense of self-worth and independence from the family structure. The shift toward more professionalism in home care is indicative of the increasing status that is identified with child care employment. At best, in licensed home arrangements, children are given personal care and a planned program.

Advantages

In licensed home environments, there are fewer regulations, less paperwork, less responsibility, less risk (because there are fewer children and staff), and a greater sense of control. Unlike directors of nonprofit group centers, home providers receive the benefits of being self-employed and only marginally attached to a child care network. They have a great deal of freedom in selecting the families they serve, in setting tuition, and in administrative decision making. They are not bound by contractual agreements or job descriptions. They can work around their own family's needs by closing a center during holidays and special events that are too important to miss. Even with this flexibility, a good provider will have little difficulty finding children.

Many parents prefer home care for children of all ages because it does not resemble a school. There is less structure and more time for spontaneous play than in group centers. For the young child, the environment is less overwhelming than in a large group center and therefore less problematic. Children are likely to make a successful adjustment when there is a primary adult present all day, personal attention, and a consistent environment. Children also identify with familiar activities they have experienced in their own homes—trips to the store, park outings, cooking and baking, washing and cleaning, watching repairmen, and visiting neighbors. For the school-age child, there is more opportunity for independence. If a child care home is within walking distance to a school, a child may enjoy after-school activities and occasional visits with friends—opportunities that make him feel grown-up and important.

A home environment offers a child consistency and security. A child and a provider can quickly bond in healthy and positive ways. To a young child, a provider is a friend and role model similar to his real mom.

In addition, a home environment offers parents more flexibility in accommodating working schedules and in caring for children who are not feeling well. There is usually no contract to sign and more forgiveness if tuition is late.

Disadvantages

Unless a child is with a friend or a relative in a familiar home, there are many reasons for feeling anxious about a home-care facility. In both licensed and unlicensed homes where few adults are present, there is little accountability. In licensed homes, there are few inspections to ensure compliance; in unlicensed homes, there are virtually no safeguards to ensure child safety. A parent has no way of knowing whether children are seat-belted on automobile outings, left alone in homes, or at risk in the company of a school drop-out who spends his time watching television. Nor does a parent have any way of knowing how many children are present throughout the day or whether the home is child-safe. Consequently, a parent/provider relationship must be built on trust.

From a child's perspective, there are fewer peers and adults to interact with, fewer toys and activities, and often less to do than in group centers. In small environments, there may be more nurturance but less intellectual challenge and social stimulation. Friendships often are made from necessity rather than from choice when there is no one else to play with. Providers, too, may feel unable to provide the quality of care that children need. They may not be able to take children to libraries or recreational facilities where there is an opportunity for adult interaction. On a full-day, full-week schedule there is hardly time for professional meetings, luncheons, and workshops. As routine sets in, a home provider may see little reason for improving the services families are paying for.

In time, a home environment can become stagnant and unsatisfying—more like babysitting than *educare*. And . . . there is no custodian to shovel snow, clean floors, and visit with; there is no opportunity to eat in the "big kids' cafeteria"; there is no opportunity to hug an older brother or sister; there is no opportunity to visit a haunted house on Halloween or to attend a special show in an all-purpose room.

A Profile of Group Care

The number of group centers is rapidly increasing, especially in urban areas. A licensed group center is somewhat more safeguarded against risks than a home environment; there are more adults present, more regulations, and fewer unknowns. Competition in the marketplace, licensing requirements, the cost of insurance, and the constant concerns about personal liability, serve as additional safeguards for children's well-being.

Advantages

Group centers offer a program similar to traditional nursery-school programs— group activities, play centers, arts and crafts, storytime, a season or study theme, lunch/rest, and a somewhat less structured afternoon. Because teachers are required to have some training in child development, a parent expects early childhood needs to be met. In group care, children naturally develop social skills at an early age. They are exposed to more materials and activities than are children in home environments. A required indoor/outdoor space provision prevents overcrowding.

Parents are kept informed about scheduled activities and events and encouraged to participate in center functions. A formal enrollment agreement establishes administrative policies. A parent handbook provides information about a center's program and child-related policies. Written policies and procedures promote trust and confidence.

Disadvantages

Space is always a common concern for group centers. Most states require a minimum of 35 square feet of interior space and 75 square feet of exterior space per child—hardly adequate for large-motor play, activity centers, common space, personal space, and vigorous outdoor play. Consequently, many group centers operate under such crowded conditions that children's overall development is compromised. In multi-age centers, it is not unusual for school-age children to share equipment with preschool children. When space and materials are limited, adjustments must be made in order to meet children's developmental needs. When conditions are inadequate, children do not experience a comforting, homelike environment. If given the choice, they would probably choose to be somewhere other than day care.

Similarly, staff become negative, fatigued, and ill-tempered in crowded conditions. Staff turnover and dissatisfaction are more the rule than the exception in group centers. Ultimately, the child is the loser. In a poorly planned, impersonal environment, there is little space for self-development, for personal interaction, or for messing around. Child development expert, Jim Greenman, writes:

> Today we have institutionalized our children; there is no other word for it. Many children almost from birth, are in a world of organized experiences and managed groups—child care, preschool, after-school programs, camps, swim/ gym and other classes.
> . . . What is missing in the real world of people and nature and machines is an opportunity to explore that world and be a part of it. In the past children did not need special places for play. They lived amidst shops and tradespeople

and mothers and fathers working around the home. And they had the time and freedom in their lives to mess about.[5]

MATCHING A PROGRAM TO ITS ENVIRONMENT

Working with Space

A program is shaped, in large part, by its environment. Every building has advantages and disadvantages. Innovative and practical use of space is essential to a well-functioning program. If outdoor space is limited, a director can compensate by setting up a large-motor room for indoor play during heavy-use preschool hours. With some adjustment, the same room can be used as an income-producing school-age room after 3:00 P.M.

The size of classrooms influences program planning. Small rooms serve the needs of toddlers through three-year-olds while larger rooms are best for larger numbers of children such as four- or five-year-olds. An all-purpose room can be divided into several smaller rooms for school-age children. Auxiliary space such as a large storage room can be used as office space, restrooms, or additional classroom space. It may, for example, be set up as a small homework room, an art room, or a book nook. Pillows, murals, and a lamp will help to make the little add-on the most popular spot on campus.

If space can be apportioned to meet multi-age needs, a program is more likely to maintain full enrollment. A program that offers full- and part-time preschool care will open space for school-age children and better serve the needs of working parents. Room dividers such as bulletin boards or freestanding screens can be used to change space to accommodate multi-age levels.

Other Considerations

Selecting a program is something like weaving a tapestry; each component must feed into the master design. The following questions need to be considered:

- What ages of children will the program serve?
- Is the program suited to the space available?
- What alterations should be made and at what cost?
- What will the hours be? What will the calendar year be?
- Will there be openings for special-needs children, for families in need of financial assistance, for subsidized, voucher arrangements with a county or local agency?
- Will hot meals be served?
- What support staff will be needed—a nurse, a cook, a custodian, a bus driver, an educational consultant?
- What will the staff/student ratio be?
- What staffing pattern will be implemented?

- During what periods of the day will maximum staff be required?
- Can staffing be staggered to accommodate fluctuating periods of the day (opening, closing, rest-time)?
- What are the qualifications for employment?
- What plans have been made for in-house training?
- What salary scale is being considered?
- What benefits are being considered?
- Will the provider seek accreditation from NAEYC or other licensing agencies?
- What is the cost of accreditation and what are the benefits?
- How can the program be cost-effective without sacrificing quality? Where can savings be realized?
- What interns or volunteers can assist in staffing a center?
- Will there be free transportation to and from the center for kindergarten-age children and for elementary-age children? If not, should a bus be leased with an option to purchase?
- Will there be a summer program? How will it be different from a center's regular program?
- What equipment will be needed, and where can it be purchased?
- What materials and resources are needed?
- What is available in the community?
- How can parents be most effective in program development and public relations?

Most programs operate on a full-year basis from 7:00 A.M. to 6:30 P.M. Centers are open on days of inclement weather and on most holidays with the exception of Labor Day, Christmas, Easter, Memorial Day, and Independence Day. It is wise to close a center for a few days between semesters. Extra days, during Christmas and Easter holidays and before and after summer vacation, provide staff with a much needed break and enable a center to clean, repair, and refurbish the environment. If parents are given a calendar at the beginning of a term, they can make arrangements for child care on days when a center is closed.

A program that offers both preschool and school-age care will have to plan for half days, inclement weather, and holidays when school-age children need additional hours of care. During these times, there may be more children than a license allows. By limiting hours in one class—i.e., setting up a part-time, 7:30 A.M. to 12:30 P.M., three-year-old class—or by asking for additional space on these days—i.e., a gym or all-purpose room—a provider will have space for additional needs.

When planning a program and assigning space, it is important to consider all possibilities; a part-time parent user wants to change to full-time care, a part-time parent needs to extend her child's hours to include naptime on certain days, a full-time parent wants to reduce her child's hours to accommodate a change in her working schedule, a kindergarten group arrives a half hour earlier than anticipated and no interim space is available. The more variables there are in a program, the more complicated is the planning and organization.

MARKETING A PROGRAM

A program with a reputation for standards of excellence will need little additional publicity than what takes place naturally when people are connected in meaningful ways. Therefore, the best and least expensive way to promote a center is through a parent/center network. Some ideas for marketing a center are to:

- Communicate effectively with parents by sharing leadership and by involving parents in activities and events that encourage communication and interaction.
- Inform parents about a center through written correspondence, through workshops, and through parent/teacher conferences.
- Request parents' assistance in informing new parents about a center.
- Invite parents and friends to a weekly social held at convenient time—it may be as simple as an afternoon tea party held around 5:00 P.M. on Fridays.
- Plan a special parent/center project each semester that involves the community—i.e., sponsoring a community outreach program (collecting food for poor families, coordinating activities with a homeless shelter), planning an annual sports event for adult/child participation, starting a special club (a scouts group, an environmental or a hiking club), and/or planning a staff recognition picnic.
- Assemble an annual "important activities" book with photos, illustrations, and writings describing special events.
- Design a logo that is used on stationery, mailings, and at special events to create a sense of identity and belonging, e.g., a sun, an owl, or children holding hands; a symbol also can be printed on backpacks, shorts, shirts, and a center's flag.
- Post notices of special events and activities on a parent bulletin board.
- Distribute a monthly newsletter.
- Distribute a handbook that describes a center's philosophy, program options, curriculum, policies, and procedures.
- Distribute parent/child/center articles for parent edification. These articles may be discussed during a parent roundtable held once a month.
- Be administratively efficient and sensitive to parents' needs—i.e., by responding to calls and pop-in visits in a meaningful and caring way.

Some ideas for marketing a center in a community are to:

- Advertise in local papers.
- Promote a center through county bulletins and newsletters.
- Distribute flyers in public places.
- Plan a special event and invite the whole community.
- Invite interested parents and friends to an annual Open House—a day when a music or drama teacher visits classrooms or when there is a special event.

DESIGNING FOR QUALITY

The concept of quality child care has generated considerable interest among educators and parents. Easy-to-obtain pamphlets provide parents a list of features and questions that attempt to address the issue. Since most centers would describe themselves as quality centers or know enough, when asked, to project a quality image, parents are left with the difficult choice of choosing one center over another. A "position paper" published by The Association for Childhood Education International (ACEI) and referred to in Gotts (1988) describes a quality center. In center-based programs care must be:

1. Developmentally focused and culturally salient;
2. Offered by qualified adults who are wise and caring;
3. Provided in environments designed and equipped for learning, arranged for safety and privacy as well as activities and interaction;
4. Professionally directed and managed;
5. Assisted by community service providers.

Moreover, such programs must attend to health, nutrition, and social concerns and encourage lively parent involvement. They must be educational in the broadest sense.[6]

Features of Quality

In concrete terms (defined elements of quality that can be interpreted and implemented by providers), there is agreement that quality can be viewed from both structural/environmental and human/interactional perspectives. Within these categories there are ten specific indicators discussed below that are identified with quality.

Licensing

State licensing is identified with legal protection, accountability, regulatory standards, and the safe caregiving of young children. Licensing establishes a basic level of quality that often is not present in unlicensed facilities. It is commonly understood that all group centers are licensed and the majority of family home centers are not. Research supports a licensed environment over an unlicensed environment as a measure of quality.

Findings from The Chicago Study of Child Care and Development[7] indicate that children in licensed center programs do better than children in homes across a variety of child-development measures (language, intelligence, social competence, independence). It was found that children in centers, as contrasted to children in unlicensed homes, spend more time in group activities—including more teacher-initiated activities such as, singing and being read to—and less time watching television and playing with an adult. Children's experiences in licensed group centers were found to be more structured than in home-care arrangements and more likely to be guided by an explicit educational curriculum. In group centers, staff are expected to have training in child development, a college background, and experience in the field. In licensed home centers, it is assumed that providers meet similar qualifications for working with children, implement child development programs, and are receiving ongoing training in the field.

Group Size

A National Day Care Study (NDCS, 1977) involving 1,800 preschool children from Atlanta, Detroit, and Seattle conducted over a four-year period found that group size is the most powerful and pervasive factor in measuring quality.

> In groups where the absolute number of children was small, children were more cooperative and responsive to initiatives by adults and other children, more likely to engage in spontaneous verbalization and creative/intellectual activity, and less likely to wander aimlessly or to be uninvolved in activities than were children in larger groups.[8]

The study also showed that children in small groups make more rapid gains on standardized tests than their peers in larger groups. In this study, favorable adult/child ratios in large groups did not offset the negative effects of large groupings.

The National Research Council suggests a "range for group size of: 6 to 8 infants, 6 to 12 one-year-olds or two-year-olds, 14 to 20 three-year-olds, and 16 to 20 four- or five-year-olds."[9]

Staff/Child Ratio

The National Day Care Study also found higher ratios of children to adult caregiver to be associated with more distress and apathy in young children with fewer opportunities for staff/child interaction. "The following ranges are recommended by The National Research Council: 4 infants or one-year-olds per caregiver, 4 to 6 two-year-olds per caregiver, 5 to 10 three-year-olds per caregiver, and 7 to 10 four- or five-year-olds per caregiver."[10] In "Quality Criteria for School Age Programs," Project Home Safe[11] recommends the following staff–child ratios:

Age of Children and Youth	Group Size					
	16	18	20	22	24	26
5 years	1:8	1:9	1:10			
6–8 years		1:9	1:10	1:11	1:12	
9 years and up			1:10	1:11	1:12	1:13

Caregiver Behavior

ACEI's position paper on "The Right to Quality Child Care" states that regardless of the setting, the quality of adult–child interactions is the most vital ingredient in an assessment of quality.[12] In small group settings, there is time for conversation, for exploration and discussion, and for social development. A teacher is able to manage tasks and to complete objectives. Learning and behavioral problems are quickly noticed and dealt with when a teacher has time to interact qualitatively with a child. Because children are less hurried and programmed, there are fewer discipline problems and more opportunities to reinforce good behavior.

Qualifications and Training

Research studies recognize caregivers' training in child development and their overall years of education as important to children's experiences and development.[13] It has been found that qualified caregivers demonstrate positive social interaction with children. They tend to spend more time praising, talking to, comforting, and responding to children than do untrained caregivers. Specialized adult training is correlated with children's higher achievement and better test scores. In the National Child Care Study, it was found that formal training at the college or university level was less significant than specialized training in child development.[14] For further information, see pages 18–20 of *Accreditation Criteria and Procedures of the National Academy of Early Childhood Programs.*

Space

Standards for determining the number of children that can be accommodated in a defined area have been established by most states as minimum of 35 square feet of usable indoor space per child and 75 square feet of outdoor space per child. Usable space is the space that exists exclusive of fixed items such as cupboards, sinks, built-in shelves, and room dividers. Many directors see the advantage of opening indoor and outdoor space to accommodate play-oriented curriculums. Crowded, poorly designed space inhibits children's movement, curiosity, and development. The NAEYC recommends that an indoor and outdoor environment be designed to promote "easy, constructive interactions among adults and children."[15] This may best be accomplished by setting up activity areas for quiet and active play and by providing adequate space.

Developmentally Appropriate Curriculum

The NAEYC has developed guidelines for developmentally appropriate practice in programs serving children from birth through age eight. The criteria represents the consensus of early childhood professionals with regard to standards of quality in areas of curriculum, staffing qualifications, staff/student ratios, staff/child interactions, parent/center interactions, the physical and human environments that surround the child, and issues of health, safety, and nutrition. Refer to *Accreditation Criteria and Procedures of the National Academy of Early Childhood Programs* (NAEYC #92) and *Developmentally Appropriate Practice in Early Childhood Programs Serving Children Birth through Age Eight* (NAEYC #224) for more information.

With regard to curriculum guidelines, NAEYC's criteria for a quality program recommends active, hands-on learning experiences that encourage exploration and learning through discovery. Children should experience a variety of activities and materials that complement age, interests, and learning styles. Activities should be balanced throughout the day. Children should be responsible for the care and maintenance of their environment. Children should experience both child-initiated and teacher-guided activities in a multicultural environment that recognizes and respects diversity. Children should "learn through play that is organized by adults to teach them language concepts, skills, and self-confidence."[16]

Parent Participation

There is a positive correlation between a child's progress in a child care center and parents participation in a child's center environment. An interactive, supportive partnership is essential to a child's continued well-being in an out-of-home environment. In quality centers, parents are expected to participate in all facets of the child care program. The NAEYC recommends that parents be given a careful orientation to a center; continue to be informed about a center's policies, procedures, activities, and events; become welcomed visitors and participants; communicate closely with a center's staff; and, as needed, discuss children's progress through conferences held at least once a year or more frequently if needed.[17]

Health, Safety, and Nutrition

In quality centers, attention must be given to preventing illness, caring for sick children when necessary, handling emergencies, and educating children about health, safety, and nutrition. The following guidelines are recommended by most state licensing agencies: licensing programs; maintaining health records on children and staff; updating written policies and procedures; periodically evaluating policies and procedures; being attentive to transportation and field-trip safety; maintaining a child-safe environment, i.e., reporting accidents and signs of abuse or neglect; inspecting equipment and materials for safety, being alert to poisonous or unhealthy elements in an environment, practicing good hygiene and sanitary procedures, posting emergency numbers and procedures; following licensing guidelines; providing children well-balanced, healthy meals and snacks that are recommended by nutritional experts such as the U.S. Department of Agriculture. For meal and snack recommendations and requirements for food service and preparation, see *Accreditation Criteria and Procedures*, Appendices C and D (NAEYC #92). For additional information on health, safety, and nutrition, see pages 28 to 36 of *Accreditation Criteria and Procedures*.

Evaluation

A quality center considers ongoing evaluation of staff effectiveness and children's progress an important administrative responsibility. Many centers request evaluations from parents as well. The NAEYC recommends that teacher evaluations include self-assessment and classroom observation by a director (or another person in leadership), with an opportunity for private discussion. NAEYC also recommends that children's progress reports be kept on file and shared with parents. Centerwide evaluations are also recommended.[18]

An NEA Forecast for Early Education in the Twenty-first Century

In a statement that addressed goals for early childhood education in the public schools, Keith Geiger (1991) includes child care as an integral part of the public-school delivery and credentialing system. NEA standards include:

- Early childhood education programs in the public schools must address the needs of both parents and child.
- High-quality programming should properly integrate day care and educational components and be supported by the resources and staff necessary to accomplish the delivery of both kinds of services.
- Both teachers and administrators associated with the public schools and early childhood programs should complete a distinguishable program and should hold a distinguishable state-preparation issued license to practice.
- School districts should offer at their expense appropriate courses in training for educational support staff working in early childhood program.
- Assessment methods used in early childhood programs should be appropriate to a child's developmental needs. The use of norm-referenced, standardized testing instruments in early childhood education programs is inappropriate.
- Teaching, administrative, and support staff working in early childhood education should be compensated in the same manner according to the same standards established for other similarly situated school district personnel.
- Parents should be actively involved in a partnership with teachers and support staff in the design, delivery, and evaluation of all early childhood services provided by the public schools.
- The public schools should serve as a coordinating service for all community services responsible for serving parents and children. In time public schools should become the linchpin of community activity aimed at meeting the needs of young children.[19]

SUMMARY

Designing and opening a child care center can become a totally absorbing and satisfying experience. As individuals develop concepts and work through ideas, they begin to envision a center as a home. In the process, their focus moves from the building itself to the program it will encompass and to the people it will encircle.

Families enter a child care facility from the outside. A building creates an image that is meant to attract clientele. Inside a child care center, however, there is another image that is less visible to the public. This image should reflect the real, untouched, untarnished world of childhood; a world of special moments that creates a day for children that is at once unique, special, and memorable; a day unlike any other day. "Everyday is all we have to give our children" (from *Everychild's Everyday*).

NOTES

1. Barbara Willer, Sandra L. Hofferth, Ellen Kisker, Patricia Divine-Hawkins, Elizabeth Farquher, and Frederick B. Glantz, *The Demand and Supply of Child Care in 1990* (Washington, DC: NAEYC, 1991), p. 3.

2. Barbara Willer, "An Overview of the Demand and Supply of Child Care in 1990," *Young Children* 47(2) (January 1992): 20.

3. Willer, et al., "Demand and Supply," p. 21.

4. Roger Neugebauer, "Churches That Care: Status Report #2 on Church-Housed Child Care," *Child Care Information Exchange* 81 (September–October, 1991): 41.

5. James T. Greenman, "Institutionalized Childhoods: Reconsidering Our Part in the Lives of Children," *Child Care Information Exchange* 45 (September 1985): 24.

6. Edward E. Gotts, "The Right to Quality Child Care," *Childhood Education* 64(5) (June 1988): 268–75.

7. Cited in K. Alison Clarke-Stewart, "In Search of Consistencies in Child Care Research," *Quality in Child Care: What Does Research Tell Us?* (Washington, DC: NAEYC, 1987), p. 109.

8. Richard R. Ruopp and Jeffrey Travers, "Janus Faces Day Care: Perspectives on Quality Care," in *Day Care: Scientific and Social Policy Issues*, ed. E. Zigler and E. Gordon (Dover, MA: Auburn House, 1982), pp. 80–83.

9. National Research Council, *Caring for America's Children* (Washington, DC: National Academy Press, 1991), p. 18.

10. Ibid., p. 19.

11. "Quality Criteria for School-Age Child Care Programs," in *An Initiative of Project Home Safe: A Program of the American Home Economics Association*, ed. Kay M. Albrecht (Alexandria, VA: Funded by Whirlpool Foundation, 1991), p. 16.

12. Edward E. Gotts, "The Right to Quality Child Care," p. 269.

13. National Research Council, *Caring for America's Children*, p. 20–21.

14. Ruopp and Travers, *Day Care*, p. 82.

15. Sue Bredekamp, "An Overview of NAEYC's Criteria for High Quality in Early Childhood Programs," in *Reaching the Full Cost of Quality*, ed. Barbara Willer (Washington: DC, NAEYC, 1990), p. 47.

16. Ibid., pp. 42.

17. Sue Bredekamp, ed., *Accreditation Criteria and Procedures of the National Academy of Early Childhood Programs* (Washington, DC: NAEYC, 1984), pp. 15–17.

18. Bredekamp, "An Overview of NAEYC's Criteria," p. 49.

19. Keith Geiger, "Early Childhood Education and the Public Schools," in *Perspectives on Early Childhood Education*, ed. David Elkind (Washington, DC: National Education Association, Early Childhood Education Series, May 1991), pp. 234–35.

RESOURCES

American Academy of Pediatrics. "Standards for Day Care Centers for Infants and Children." Evanston, IL, 1980.

Bergstrom, J. M., and L. Joy. *Going to Work? Choosing Care for Infants and Toddlers.* Washington, DC: Day Care Council of America, 1981.

Bredekamp, Sue, ed. *Developmentally Appropriate Practice in Early Childhood Programs Serving Children from Birth Through Age Eight.* Washington, DC: NAEYC, 1987.

Bredekamp, Sue, ed., *Accreditation Criteria and Procedures of the National Academy of Early Childhood Programs.* Washington, DC: NAEYC, 1984.

Bronfenbrenner, W. "Discovering What Families Do," in *Rebuilding the Nest: A New Commitment to the American Family,* ed. D. Blankenhorn, S. Bayme, and J. B. Elshtain. (Milwaukee, WI: Family Service America, 1990).

Bronfenbrenner, W. *The Ecology of Human Development.* Cambridge, MA: Harvard University Press, 1979.

California State Department of Education. "Child Development Program Quality Review." Sacramento, CA, 1982.

Children's Defense Fund. *A Vision for America's Future.* Washington, DC: Children's Defense Fund, 1989.

Children's Defense Fund. *S.O.S. America!* Washington, DC: The Fund, 1990.

Child Development Associate National Credentialing Program. CDA Competency Standards and Assessment System. Washington, DC: NAEYC, 1983.

Endsley, R. C. and M. R. Bradbard. *Quality Day Care: A Handbook of Choices for Parents and Caregivers.* Englewood Cliffs, NJ: Prentice-Hall, 1981.

Garbarino, J. "Early Intervention in Cognitive Development as a Strategy for Reducing Poverty," in *Giving Children a Chance: The Case for More Effective National Policies,* ed. G. Miller. Washington, DC: Center for National Policy Press, 1989.

Prescott, E., E. Jones, and S. Kritchevsky. *Day Care as a Child-Rearing Environment.* Washington, DC: NAEYC, 1972.

Prescott, E. "Relations Between Physical Setting and Adult/Child Behavior in Day Care," in *Advances in Early Education and Day Care,* Vol. 2, ed. S. Kilmer. Greenwich, CN: JAI Press, 1981.

Ruopp, R., J. Travers, F. Glantz, and C. Coelen. *Children at the Center: Final Report of the National Day Care Study,* Vol. 1. Cambridge, MA: ABT Associates, 1979.

Schorr, L. B. *Within Our Reach: Breaking the Cycle of Disadvantage.* New York: Doubleday, 1988.

Shapiro, R. J., "The Family Under Economic Stress," in *Putting Children First: A Progressive Family Policy for the 1990s.* Washington, DC: Progressive Policy Institute, 1990.

Weikart, D. *Quality Preschool Programs: A Long-Term Investment.* New York: The Ford Foundation, 1989.

Zill, N., and C. A. Schoenborn. *Developmental, Learning, and Emotional Problems; Health of Our Nation's Children, 1988,* Advance Data from Vital and Health Statistics, No. 190. Hyattsville, MD: U.S. Department of Health and Human Services, National Center for Health Statistics, 1990.

A good administrative structure sets up clear lines of accountability and authority. It should be well developed to ensure that people both within and without the organization know who is responsible for what.
— *The Virginia School-Age Child Care Project*

5

LEGAL AND OPERATIONAL CONSIDERATIONS

LEGAL CONSIDERATIONS

How to form an organization for the purpose of running a day care center is determined by various state law and procedures. The three legal forms of private organizations are proprietorship, partnership, and corporation. These categories are defined by Decker and Decker in *Planning and Administering Early Childhood Programs* as follows:

1. Under a *proprietorship,* a program is owned by one person. This individual has no partners and is not incorporated. Sole proprietorship may have a one-person owner and operator, or a large staff with one person as owner. In a proprietorship one individual is fully responsible and liable for all actions.

2. In a *partnership,* two or more persons join together for the purpose of operating a program. A partnership may involve minor children, a sole proprietorship, or even a corporation as partner. There are both general and limited partnerships.

3. A *corporation* is a legal entity established on a for-profit or not-for-profit basis. Corporations exist as legal entities forever unless dissolved by the board or a court. Most private early childhood programs legally organized as corporations are independent (i.e., are not part of other businesses). However, worksite day care programs may be organized as a division of the parent corporation, a subsidiary corporation, or an independent, not-for-profit corporation. The corporation protects its members from certain liability by creating a decision-making and accountable board of directors when the program is incorporated with a state.[1]

The four steps involved in incorporating a day care program identified in *The Legal Handbook for Day Care Centers* are:

Preparing articles of incorporation
Preparing bylaws
Conducting an initial incorporator's meeting
Filing of articles and other documents

The *Articles* define the purpose for which the organization is formed, the powers that the organization will have, and the members of the organization. The *bylaws* are rules that determine who has the power to make decisions and how and when these decisions are to be made. An *incorporator's meeting* is the legal channel for bringing the corporation into existence. Once the state approves incorporation and a corporate charter is issued, the incorporators go out of existence. After approval, all authority in the organization lies with its members, if it has [hired] any, and with its board of directors. The *filing of articles* is a formality that requires the official filing of all legal documents with a state office.[2]

A franchise and a chain are common organizations in the field of child care. Decker and Decker define them as follows:

1. A *franchise* is an organization that allows an individual or an entity to use its name, follow its standardized program and administrative procedures and receive assistance (for example, in selecting a site, building and equipping a facility, and training staff), for an agreed-upon sum of money and/or royalty.
2. A *chain* is ownership of several facilities by the same proprietorship, or corporation. These facilities are administered by a central organization. Kindercare is an example of a chain.[3]

Large national chains increased rapidly during the decade of the eighties. The largest chain has more than 100 centers.[4] Mid-sized chains also increased significantly. These companies operate child care facilities on a regional, multi-state and/or single-state basis. They generally serve a large number of preschool and school-age children, offer twelve-hours per day of care by trained professionals, and provide a balanced educational/nutritional program. Many parents feel that the quality of service offered by a chain is more extensive and reliable than what is offered in small group centers.

Profit and Nonprofit Status

A Profit Status

Most for-profit child care centers are small facilities generally owned and operated by a single provider or jointly owned by a husband and wife. The individual(s) has exclusive authority to operate a center under her or his own standards as long as the standards are in accordance with licensing regulations. On a larger scale, profit centers may include chains, centers at work-sites or other arrangements that are set up for the combined purpose of serving the community and conducting a business. Decker and Decker define a for-profit center as follows:

> A closed corporation in which a family or small group own stock or an open corporation in which the stock is traded on exchanges. If the corporation makes a profit, it must pay taxes on the profit. . . . In a closed corporation with a subchapter "S" status, granted by the IRS, the corporation may distribute its profits or losses according to the proportion of stock held by individual stockholders, who in turn pay taxes or file a depreciation schedule.[5]

Regardless of the size, all profit organizations expect to receive a reasonable return on their investment. Legal requirements for operating for-profit centers vary from state to state.

A Nonprofit Status

Nonprofit centers vary in their organizational structures. There are single centers governed by voluntary boards of directors, centers administered by church boards, hospitals, YMCAs, colleges, public schools, community service organizations, government agencies, and military bases.

Under IRS, 501(c)(3), a nonprofit organization must define itself in legal documents as a charitable, educational, literary, religious, or scientific organization. To qualify as an educational institution, the Articles of Incorporation of an organization must describe purposes that are primarily educational rather than custodial in orientation. Accordingly, a center must have a curriculum and a regularly scheduled staff of teachers and students.[6] To qualify for tax-exempt status means an organization is not required to pay federal or state corporate income taxes and/or some state sales taxes. This tax status offers other advantages as well. Nonprofit organizations can conduct fund-raisers, and they can apply for foundation or grant money. They are preferred tenants in county organizations, churches, colleges, government agencies, and philanthropic agencies. Although nonprofit centers do not show a profit at the end of a year, they can put money back into their program in the form of bonuses, merit awards, scholarships and/or special activities for staff development (training, retreats, and so on).

Other Legal Requirements

There are some additional responsibilities that are mandated for both for-profit and nonprofit organizations at national and state levels. The *Legal Handbook for Day Care Centers* defines them as follows:

1. *Filing for an employer identification number:* Every organization is required to obtain a federal employer identification number (EIN). An EIN is obtained by filing Form SS-4 with the Internal Revenue Service.

2. *Registering for state unemployment insurance:* An organization is required to register with the state unemployment insurance office. Registration includes filling out a questionnaire about the activity of an organization, the number of its employees in part- and full-time positions, and the organization's tax status.

3. *Initiating social security:* A center that has employees earning in excess of $50 per quarter is required to participate in the social security system through payment of a Federal Insurance Contributions Act (FICA) tax. This tax is paid equally by an employer and by an employee.

4. *Withholding Exemption Certificate.* Every employee must fill out a withholding exemption certificate that is the basis for determining how much is to be withheld from paychecks for federal and state taxes.

5. *Periodic Tax Returns.* Employers are required to file a federal payroll tax return, Form 941, with a regional IRS Service Center on a quarterly basis each year.

6. *Annual Tax Returns.* Every organization, regardless of status, is required to file an annual tax return, Form 990. For a center operating as a partnership, the partners must file a partnership return each year. For a center operating as a proprietorship, the owner must file Schedule C, Form 1040.[7]

Licensing

Licensing provides legal protection for children and for centers. Licensing statutes are written and enforced by state regulatory agencies to safeguard the health and well-being of children in home and group facilities. The primary regulatory agency for establishing and enforcing standards and for issuing or revoking licenses at the state level is the Department of Health and Human Services. Regulatory guidelines provide baseline protection by stipulating the conditions and identifying the components for quality control.

State licensing regulations include but are not limited to: a definition of terms, a center's legal status, proof of insurance, documentation of fingerprinting, medical documentation for children and staff, indoor/outdoor-space requirements, student/teacher ratios, staffing patterns, administrative requirements (posting telephone numbers, maintaining a safe environment, enforcing policies and procedures), personnel qualifications and training, recordkeeping, snack and meal requirements, program guidelines, basic equipment and materials, health and sanitation requirements, procedures to follow for child abuse or neglect, recording accidents and communicable diseases, and procedures for enforcement—revocation, suspension, and appeal.

The licensing process is tedious and time-consuming. From start-up to opening a center, a period of six months to a year may be required to complete the process. There will be interviews, paperwork, permits to obtain, preopening inspections, and ongoing consultations with an assigned coordinator who is most likely a child development specialist as well as a health department specialist.

Each state has its own system for implementing and enforcing its regulatory requirements. Evaluations are generally thorough and comprehensive. Violations are discussed and remedied within a specific period of time. In cases of serious infractions, such as child abuse or overenrollment, a center may be fined, prosecuted, closed, or put on a probationary status. A director has the right to appeal the action. In most cases, infractions are unintentional, minor, and easily corrected. For example, a director may not have safety caps on all electrical outlets, an exit sign may have been overlooked, a sandbox may be uncovered, and/or a playground may need more ground protection than currently is visible.

In addition to a license review, a building must be inspected periodically for safety and sanitation requirements. Inspections may include an evaluation of lighting, water systems, bathrooms, food service and storage areas, heating units, fire safety devices, classroom materials, and general cleanliness. Unlike licensing coordinators who work with directors on an ongoing basis, safety inspectors arrive unannounced and tend to be unforgiving. A center may be closed on the spot when an inspector notes noncompliance. For example, a smoke-alarm system may be malfunctioning; there may be evidence of rodents or safety or sanitary violations.

Insurance

Child care workers increasingly are concerned and unduly alarmed about personal liability. Some adults are reluctant to demonstrate physical attention or be alone with children. Anxiety extends to children's activities. They are not allowed to engage in natural play because teachers fear injury and accusations of negligence. Climbing, gathering sticks, exploring a little beyond one's backyard—the ABC's of childhood—are not permitted in many centers. Most directors probably would acknowledge that out-of-center events that involve transportation or some risk have been drastically reduced. Children fall when they ice skate, they may be allergic to hay or farm animals, and they might get lost in a museum.

A child care program cannot function effectively for children if adults are consumed by anxieties and fears of personal responsibility. To work in a child care center is to acknowledge that even under safe conditions, accidents happen. A child falls when a teacher turns her back, equipment unexpectedly breaks, and children can get hurt by their peers. By being cautious and conscientious, adults can feel less apprehensive about adventuring with children. Proper maintenance and periodic reviews about safety, common sense as well as comprehensive insurance will ensure a relatively risk-free environment.

By building in safeguards that ensure reasonable care, a center's leadership can feel confident about its administrative practices. They will feel confident that accidents are recorded; and that there is careful documentation of accidents, of episodes between a child and a teacher (a child kicks a teacher and a teacher attempts to restrain the child), or of incidents between a child and a child (a child bites another child). They will feel confident that rules and regulations governing child care centers are carefully reviewed and shared with staff, that insurance is adequate, and that everything possible has been done to minimize personal responsibility and minimize the risk of personal liability.[8]

In response to public lobbying and the day care crisis, a growing number of companies offer comprehensive insurance plans especially designed for child care centers. A comprehensive policy generally includes liability insurance, accident insurance on children, and vehicle and property insurance.

Liability Insurance

The material provided in this section is derived from *Insuring Your Program: Liability Insurance* (1992 revision) published by The Child Care Law Center. For a list of other publications available see Resources at the end of this chapter.

Is liability insurance required? State regulatory agencies require proof of liability insurance before a license can be granted. Coverage of at least $300,000 per injury is recommended by most state Departments of Social Services. A minimum limit of $500,000 per occurrence for bodily injury and $500,000 aggregate is recommended by most insurance carriers and by some states.

How does liability insurance protect a center? If a center has general liability insurance, an insurance company will defend the insured. If the court decides a center is liable (meaning there is evidence of negligence), the company will pay the amount of the judgment up to the limits of the liability.

What does it mean to be negligent? When a provider fails to use reasonable care and a child is consequently injured, the provider is said to have breached his or her duty of care, or acted negligently.

Who is covered? A program's general liability insurance will provide coverage if the program is sued because of the negligent acts of its employees, but only when they were acting within the scope of their duties. However, if employees are also sued as individuals, the policy usually will not pay for their defense or any judgment against them. This can be remedied by adding a center's employees as additional insured on the general liability policy. Volunteers are not covered by a program's liability insurance, even if the employees are added as insured. A center may want to purchase a special volunteer liability policy. Board members and officers can be sued individually. A general liability policy will protect board members and officers where the corporation is charged with negligence of the employees. Officers can be protected by indemnifying them in the corporate bylaws. This means the program will pay for legal costs if officers or members of a board are sued.

General Liability Coverage.   General liability policies usually cover four kinds of costs when the insured's negligence causes injury:

1. Bodily injury to others, which includes physical injury, pain and suffering, sickness, and death;
2. Damage to other people's property, including both destruction and loss of use;
3. Immediate medical relief at the time of the accident; and
4. The cost of legal defense if sued.

Comprehensive General Liability.   Coverage is extended to include injuries sustained away from the program site (such as fieldtrips).

Other Liability Insurance includes a personal injury policy, products liability, contractual liability, owner's and tenant's liability, and fire legal liability.

It is important to know that liability insurance policies do not cover accidents where no one is at fault, transporting children in automobiles (which should be written as a separate policy), and property damage (property insurance is always written as a separate policy).

Vehicle and Property Insurance

The material in this section is derived from *Insuring Your Program: Vehicle and Property Insurance,* published by The Child Care Law Center (Kathleen A. Murray, Esq., and Carol S. Stevenson, Esq.; revised by William Kelly, January 1986).

Is automobile insurance necessary? If a program transports children by car, such as on field trips or to and from public schools, a provider must purchase auto insurance. If an accident occurs when employees or volunteers are driving their own cars, it is likely that the program itself will be named as a defendant along with the driver in any lawsuit. A good policy will cover most of the costs following an auto-related injury to a child. Often insurance companies will include a deductible—an amount the insured must pay before the coverage takes over—in the policy.

What are the mandatory forms of auto insurance for program-owned autos? Most states require bodily injury liability, property damage liability, and uninsured motorist protection. Additional forms of coverage are available such as collision, medical payments, fire, and theft.

What types of coverage are available when employee- or volunteer-owned autos are used? There are three types of coverage but each requires the car owner to carry some amount of insurance: 1) employee's nonowned auto insurance (usually purchased as an addition or rider to the program's general policy), 2) social service excess liability coverage (purchased by a nonprofit organization to extend a program's own general liability or program-owned auto policy to give driver's additional protection), and 3) hired-auto liability insurance (sold as an addition or rider to the program's general liability policy).

How much coverage is recommended? Experts suggest $300,000 bodily injury per person, however, a program that uses cars a great deal should increase minimal coverage to $500,000 or $1 million.

When is property insurance needed? If a building is owned, it should be insured against fire and other perils. If a building is leased, the landlord usually will carry insurance on the building itself. Some leases, however, require that tenants purchase their own or additional insurance on a building.

What types of property insurance are available? Insurance can be purchased to protect a provider from three kinds of damage: damage to a building, damage to equipment, and consequential damage. Coverage on named-perils should include fire and lightning, vandalism and malicious mischief, and extended coverage.

How much coverage is recommended? After a formal appraisal of a building, a policy will be written at the amount fixed by the appraisal. Property should be insured for a minimum of 80 percent of its value.

Contracts

The contracts recommended for child care organizations are a Parent Enrollment Agreement and a Staff Contract for Employment. For samples of these contracts see Appendix A.

OPERATIONAL CONSIDERATIONS

Preparing a Budget

A budget estimates expenses and allocates income for a school year. In most centers, a budget is prepared and monitored by a director. If the center is a corporation, it is reviewed and approved by a governing board. A budget should realistically reflect a center's objectives and standards and provide for contingencies such as underenrollment and unexpected emergencies that may cause a breakdown in operation. A director should work continuously with an accountant in setting up, monitoring, and evaluating a budget and in preparing annual reviews and reports that accurately reflect a center's financial status.

If a provider is starting a center, he or she will need assistance with all aspects of financial planning. Pre-opening costs will need to be figured into the first-year budget. These costs are difficult to estimate but generally include: legal, accounting, and consulting fees; licensing and permit fees; advertising and mailing costs; pre-opening salaries; and other building-related costs.

A critical line item will be salaries; generally they consume 65 to 85 percent of a center's expenses. In a quality center, salaries are commensurate with training, experience, and professional standards in related fields. In an informative book, *Day Care Personnel Management,* Travis and Perreault give this advice:

> A salary plan is an attempt to establish salaries in a systematic way with attention given to levels of pay in the community and the relative worth of each job within the center. A salary plan is designed to be fair and consistent in its treatment of employees and is built on a classification of jobs that shows the degree of difficulty and responsibility of various kinds of work which employees do.[9]

Considerations in budget planning are:

- Determining a center's legal status;
- Approximating fixed (unchanging) and variable (changing) expenses that are essential to setting up and running a child care center;
- Finding out what other centers are paying staff—centers that are established in a community and recognized for quality;
- Determining what support staff is needed;
- Prioritizing needs;

- Making early decisions with regard to personnel benefits, incentives, qualifications, and training needs;
- Making an early decision with regard to accreditation;
- Drafting of several sample budgets before making final decisions;
- Setting fees tailored to a program and to the community it will serve.

In determining a fee structure, a director will want to become familiar with these payment systems:

- a flat-fee plan in which all parents pay the same tuition;
- a sliding-fee plan in which parents pay on a graduated scale according to their financial ability;
- scholarship plans offered on a limited basis to parents who qualify for assistance.[10]

Because parents vary in their ability and willingness to pay fees on time, a center should require that parents sign a contract and are informed, in writing, about policies and procedures that govern a center. (See Appendix A.)

For helpful guidelines to understanding the budget process, see *Managing the Day Care Dollars: A Financial Handbook,* by Gwen G. Morgan, and "Tools for Managing Your Center's Money," by Roger Neugebauer.

Expenses

Expenses include fixed and variable items (see Sample 5–1). A fixed expense is a fairly constant monthly line item, such as rent, phone service, equipment rentals, monthly salaries, mandatory tax withholdings, employee benefits, leasing a bus, interest on a loan. A variable expense is one that fluctuates from month to month: per diem salaries for staff who do not work on regular schedules, consumables, utilities, making copies, maintenance, equipment replacements. Variable costs increase in proportion to the level of services provided.

Income

The income side of a budget reflects revenue from various sources, such as parent fees, registration and insurance fees, special government or state funding, and monies from in-kind services and fund-raising (see Sample 5–2). A center breaks even when its income equals its expenses, i.e., when revenue equals costs.

Hidden Costs

These are costs that cannot be anticipated or planned for in a budget. For example, a drama teacher needs to spend additional time to organize a center event, a teacher may ask to attend a special workshop, a parent may withdraw a child without notice, a piano may need tuning, and/or a refrigerator may need to be replaced. A reserve fund must be held for unexpected "happenings."

SAMPLE 5–1 Typical Expense Items

Salaries:
Administrative (director, administrator, bookkeeper, other)
Educational (teachers, assistants, aides, specialized teachers)
Support services (custodial, consultants, cook, nurse, bus driver, substitute teachers)

Operational Costs:
Rent
Utilities/phone service
Contracted services (trash removal, milk delivery, snow removal)
Teacher resources and materials
Insurance
Legal/accounting fees
Mandatory fringe benefits (FICA, unemployment insurance)
Other benefits (health, vacation pay, maternity leave, sick/personal leave days)
Advertising and marketing
Tuition assistance plans
Food services
Consumables (office, kitchen, media center, and classroom supplies)
Equipment and classroom materials
Petty cash fund
Transportation costs
Field-trip costs
Special in-center events
Training and staff development
Emergency, hidden costs
Summer camp costs not included in ten-month operation budget
Start-up costs

SAMPLE 5–2 Income Sources

Parent fees
Registration and insurance fees
Funding sources
Grant money
Fund-raising
Other

Enrollment Variables

Enrollment varies considerably, especially during the first year or two. A director should calculate a center's projected utilization rate in order to determine enrollment. It is not unusual for most programs to operate at 70 to 80 percent of enrollment capacity. By monitoring enrollment, by formalizing a contractual agreement, by requiring parents give advance notice of withdrawal, and by requiring advance deposits on tuition, a director will minimize variables. For further information, see *Managing the Day Care Dollars* by Gwen Morgan.

An Inventory of Revenue and Expenses

When preparing a budget for the first year of operation, a provider should consider the following questions:

- What is the fee scale and what is it based on?
- Will there be a registration fee?
- Will parents be required to pay tuition in advance?
- Have insurance, legal and accounting, and start-up costs been averaged into an annual budget?
- What are the revenue sources?
- What are the terms of the lease, and what are the monthly costs for leasing and operating a center?
- Is there a scholarship plan?
- What percentage of the budget has been allocated for hidden costs, for enrollment fluctuations, for staff incentives?
- Is the program efficient?
- What salary scale will be implemented?
- What benefits will be offered?
- What auxiliary staff may be needed?
- What amount of money is being allocated for equipment, consumables, office supplies, staff development, program development, transportation, fieldtrips?
- How much will be allocated for petty cash each month?
- What are the plans for meals and snacks?
- Will there be children with special needs? What needs? Will they be mainstreamed or require special services?
- What additional training or staffing will be required?
- What plans have been made for marketing the center?
- What additional resources are needed?
- What special events have been planned?
- Will the center be accredited as an educational institution?
- What pertinent child care laws and regulations will need to be met and at what cost?

Other Considerations

Benefits

A director will need to give serious consideration to required and desired staff benefits. Required benefits include:

1. *Unemployment insurance:* money received by an individual from the state during the time that he/she is actively seeking employment. In cases of dismissal during employment (layoffs), a center assumes some of the financial responsibility by paying a higher insurance rate. In the interest of a center, new employees should be contracted for a limited trial period, e.g., one to three months, before being given a contract.

2. *Worker's compensation:* insurance payments to an employee who has been injured or in some way disabled on the job. It is usually mandatory if an organization has ten or more employees.

3. *Social security:* a retirement benefit shared by employer and employee (FICA). A percentage in the range of .0765 of a gross salary is contributed by the employer each pay period.

Desirable benefits to offer include: sick and personal leave pay—e.g., one day per month—remitted or reduced tuition for staff's children, health insurance, a retirement plan, an annual contract with a paid vacation, incentives at the workplace, and/or training incentives (Travis and Perreault, 1987).

Training

Increasingly, professional training is identified with quality. A director must approximate staff needs and decide what percentage of a budget can be set aside for training. The level of expertise and professionalism already in a center will reduce the cost of training. Often new centers must provide financial assistance to qualify staff to work in a center, e.g., a first-aid course or a curriculum course. A director also may find the need to facilitate program development by requiring staff members to take basic courses in child development or classroom planning. If a course is required, a director has an obligation to provide some financial assistance.

Accreditation

If accreditation is a goal, salaries and benefits will need to reflect the status earned. In an accredited center teachers can expect good working conditions, a fair salary, benefits, and opportunities for continued training. Parents expect a written curriculum and opportunities for participation and input. As centers move up in quality, they tend to extend their "wish" list to include a computer, program specialists, a staff lounge, furniture upgrades, and a large coffeepot.

Establishing Professional Standards

A center will have to pay adequate salaries to attract and hold on to competent personnel. Most established centers offer contracts that ensure a guaranteed monthly salary throughout a working year. Because salaries vary considerably within regions, a director will have to use discretionary judgment in setting salary scales. Monthly contracts usually are calculated based on an hourly rate times 20 days. That is, a teacher earning $10.00 per hour, working an eight-hour day would receive a monthly gross salary of $1,600.00. Monthly salaries should include pay for holidays and inclement or emergency closing days when teachers are not expected to work.

Large centers might find it simpler and more efficient to pay staff on an hourly basis. Under this plan, staff still should receive an annual contract, sick and personal leave days, and adequate benefits. In most cases, part-time help—high-school aides, substitute teachers, or specialized teachers—are not given standard staff contracts that include responsibilities, benefits, and job descriptions. For detailed information on child care management, see *Day Care Personnel Management* by Nancy Travis and Joe Perreault.

Practicing Financial Management

A director will need to develop a bookkeeping system that is systematic without being overly complicated. She will need to become a budget expert so she can maintain and balance a checkbook, pay bills, and be certain there are sufficient funds to meet a center's present and future obligations. A director should know how to receive and record payments (tuition), how to deposit fees, how to process a payroll, and know how and when to pay taxes and bills. This entails recordkeeping, monitoring and, if the center is a large group center, professional assistance from an accounting firm.

In most child care centers, there is little margin for error. A realistic budget that allows for contingencies also provides a *framework* for effective financial management. A recordkeeping system that accurately reflects a budget as well as deviations from a budget serves as a *tool* for effective financial management. A cash flow analysis enables a director to project a center's financial status (expected receipts and expected disbursements). A monthly status report helps a director pinpoint areas where expenses are exceeding projections or where income is falling behind.[11]

A Cash Flow Analysis

A cash flow analysis is a method of monitoring income and cash disbursed so that there is adequate money to meet needs. It usually is done on a month-by-month basis. A director is advised to make a flowchart to determine when income will be received and when cash will be dispersed. The chart will show expected receipts, expected disbursements, a monthly cash balance, an opening cash balance, and a cumulative cash balance. The key item is the cumulative cash balance at the end of each month. This will let a director know whether or not the budget is working.[12]

A Monthly Status Report

A monthly status report is a monitoring tool that gives a director a monthly accounting of a center's financial position. A bookkeeper records a center's income, expenses, and net gain or loss in a given month to determine if a center is still operating within its budget. The report can be set up to provide a center's cash flow in a given month, its projected cash flow for that given month, the amount of variation (the difference between the two), and the percentage of variation (the percentage by which the actual amounts vary from the projected amounts).[13]

Practicing Sound Management

In order to ensure that a center is operating from a sound financial position, a director should be attentive to all aspects of calculating and monitoring a budget by:

- Preparing a realistic budget that reflects fixed, fluctuating, and hidden costs;
- Hiring and firing judiciously;
- Evaluating staff before hiring to avoid dismissals;
- Soliciting in-kind services wherever possible;
- Setting up a bookkeeping system that is monitored frequently;
- Making changes as needed to keep a budget balanced;
- Being certain check books are balanced each month;
- Having an accountant or a back-up person review a bookkeeper's work;
- Having an annual audit or review done;
- Being certain all incoming tuition is duly recorded each month by name, amount, and date.
- Having two people with check-signing and withdrawal authority;
- Making copies of deposit slips that record income;
- Monitoring enrollment carefully by taking daily attendance and by asking parents for advance notification before a child is withdrawn;
- Paying salaries on or after the fifth of the month to ensure an adequate cash flow to meet monthly expenses;
- Advertising a program in local child care resource centers to facilitate maximum enrollment;
- Being cautious about committing more benefits to staff than can be afforded;
- Monitoring petty cash disbursements carefully and putting a ceiling on the amount a staff member can spend in one month;
- Having parents sign agreements that clearly state when and how tuition is to be paid;
- Implementing a penalty fee for checks returned or for late payment; and/or
- Not making promises that are hard to keep: authorizing new toys, approving staff luncheons, paying more than is necessary toward staff training courses.

Written Policies and Procedures

Every center will need written guidelines in order for parents and staff to become familiar with a center's policies and procedures. The most important materials are: a parent handbook; a staff handbook; and health, nutrition, and safety guidelines (see Appendix A). In addition, a director must maintain a recordkeeping system for children, staff, and center-related files.

Children's Records

Each child should have a personal folder that includes: an immunization record, an emergency record card, special instructions from parents, a blanket fieldtrip permission form, a record of accidents, an ongoing anecdotal record (i.e., developmental milestones, special interests, behavioral changes, speech and motor development, eating and resting patterns, social and mental development, any specific concerns), a report on parent/teacher conferences, and an annual progress report.

Personnel Records

Each staff member should have a personal folder that includes: an application with references, a contract, an updated medical record and tine test, a W-4 form, a record of first-aid and CPR training (to be updated every three years), a transcript from a college or university, a background check as required by a state, a signed statement that employee has received orientation training, and records of evaluations, warnings, attendance, training, and special recognition or awards.

Center Files

A filing system may include: correspondence, resources, bills, receipts, petty cash disbursement sheets, financial reports, leadership reports, parent newsletters, calendars, licensing information/reports, updates on child care health, safety and nutrition, planned events, items for follow-up, an accident log, personnel records, children's records, a folder with confidential information and a community relations file.

SUMMARY

With consultation, commitment, and perseverance, a director can design a program that works for children, parents, and staff. The program should reflect the director's standards, philosophy, and background in the field. If a program is recognized for quality, it will quickly take off on its own. A director will continue to guide its direction and ensure its well-being but a good center will not have to be "sold" to parents. Parents will seek it out.

NOTES

1. Celia Anita Decker and John R. Decker, *Planning and Administering Early Childhood Programs,* 4th ed. (Columbus, OH: Merrill Publishing, 1988), p. 173.

2. Lawrence Kotin, Robert Crabtree, and William F. Aidman, *The Legal Handbook for Day Care Centers* (Washington, DC: U.S. Department of Health and Human Services, 1981), Chapter II. (Edited and revised by Karen S. Stone of DeBoe & Stone, CPAs, Washington, DC: October 1986).

3. Decker and Decker, *Planning and Administering . . . ,* pp. 173–74.

4. Daniel F. Kingsbury, Sally Kweskin Vogler, and Christine Benero, *The Everyday Guide to Opening and Operating a Child Care Center* (Lakewood, CO: 21st Century Products and Publications, 1990), p. 48.

5. Decker and Decker, *Planning and Administering . . . ,* pp. 188–89.

6. Ruth K. Baden, Andrea Genser, James A. Levine, and Michelle Seligson, *School-Age Child Care: An Action Manual* (Dover, MA: Auburn House, 1982), p. 131.

7. Kotin, Crabtree, and Aidman, *The Legal Handbook . . . ,* Chapter III.

8. L. Carol Scott, "Injury in the Classroom: Are Teachers Liable?" in *Administering Programs for Young Children,* ed. Janet F. Brown (Washington, DC: NAEYC, 1986), pp. 100–108.

9. Nancy Travis and Joe Perreault, *Day Care Personnel Management* (Atlanta, GA: Save

the Children, Child Care Support Center, 1981), p. 17.

10. American Child Care Foundation, Inc., "Financial Resource Development: Finding the Dollars to Create a Quality Program," *Perspectives on School-Age Care, 1991* (Reston, VA: Virginia School-Age Project [1801 Robert Fulton Drive, Suite 400, Reston, VA 22091]).

11. Roger Neugebauer, "Managing Money as If Your Center Depended on It," *Exchange Press,* Reprint #2 (March 1986), pp. 1–5.

12. Marlene Scavo, and David Delman, eds., "Money Management Tools: Cash Flow Analysis," *The Exchange Press,* Reprint #2 (March 1984): 13–16.

13. Roger Neugebauer, "Money Management Tools: Monthly Financial Status Report," (March 1981) pp. 17–20.

RESOURCES

Legal

The Child Care Law Center (22 Second Street, 5th Floor, San Francisco, CA 94105, 415/495-5498) publishes and distributes:

    Child Care Contracts: Information for Providers
    Collecting Fees Owed
    Legal Aspects of Caring for Sick and Injured Children
    Insuring Your Program: Liability Insurance
    Insuring Your Program: Vehicle and Property Insurance
    Finding and Using Legal Resources for Child Care
    Child Care Contracts: Information for Parents
    501(c)(93) Status and How to Get It
    The Child Care Tax Credit
    Deed Restrictions
    Summary of Tax Provisions for Employer-Supported Child Care with Model Dependent Care Assistance Plans
    Reporting Child Abuse
    Family Day Care Zoning Advocacy Kit and Guide
    Child Care Resource and Referral Legal Guide
    Child Custody Disputes

Cohen, Abby J., Esq. *School-Age Child Care: A Legal Manual.* Wellesley, MA: School-Age Child Care Project and Child Care Law Center, 1984. (Available from the Center for Research on Women, Wellesley College, Wellesley, MA 02181.)

For Financial Management and Fundraising

Finn, Matia. *Fundraising for Early Childhood Programs.* Washington, DC: NAEYC, 1984.

Flanegan, Joan. *The Grass Roots Fundraising Book.* Chicago, IL: Contemporary Books, 1982. (Available from Toys n' Things, 906 Dale Street, Box 23, St. Paul, MN 55103.)

The Grantsmanship Center. *How to Develop an Effective Funding Strategy. See also, Programming Planning and Proposal Writing* and *A Guide to Accounting for Nonprofits* (Available from The Grantsmanship Center, 650 South Spring Street, Suite 507, Los Angeles, CA 90015.)

Heywood, Ann M. *The Resource Directory for Funding and Managing Nonprofit Organizations, 1982.* (Available from the Edna McConnell Clark Foundation, 250 Park Avenue, New York, NY 10017.)

Morgan, Gwen G. *Managing Day Care Dollars.* Cambridge, MA: Steam Press, 1982.

Neugebauer, Roger "Tools for Managing Your Center's Money" (Reprint #2); "Employer Child Care" (Reprint #9); "Fundraising" (Reprint #10). (Available from the CCIE, P.O. Box 2890, Redmond WA 98073.)

For Insuring a Center

Chapman, Terry S. *Am I Covered for . . . ? A Guide to Insurance for Nonprofit Organizations.* Madison, WI: Society for Nonprofit Organizations. (Available from the Society for Nonprofit Organizations, 6314 Odana Road, Suite 1, Madison, WI 53719.)

Lane, Marc J. *Legal Handbook for Small Business.* (Available from: AMACOM, 135 West 50th Street, New York, NY 10020.)

Reynolds, S. W., and J. Strickland "Buyers' Guide to Child Care Liability: Discover What's Under the Cover!" *Exchange* (January/February 1991): 56–59.

Resources for Child Care Liability Insurance:

Directors Network/CRI National Insurance Program for Child Care Centers, 818 North Mountain, Suite 203, Upland, CA 91786 (800/448-5306).

General Star National Insurance Company, 1166 Avenue of the Americas, New York, NY 10036 (800/631-8890).

Lexington Insurance Company, 2601 Fourth Avenue, Suite 200, Seattle, WA 98121 (800/275-6472).

Reliance Insurance Company, P.O. Box 723035, Atlanta, GA 30339 (800/476-4940).

Scottsdale Insurance Company, 8877 North Gainey Center Drive, Scottsdale, AZ 85261 (800/423-7675).

Administering a Child Care Center

Baden, Ruth K, Andrea Genser, et al. *School-Age Child Care.* Dover, MA: Auburn House, 1982.

Brown, Janet F., ed. *Administering Programs for Young Children.* Washington, DC: NAEYC, 1984.

Caplow, Theodore. "How to Be an Effective Supervisor," *Child Care Information Exchange* (January 1986): 3–6.

Christian, Walter P., and Gerald T. Hannah. *Effective Management in Human Services.* Englewood Cliffs, NJ: Prentice-Hall, 1983.

Day Care Council of New York. *Handbook for Day Care Board Members,* rev. 1984. (Available from the Day Care Council of New York, Inc., 22 West 38th Street, New York, NY 10018.)

Decker, Celia A., and John R. Decker *Planning and Administering Early Childhood Programs,* 4th ed. Columbus OH: Merrill Publishing, 1988.

Host, Malcolm. *Day Care Administration.* Washington, DC: U.S. Deptartment of Health, Education and Welfare, 1971.

Johnston, John M. "Assessing Staff Problems: Key to Effective Staff Development." *Child Care Information Exchange* (March 1984): 1–3.

Kingsbury, Daniel F., Sally K. Vogler, and Christine Benero. *The Everyday Guide to Opening and Operating a Child Care Center.* Lakewood, CO: 21st Century Products and Publications, 1990.

Lurie, Robert. *Making Child Care Work: Managing for Quality,* 1985. (Available from Resources for Child Care Management, P.O. Box 669, Summit, NJ 07901.)

Storm, Sherry. *The Human Side of Child Care Administration.* Washington, DC: NAEYC, 1985.

Travis, Nancy and Joe Perreault. *Day Care Personnel Management.* Atlanta, GA: Save the Children, Child Care Support Center (1182 West Peachtree Street, NE, Suite 209, Atlanta, GA 30309), 1981. (Currently available from Gryphon House, Inc. P.O. Box 217, Mt. Rainier, MD 20822.)

A quality program is built upon competent, caring and skillful leadership. Good managerial skills produce desired outcomes. When an organization is efficiently managed, there is more incentive for staff to become committed to their job.

P A R T   III

LEADERSHIP AND STAFF DEVELOPMENT

You may not feel like a leader. Given the crisis management way in which you often spend most of your time, you may feel more like a paramedic, a plumber, an accountant, a fundraiser, a bureaucrat appeaser, a lawyer, or a supply clerk. If your nursery school or child care center is to survive, you must perform well in all of these roles. Yet, when it comes to the quality of care children receive in your center, it is your performance as a leader that really matters.

— *Roger Neugebauer*

6

PARTNERS IN LEADERSHIP

A BOARD OF DIRECTORS OR GOVERNING BOARD

Purpose

Organizations often are created by people who have a common interest, a purpose, and a plan for achieving their goal. The first step in organizing a center is to gain a legal status from which to operate. In the field of child care, leadership is entrusted not only to a director but to a board of directors as well. A board is the governing and policy-making arm of a center. The board sets in motion an organizational framework with clear lines of authority and responsibility. The director of a center is the liaison between a board and a center. She is hired by, and is accountable to the board. A board's primary responsibilities are to oversee an organization, to ensure the safety and well-being of its children and staff and to promote standards of excellence at all levels of operation.

Many centers have governing bodies but not all have a board of directors. A program may be administered by a partnership, a sponsoring agency (a parent cooperative, a public school, or a recreation department), a community agency, a business or corporation, a government agency, a hospital, a university, or a church. Each entity has its own management system that meets the legal requirements for operating a specific kind of child care center in a given state. The degree of authority conveyed to a board varies. Some boards may have as few as three members and only nominal responsibility while other boards may expand its membership to include members of the community and child care professionals outside of the center. In the latter example, a board would be more active and visible in a center's functioning. A director setting up a new center exercises a great deal of leadership in appointing board members and in defining their authority.

Responsibilities

Decker and Decker identify the primary functions of a board of directors. A governing board:

1. Formulates major policies for achieving overall goals of a program. The board must develop or adopt the program's basic philosophy and provide an outline of services.

2. Adopts all proposed policies planned by the director. Usually the director formulates policies, but the board must adopt all policies prior to execution.

3. Supports the annual budget. Usually the director formulates the budget, and the board approves it before implementation. The board can also authorize expenditures exceeding the specified limits of the budget.

4. Approves all personnel hired. The director selects staff within the guidelines set by the board, and the board acts on a director's recommendations and issues the contracts.

5. Develops criteria for evaluating the program. The director is expected to inform the board of various assessment instruments. Once the assessment instrument is selected by the board, the director implements the evaluation.

6. Participates in community relations. The board represents the program in the community.[1]

Composition

Members of a board can be selected from within an organization, a child care community, or from a community-at-large. Directors are inclined to include professionals skilled in areas needed for management or program development, i.e., an accountant, a lawyer, an educator in the field, a pediatrician, a child development specialist. Board members are invited to serve for a designated period of time, subject to renewal. If the founding members of a center want to enlarge a board, they may require that membership be apportioned. For example, a board may consist of two permanent members integral to a center plus elected members consisting of two parents, a lawyer, an accountant, two community leaders, and two child care experts. Board members generally serve on a voluntary basis, receiving an honorarium for each meeting that is attended. Meetings must be held at least three times per year.

A board relies on a director to manage a center in good faith and in an exemplary manner. Because board members are not involved in the daily operation of a center, they entrust a director with considerable decision-making authority. A competent director works in close harmony with a board, keeping members informed about pertinent issues and calls emergency meetings as needed. Members are invited to participate in special events. The relationship between a director and a board should be respectful, confidential, and supportive.

A DIRECTOR

A Profile

A director is quick to grasp the magnitude of the responsibilities and realizes that a typical child care center is filled with the same emotions and activities that have engaged families throughout history. Day care is at once frenetic and immensely fulfilling. It is ordinary: a fish dies when it is hugged, a child misses a bus, a report card is lost on purpose, and bugs are getting in through a hole in the screen that was never patched. It is extraordinary: a child's smile, a touch of wonder, a moment of perfection. It is a place where little things matter and where big things, like buying a van, must be put off until much later. It is a place where responsibility is keenly felt by leadership—a place where people's lives intersect in meaningful and unpredictable ways. It is a place where families, children, and staff depend on a director for leadership and support.

A director shares the hopes, the visions, and the disappointments that touch people's lives every day. As with most public services, a director listens and responds to those who, for whatever reason, need assistance—providing emergency care, stretching a budget to help a parent in need, adjusting tuition to accommodate just one more child.

A director is central to a child care organization and establishes the tone and the climate that will shape and direct a center. What is important to a director becomes important to an organization. Her ideals, standards, and point of view become models for staff development and for program development.

Leadership Roles

A Board Member

A director is a member of a board of directors. She/he prepares an agenda, submits a progress report, prioritizes items for discussion, makes recommendations, prepares an annual budget, and informs members about issues that are critical to the growth and well-being of a center. In key policy-making issues, a director's opinion is extremely influential. As the primary liaison between a center and a board, a director exercises power judiciously. If she is persuasive in promoting ideas for a center, it is not because a director is autonomous, but because she has earned the respect of board members.

A director often calls upon particular board members for counsel and advice. Decision making and problem solving are the most constant and challenging aspects of leadership. Rarely does a day pass without a crisis of sorts. Without attention, a crisis can fester into a centerwide problem. A board member often can perceive a problem from a different perspective, helping a director focus on and analyze a problem and come to terms with it. A staff member who is constantly late and not attentive to administrative policies—as nice as she may be—must be told this behavior is not acceptable. A parent who is a friend of the director must receive the same treatment regarding late tuition as any other parent. A child, who is placing other children at risk, as painful as it is, may have to be terminated from care. A board member can provide the objective input needed for critical situations requiring thoughtful attention and decision making.

An Administrator/Educator

A director must function as both an administrator and an educator even if someone else has been hired to fill either role. No one but a director can translate her visions and goals for a center into a system of management that works for everyone. This is done by continually assessing the strengths and weaknesses of a center, by delegating responsibilities, and by hiring judiciously. Similarly, no one can translate a philosophy and curriculum into a child-appropriate program better than a director.

In the role of administrator, a director will:

- Set up a budget and a bookkeeping system;
- Hire, train, and supervise staff;
- Write policies and procedures that are requisite to running a sound operation;
- Write and enforce job descriptions;
- Comply with licensing regulations;
- Order and purchase equipment and materials;
- Attend management seminars pertinent to the field;
- Maintain a thorough recordkeeping and filing system;
- Review and distribute information that pertains to health, safety, nutrition, and program development;
- Prepare a registration packet;
- Develop a plan for marketing a center;
- Maintain adequate enrollment;
- Oversee and evaluate a monthly budget; and
- Communicate with parents on a regular basis.

For administrative guidelines, see *Policies and Procedures for Early Childhood Directors* compiled by the Early Childhood Directors Association.

Notwithstanding the importance of administration to a child care operation, a director's primary responsibility is the care and education of children entrusted to a center. Celia and John Decker phrase it this way:

Providing leadership in program planning, implementation, and evaluation is undoubtedly the major task of the early childhood administrator. Staff, housing, equipment, assessment practices, parent education programs, and everything else involved in operating a program can be justified only in terms of their contribution to a child's development. And, although program planning is the pivot for all other administrative functions, perhaps no other aspect of early childhood planning is beset with so many problems and so much confusion.[2]

In the role of educator, a director will:

- Develop and implement a curriculum;
- Develop a media center for staff use;
- Provide opportunities for training and workshops in areas that reinforce the center's program;
- Provide resources that implement and reinforce a center's program;
- Attend workshops and conferences in the field;
- Plan workshops and provide training opportunities for staff development;
- Evaluate programs and communicate daily with teachers;
- Encourage and support staff for exemplary work; and
- Consider and, if appropriate, pursue accreditation.

A director's primary task is developing an educational design and writing a curriculum guideline. If a center has both preschool and school-age children, it is necessary to develop a multiage curriculum. A curriculum guideline defines a center's philosophy, objectives, and specific areas of emphasis. It identifies areas of child development critical to program development and provides ideas and suggestions for classroom implementation. It provides a system of evaluation as well as techniques for disciplining and working with children in child care environments. Within this framework, teachers are required to develop their own programs to reinforce and expand a center's curriculum and philosophy.

An educational design and curriculum must provide child-appropriate experiences, activities, and materials. It must:

- Reflect a philosophy of education;
- Reflect the writings and positions of leaders in the field;
- Be substantiated by research and development;
- Reflect an understanding of child development;
- Address the total needs of children;
- Reflect a child-centered environment;
- Be articulated in writing;
- Be responsive to ethnic and cultural diversity;
- Include opportunities for training staff;
- Provide teaching guidelines;
- Reflect a child's full-day needs by providing opportunities for education, enrichment, recreation, and nurturance;
- Provide opportunities for community outreach, community involvement, parent participation, and staff development; and
- Provide a plan for a center's growth and development.

For other information on developing educational guidelines, see *Developmentally Appropriate Practice in Early Childhood Programs Serving Children from Birth Through Age Eight* edited by Sue Bredekamp.

Preparing for Leadership

Before entering or advancing in the field, a person may want to engage in a self-screening process to determine suitability for leadership. The following five sections describe some of the areas to address.

Motivation

Questions might include: What do I hope to accomplish? What am I willing to sacrifice to meet my objectives? How committed am I to the child care profession? How can I motivate staff to support my program and to help me achieve my goals?

Characteristics

Questions might include: What areas do I excel in that might become leadership tools? What areas might I improve? Do I have the qualities that attract and motivate people—that sustain relationships? Do I generate confidence? Do I value the opinions of others? Am I willing to share leadership? Am I able to delegate responsibility? Am I a taskmaster or do I procrastinate when it comes to making decisions? Do I have strong convictions and an ability to persevere? Do I have an instinct and talent for leadership? Am I willing to take risks to further my goals? Am I assertive when I need to be? Am I empathetic? Do I have stamina and energy? Can I communicate effectively? Am I quick to prejudge or am I objective in solving problems? What do I feel are the most important characteristics of leadership?

Knowledge and Experience

Questions might include: Do I have the background, knowledge, training, and skills requisite to directing a center? Do I have a philosophy of education? Do I have adequate training? What strategies would I implement for staff training? How would I evaluate a program's effectiveness? How would I find staff to implement my program? How would I gain backing and support from parents? What resources do I have to promote my program? What models will I follow in developing a program? What age-level would I want to teach and why? What is the purpose of child care, the role of a director, the role of teachers, the role of parents?

Basic Skills

Questions might include: Do I have the administrative skills required to manage a center—can I interpret and organize information; can I communicate and write policies and procedures, parent newsletters, and routine correspondence? Can I set up and maintain a filing system? Do I keep accurate records in my personal life? Can I work efficiently in a distracting environment? Can I organize time and set up priorities? Am I able to delegate tasks to others? Do I have knowledge in bookkeeping, in office management? Do I have supervisory skills? Do I have computer skills? Am I willing to get training in areas that I perceive to be deficient?

Talents and Interests

Questions might include: What special talents do I have? How might they be used in a child care setting? What are my interests . . . arts and crafts, camping, creative writing, photography, travel, sailing, hiking, geology, sports, cooking, drama, reading, painting, sculpture, music, gardening, woodworking, puppets, environmental projects, theatre . . . ? How might my interests be used in a child care setting? How would I describe a creative program at preschool levels, at school-age levels? How important is self-expression to children's growth and development? What community resources are available to develop interests and talents?

Developing a Philosophy

A philosophy is a statement of belief that expresses the principles and values of an organization. A philosophy provides a framework for a program, for working in a center, and for establishing its goals and objectives. A philosophy gives a center a sense of direction and purpose (see Example 6–1). A statement of philosophy should be included in a parent and staff handbook (see Appendix A).

EXAMPLE 6–1

Philosophy

The purpose of this program is to help children discover the joy of learning through foundational experiences that encourage and motivate their interests and curiosity. Within *their* environment, children are encouraged to become active learners. They are encouraged to ask questions, to express ideas, and to solve problems. They are guided and reinforced by caring teachers who are trained in child development. As children shape their own experiences, they begin to integrate knowledge and understand relationships. They find out why things work and why things don't work. As children begin to master their world, they develop competencies and habits that will prepare them for life-long learning. With each new experience they are building on a base of knowledge that began in the early years.

In a child-centered environment, play is considered a natural springboard for learning, for creative development, and for social development. As children play, they develop friendships and learn to value one another. They use language to communicate ideas and critical thinking to test out ideas. They cooperate to complete projects and to gain friendships. Most important, when children feel a sense of control over their play world, they develop a sense of mastery and pride. They begin to believe in themselves and in others. They are willing to extend themselves in ways that reinforce and complement a child care setting. In an atmosphere of trust and support, children begin to trust themselves.

EXAMPLE 6–2

A Center's Goals

Under the guidance of nurturing and competent adults, the center hopes to encourage among its students: a spirit of lifelong learning; a core of values that will become part of the child; a commitment to good citizenship; a belief in one's self and in one's community; a sense of responsibility; an appreciation for all living things; a respect for one's environment; a desire for knowledge that continues through life . . .

Defining Goals

Goals are statements of intent that reflect and reinforce a center's philosophy (see Example 6–2).

Defining Objectives

Objectives are statements of intentions that reflect a center's program at specific age levels (see Example 6–3). At early levels of development, objectives should never be confused with goals. Objectives are merely guidelines and should be written with the intention of encouraging or promoting development, e.g., replace the phrase "a child will learn" with a less predictive and more appropriate phrase such as, "In this program a child is encouraged to . . ." or "In this program a child will be exposed to . . ."

EXAMPLE 6–3

Program Objectives

This program is designed to provide children with an enriching selection of activities and materials to foster learning, creativity, and self-awareness. At this center, a teacher views herself as a facilitator, a guide, and a role model.

Social and Emotional Development. Children are encouraged to:
- Play and learn cooperatively;
- Interact without a competitive, demanding attitude toward others;
- Value and care for property;
- Value and support friends;
- Share with and care for others;
- Become active learners with agile minds;
- Communicate problems and tensions before they escalate into major confrontations;
- Develop self-control;
- Find ways to express anger that are not hurtful to others;

- Respect and honor rules of conduct;
- Talk about things that are bothering them;
- Express feelings and moods without inhibition;
- Develop an awareness of how one's feelings and attitudes affect others;
- Develop positive values;
- Feel good about themselves, their center, and their friends;
- Participate in making agreements and in establishing rules of conduct; and
- View their center as an extended family and its members as friends.

Reasoning and Thinking Skills. Children are encouraged to:
- Engage in hands-on learning and play;
- Make wise choices and accept the consequences;
- Explore, investigate, and solve problems;
- Practice critical thinking as they play and work;
- Learn to be flexible in attitude formation and creative thinking skills;
- Learn to communicate thoughts and ideas in ways that can be understood and respected by others;
- Develop interests and talents fully; and
- Become a self-manager, an initiator, a motivated student who does not require rewards for a job well done.

Language and Communication Skills. Children are encouraged to:
- Become active, responsive listeners;
- Communicate ideas and feelings;
- Develop comprehension skills;
- Read books;
- Develop and enrich language skills;
- Practice creative writing; and
- Learn language skills through creative experiences.

Physical Development. Children are encouraged to:
- Develop and coordinate body movements;
- Be physically active during indoor and outdoor play;
- Develop fine-motor and gross-motor skills through materials, equipment, and special activities designed for various stages of growth;
- Engage in a wide variety of group games and activities; and
- Develop social skills through cooperative games.

Creative Development. Children are encouraged to:
- Express themselves through art, drama, music, crafts, play, literature, and other arts-related experiences;
- Develop an interest in and knowledge of artists who have contributed to our culture;
- Develop sensory discrimination;
- Develop talents and interests; and
- Use self-expression as a way of understanding and interpreting one's world.

Practical Life Skills. Children are encouraged to:
- Learn to care for and about themselves;
- Develop good hygiene and habits when caring for their bodies;
- Identify appropriate behavior;
- Avoid inappropriate behavior;
- Develop standards of conduct that ensure well-being;
- Be attentive to good eating habits;
- Learn to regulate activities so that there is time for quiet and active play;
- Learn to make appropriate decisions, to practice healthy habits, and to develop lifelong skills.

Management/Leadership Skills

Communication Skills

A successful director knows how to communicate and implement ideas for an effectively functioning, environmentally sensitive system of leadership.

Writing. A director communicates a great deal about herself through writing. A writing style reflects one's training, personality, point of view, and general ability. A director must know how to write quickly and well whether it is jotting down a memo, recording minutes, or preparing an important document such as a contract.

A good way to learn to write for a child care setting is to develop the guidelines that are distributed to staff and parents. A director will soon learn that when policies are clearly stated, there is less to complain about and less to challenge. A staff member knows what is expected and a parent knows what is expected.

When staff members receive handbooks and written information about a program, they will take their own writing more seriously. They will be more attentive to spelling, grammar, and syntax. A director will not need to edit calendars and newsletters as frequently and parents will view a center with greater respect.

Verbal Skills. A director communicates a great deal about herself through the style of oral communication. The way a director expresses thoughts at meetings and in leadership contexts reflects abilities, strengths, and shortcomings. An informed, knowledgeable director will keep abreast of trends and issues in the field so that she can speak with authority and sincerity.

The manner in which a director expresses herself in a center reflects personality, leadership style, and priorities. A friendly director, who is highly respected, will find time for informal visits with staff and parents. The office will be open to children and adults, and the director will be a visible and an active part of a center.

Nonverbal Communication. Nonverbal communication can be very revealing; it can convey a positive, negative, or apathetic image. A respected director should convey a sense of confidence, dignity, determination, energy, and friendliness.

What is most important is that she conveys a sense of authenticity; a director is a person who values honesty and practices fairness.

Organizational Skills

A successful director must have management skills and must learn to prioritize her time and responsibilities. She must determine what items require immediate attention and what items can be put on hold. Personnel disputes, a disgruntled parent, a classroom crisis, an important phone call, recording an accident, or registering a new child all fall into an "immediate action" category. Writing newsletters, filing, finding a substitute teacher, or planning a fundraiser fall into a less important "not now" category. A competent director will review and evaluate her system of management periodically, soliciting professional assistance when needed.

A quality program is built on competent, caring, and skillful leadership. Good managerial skills produce desired results. When an organization is managed efficiently, there is more incentive for staff to become committed to the job. There is more likelihood of better working conditions, better salaries, and more benefits which, in turn, increase motivation. Productivity increases when teachers are a part of decision making and planning. A director who is estranged from her staff will not be able to translate her ideas into a workable program.

A director *develops* and *defines* an organizational climate by articulating a vision or purpose that can be commonly shared. In an article, "The Power of the Purpose," Susan Gross defines *purpose* as an organization's driving force.

> Organizations, in essence, are a series of relationships built around a common purpose. It is purpose that brings people together to create an organization; moves them to foster and sustain the relationships necessary for effective, productive work; revitalizes them when they're tired or discouraged; and compensates for their long hours and low pay.[3]

Interpersonal Skills

A successful director must have interpersonal skills that enable her to work effectively with many people from various backgrounds and disciplines. These skills involve management strategies that promote efficiency and high levels of performance.

Planning, Conflict Resolution, Support Strategies.   A skillful director will influence colleagues by careful planning and communication, by monitoring and evaluating performances, by resolving conflicts through open and objective dialogue, and by exercising strong leadership in interpersonal relationships. A survey of Fortune 1000 companies published in *Success!* identifies practices for generating and sustaining a high level of performance.[4]

Planning

1. Make clear the role each person will play in accomplishing a task.
2. Understand which decisions can be made alone and which cannot.
3. Strive to set team or group goals as well as individual goals.

4. See the value of bringing together people with different opinions.
5. Demonstrate commitment and persistence in achieving goals.
6. Communicate priorities consistently.
7. Insist that group members make every effort to solve problems before taking them to higher management.
8. Treat requests to change plans and goals with an open mind when circumstances seem to warrant change.

Conflict Resolution

1. Encourage reluctant co-workers to express or defend their opinions.
2. Encourage the open airing of problems and differences of opinion.
3. Respond in a nondefensive manner when others disagree.
4. Try to influence others through knowledge and competence rather than through official status.
5. Be willing to share one's powers in the interest of the overall organization.
6. In conflict situations, look for points of reconciliation rather than differences.
7. Encourage decisions based on logic and the weight of evidence.
8. Encourage the reaching of decisions through blending ideas.
9. Seek new ways to resolve conflicts.

Support Strategies

1. Behave in a trust-inspiring way.
2. Be supportive and helpful to others as they perform their jobs.
3. Encourage innovation and calculated risk-taking in others.
4. Consider others' views according to their logic, not personal preferences.
5. Consider opinions of others open-mindedly before evaluating them.
6. Evaluate the views of others according to their knowledge and competence, rather than according to their positions.

Practical Skills

A successful director knows how to delegate and when to ask for help. No one should attempt to run a group center without some salaried support service. An "in" basket can overflow and overtax a director. Many valuable opportunities are lost to a wastepaper basket because there isn't time to read mail or in-house correspondence. Additional help might include:

Hiring an Administrator.   This is a position that requires office, computer, and bookkeeping skills and a pleasant demeanor. An administrator is critical to the effective functioning of a center. She is the person most visible and available to parents and staff. If she presents an image of cordiality and competency, an administrator will attract parents to a center. She will know how to describe a center's philosophy and how to articulate its program. Working closely together, an administrator can become a director's spokesperson and colleague. Administrative responsibilities may include monitoring enrollment, responding to staff needs, bookkeeping, general office duties, maintaining a safe environment, and overseeing the daily financial management of a center.

Hiring a Health Consultant.   Preventing illness and monitoring health policies is a time-consuming and critically important aspect of leadership. A health consultant who has a background in child care can monitor children's health records; inform employees about new rules and regulations pertaining to health, safety, and nutrition; evaluate classrooms for compliance; oversee medication and accident reports; review and update employee records; spot check a first-aid kit; and alert a director to potential indoor and outdoor hazards. A consultant should be thoroughly familiar with state licensing requirements and should have the best resources to draw on.

For more information on comprehensive health and safety guidelines, see *Caring for Our Children,* a collaborative project of The American Public Health Association published in 1992; *Healthy Young Children: A Manual for Programs,* edited by Abby Shapiro Kendrick, Roxane Kaufmann, and Katherine P. Messenger; and *Health and Safety in Child Care* by Susan S. Aronson.

Expanding Leadership

A successful director will consider still other ways to obtain help in managing a center and might decide to expand the leadership role by:

Appointing a Teacher Advisory Committee.   When a director has a reliable administrator, she can expend her energies on program development and leadership. A Teacher Advisory Committee (TAC) may become a valuable asset to a director. The most likely and promising candidates to serve in this voluntary capacity are teachers who have worked closely with a director for some time. They are individuals who respect and believe in a program and its leadership. A TAC can be structured in two ways: 1) It can serve primarily as an advisory committee to a director; in this capacity it can make recommendations and mediate disputes. 2) It may be established as an Executive Committee with broad powers in areas of policy and decision making; in this capacity, one member may be elected to serve as a staff representative on a board of directors.

Appointing a Parent Advisory Committee.   A Parent Advisory Committee (PAC) also can prove to be a valuable channel for inter-center communication, program development, and leadership. By inviting parents to participate in a center's life, a director is acknowledging their importance to a center. A PAC may be composed of a parent representative from each classroom or may include alumni or community friends who have contributed to a center's development.

Parents can serve a myriad of needs that complement and expand a center's services. They can provide leadership in classroom activities, in fund-raising campaigns, scholarship funds, cultural arts programs, and community projects that benefit both children and staff. They can organize family/center functions such as picnics, parties, hikes, and camping trips. They can serve as liaisons between a center and a public school. They can become resource people for children's enrichment and entertainment. A member of a PAC may be elected to serve on a board of directors as a parent representative.

Introducing a Parent Teacher Association. A partnership concept may develop into a Parent Teacher Association (PTA) organizational structure that clearly acknowledges the role of parents as leaders in their child's education. As such, parents would have a decisive role in developing a program, in hiring staff, and in determining how money is to be spent. In an established program, a PTA may have a quasileadership role that is shared with a board of directors. Under this plan, a PTA might be responsible for fundraising and program development while a board would continue to exercise control over the budget and major policy issues.

Personal Attributes

To complement and reinforce management skills, a director must have personal attributes that attract colleagues, parents, and children; generate respect; and build confidence. These qualities might include: conviction, commitment, determination, empathy, creativity, resourcefulness, and a sense of self-affirmation.

Conviction, Commitment, and Determination

A child care center needs gentle, competent, and strong leadership. A director with a sense of conviction and purpose will naturally appeal to and attract people like herself. With high standards and an ability to communicate effectively with everyone in a child care environment, a director will build a network of support.

A director with commitment is prepared to invest time and energy in the project to accomplish goals and will seek and gain the support and cooperation of people who can help. A director is able to prioritize objectives to maximize efficiency and distribute resources so a program will continue to grow. If a director is committed to developing a quality center, she will find a way to make the changes that will make her vision a reality. Ultimately, it is a director who is the force behind a center's growth and development.

A director with determination has a firmness of purpose that keeps her on task and, as a problem solver, is able to overcome obstacles and disappointments. She is not easily daunted; a positive attitude and inner strength are respected and admired by staff and parents as well. Capable of exemplary, conscientious leadership, a director is a person that others are willing to and want to follow and support.

Empathy

It is difficult to imagine a child care center without a friendly, smiling director walking around its halls, replacing paintings that have fallen on floors, and assuring children and staff that all is right with the world.

A staff is capable of performing at consistently high levels if they feel important to an organization. A child care teacher or assistant wants to feel acknowledged, accepted, and respected. She wants to be a part of a center's life; a teacher wants to make and communicate observations; she wants to make recommendations and feel a part of leadership. A teacher doesn't want to be passed by or ignored. By being sensitive to staff needs and to their importance to a center, a director will develop bonds of communication that can only continue to grow.

A director can acknowledge the staff in many ways: by small but important gestures such as personal notes or special rewards—luncheons, dinners, merit rewards, or citations in parents' newsletters. By daily communication with staff members, a director will become more of a colleague and less of a boss. By sharing herself in meaningful ways, a director is opening space for friendship.

Creativity and Resourcefulness

A creative director is open to change, constructive criticism, and new ideas. She has a flexible, probing mind that enjoys a challenge. She enjoys the process of leadership and the personal benefit that is derived from each accomplishment. Every child, every experience, and every day opens up new possibilities for renewed growth.

Every now and then a director needs to review her purpose and commitment to a center. By so doing, she will come to terms, once again, with her own creative potential. She will get in touch with the fact that creativity is not a product—it is a process that is cultivated in an environment that encourages originality and creative thinking. Characteristics identified with creativity are: an *open mind,* a *flexible attitude,* a desire for self-expression, a *curious nature* and *inquiring mind,* an ability to view a problem from *many perspectives,* a desire to *play with ideas,* a desire to *experiment with absolutes,* a *willingness to take risks,* and a *desire to understand rather than to achieve.*

A director who has a number of these characteristics will become a creative role model for staff and children. The feelings about creativity will filter down to remote corners of a room. Each area will become an important part of a harmonious whole.

Self-affirmation

With commitment and self-affirmation, a leader ultimately acknowledges her importance to a center and her unique contribution to its growth. By so doing, a director affirms herself. Self-affirmation is immensely rewarding and satisfying. It has to do with a ripening process that one has to experience to comprehend. A director who gradually sees a center as an extended self and its own unique community, no longer needs accolades. At a certain point in time, a director arrives at a position of *authenticity.* Big problems become less traumatic and little problems far more manageable. Interestingly, with time, self-acceptance and a sensitivity to the whole environment, feelings of fulfillment and success come. Everyone embarking on a child care career should reread the touching, timeless classic, *The Velveteen Rabbit* by Marjery Williams, in which becoming real is described as a process that happens over a period of time.

> . . . When a child loves you for a long, long time, not just to play with, but REALLY loves you, then you become Real.

THE STAFF

Extending Leadership

A child care director is making a mistake if she does not accord special recognition to the staff through shared leadership. It doesn't take long for anyone who has experience in the field to recognize that teachers are absolutely critical to a center's functioning, survival, and growth. When a favorite teacher leaves a center, there is a sense of loss not unlike the loss of a family member. Over the years, the teacher probably has developed a network of colleagues who credit her with the popularity of a center. Even though her status may be somewhat overstated, the teacher's absence is keenly felt by an entire center. If several good teachers leave a center within a short period of time, parents begin to doubt a center's credibility. From a parent's perspective, their child has lost a trusted friend—someone who cannot easily be replaced.

Actually, finding and holding onto good teachers and assistants is a persistent problem in child care centers. Breaking new staff members in to a system as complex as child care takes a great deal of time and patience. In a large center, transitions require inordinate detail—dealing with schedules, meeting busses; handling emergencies (a child misses a bus); taking attendance; checking on children who don't show up; helping children to adjust to a changing environment; being attentive to lunch boxes, backpacks, notes, and personal belongings. A skillful teacher can control a frenetic period during the day without appearing stressed; a new teacher cannot. One must conclude that a teacher who is dependable, trustworthy, and seasoned is an indispensable member of the group. Thumbing through a batch of résumés, a director may feel confident that she can find a cheaper and equally qualified replacement. After a few interviews, however, she will learn that a person who appears to have everything on paper may be short on experience, patience, and common sense. A wise director will make teachers feel integral and important to a center by letting them participate in leadership and other incentives. She will ask their advice, treat them like equals, and make them aware of their importance. At some point, a director will ask respected members of a staff to serve on planning committees or to become assistants in various areas of program development—i.e., organizing and evaluating workshops, developing and evaluating curriculum.

Factors that Contribute to Low Morale

A Poor Image
The focus of concern in child care during the decade of the eighties has centered on the child. By comparison, concerns about staff have been given far less attention. Those in the field realize the importance of centerwide improvement and are seeking to make changes throughout the system: in leadership, staffing, and the total child care environment.

A nationwide effort to upgrade staff through accreditation has met with some degree of success, particularly with NAEYC's exemplary credentialing system. However, centers that should be stretching for accreditation are not doing so fast enough because the child care system is not professionally oriented. The number of unskilled and untrained people in the field and the cost of upscaling a program preclude participation in centerwide training. Without incentives, such as compensatory pay for training, staff probably are not going to invest additional time or money to upgrade their professional status.

The poor image and inadequate leadership that has permeated child care over the years are primarily responsible for its poor quality. It is astounding to learn that college-educated teachers are working for $7.50 or less per hour, that turnover in many centers is close to 50 percent per year, and that many talented young professionals are forced to leave the field because of objectionable working conditions and insensitive leadership. These conditions are so entrenched and widespread in some areas that only corrective action at national levels will force a change. Centers that recognize deficiencies and are willing to make changes, regardless of cost, will begin to change the image; by requiring professional credentials, by making training available, and by recognizing and rewarding quality teaching.

Poorly Trained Leadership

A team is as good as its coach. Child care is attracting leadership, in large part, because the job market is open and qualifications are minimal. Qualifications vary among states, but there are states that do not yet require directors to have college degrees or special training in child development. Many supervisors, in fact, have entered the field as aides and moved up the ladder with minimal training and from backgrounds that exclude education.[5] An art teacher, a nurse, a psychology major, a social worker, or a recreation specialist may have a great deal to offer a child care center, but without an early childhood background, children's total needs are being compromised. A person who teaches without appropriate training will use an approach that is more intuitive and experiential than educative. In assessing supervisors in early childhood programs, Joseph J. Caruso states:

> It is very clear that directors and other supervisors learn much of their supervisory craft through trial and error, experiencing great anxiety, and oftentimes, pain in the process.[6]

In recognition of the need for qualified teachers and consistent standards throughout a child's early education (birth through age eight), the Association of Teacher Educators and the National Association for the Education of Young Children recommend the establishment of specialized early childhood teacher certification standards.[7] Early childhood will be perceived as a continuum that includes grades one through three as well as the early years. Therefore, teachers must have specialized knowledge in child development that includes theory and content as well as an understanding of cultural differences. The organizations perceive this certification as distinctive from existing elementary and secondary certifications. Universal standards will accelerate the movement toward quality child care at its most basic level—teacher training and staff development.

Poor Communication

While directors tend to view their role from a macro level that encompasses an entire organization, teachers tend to operate on a micro level, focusing on an immediate environment. Efficient appliances, reliable aides, and prompt reimbursement for groceries matter to teachers. Getting a director's attention and approval also matters to teachers. Directors may fail to recognize the correlation between job satisfaction and performance, while teachers do not always appreciate the nature and scope of a director's responsibilities. In the busy world of child care, each tends to walk a different path, often with little or no contact throughout the day. A director may fail to give more than a passing glance at a project that obviously is important to a teacher. She may be too preoccupied to notice signs of burnout that are beginning to surface, e.g., tardiness, absenteeism, a decline in creativity and productivity, negative comments, irritability. Similarly, a teacher may fail to notice the visible strains of leadership that cross a director's face.

Stress

Emotional and physical stress are no strangers to those who work in the field of child care. Teachers work long hours and directors longer hours. Close environments are breeding grounds for dissatisfaction and irritability. Demanding children (and sometimes parents) can exhaust tolerance levels. Routine classroom responsibilities (in themselves a full-time job) begin to escalate—more is required, more is not enough. A director adds to the problem by requiring that teachers take courses, write progress reports, plan lessons, shop for food, attend meetings, and be available for evening calls from parents. Increasing responsibilities typically are not offset by compensation. Directors expect staff to become labor intensive because there is simply no other way to get the job done. Teachers are rarely asked to cooperate; they are expected to share in the burden of running a center. In the fast-paced world of child care, a late parent may not receive a friendly greeting from a tired teacher. Gradually teachers become overwhelmed and sometimes incapacitated by a job that leaves no time for rest and personal growth.

Fatigue brings on stress and for some, burnout—a condition that slowly takes over one's spirit and capacity for work. An unhealthy mental condition may bring on physical symptoms, such as headaches and backaches, necessitating chronic absenteeism. When a teacher's performance level drops, she becomes petty and narrow toward others. She criticizes leadership, parents, and colleagues alike. She is less patient with children and easy to anger. Slowly, a once pleasant atmosphere becomes contaminated by poor morale. For information on developing strategies to avoid stress at the workplace, see *Avoiding Burnout* by Paula Jorde-Bloom.

Insensitivity

In a low-performance center, a director may ignore the conditions that cause poor morale or may react by attempting to change too much too soon. When exercising authority, she may begin to treat colleagues more like children than responsible adults. Staff may be required to sign in and sign out using a time clock. Petty cash disbursements may be overly scrutinized. Staff evaluations may be written in a disparaging manner that lowers esteem and reduces incentive. A center cannot function as a healthy unit when members of a staff feel insecure and unappreciated. Incapable of pleasing others, a teacher may act like everything is fine when in reality, she is losing confidence in herself and in her job.

Expecting too Much from Staff

Directors who are unwilling to hire support staff to assist with routine management tasks expect more than is healthy from a staff. Teachers may be asked to become custodians, shoppers, fill in for the director, or messengers. They may be asked to make cookies for social functions, run to the post office, and attend meetings for the director. In effect, they are catchalls for unfair administrative practices. Conversely, when routine chores are fairly distributed and when teachers understand why they are being asked to take on additional work, there is more support. By bringing teachers into a center's decision-making process, a director is more likely to gain support and respect for her management style and is more likely to get the help she needs without asking.

Feeling Unworthy and Unappreciated

Oftentimes, directors and parents fail to acknowledge a teacher or assistant's contribution to a center. A simple "thank you" can mean a great deal to a person's pride and self-esteem. Sincere gestures of recognition and support go a long way toward building relationships. Unfortunately, feedback may be understated (saying too little) or overstated (saying too much). An insincere response is worse than no response. Unless a director can find time to express genuine messages, she should not make the effort. By not making the effort, however, a director is setting herself up for an eventual turning point in an employee's performance and in her relationship with that employee.

Poor Working Conditions

Budget-conscious child care centers are not known for adult furnishings or amenities. Budgets are set up for children's needs and not for adults' needs. Rarely are there adult-sized tables and chairs, furniture, or rest areas. Consequently, adults tend to feel overlooked when it comes to natural (and necessary) courtesies such as private bathrooms, coat racks, or closets for personal belongings. When there is "grown-up" furniture, it usually is donated—an old sofa with worn fabric and soft, sink-in cushions that are perfect for cats. Even an old sofa, however, may be present today but gone tomorrow. It may be moved from a teacher's lounge to become a "soft area" for school-age children.

Most child care centers are overcrowded, understaffed, and poorly equipped. Such settings become natural hosts for germs and infectious illnesses. As germs multiply in contained areas, teachers and children become more susceptible to common illnesses such as colds and flus. Consequently, prolonged periods of illness are not unusual in child care environments. Sickness is a chronic problem in group centers especially for new teachers who do not have sufficient immunity to withstand many childhood illnesses. Getting sick is probably the worst thing that can happen to teachers because, chances are, there are no health benefits to lessen the cost of medical care. And, there is probably no sick pay either. Under these circumstances, teachers elect to work when they are sick. Teaching under adverse and unhealthy conditions becomes a test of endurance.

Low Wages

Teachers tend to undervalue themselves but have to bear some responsibility for the low wages that have become identified with the field of child care. Somehow teachers have allowed themselves to be seduced into thinking that job satisfaction is not equated with fair compensation but with the pleasure derived from working with young children. It is sad to think a teacher may feel satisfied earning $8.00 an hour, especially if someone at another center is earning only $6.00 an hour. True, there is little opportunity for collective bargaining in the field, but if teachers were brought into the power structure of an organization, they would be in a more favorable position to initiate changes at the workplace. A leadership team of teachers, for example, might initiate changes at management levels that might trickle down to staff in the form of salary increases or compensatory time, e.g., two hours per week for class preparation time or one day a month for personal leave.

Conversely, a director who is not responsive to the needs of staff will be forced into a situation of hiring and rehiring, training and retraining. Under adverse conditions, the spirit that attracted a person to a center's leadership wanes. She may begin to think of alternatives that are less problematical, more rewarding, and far less stressful.

Managing Time

A chronic factor that increases dissatisfaction and stress is one of time. Time management is very important in child care centers because of the number of transitions that take place naturally each day, i.e., staffing changes, room changes, activity changes. For a teacher there is rarely time to accomplish daily objectives and for a director there is rarely time to visit classrooms or interact with colleagues. A typical child care center magnifies the problem by posting an abundance of time charts: schedules for medicines, staffing transitions, bus routes, lunches, outdoor play, program hand-ins, staff functions, and changes in schedules.

Time is also a problem after working hours. In addition to domestic routines, many teachers hold another job, attend college, participate in aerobic classes, and attempt to maintain some semblance of a social life outside the classroom.

Although a director has little control over nonworking hours, she can exercise leadership at the workplace by ensuring that staff are not overworked and over-stressed. She can schedule staffing patterns so that a staff member doesn't work more than eight hours at one time, allow a half hour for lunch and periodic breaks throughout the day. In addition, a director can facilitate a healthy working environment by providing sick and personal leave days for teachers and aides.

What Do Surveys Tell Us?

In an extensive prekindergarten survey, Professor John M. Johnston of the University of Wisconsin identifies and describes the seven major sources of staffwide dissatisfaction:

1. *Subordinate staff relations:* finding time to adequately supervise and train staff, not being able to count on staff to follow policies and procedures;

2. *Control and nurturing of children:* the consistency of problems related to classroom management and control such as, getting children to follow rules as well as nurturance concerns such as fears and anxieties;

3. *Remediation:* knowing how to help special or atypical children and how to communicate these concerns with parents;

4. *Persistent problems between leadership and staff* particularly when staff are not a part of decision making and are not given program guidelines and feedback on performance;

5. *Parent cooperation:* parents show little attentiveness to following procedures—bringing sick children, picking up late, saying a child is toilet trained when she is not, paying fees on time.

6. *Management of time:* difficulties associated with finding time for planning, picking up, administrative chores, and routine tasks.

7. *Management of routines:* problems managing the many tasks associated with a prekindergarten program, such as toilet training, rest or nap time, and meal-times.[8]

Ways to Improve Interstaff Relationships

Personalize an Environment

Teachers in child care centers must function at high levels of energy and productivity. In positive working environments that value teachers, teachers are more likely to tolerate job-related aggravations and shortcomings. A personal area for privacy and belongings is just as important to teachers as it is to children. For children, a cubby satisfies the need; for staff, a lounge satisfies the need. A day care lounge should be designed as a place for rest and refreshment—a place away from children, telephones, and noise. A caring director should make an effort to furnish a lounge modestly though tastefully—some pictures, posters, a flowering plant, soft chairs, a lamp, a radio, a staff phone, and special snacks.

Support Teachers

A director can best acknowledge the importance of teachers by providing adequate salaries and compensation. She knows it is primarily teachers who attract parents, ensure a steady enrollment, and provide the glue that holds a center together. Directors who fail to recognize the significant contribution teachers make to the livelihood and pulse of a center are limiting their chances for success in the field.

Reduce Stress

By promoting an open, comfortable environment with few transitions, a director will significantly reduce tension. By eliminating classroom clocks, a director will force teachers to think in terms of hours rather than minutes. Without structuring activities into every half hour, something wonderful happens in a room. Staff and children begin to enjoy each other; they take time to interact and to share special moments. They become less critical and feel more relaxed about their relationships. From uninterrupted quality time comes friendship and fulfillment.

Extend Recognition

A standard method for ensuring quality performances is to provide bonuses or merit pay increases. In a team environment that stresses the importance of each individual to an entire organization, bonuses are not necessary expressions of appreciation. If a bonus means singling out some individuals, the other staff members feel left out. A better way to honor staff is to have a centerwide event every six months—a potluck dinner or a special outing. A center that sends messages of high standards and high expectations is already rewarding staff.

Teachers themselves should participate in the selection of incentive plans that are available to *all* members of a staff. There may be a monthly drawing for something useful—a subscription to a magazine, a book, a tape recorder, dinner for two, or a ticket to a concert. A staff committee may decide to initiate a "teacher of the month" or a "bright idea" contest that teachers and aides can participate in. The winners may receive a "lunch for two" gift certificate or a half day's leave for a shopping spree (the latter at their own expense). Staff winners also may be given special recognition in a parent/staff newsletter or on a parent bulletin board.

Create a Feeling of Interdependence

Many of the negative factors identified with child care will dissipate when a center is perceived as a place where people interact and reinforce one another. In order to retain competent staff, a director must provide attractive working conditions and adequate salaries. She must see the wisdom of inviting staff to participate in the growth and development of *their* center. The results of developing leadership from *within* an organization will reinforce and strengthen a center's commitment to excellence.

A partnership concept of leadership will increase a director's stature and importance to a child care community. Her leadership will continue to grow by example as she becomes a model leader. "I have observed," writes David Ogilvy, "that no creative organization, whether it is a research laboratory, a magazine, a

Paris kitchen, or an advertising agency, will pr
is led by a formidable individual."9

Develop a Team

By improving the overall working conditions, a d
role staff plays in the continued growth and wei

A director will . . .

- Provide better working conditions;
- Increase salaries commensurate with education, ＿ ＿ ＿ performance;
- Consider an annual contract that includes perso..al and sick leave days as well as paid holidays;
- Provide free or reduced child care benefits to employees;
- Eliminate misunderstandings by providing written guidelines;
- Provide an incentive system by including staff members in a center's leadership, by offering opportunities to advance in the field, and by planning centerwide events;
- Consider closing a center during the Christmas or Easter holidays;
- Respect employees and make them feel important;
- Provide feedback that emphasizes strengths rather than weaknesses;
- Evaluate fairly and honestly;
- Provide channels and places for communication;
- Provide a means for staff to express grievances or to make suggestions;
- Provide opportunities to resolve conflicts amicably;
- Consider the consequences of being overly demanding or uncompromising in interpersonal relations;
- Consider the consequences of overstructuring a program from the perspective of both staff and children;
- Consider the consequences of a competitive, nonsupportive environment;
- Plan staff meetings that center on subjects of common interest and concern;
- Establish relationships of trust and respect within an environment; and
- Encourage teachers to cross self-imposed boundaries that limit and restrict creative teaching.

Teachers will . . .

- Become positive and supportive members of a team;
- Hand in assignments on time;
- Implement a program that reflects high standards;
- Avoid petty gossip that is injurious to others and unproductive to a center;
- Respect a center's need for confidentiality in parent-, child- or staff-related matters;
- Keep growing professionally: attend workshops, subscribe to educational magazines and journals, try new ideas;
- Be objective in evaluating one's own performance;

en to criticism and suggestions from a director;

aintain a harmonious relationship with parents;

Discuss problems and concerns with a director;

- Become familiar with the rules and regulations that govern a center;
- Review one's responsibilities periodically as defined by a job description;
- Become better organized so that there is more time for personal growth; and
- Uphold a center's philosophy and its high standards.

And parents will . . .

- Develop ongoing communication with a center's director and staff;
- Read memos and calendars, and ask questions;
- Recognize and praise teachers at appropriate times and in appropriate ways;
- Become familiar with a center's goals and objectives;
- Support teachers by contributing time in a classroom or by chaperoning on fieldtrips;
- Avoid sending a sick child to a center;
- Be attentive to providing a change of linen for resting cots, to dressing children for active play, and to sending extra clothes;
- Be attentive to packing a nutritional lunch that is attractively wrapped and packed;
- Be attentive to getting a child to bed on time so that he doesn't begin the day feeling tired and out of sorts;
- Keep teachers informed about changes in family patterns or about changes on emergency record cards;
- Be attentive to getting each day started in a positive way.

PARENTS

A child's experience in a child care center is most beneficial when there is respectful communication between a center and its parent body. Parents who are involved in their children's education are sensitive to children's developmental needs. They recognize the importance of a healthy and happy childhood and the critical role a center plays in a child's total development.

Building a strong relationship between a center and its parent body is not always an easy task. Planning for family/center engagements, activities, and advisory board meetings requires considerable time and organization. Working parents often are difficult to contact and not always reliable. Promises to attend a center-wide event may be broken because of another equally important commitment. Nor are occasional visits to a child's center as positive as they might appear. Short, periodic visits become problematic—for the child who does not have a parent visiting, for the child who must share a parent with playmates, and for the parent who must give her more favorable attention. Initial pleasure often is offset by a child's unwillingness to separate from a parent and a parent's reluctance to leave a child in distress.

Nonetheless, it is the responsibility of a center to facilitate a positive relationship with parents. As primary caregivers, parents need to be encouraged to participate in their child's center. A staff must understand that a friendly, sincere relationship between a teacher and a parent will help the adjustment process for a parent and a child. This can best be accomplished by accepting parents as they are, recognizing that there is no formula for successful parenting. Many centers avoid close contact with parents by limiting access to a program or by imposing too many rules and regulations; e.g., parents cannot go into classrooms to pick up children or parents may not linger in classrooms. Restrictive policies that make parents feel uncomfortable or unwanted tend to break down communication. In a close family-like environment, parents should feel welcome and a part of their child's world at all times. There should be time for unhurried departures and pickups. Informal, friendly encounters between a parent and staff members generate good feelings.

In an informative article, "Planning for the Changing Nature of Family Life in Schools for Young Children," Mick Coleman, Ph.D., reminds us of our obligation to families:

> We know that children feel respected when their families are respected—which means reaching across diverse cultural, lifestyle, and economic differences, using all of our resources outside the classroom, including family life professionals, to create linkages between family and school environments.[10]

Conflicting Pressures

Many parents find a healthy balance between work and childrearing responsibilities but for some parents, work must be a priority. Many employers are not willing to provide flexi-time for parents to visit a center or to spend quality time with a child. They are not understanding when parents are called to pick up a sick child or forced to take emergency leave. For these parents, dealing with child care can be a painful experience. Physically and emotionally separated from a child for ten hours a day five days a week, they are not able to achieve a healthy balance between child care and career. These parents are especially in need of a center's support and understanding. An occasional telephone call, a note, or a special greeting from center personnel will lessen the anxiety they feel.

There are many ways that parents can contribute to their child's program. Parents who are regular volunteers in a classroom and parents who volunteer on an occasional basis should be given equal recognition. Parents who are unable to volunteer can be made to feel important in other ways. They might be asked to send in treats for holidays or to find some time at home to assist with office needs.

Valuing Parents

Research confirms the benefit of encouraging parent involvement in a child care center. Parents involved in their child's schooling demonstrate increased sensitivity to their children's developmental needs; a greater acceptance of their children's behavior and emotions in general; increased ability to recognize and respect individual differences in their and others' children, and increased communication with their children through reasoning and encouragement rather than through authority.[11]

These findings reinforce the value of building a partnership with parents by recognizing parents as primary influences in their children's lives, by including parents in decision making and program development, and by ensuring parents open visitation rights to their child's center.

Promoting Communication

With a little thought and ingenuity, ways can be found to make all parents active participants (and even partners) in their child's center. A letter of introduction is a good way to begin a positive, mutually supportive relationship. The letter might begin by acknowledging the difficulties of balancing work and childrearing by letting parents know the child care center can become a support group as well as a service to working parents. Opportunities for both in-center and out-of-center participation may be suggested, e.g., volunteering in classrooms, repairing broken toys, mending books, making telephone calls to other parents, shopping for groceries, going to the library, making a special snack for classroom events. A get-acquainted letter also might ask parents to share information about themselves.

- What are your interests and talents?
- What time might be available for assisting in classroom activities? in center-wide activities?
- What area(s) are you interested in supporting with your services: fundraising, chaperoning, helping in a classroom, membership on an advisory committee, clerical assistance, room parent, building and equipment maintenance, bulk shopping, telephone helpers, serving on a cultural arts or scholarship committee, a resource person for fieldtrips and special events, an office helper, a sickroom aide, a scenery or costume helper, a tutor, a classroom assistant helping with vision and hearing testing or giving personal time to children with special needs, a host or hostess for special events, a classroom parent, a newspaper editor, a photographer, a furniture maker, a media center helper, a liaison with a PTA, a club leader for school-age children in areas—foreign language, scouts, drama, dance, group piano, aerobics, science, helping hands, a writer's group, woodworking, cooking, sewing, embroidery, glassmaking, pottery, gardening, sports?

A letter may conclude by inviting parents to an open house and thanking them for their support.

Once a relationship has been established, a center will want to foster continued communication through: newsletters; calendars; children's writings, e.g., a daily journal; a parent bulletin board; a parent lending library; a weekly open-house day when parents can stop in to play with their children; special events such as grandparents' day, workshops, picnics, plays; a community car wash; Saturday hikes and Monday morning breakfast, giving parents time to linger a little longer with their children before the beginning of another busy week. In addition, teachers may be required to visit children in their homes as a way of developing closer relationships between center and home. Finally, centers need to make a concerted effort to be "open" by reducing barriers that separate parents and staff. Rules and regulations can be "toned down" so that parents don't feel they have to make an appointment to see their child.

Parents' Rights and Responsibilities

To promote good family/center relationships and to clarify a center's policies a director may want to post a list of parents' rights and responsibilities.

Parents' Rights

At this center parents have the right to:

- Visit their child at any time;
- Evaluate a center (see Sample 6–1);
- Bring concerns or complaints to the attention of the director or to the board of directors;
- Access their child's records at any time;
- Expect confidentiality in the handling and recording of sensitive or personal information;
- Choose not to have personal information concerning their child disseminated;
- Feel welcome when visiting the center;
- Receive a written statement of policies and procedures;
- Be informed about all fieldtrips and special events;
- Become active participants in their child's classroom experiences;
- Contribute leadership by serving on the center's advisory committee, by serving as classroom helpers, or by serving as center helpers;
- Participate in workshops designed for parent/staff training;
- Feel confident that their child's center is in compliance with licensing regulations;
- Feel confident that all staff members conduct themselves in a professional, exemplary manner;
- Feel confident that parents will be informed immediately when children are sick or injured;
- Feel confident that the center's staff is well trained in areas of safety, health, and nutrition;
- Feel confident that their child is in a developmentally appropriate environment that is meeting his or her full needs;

- Feel confident their child is disciplined in a gentle but firm manner that is not physically harmful, emotionally abusive, or developmentally inappropriate;
- Feel confident that children are receiving appropriate guidance, training, and nurturing;
- Receive a written progress report in January and May;
- Attend a parent/teacher conference in January and in May;
- Meet periodically with staff to review children's progress and to review a center's curriculum;
- Evaluate and communicate feelings and concerns about a center, its staff, its environment, and its program;
- See evidence of an open, nondiscriminatory policy in admissions, in hiring staff, and in interpersonal relations;
- See evidence that staff members have been screened for criminal records and have met health and first-aid requirements;
- See evidence that a center and its staff are licensed and adequately insured.

Parents' Responsibilities

At this Center parents are asked to:

- Follow the rules and procedures outlined in the Parent Handbook;
- Communicate concerns or criticisms to a director or a teacher rather than to other parents;
- Avoid socializing or conferring with staff at inappropriate times;
- Notify the center if a child has contacted a contagious disease or an infectious illness;
- Keep children with an infection or a fever at home so other children and teachers do not become infected;
- Spend quality time with children during evening hours and put them to bed at a reasonable time;
- Keep children's records and emergency information up to date;
- Inform the center if there are changes in family patterns or if there are upsetting situations at home;
- Inform the center about changes in schedules, pick-up routines, or any other area that is child-related;
- Pay tuition on time;
- Pick children up on time;
- Contribute quality time to the center;
- Be supportive of the center, its leadership, and its staff.

Relationships are strengthened by formal written communication. In a parent/center relationship, a Parent Handbook clarifies policies and procedures and an Enrollment Agreement establishes a formal contractual relationship between a parent and a center. (For samples, see Appendix A.)

SAMPLE 6-1   A Parent Evaluation

Code: Check   ✓

Check Minus   ✓—

Dear Parents,

The purpose of this evaluation is to determine how this Center can better serve the needs of its children and their families. Please complete this form and return to the Center by _____. Thank you for your continued cooperation and support.

_____ I am pleased with my child's adjustment and with the general quality of this Center.

_____ I have a comfortable and supportive relationship with my child's teacher(s).

_____ I understand the philosophy and objectives of this Center.

_____ I am familiar with this Center's curriculum.

_____ I have been informed about this Center's discipline policy.

_____ I understand the administrative policies and procedures of this Center.

_____ I receive written information about classroom activities.

_____ I feel that this Center is very attentive to the safety and well-being of my child.

_____ I feel welcome when I visit my child's classroom or participate in Center events.

_____ I have been invited to a conference with my child's teacher.

_____ I feel satisfied that my child's teacher will provide me ongoing information about my child's adjustment, development, and special needs.

_____ I attended and benefited from Open-Center night.

_____ I plan to register my child in this Center next year.

Suggestions:

Concerns:

Comments:

Name: _____

Date: _____

Child's Teacher: _____

SUMMARY

Young children prosper when centers value and nurture continuous and caring interaction among the primary adults in their lives. They gain knowledge and understanding from the role models around them throughout the day. Children perceive themselves as members of a group that resembles an extended family. In this extended family, teachers know family members and parents know classroom friends. Instinctively, children identify with and place their trust in a center/home environment that provides consistency and love.

Directors, staff, and parents must envision themselves as cooperative partners in the care, nurturing, and education of young children. They must share common goals, recognizing that each partner in the team has something important to contribute to the life of a child throughout the formative years. Such collaborative interaction and shared responsibility will give children a sense of continuity between a home and the school environment, and they will prosper in an environment that is consistent and reinforcing.

NOTES

1. Celia A. Decker and John R. Decker, *Planning and Administering Early Childhood Programs* (Columbus, OH: Merrill Publishing, 1976), 169–70.

2. Ibid., 34.

3. Susan Gross, "The Power of Purpose," *Child Care Information Exchange* (July 1987): 26.

4. From "A Survey of Fortune 1000 Companies" published first in *Success* in 1986. Reprinted with permission from *Success* magazine, copyright © 1986 by Hal Holdings, Inc.

5. Joseph J. Caruso, "Supervisors in Early Childhood Programs: An Emerging Profile," *Young Children* 46(6) (September 1991): 22.

6. Ibid.: 23.

7. "Early Childhood Teacher Certification—A Position Statement of the Association of Teacher Educators and The National Association for the Education of Young Children," *Young Children* 47(1) (November 1991): 17.

8. John M. Johnston, "Assessing Staff Problems: Key to Effective Staff Development," *Exchange* (March 1984): 1–4.

9. David M. Ogilvy, "The Creative Chef." In *The Creative Organization*, ed. G. A. Steiner (Chicago: University of Chicago Press, 1965), p. 4. (Cited in "How to Be an Effective Supervisor," in *The Best of Exchange*, Theodore Caplow. Reprint #3, January 1986.)

10. Mick Coleman, Ph.D., "Planning for the Changing Nature of Family Life in Schools for Young Children," *Young Children* 46(4) (May 1991): 20.

11. G. S. Morrison, *Parent Involvement in the Home, School and Community* (Columbus, OH: Merrill Publishing, 1978). As cited in *Developmentally Appropriate Teaching in Early Childhood* (Washington, DC: National Education Association of the United States, 1992), p. 61.

RESOURCES

For Directors

The American Public Health Association. Washington, DC (1015 Fifteenth Street, NW), 1992.

Aronson, Susan S. *Health and Safety in Child Care*. New York: Harper-Collins, 1991.

Decker, Celia A., and John R. Decker. *Planning and Administering Early Childhood Programs*. Columbus, OH: Merrill Publishing, 1988.

Early Childhood Directors Association. *Policies and Procedures for Early Childhood Directors*. St. Paul, MN: Toys 'n Things Press (distributor), 1990.

Jorde-Bloom, Paula. *Avoiding Burnout*. Lake Forest, IL: New Horizons, 1989.

Kendrick, Abby Shapiro, Roxane Kaufman, and Katherine P. Messinger, eds. *Healthy Young Children: A Manual of Programs*. Washington, DC: NAEYC, 1988.

Kingsbury, Daniel F., Sally K. Vogler, and C. Benero. *The Everyday Guide to Opening and Operating a Child Care Center*. Lakewood, CO: 21st Century Products and Publications, 1990.

For Parents

Baldwin, Rahima. *You Are Your Child's First Teacher*. Berkley, CA: Celestia Arts, 1989.

Bettelheim, Bruno. *Uses of Enchantment*. New York: Knopf, 1975.

Brazelton, T. B. "Working with the Family." In *The Infants We Care For*, ed. L. L. Dittmann. Washington, DC: NAEYC, 1973.

————. *Working and Caring*. Reading, MA: Addison-Wesley, 1985.

Caldwell, B. M. *Home Teaching Activities*. Little Rock, AK: Center for Early Development and Education, 1971.

Carter, M. "Face-to-Face Communication: Understanding and Strengthening the Partnership." *Exchange* 60 (March 1988): 21–25.

Child Development Associate Consortium. "Parents Ask . . . C.D.A. Answers." Washington, DC: NAEYC, 1978.

Croft, D. J. *Parents as Teachers: A Resource Book for Home, School and Community Relations*. Belmont, CA: Wadsworth Publishing, 1979.

Curry, L. J., and L. A. Rood *Head Start Handbook for Parents*. Mt. Rainier, MD: Gryphon House, 1975.

Everett-Turner, L. "Parent-Teacher Partnerships." *Early Childhood Education* 19(2) (Summer 1986): 19–23.

Galinsky, E. "Parents and Teacher-Caregivers: Sources of Support." *Young Children* 43(3) (March 1988): 4–12.

Hatfield, L. M., and S. P. Sheehan "Parent Information Manual: A Vital Link Between Home and School." *Exchange* 49 (May 1986): 29–31.

Honig, Alice S. *Parent Involvement in Early Childhood Education*. Washington, DC: NAEYC, 1975.

Johns, N., and C. Harvey. "Engaging Parents in Solving Problems: A Strategy for Enhancing Self-Esteem." *Exchange* (November 1987): 25–28.

Neugebauer, R. "Coping with the Chronic Complainer." *Exchange* 46 (November 1985): 37–39.

Office of Child Development. "A Guide for the Development of Parent and Child Centers." Washington, DC: U.S. Department of Health, Education and Welfare, 1968.

Spock, B. M. *Raising Children in a Difficult Time: A Philosophy of Parental Leadership and High Ideals*. New York: W. W. Norton, 1974.

Steiner, Rudolph. *Knowledge of Higher Worlds: How Is It Achieved?* London, England: Rudolf Steiner Press, 1969.

Sutton, L. E. "Day-to-Day Communication with Parents." *Exchange* (October 1984): 15–18.

Weaver, C. "Parent-Teacher Communication." *Childhood Education* 3 (1968): 420.

For Staff: Magazines and Journals

Child Care Information Exchange: The Director's Magazine. Exchange Press, Inc., 17916 NE 103rd Court, Redmond, WA 98052-3243.

Childhood Education. Journal of the Association for Childhood Education International,

11141 Georgia Avenue, Suite 200, Wheaton, MD 20902.

Children Today. U.S. Department of Health and Human Services, 200 Independence Avenue, Washington, DC.

Day Care and Early Education. Human Science Press, 72 Fifth Avenue, New York, NY 10011.

Early Childhood Research Quarterly. Ablex Publishing, 355 Chestnut Street, Norwood, NJ 07648.

First Teacher. P.O. Box 6781, Syracuse, NY 13217-7915.

High/Scope: A Magazine for Educator. High/Scope Press, 600 North River Street, Ypsilanti, MI 48198.

Instructor. Scholastic Inc., 730 Broadway, New York, NY 10003.

Pre-K Today. Scholastic Inc., 730 Broadway, New York, NY 10003.

School-Age Notes. A Newsletter for Child Care Professionals, P.O. Box 40205, Nashville, TN 37204.

Teacher Magazine. 4301 Connecticut Avenue, NW, Washington, DC 20008.

Teaching Pre-K–8: Early Years, 40 Richards Avenue, Norwalk, CN 06854.

Young Children. NAEYC, 1834 Connecticut Avenue, NW, Washington, DC 20009-5786.

. . . Early childhood teachers must be adequately informed about the unique developmental characteristics of young children and the implications for curriculum and instruction. Furthermore, this knowledge must embody an understanding of variations due to cultural differences and/or the presence of a handicapping condition. These are not separate aspects of a child's life and therefore should be merged into teacher education programs.

— A Position Statement of the Association of Teacher Educators and the NAEYC (1991)

7

STAFF DEVELOPMENT

QUALIFICATIONS

It is now considered appropriate practice to hire staff based on specific qualifications that are differentiated by training and levels of experience. The NAEYC identifies four levels of professional responsibility by title and training requirements (see Figure 7–1). For more information on staff qualifications and development and on policies and procedures for accreditation, see *Accreditation Criteria and Procedures of the National Academy of Early Childhood Programs* (Bredekamp 1984).

A **Director** is considered an early childhood specialist—a person who supervises staff and administers an educational program that reflects the principles of child development. Qualifications and training requirements need to include: a course in business administration or equivalent on-the-job training, a minimum of four courses in child development and/or early childhood education; and two to three years of experience as a teacher of young children of the age group(s) in care. A director should be at least 21 years of age, hold an undergraduate degree in early childhood education, elementary education, child development, recreation, or other child-related fields. In small group centers, a combination of college course work and experience under qualified supervision and not less than two years' experience working with young children may qualify a person to be a director.[1]

A **Teacher** plans and implements a curriculum and assesses the needs of children in her care throughout the day. She should show competence in caring for and educating young children and be able to communicate effectively with parents. In addition to early childhood credentials, a teacher should have at least one year of experience working in a child care setting. College graduates seeking employment

FIGURE 7–1   Staff Qualifications

Level of professional responsibility	Title	Training requirements
Pre-professionals who implement program activities under direct supervision of the professional staff	*Early Childhood Teacher Assistant*	High school graduate or equivalent, participation in professional development programs
Professionals who independently implement program activities and who may be responsible for the care and education of a group of children	*Early Childhood Associate Teacher*	CDA credential or associate degree in Early Childhood Education/Child Development
Professionals who are responsible for the care and education of a group of children	*Early Childhood Teacher*	Baccalaureate degree in Early Childhood Education/Child Development
Professionals who supervise and train staff, design curriculum, and/or administer programs	*Early Childhood Specialist*	Baccalaureate degree in Early Childhood Education/Child Development and at least three years of full-time teaching experience with young children and/or a graduate degree in ECE/CD

Source: From *Accreditation Criteria and Procedures of The National Academy of Early Childhood Programs,* ed. Sue Bredekamp. Copyright 1984 by The National Association for the Education of Young Children. Reprinted with permission of NAEYC.

in the field should have completed an undergraduate internship under the supervision of a certified teacher and should demonstrate skills in and knowledge of working with young children before being given complete responsibility for a class.

An Associate Teacher, with certain qualifications, also may be responsible for a group of children. At this level of experience and training, an associate teacher should work under supervision by a director or head teacher until she has earned a CDA credential or an associate's degree in early childhood education. She also should be expected to have the qualities requisite to teaching in a child-centered environment.

An Assistant (or Aide) is not responsible for a group of children but is responsible for maintaining harmony in a classroom; providing support for the teacher in charge; and for sharing in the care, safety, and healthy development of children in her group. Assistants should be given the opportunity to interact with children, to plan special projects, and to participate in conferences.

In-service training for all employees should include a minimum of four workshops per year. The workshops should be approved by a director and certified by a licensing agency. In addition, all employees are required to take first-aid training and CPR. For more information on qualifications for directors, staff, and home care providers, see *Caring for Our Children* (1992).

CAREER ADVANCEMENT

With training and experience, employees who distinguish themselves as competent professionals will advance in the field. By observing staff both informally and formally in a classroom and in a centerwide context, a director can discern an employee's effectiveness in meeting her job description, in working with children, and in maintaining interpersonal relationships. A director can single out an employee for leadership by asking her to attend workshops, to lead workshops, or to serve on a Teacher Advisory Committee (TAC). In time, this person may be asked to become an assistant to the director, a program coordinator, or director of a satellite center.

As early childhood education continues to be valued as an integral part of the learning continuum, there will be uniform standards and salaries throughout the country. In a "position statement" adopted in July/August 1991, the NAEYC recommends that state departments of education develop consistent standards for early childhood teachers across the country to ensure that:

- The unique learning styles of children ages birth through eight are certified as distinct from other levels of elementary and secondary education;
- Certification standards are age- and content-congruent so that teachers are properly trained in the field;
- All early childhood preparation programs meet the standards set forth by NAEYC and The Association of Teacher Educators;
- All early childhood teacher preparation programs recognize the vital link of the care and education of children;
- States work with two- and four-year institutions to provide a continuum of teacher preparation opportunities and professional growth and development;
- States coordinate the departments that award credentials to teachers in child care settings and in public and private schools.[2]

For more information on qualifications, salaries, and benefits, see "Estimating the Full Cost of Quality" (Willer, 1990).

THE ROLES AND RESPONSIBILITIES OF QUALITY TEACHERS

An effective educator in a child care environment must acquire a range of skills and a level of professional competency that encompasses all facets of child development. In *Early Childhood at Risk: Actions and Advocacy for Young Children,* Professor Victoria Jean Dimidjian aptly describes early childhood teachers as developmental interaction specialists. She defines their roles by these categories:

- Observer
- Environmental designer
- Facilitator
- Nurturer
- Inquiry-based explorer
- Intellectual guide and stimulator
- Information provider
- Modeler of social skills
- Disciplinarian
- Assessor/diagnostician
- Resource and referral provider
- Staff/team member[3]

These functions require not only considerable training but instinct as well. An instinctive teacher is naturally child-sensitive; she knows how to manage a classroom and how to interact with children. She is not quick to label or judge children in her care. Rather, she is objective and open minded, recognizing that behavioral changes are not unusual in child care environments. The teacher knows how to help children work through the everyday experiences that cause upsets. Using both wisdom and training, she extends herself for a child in need and, more often than not, experiences success.

In a developmental environment, a teacher and an assistant perceive their relationship as interdependent and supportive. An assistant may have insight about a child that a busy teacher has missed. She may notice changes in development and changes in behavior because she is with the child for a longer period of time during various transitions. A wise teacher will cultivate a strong relationship with her colleagues, one that creates a sense of togetherness.

RECRUITING AND HIRING STAFF

Characteristics of Quality Teachers

Teachers who work with young children should be:

- Sensitive to the individual needs of children in a child care environment;
- Professionals trained in child development and experienced in working with children;

- Skilled in classroom management;
- Kind and considerate toward children, colleagues, and parents;
- Affectionate and positive role models for children to place their trust in;
- Prepared and organized in their approach to teaching and training children;
- Skillful in bringing out the best in young children;
- Able and resourceful in developing a creative and challenging program;
- Flexible in their approach to teaching and learning;
- Aware of the importance of teaching children responsibility, values, and good work habits;
- Aware of the importance of encouraging independence, initiative, and problem solving skills;
- Able to plan and implement fieldtrips that complement a program and enrich children's lives;
- Able to use the creative arts as a primary vehicle for self-expression, self-development, and creativity;
- Able to work effectively with staff;
- Aware of the importance of promoting multicultural awareness and ethnic identity throughout a program;
- Creative architects in planning and equipping activity centers for children to explore and enjoy;
- Creative in developing ideas and original materials for children to interact with and derive knowledge from;
- Able to initiate ideas for children to develop in their own ways;
- Talented in bringing out the talents in others;
- Able to make each child feel important and good about himself;
- Able to help children to value and love all people;
- Skillful at eliminating stereotypes and biases;
- Skilled in behavior management and conflict resolution;
- Humorous and patient in mannerisms and style;
- Loving and accepting toward children and adults.

Prescreening

A director should screen an applicant before scheduling an office interview. After a brief, initial screening, a candidate for employment should be scheduled for an interview with the director and mailed an application form (see Sample 7–1). The application should carefully phrase or avoid asking questions that might be considered discriminatory in nature—race, religion, age, sex, family status.

Recruiting Staff

The purpose of an interview is to determine an applicant's eligibility for employment and to assess individual strengths, talents, and limitations. During this process, the director makes observations about an applicant's training, experience, suitability for the child care profession, knowledge of the field, unique features,

SAMPLE 7–1   Elements of an Application for Employment

- Name, address, telephone number, and social security number
- Citizenship status
- An age range (i.e., over eighteen years of age)
- First and second languages
- Last previous address
- Means of transportation to and from work
- Number of children in family
- Ages of children
- Formal training and certificates earned
- Courses in child development
- Talents, interests, and attributes
- Information about an applicant's present job status
- Information about previous jobs
- Position applying for at a center
- Preferred schedule and ages to work with
- Availability
- Reasons for selecting child care as a profession
- Statement of general physical and mental health
- Information about an applicant's knowledge of a center, i.e., mutual acquaintances, and so on
- Two professional and two personal references
- Phone numbers during the day and evening
- Other pertinent information
- A closing statement that provides information about when and how an applicant will be contacted.

and personal attributes. Based on knowledge gained, she visualizes a person in a specific teaching situation that complements her qualifications.

Equally important is an applicant's opportunity to become familiar with, and evaluate, a center according to her own perceptions and ideals. A director should give the applicant a tour of the center, pointing out personal touches that make it unique. She should allow time for a brief introductory session on center policies and procedures, and for answering questions.

Within an open hiring policy, reasonable efforts should be made to recruit staff of both sexes and to include persons from various cultural backgrounds. A center that advocates for diversity in staffing policies will facilitate multicultural awareness and understanding among children.

Verification

Before presenting an applicant with a contract, a director should carefully check references. A reference check should include:

- A verification of employment;
- Specific information regarding competency, attitude, reliability, organizational skills, responsibility, and relationships with colleagues and parents;
- Potential for leadership;
- General health and physical stamina;
- Areas that may need improvement;
- Other information that might influence decision making;
- Suitability for rehiring;
- Suitability for child care.

A Prehiring Visit

Before hiring, a director should arrange for an applicant to spend a morning in a classroom. She may be asked to share an activity with children such as a flannel board story, a group project, or a handmade game. The head teacher will observe the applicant in group experiences and during free-activity time when children are playing in groups. She will ask questions and answer questions, making an effort to make her guest feel comfortable, noticing if she:

- Has a gentle and positive manner with children.
- Is an effective group leader.
- Has a good grasp of foundational skills.
- Has a style that invites rather than imposes learning.
- Has a teaching style that encourages interaction and dialogue.
- Projects a sense of self-control and confidence.
- Encourages creative thinking.
- Recognizes and expands children's ideas.
- Attracts children and holds their attention.
- Enjoys children.

At the end of the session, the supervising teacher records her observations, noting reasons to hire or not hire a candidate. A thoughtful evaluation written at the time of decision making will help in the selection process. It also will document reasons for hiring one applicant instead of another. If the applicant is offered a position, she should be informed that the first month of employment is a trial period for both parties. Some centers refer to this period as probationary.

Hiring Staff

At the time an applicant is accepted for a position, she will be given a job description, a formal contract, and an employee handbook (see Appendix A). A job description describes in detail the responsibilities of an employee, the expectations of an employer, and the policies of an organization. An employee contract is a binding agreement between an employee and an employer that states the terms of employment, areas of responsibility, and policies and procedures regarding employment and dismissal. An employee handbook is a guide that clarifies policies, procedures, and teaching responsibilities; it contains health, safety, and nutritional information.

As part of the introductory process, the applicant is assigned to a lead teacher who serves as a mentor. The teacher is available for counseling, sharing ideas, answering questions, and making suggestions. With few questions left unanswered and with a clear understanding of her role and responsibility, the employee can embark on her new job feeling reasonably confident she has made a good choice.

TRAINING

Training is an extremely important medium for professional growth and development. It should be designed to:

- Reinforce a center's goals and philosophy;
- Stimulate thinking in areas of child development;
- Encourage open dialogue and flexible thinking;
- Ensure that staff continues to develop the knowledge, skills, and techniques requisite to working with young children;
- Provide practical knowledge in areas of health, nutrition, and child care;
- Provide a constructive outlet for common concerns;
- Encourage staff members to express opinions and exchange ideas;
- Let staff know that their ideas are valued;
- Provide a platform for healthy dissent, brainstorming, and problem solving;
- Provide valuable resources for the continued growth and development of a center and its staff;
- Provide an opportunity for staff to interact and to get to know one another and a center's leadership.

A center should design a system for training personnel that includes orientation training and ongoing training at the workplace as well as opportunities to attend workshops and conferences at local, state, and national levels.

Orientation Training

Before working with children, all new employees should be thoroughly oriented to a program and briefed on their responsibilities. An orientation session provides an overview of a center's policies and procedures and acclimates a new employee to her surroundings. It can be conducted by a director or by a lead teacher who is knowledgeable about a center and can communicate effectively. An employee should be carefully briefed about preservice personnel requirements; routines; recordkeeping; training requirements; staff meetings; attendance procedures;

methods and procedures for handling food, for administering medicine, for handling a sick child, for handwashing, for reporting accidents, for indoor and outdoor supervision, for ensuring a safe environment, for discipline, for emergencies, for reporting child abuse; program requirements; and specific job responsibilities (e.g., preparing calendars and lesson plans, holding conferences, working with parents). In addition to an employee contract and a job description, a new employee should receive written materials that clarify general policies and staff requirements, HSN guidelines, a curriculum guide and samples of units, lesson plans, calendars, conference reports, and so on.

Ongoing Training

General Staff Meetings

General staff meetings customarily are scheduled once a month at a time convenient to employees. A workable time is usually around 6:00 PM when many staff members already are present. After a snack and a few moments to unwind, staff members are ready to interact as long as the meeting doesn't last too long. The director prepares and distributes an agenda and presides over staff meetings. Items for discussion usually include: a general progress report, center business, and general topics of interest or concern. It is a good idea to include staff members on an agenda. A staff member may be asked to give a report on a workshop or on a subject of interest.

Staff meetings provide important opportunities for employees to share common interests and to interact with one another. Meetings often become a forum for discussion, debate, and problem solving. It is important that staff members leave meetings with a good feeling about themselves, their work, and their colleagues.

In-service Certified Workshops

Workshops are planned by a director or by a center's leadership team. The topics and presenters are scheduled well in advance so that staff can become knowledgeable and enthusiastic participants. A director may select topics based on classroom evaluations, new trends, or she may solicit ideas for subjects from her staff. Most centers plan two to three workshops per year and also offer employees the opportunity to attend out-of-center workshops. Employees receive a certificate of attendance, which is filed in their personnel record and reviewed at the time of relicensing. A good way to meet the cost of workshops is to ask each employee to contribute a modest amount, i.e., $10.00 per workshop. The center should be prepared to finance the remainder.

In-house Workshops

When formal training requirements have been met, a director may want to schedule several in-house workshops that might be led by a parent, an interesting personality from the community, a specialist in the field, or a member of the staff. Many staff members feel more comfortable presenting a workshop with a colleague. One member of the team may be a presenter and the other, a moderator.

Videotapes, handouts and hands-on activities always add flavor and fun to workshops. Each participant should fill out an evaluation form to share with the presenter(s), and the director should give the presenter(s) a note of appreciation.

Suggested Topics for In-house Workshops

1. How to conduct a parent/child conference
2. Integrating the arts in the classroom
3. What to do about nap-time
4. Professional conduct in the workplace
5. The problem with transitions
6. Using parents to assist in a classroom
7. New books for a media center
8. Storytelling and other creative experiences
9. Making puppets the easy way
10. An introduction to poetry
11. Integrating the arts: poetry, music, dance, and art
12. The value of self-evaluation: Am I as good as children think I am?
13. Games and activities for school-age children
14. Games and activities for mixed-age groups
15. Rainy-day activities
16. Projects that cost next to nothing
17. Making a prop box
18. Cooking for fun: "The Rite Bite"
19. Ideas for nurturing children
20. Exploring our community
21. Exploring our own backyard
22. "Once Upon a Time" group storytelling
23. What to do when you've run out of creative ideas
24. Physical fitness for staff and children
25. Community outreach projects
26. Making maps, charts, and bar graphs from the eyes of a child

Suggested Topics for In-service Workshops

1. Learning through play
2. What is creativity?
3. A child-safe environment
4. Dealing with difficult behavior
5. Signs of distress and/or dysfunction
6. An open versus a closed environment;
7. Moments of madness—how teachers cope with stress
8. When projects don't work, are expectations too high?
9. Teaching values to children
10. How to cope with sadness and loss
11. Integrating children with special needs into a classroom

12. Outdoor play: beyond the sandbox
13. Cloud pictures: looking at one's world from the e[...]
14. Writing and producing a play
15. Changing sets for summer fun: how to design a summer pr[...]
16. Guess what I found on a discovery walk?
17. Sharing space: finding places and spaces for school-age children
18. Fieldtrips with a purpose
19. What is language?
20. A thinking classroom
21. Ideas for conferences and evaluation

Out-of-center Workshops

Staff members love to attend workshops and conferences. The experience of interacting with prominent educators and writers whose books are on center shelves or
in local bookstores is extremely inspirational for staff. They return to their center
with books that are right off the press, a bag full of collectibles, and a wealth of new
ideas that they cannot wait to share with colleagues.

The real value of training is that it generates knowledge and awareness
through the interplay of personalities and ideas. It makes a person want to know
more. In the process of gaining insight, teachers become sensitive to their own
biases and inadequacies. A teacher may return so liberated that she is finally able to
make changes—in her program, in her classroom, and in herself. She may take
guitar lessons, write children's books, or dress more comfortably so that she can
engage in floor-time with children. She may abandon her lesson plans and experience being herself . . . without props, without a preplanned art project. Similarly,
a director may look at a troublesome staff member from a new perspective: She
may discover hidden qualities to work with or she may decide enough is enough
and move toward dismissal.

Training is most beneficial when a staff person has arrived at a readiness level
for self-growth and development. This is the time when the mission and purpose
of a center become a part of its foundation. Teachers have passed beyond the basics
and begin to experiment with new thoughts and ideas. Each experience has a
rippling effect on a total environment. Teachers themselves become experts in
training because they are the designers and architects of their own programs.

EVALUATION

Of Staff

Its Purpose and Value

Evaluation is a method of measuring progress, clarifying objectives, and improving
overall performance. It should be used as a medium for monitoring and improving
the quality of teaching in a center. It is the responsibility of a director to evaluate
teachers in an honest and systematic way that emphasizes strengths but also

who is not performing up to expectation needs to
ɔrrect the problem. It is the responsibility of a
record and share her observations with an em-
suggestions for improvement as well.
cognize the many factors that come into play when
care setting. She may concentrate her evaluation on
ctions without considering the total environment—
ɔosition of a group, the effectiveness of an aide, the
ɪds of children, health and nutrition factors, family
ɪtal readiness levels, noise levels, required transitions,
ɪterials and equipment, storage facilities, and the use of a
. In child care centers, there are many variables that affect
ɔerformance levels. By evaluating a teacher in the context
ot tɪɪ nt, a director will become more *objective* in her assessment.

Communicating Concerns to Teachers

The following suggestions serve as useful guidelines:

1. Clarify the situation: Does the employee understand her responsibilities? Is there a personal problem that is affecting performance? How well has the employee performed in the past? Is too much expected?
2. Emphasize the good things that are happening in a class.
3. Make suggestions rather than demands.
4. Be sensitive to the moment: Is this a fair appraisal? Is this the right time to address the matter?
5. Be concise and diplomatic in presenting concerns to a teacher: This is a time to tactfully exercise authority.
6. Refer to a curriculum guide or a job description to substantiate one's position.
7. Allow space for discussion and problem solving.
8. Be ready to acknowledge a teacher's point of view and to change one's own position if that is the appropriate course of action.
9. Clarify what changes will be made and when.
10. Offer assistance: resources, materials, ideas.
11. Reaffirm a teacher's importance to the center.
12. Design a plan and a time frame for correcting deficiencies.
13. Take corrective action if necessary: place an employee on probationary status or, under justified circumstances, dismiss an employee immediately;
14. Follow up as needed.

Attentiveness to Staff

A director who seldom visits classrooms or interacts with staff will find a formal evaluation process tedious. In a healthy organizational climate, evaluation needs to be informal and ongoing. A director supports and, when necessary, criticizes teachers, always remembering that forgiveness is a key factor in any human relationship. A director promotes good teaching and harmonious relationships by:

- Informing staff about the system of evaluation that is practiced at a center;
- Periodically providing teachers with feedback about their performance and their program;
- Setting a time and place for informal meetings with staff;
- Spending time in classrooms and on the playground;
- Making suggestions by note or by conversing with a teacher in a positive, nonthreatening manner;
- Asking a teacher for her ideas;
- Acknowledging and reflecting on comments and ideas;
- Taking a deep breath or a short walk before confronting a teacher with criticism;
- Avoiding biased or emotional judgments;
- Using videotapes as a medium for evaluation;
- Creating environments that are supportive and nonthreatening to staff and children;
- Distributing articles that reinforce the philosophy and program of a center;
- Putting one's self in the role of a teacher;
- Giving teachers a sense of ownership through leadership;
- Becoming a good listener.

Affirming Staff

A director is responsible for the quality of teaching that surrounds a center. She trains, supervises, and cultivates the staff she has chosen. When morale declines and a center is no longer "fertilized" by creative ideas and a desire to learn, a director is primarily responsible. Only when she self-examines and begins to make changes, will she begin to replenish and restore a center's energy. Making employees feel appreciated is an important first step. When acknowledged, most staff members will become resourceful and reliable employees who do not need a great deal of supervision. When an organization begins to work in tandem, there is little time for criticism and pettiness. In this context, training becomes an extension of what teachers already know; it is looked at as another opportunity for growth and development.

A Formal Evaluation

A formal evaluation should articulate a center's program and philosophy. A director cannot expect teachers to perform at high standards if they are evaluated by standards that do not reflect the program. An evaluation form should encompass a center's philosophy, program, points of emphasis, job descriptions, and specific responsibilities that have already been communicated to teachers. If a teacher is responsible for writing a monthly calendar, planning one special event per month, and developing a unit every six weeks, these areas must be included in a formal evaluation. If a teacher is to conduct her class according to the principles of child development, a checklist must include this area (see Appendix B). Similarly, if a teacher is required to set up activity centers, a checklist must include an assessment of her effectiveness.

An evaluation form may take a great deal of time to prepare, especially if it is written to incorporate a center's philosophy. Evaluations require more than a check or check minus. There should be space for general observations and comments on the:

- Quality of the interactions between a teacher and her children;
- Quality of the interaction between a teacher and an aide;
- Atmosphere and feeling that is projected from a room;
- Presence of creativity and originality;
- Expressions on children's faces;
- Opportunities a teacher provides children for:

    - Relaxed, unhurried experiences;
    - Exploring and developing their own interests;
    - Self-expression;
    - Thinking and reasoning;
    - Making choices and solving problems;
    - Cooperative learning;
    - Social development;
    - Quiet time and time alone.

A Guideline for Conducting a Formal Evaluation.   A director should inform teachers when she will be conducting formal evaluations. By giving notice, a director is working with her staff. She is giving them time to review their responsibilities and to freshen up their classrooms and performances. Evaluations should be conducted at least twice a year. An evaluation in early spring assists a director in determining placements for the following year. A formal evaluation report should be completed and filed in a teacher's personnel record. During an evaluation, a director should:

- Have a checklist, a note pad, but also take mental notes and try to be gracious and unintimidating;
- Converse, compliment, and reinforce at appropriate times;
- Be positive and friendly, establishing an atmosphere of mutual interest and support;
- Greet and interact with children;
- Thank the teacher for a lovely visit.

After an evaluation, a director should:

- Record her observations;
- Set up a meeting with the teacher to communicate strengths and deficiencies;
- Problem solve together through constructive interaction, developing a plan for correcting deficiencies;
- Provide resources;

- Offer to purchase materials and equipment as needed;
- Become an enthusiastic participant in the follow-up process—encourage the teacher by complimenting her ideas and praising her creative abilities;
- Record the process of change.

For a sample of a formal evaluation, see Appendix B.

An Informal Evaluation

Informal evaluations are less comprehensive but just as important as formal evaluations. They usually are not scheduled in advance. The advantage of making unannounced classroom visits is that a director gets to see a group interact in natural circumstances. She may walk in on tears, a spill, or an unsmiling teacher. Taking the scene in stride, a director will look beyond the moment at: adult/child interaction, the quality of teaching, the arrangement and selection of materials and activities, the attitudes and feelings of the children, the sense of ambience in a room.

A director should carry a note pad at all times so she can jot down thoughts and observations for possible follow-up. A brief note of appreciation is always a good idea. Words like, "Thank you for a lovely visit," "I enjoyed having snack with the children," make teachers feel good about themselves and their program. A director should not wear out her welcome by staying too long or coming too frequently. For a sample of an informal evaluation, see Appendix B.

Informal Office Visits

An even less formal but extremely effective way of getting to know staff is to provide a time for office visits with staff members. This is a good way for concerns to be aired before they escalate into major problems. Office visits also can provide an opportunity for personal communication. A teacher may return from a workshop feeling extremely challenged and enthusiastic. A few moments with a director will not only reinforce her mood but motivate her toward extended learning. Through candid, open sharing, a director develops a sense of a person's character and potential. A welcome mat, a cup of tea, and a few minutes of sharing between a director and an employee may be more informative than lengthy in-class observations.

Of One's Self

A Self-evaluation

Perhaps the most enlightening and educative way of assessing one's performance is through a self-evaluation process. In a trusting environment, people perform at high levels because they have *high* standards. A teacher knows when she is delinquent in her duties, when she is feeling inadequate for a task, and when she is performing at a marginal level of proficiency. She also knows that only by correcting deficiencies will she feel good about her performance and comfortable with herself. When a teacher signs up for a workshop, subscribes to an educational periodical, is cooperative and willing to help, is generous toward others, purchases books and carries in a sack of resources and materials every morning, she is making a statement about her commitment to herself and to her job. A self-evaluation form can be filled out by a teacher and, if willing, may be shared with a director and her colleagues. For a sample of a self-evaluation, see Appendix B.

Of an Organization

The leadership of an organization should have some way of evaluating the overall performance of a center and the performance of its director. An organizational checklist that addresses key areas of leadership and management is one way of evaluating a center. A checklist can be completed by a director and a select number of teachers who represent the larger staff, for presentation before a board of directors.

In order to present an objective evaluation to a board, a director should be attentive to these ongoing areas of leadership that may require attention:

- Keeping a board informed;
- Reviewing and updating a center's policies and procedures;
- Networking with parents and teachers to assess needs;
- Being attentive to written reports, evaluations, and licensing requirements;
- Reviewing and assessing the status of a center with staff leaders;
- Developing a plan for improvement and/or expansion;
- Reviewing periodically a center's philosophy, objectives, and goals;
- Attending conferences and workshops in the field;
- Attending leadership conferences;
- Advertising or marketing the program as needed;
- Being alert to new trends or changes that might impact on a center;
- Brainstorming frequently with people whose opinions are valued;
- Testing out a director's effectiveness and popularity by asking staff to evaluate a center.

For a sample of an organizational evaluation, see Appendix B.

Of Children

Holding Conferences

Conferences are important channels for communicating with parents about a child's adjustment and progress in a child care environment. In addition, a conference is an opportunity for a teacher to gain more information and insight about a child and an opportunity for parents to learn about a program. The challenge for a teacher is to communicate effectively and honestly. She will want to stress the positive aspects of a child's development, but she also will want to provide an objective assessment that points out areas of concern. A teacher will gradually learn how to communicate concerns to parents, some of whom may blame themselves for a child's problems. When necessary, she will provide resources and special assistance and recommend a plan for correcting deficiencies that can be followed through at home. For example, a child with poor motor skills will need materials and equipment that are specifically designed to develop eye-hand coordination. A center may lend toys for weekend use or suggest fine-motor games and toys that can be purchased at a local store.

Most important, a teacher and a parent should end a conference by agreeing to work together, to reinforce and support a child's interests. A summary of each conference should be placed in a child's file and retained for at least one year after a child's departure from a center.

Preconference Considerations

A conference should not be handled in a routine, checklist format. Parents have the right to know what a program is about so that they too can evaluate and reinforce a child's learning. By outlining areas of emphasis, a teacher will be better able to communicate a center's objectives and a child's progress. Areas to include might be:

Self-development: Degree of independence, initiative, self-management child manifests toward self and environment. What particularly interests the child during self-initiated play and practical life experiences (i.e., washing tables, setting tables, sorting and classifying objects during pick-up)? What is child's attitude toward cooperating and helping with tasks? Why is this area of training important in a child care environment? How can parents help children toward self-management and responsible behavior? What responsibilities are children given in this classroom? How much time are they given to complete tasks and to clean up?

Social Development: Degree of social maturity child expresses. How and to whom does child demonstrate sharing and friendship? How is caring and friendship nurtured in this classroom? How can parents encourage this important area of development? How is self-esteem and social awareness developed in this classroom (i.e., Star of the Week, sharing day, parent visits, celebrating birthdays, helping children to accept and understand differences, projects and activities that invoke emotions and feelings)?

Physical Development: Degree of large- and small-motor abilities child is acquiring. What opportunities for both areas are available in this program? What is child particularly good at or interested in? How can parents encourage this important area of development? How are nutrition and good health practices encouraged in this classroom?

Emotional Development: Degree of adjustment child is making to his or her child care experience and environment. Is child developing self-control, patience, and self-awareness? Is child able to play alone for extended periods of time? Is child able to sustain group or peer play for reasonable periods of time? How is emotional growth encouraged in this classroom? How do parents assess this important area of development from a home/family perspective?

Cognitive Development: Degree of awareness, alertness, inquiry, and exploration child exhibits toward mastery and understanding his or her physical environment. What formal and informal learning opportunities are available for children's cognitive development? What areas may or should be given extra attention by teachers and parents? Why? What basic skills are introduced to children and in what way (i.e., language, math and science concepts, spatial relationships, ordering, classification, problem solving, memory, and critical thinking skills)? How are children encouraged to think creatively and independently in this classroom?

Language Development: Degree of language competency expressed by child. Does the child attend to a story? Can he or she project endings, show interest, identify with characters, recall a sequence of events (if appropriate)? Does the child participate in group circle? What whole-language program is incorporated into this program? How are phonics integrated into the language-arts program? What is important in a child-centered reading program (i.e., the process, enjoying language, reading and telling stories in unique and motivating ways, encouraging children's interest in books, stimulating thinking and encouraging children to express themselves through language)? What specific activities may parents want to adapt for use in a home language program?

Creative Development: What degree of interest and involvement does child exhibit toward dramatic play, toward storytelling experiences, toward painting, toward music and poetry, toward original thinking, toward discovery opportunities in the classroom and on the playground? How important is creative expression in this classroom? What areas might parents want to cultivate? What is creativity?

Suggestions for Effective Conferences

Some or all of the following may be useful when preparing for a conference with a child's parents:

- Prepare well in advance for parent conferences; observe and evaluate children's progress during the preceding months and especially during the preconference period.
- Keep a daily record of children's progress, noting milestones, interests, friends, concerns, and behavior changes.
- Review the center's curriculum guide and refer to its developmental checklist when observing children, noting areas that may be of concern.
- Spend individual time with children before a conference so that information can be updated and verified by the child's primary teacher; be certain children can perform basic skills that are age-appropriate and observe their thinking patterns and language development.

- Keep an ongoing file of children's drawings, anecdotes, original writings, and so on to share with parents.
- Be able to point out the important objectives of a program.
- Emphasize the special qualities of each child by pointing out interests, attitudes, talents, and friends.
- Be relaxed and nonjudgmental with parents.
- Observe but *do not* label children.
- Make recommendations in positive and supportive ways.
- Be prepared to provide resources for learning or emotional problems, for special events or activities that might interest a child, and for parent/child fieldtrips.
- Allow time for natural "in-time" maturation, i.e., avoid hasty decision making and recommendations.
- Begin and end a conference on a positive note.

A Developmental Checklist

A child's progress in areas that are significant to his development usually is recorded on a developmental checklist. Because a child care center emphasizes the total child, such a list should include both general and specific categories in checklist form. The form should not be so *general* as to exclude basic skills in foundation areas or so *restrictive* as to exclude important developmental, interactional factors. A checklist should *not* label a child, grade a child, or attempt to predict a child's educational future; it should merely be a *tool* for assessing progress at a given time and for *promoting* and *enhancing* a child's development. It is also a way of assessing one's own performance. By evaluating children, a teacher evaluates *herself*. Am I meeting the needs of each child? Do I need to make changes in the environment, in my program, in my performance, in my own objectives for children?

In order to assess a child with some degree of accuracy, a teacher must be informed about developmental theories and practices. She must understand the significance of self-expression and play to a child's development. A teacher needs to understand that a three-year-old who can identify colors, shapes, numbers, or words is performing in only one small area of development. If the same child can recall information, self-manage, and work independently, a teacher may assume that a child is progressing well. Progress is *never* forever. Children dip and rise in their abilities and interests much like adults do. Checklists may or may not describe a child—they should be used with discretion or not used at all. For a sample of a developmental checklist, see Appendix B.

SUMMARY

Staff development, in its broadest context, encompasses all components of a program from the selection and training of staff to the implementation of policies, the actual interaction between each teacher and each child, and the quality of the environment that reflects a center's leadership. In a quality environment, teachers perceive their role as both nurturers and educators acknowledging that the process of maturation varies from child to child. When learning is viewed from a total child perspective, there is no one model or method that can ensure success. A good program will draw from several pathways that offer direction and promise. These pathways are guideposts that have been illuminated by leading educators in child development.

NOTES

1. *Caring for Our Children* (Washington, DC: American Public Health Association and American Academy of Pediatrics, 1992), pp. 4–18.

2. "Position Paper," *Young Children* 47 (1), November 1991: 18.

3. Victoria Jean Dimidjian, *Early Childhood at Risk: Actions and Advocacy for Young Children* (Washington, DC: National Education Association, 1989), pp. 49–51.

RESOURCES

For Training

Aronson, S. S. "Health and Safety Training for Child Care Workers." *Exchange* (October 1984): 25–28.

———. "Coping with the Physical Requirements of Caregiving." *Exchange* (May 1987): 39–40.

Berk, L. E. "Relationships of Caregiver Education to Child-Oriented Attitudes, Job Satisfaction, and Behaviors Toward Children." *Child Care Quarterly* 14(2), 1985: 103–29.

Bredekamp, S., ed. *Accreditation Criteria and Procedures of the National Academy of Early Childhood Programs.* Washington, DC: NAEYC, 1987.

Carter, M. "Honoring Diversity: Problems and Possibilities for Staff and Organization." *Exchange* (January 1988): 43–47.

Caruso, J. J., and M. T. Fawcett. *Supervision in Early Childhood Education: A Developmental Perspective.* New York: Teachers College Press, 1986.

Counselman, K. "Supervising Long-Term Employees." *Exchange* (July 1987): 11–13.

Green, S., L. M. Hatfield, and D. D. Long. "Making Conference Time Count." *Exchange* (October 1984): 11–13.

Greenberg, H. *Coping with Job Stress.* New York: Prentice-Hall, 1980.

Jones, E. *Teaching Adults: An Active Learning Approach.* Washington, DC: NAEYC, 1986.

Jentz, B. C., and J. Wofford. *Leadership and Learning: Personal Change in a Professional Setting.* New York: McGraw-Hill, 1979.

Jorde-Bloom, P. *Avoiding Burnout: Strategies for Managing Time, Space, and People in Early Childhood Education.* Washington, DC: Acropolis Books, 1982.

———. *A Great Place to Work: Improving Conditions for Staff in Young Children's Programs.* Washington, DC: NAEYC, 1988.

Kessler, D. "Lessons in Parent Communication: Insights from the Parent Co-op Model." *Exchange* (April 1989): 25–27.

Morris, S. "Recognition for a Job Well Done: Increasing Respect for Teachers." *Exchange* (October 1989): 15–17.

Hegland, S. M. "Teacher Supervision: A Model for Advancing Professional Growth." *Young Children* 39(4), 1984: 3–10.

Nash, M. *Managing Organizational Performance.* San Francisco: Jossey-Bass, 1979.

Neugebauer, R. "When Friction Flares—Dealing with Staff Conflict." *Exchange* (February 1989): 3–6.

Perreault, J. "Developing the Employee Handbook: Grievance Procedure." *Exchange* (April 1989): 41–44.

Porzel, M. *Resources for Early Childhood Training: An Annotated Bibliography.* Washington, DC: NAEYC, 1987.

Scallan, P. C. "Teachers Coaching Teachers: Development from Within." *Exchange* (November 1987): 3–6.

———. "Improving Staff Performance Part One: Providing Feedback." *Exchange* (June 1990): 15–18.

———. "How to Implement a Coaching Program in Your Center," *Exchange* (January 1988): 35–37.

Schrag, L., E. Nelson, and T. Siminowsky. "Helping Employees Cope with Change." *Exchange* (September 1985): 3–5.

Seashore, S., E. Lawler, P. Mirivis, and C. Cammann. *Assessing Organizational Change.* New York: John Wiley & Sons, 1983.

Sheerer, M., and P. Jorde-Bloom. "The Ongoing Challenge: Attracting and Retaining Quality Staff." *Exchange* (April 1990): 11–16.

Storm, S. *The Human Side of Child Care Administration.* Washington, DC: NAEYC, 1985.

Willer, Barbara. "Estimating the Full Cost of Quality." In *Reaching the Full Cost of Quality.* Washington, DC: NAEYC, 1990.

Yonemoura, M. V. *A Teacher at Work: Professional Development and the Early Childhood Educator.* New York: Teachers College Press, 1986.

By adapting theories to contemporary knowledge and practices, a child care provider will recognize the importance of meeting the individual needs and developmental patterns of children. She will view the first years of life as extraordinary and critical to a child's lifelong development.

P A R T IV

CHILD DEVELOPMENT

In the broadest sense, [child development] is the process of becoming a fully functioning human being. A child's experience combines with a child's biological givens, and from this mixture emerges an adult person, one who will face the challenges of day-to-day life—as student, worker, friend, family member and citizen. If they are to succeed in these roles as adults, children need to be rooted in the basic skills of modern life. They need to become socially competent. They must come to know who they are. They must have acquired a secure and positive sense of their own identity. In addition, they must become proficient in thinking and in speaking clearly. They must learn to understand the many ways people communicate with one another. It is in the context of this broad conception of the process of child development that we must understand cognitive development.

— James Garbarino

8

THEORIES AND PRACTICES

A THEORETICAL APPROACH TO CHILD DEVELOPMENT

Child development is a field of study that examines and interprets human growth and development from conception to adolescence. The principles of child development are derived from systematic, documented research studies that test and validate theories. Theories serve as useful guidelines for understanding the nature, interests, and needs of children at various stages of development. They help us to understand how children acquire and use knowledge and they help us to interpret behavioral characteristics. Most important, from a child care perspective, theories help us to develop strategies for working with children at all levels of development. By understanding the fundamentals of child development, educators can design and implement a child-appropriate curriculum and environment.

Theories

Theories form a baseline for a philosophy of education and for program development. Without an understanding of the nature and needs of childhood, a director cannot fully cultivate a child's development. Theories contribute to the educative process by raising questions and by opening dialogue on pertinent issues. They force educators to think about the *process* of learning from an interactional, total child perspective. In a dynamic learning environment, a teacher will examine her assumptions and be receptive to change. She will look at her classroom as a composition of unique personalities. As she focuses on individual children, she will ponder her role in and responsibility for their development: How much freedom is appropriate for active, open learning environments? What is a teacher's role in the learning process? When is an appropriate time to teach basic skills? How do children learn? How are multicultural backgrounds built into a program? Have individual learning styles been considered in program planning?

Theories Are Guidelines

Educators use theories as guidelines for program development. Theories form a foundation for education. They are intended to shape and direct programs in ways that are relevant to contemporary needs and learning styles. Today's child is socially acclimated and, in many cases, considerably more advanced than were children in Jean Piaget's generation. Most educators agree that children who have been exposed to early enrichment, through quality programs such as Head Start, are at a developmental advantage before entering a formal school experience. All children benefit from a strong learning environment that provides opportunities for language, thinking, and social development.

Adapting Theories

By adapting theories to contemporary knowledge and practices, a child care provider will recognize the importance of meeting the individual needs and developmental patterns of children. She will view the first years of life as extraordinary and critical to a child's lifelong development. A two-year-old can astound a teacher with the rate at which he can process and assimilate information. He can recall and perform routines, discriminate among physical objects, and to some degree, anticipate outcomes. He can pour and mix Jell-o and visualize its solid form if he is familiar with the process. A four-year-old can make associations, generalize information, and begin to form simple concepts. He can identify a dog by its physical appearance, compare it to a cat, and identify them both as members of the animal family. Children who experience positive interactions with people, ideas, and materials at an early age blossom into competent thinkers.

With some basic training in child development, a provider will realize that a two-year-old and a five-year-old will not behave and interact with their environment in the same way; they do not have the same degree of awareness, autonomy, or ability. A two-year-old reacts physically, spontaneously, and emotionally to his or her environment while a five-year-old is beginning to exercise reason and self-control in social settings. A two-year-old grabs or hits in anger while a five-year-old, though still a hitter uses language as a channel for cooperative dialogue with peers. A five-year-old is less controlled by his need for satisfaction and more sensitive to peer feelings. A provider, therefore, will limit the number of choices a two-year-old is given and oversee play activities. She will limit the number and length of formal group activities but will promote cooperative exchanges with peers. At the five-year level, she will increase choices, problem solving, and group interactions in both formal and informal settings. (See Figure 8–1.)

Knowledge of child development will facilitate optimal development at each stage of growth and learning. A quality environment derives from theories of learning that *enlighten* and *guide* leadership in childrearing practices. Children can become fully functioning human beings if they experience a secure and challenging total environment during their formative years. The NAEYC advocates a child development approach to early childhood education:

The National Association for the Education of Young Children (NAEYC) believes that a high-quality early childhood program provides a safe and

FIGURE 8–1   Developmental Differences between Ages 2 and 5

The 2-year-old	*The 5-year-old*

Social-emotional characteristics

Is engrossed in his own manipulations of objects.	Includes others in his explorations of the physical world.
Imitates the actions of objects and others as he sees them.	Goes beyond what he sees; invents sociodramatic themes in play.
Spends a lot of his time watching as well as acting.	Is able to pick up a lot of information from a momentary glance.
Self-directive, varies abruptly in his amenability to be influenced by an adult.	Socially tractable, waits for instructions and responds appropriately.
Strong in self-set goals, has difficulty inhibiting an action once initiated.	Can change an intended action in mid-flight at the verbal suggestion of an adult.
His emotional mood changes abruptly, but intensity is often short-lived.	His emotional mood can pervade several situations and is manifested in themes of social play and in approach to materials.

General cognitive characteristics

His goals exceed his means; preparing materials sometimes frustrates him as he attempts to reach his intended goal; is sidetracked on means.	Has mastered the simple means of preparing and wielding materials; anticipates definite products.
Has no clear sense of the continuity of past, present, and future but can anticipate physical consequences of his actions.	Is beginning to see the continuity of his own past, present, and future but has difficulty generalizing this to other persons.
Treats pictures as static shots of things rather than as momentary freezes of ongoing actions.	Can infer the course of action from a sequence of pictures.
His preferred mode of exploration is manual manipulation combined with observation.	Can visually explore the physical world in advance of manipulation in order to pick up information needed to guide goal-directed behavior.
Has difficulty coordinating his actions with those of other children in group games.	Has no difficulty coordinating his actions with those of others and is beginning to anticipate the meaning of game rules.

Language characteristics

His sentences omit adjectives and adverbs necessary for explicit communication.	Has more effective ability to express desires and ask questions.
Uses language primarily to express personal desires and immediate needs.	Uses language to gather information about things in general—for example, origins and reasons.
His language is episodic and refers to single events and objects.	His language develops an idea or question, and his sentences build upon each other around a core theme.
His language is quite bound to the spatial and temporal present or to familiar contingencies.	Can use language metaphorically and to invent novel contingencies he doesn't actually see.
Adult's language can be used to activate him if the physical setting is right.	Adult's language can be used to set task constraints and to have him modify the physical setting.

Source: From George E. Forman and David S. Kuschner, *The Child's Construction of Knowledge: Piaget for Teaching Children.* Copyright 1983 by The National Association for the Education of Young Children. Reprinted with permission of NAEYC.

nurturing environment that promotes the physical, social, emotional, and cognitive development of young children while responding to the needs of families. Although the quality of an early childhood program may be affected by many factors, a major determinant of program quality is the extent to which knowledge of child development is applied in program practices—the degree to which the program is developmentally appropriate.[1]

AFFECTIVE DEVELOPMENT

Affective education is focused on the emotional development of children. This is becoming an area of increasing importance to educators and specialists who are seeing growing numbers of emotionally troubled children in schools. Early child-rearing environments are being examined as contributing factors to emotional disorders among a growing number of children. The psychological and social ramifications of rearing children in out-of-home environments for prolonged periods of time has yet to be determined. It is known, however, that children's feelings and emotions reflect the way they *see, relate to,* and *respond to* their world. A joyful, nurturing teacher generates feelings of happiness in children. In a secure environment children feel satisfied and unthreatened. They are able to venture forth, test their capabilities, and in the process, find out about themselves.

There is agreement that a child's rate of development is strongly influenced by the quality of family life and the social institutions he has been exposed to. A child behaves as he is treated; he imitates those who surround him. He trusts relationships as long as he can depend on their constancy and predictability. If a teacher who is very important to a child becomes unpleasant or angry, a child will react to the change in mood. If the behavior continues, he will become mistrustful. The teacher's behavior may have nothing to do with the child, but it is the child who perceives and reacts to the change. He doesn't understand why things are different and is not certain how to react. He may act out his feelings by changing his own behavioral patterns—becoming withdrawn, anxious, or hostile. Children are influenced by how they are treated, by what they observe, and by what they experience. They are strongly influenced by adult role models.

A child care program should provide *many* opportunities for children to express love and feelings in uncontrived, natural ways. A tender attitude toward animals, family members, friends, and community members will foster nurturance. The concept of unity through togetherness can be understood by the youngest child if it is presented in a sensitive and empowering way—using songs and group activities that children can collectively enjoy and identify with. Children are naturally sociable and friendly. From imitating one another, they begin to role model, taking on the characteristics of others. They especially are interested in pleasing the teacher. If she values the environment, they too will become sensitized to the world around them, to its problems as well as its gifts.

One learns from theorist Erik Erikson that problems and conflicts must be resolved before a child can successfully move on to the next stage of development.

A child, lacking meaningful and sustained human contact in the early years, will not conform to normal patterns of behavior. She will not be able to empathize with others, nor will she be able to express her feelings in ways that are healthy and helpful to her development. Her values and perceptions will be distorted by early experiences. A child will need a great deal of quality time with adults before being able to exhibit positive, prosocial behavior.

Even a happy child can go through reversals in an out-of-home environment. A child may experience a sense of loss over a mother's absence and not be able to verbalize his feelings. He may become fretful and listless at certain times of the day. In child care centers, teachers and assistants must be sensitive to the moods and dispositions of children at any given time. They must extend themselves by spending personal time with a child in need *while* he is experiencing anxiety or discomfort. This can best be accomplished in an unhurried, child-centered atmosphere.

An affective child care program must meet the diverse needs and backgrounds of its members. Language-poor or disadvantaged children will require considerable teacher/child personal time before they can function independently. In contemporary environments, a teacher will have to consider ethnic backgrounds, languages spoken, cultural experiences, and home circumstances before designing a curriculum. A unit on Native Americans, for example, will have to forego a traditional stereotypical approach that portrays an inaccurate picture of "Indian" culture. It could extend beyond Thanksgiving, focusing not on Pilgrim and Indian feasting but on a comparative study of tribes in several regions of the country. Or, a unit may focus on a cross-cultural, historical perspective that reveals a heritage rich in customs and traditions.

By assessing each child from a total developmental perspective, a teacher will be better able to design a program. She will know when and how to approach emotional issues such as death or divorce. A young child who has experienced a loss may not know how to deal with expressions of sympathy. An "affective" teacher will know how to connect with a child to facilitate the healing process. She will understand that, at certain times, the best thing to say is nothing at all.

An affective program that *acknowledges* and *cultivates* a child's own unique personality while gradually introducing him to his surrounding world is probably the most important "first lesson" for child care providers. As children identify with their immediate environment, they extend their feelings and their perceptions to incorporate their surrounding world. They accept others if they feel accepted and loved. A group is shaped by individual members who gradually develop common interests and points of contact. A group has its own distinct personality and dynamic—there is *no* model that can guarantee successful teaching. A model can only create a framework or context for learning.

A center that does not cultivate the child's own personality is not practicing the principles of child development. Children are individuals before they are members of a group. Early childhood is a time of formation and expression. In the words of the great French educator and philosopher, Jean-Jacques Rousseau, childhood is a time of *unfolding*. It is not a time of *molding* young minds and spirits.

Dropping children on the doorstep of life without a sense of "me," of self-identity, is one of the saddest aspects of contemporary childrearing practices. It is taking the child out of childhood. It is replacing the very essence of childhood, the *emerging child,* with a concept of childhood that is shaped by norms defined by adults. Educational settings become depositories of rules and regulations that may keep children safe but that have little meaning to the emerging young child.

The Work of Erik H. Erikson

In his now famous book *Child and Society* (1963), Erik Erikson developed a comprehensive theory of emotional development that spans eight stages from infancy through adulthood. Erikson's emphasis on psychosocial development from a life-span perspective was strongly influenced by Sigmund Freud's work in psychoanalysis. Both Freud and Erikson viewed a child's response to distinctive stages of development as critical to personal development and to personality formation. Unlike Freud, Erikson emphasized the healthy personality affected, but not irrevocably marked, by problems in infancy and early childhood. To Erikson, meeting and dealing with a crisis at the time of occurrence was critical to continued personality adjustment and growth. Under appropriate conditions, people could reorder and adjust their lives before meeting the next conflict. The way in which a person resolves a problem will have a lasting effect on the person's self-image, personality, and view of society.[2]

Understanding and Interpreting Erikson's Stages

Stage 1: Trust versus Mistrust.   During this period (0 to 1 year), the quality of interaction between a parent and child will determine a child's attitude toward other people. According to Erikson, the infant will develop a sense of trust if his basic needs for food and care are met with comforting regularity. He is learning that people and objects exist even though they cannot be seen. The mother figure becomes an inner certainty when the child perceives her presence even though he cannot see her. Under healthy conditions, the child trusts that mother will reappear and will continue to meet his needs. The alternative to trust, mistrust, occurs when children's basic needs are not consistently met—when children cannot depend on the constancy of relationships.

Application to Child Care. The single, most important person for a young child is the primary parent, or, in a child care environment, an adult caregiver to whom the child transfers his or her security needs and attachment during the absence of the primary parent. If this basic need is threatened, a child will manifest insecure behavior patterns; thumb clutching, nervous habits, physical aggressiveness, fears and anxieties, mistrust, and other signs of dysfunction. Bonding (natural attachment) is a trusting relationship that develops between a child and a caring adult. A child's overall nurturing needs may be met by several adults. But, as is often the case, there will be one person whom a child will single out for comfort and security. The feelings generated by a special friend can remain with a child even though the adult is no longer present. Bonding in the form of trust is *essential* to young children in day care centers. Staff members who care for infants and toddlers should be hired with the expectation of a long-term commitment.

Trust is an extremely important part of human relationships at any age. It is cultivated through *continuity* and *positive* relationships. A child care program must strive for consistency in staffing, in behavioral guidelines, and in teaching methods. A child care program that is *trusting* is *loving*. Young children experience love through verbal and nonverbal communication. They want to be hugged and they want to express love to the adults with whom they have bonded. It is difficult to conceive of an early childhood environment that is not generous with its affection to young children. As children mature, they tend to have less of a need for physical contact but continue to need emotional support. In particular, boys may feel embarrassed by a teacher's touch, while, for the most part, girls continue to need their hugs from adults. Children develop *trust* when caregivers:

- Show affection—let children know you care and are there for them: to counsel, to comfort, and to participate in their joys and disappointments.
- Emphasize the importance of *cross-bonding* (child, center, and family) so that children feel a sense of unity among their relationships and their environment.
- Help children understand and cope with negative or anxious feelings in ways that preserve self-worth.
- Deal with a child's feelings *immediately;* console a child but do not make false or unrealistic promises.
- Help children learn to trust by providing consistency.
- Promote peer friendships so children can feel secure in their center.
- Plan projects that cultivate nurturing and bonding.
- Help children identify with feelings and attitudes through literature, discussions, fieldtrips, and visual aids.
- Approach emotional issues, such as divorce and separation with honesty and empathy.
- Encourage parent visitations so children can connect their center to their home.

Stage 2: Autonomy versus Doubt.   During this period (1 to 2 years), the child operates in a self-centered world of need gratification. A child's insatiable curiosity can best be satisfied by physical contact with the concrete world—a physical world that is visible and tangible. The period is essentially egocentric (the child's needs and interests are all-consuming). The child is developing self-control and self-confidence as he makes contact with the environment. He needs to be protected but not overprotected. The alternative to autonomy, doubt, occurs when children begin to feel frustrated because they are no longer in control of their world—when they no longer feel confident in their ability to make choices.

Application to Child Care. Young children exercise autonomy when they are free to investigate and not restricted by the presence of anxious, controlling adults.

Children develop confidence by doing more and more for themselves. A child learns how to manipulate and control his environment through *repeated* exposure to positive reinforcing experiences. In the process, the child must take chances and experience a few bruises along the way. If fears have been instilled in a child, he will avoid growth-enhancing experiences that promote mastery and competency. Over a period of time, a child's anxieties may become *generalized;* more and more things will make him anxious. He may stutter or wet the bed when he feels upset. He may feel uncomfortable with transitions or new situations. The opposite, too much autonomy, may be equally harmful. The adventurous child who knows no boundaries may have difficulty accepting rules designed for his safety. Testing limits, he will continue to have difficulty developing internal control mechanisms. Young children must be trained not only to take chances that are constructive and necessary to their growth but to avoid things that are harmful to their growth. They must learn to practice caution and wisdom *before* they can be entrusted with freedom.

Child care centers should encourage children of all ages to become independent managers. They should be *expected* to care for their personal belongings, to keep their cubbies tidy, and to cooperate with their classmates in maintaining and caring for their rooms. Jobs and chores should become a natural part of classroom routines. Every child should understand the value of good hygiene, good eating habits, and overall cleanliness. When they are participants in self-care and center-care, they will be able to transfer their good habits to other situations outside the center. They will become more *cooperative* at home and in their communities. They will become *trustworthy*. Children will develop autonomy when caregivers:

- Reinforce their need to explore and investigate their concrete and surrounding world on their own.
- Select appropriate materials for them to play with and learn from.
- Help them develop self-control by understanding that some behavior is acceptable and some behavior is not tolerated—like being unkind to others.
- Help them understand consequences (cause-and-effect relationships).
- Encourage them to make choices when selecting activities.
- Help them develop self-management skills within their developmental level (zippering, buttoning, folding sheets on a cot, unpacking a lunch box).
- Help them develop caution in spontaneous and social play.
- Encourage them to take responsibility.
- Encourage them to develop coping mechanisms to help them deal with stressful encounters and disappointments.

Stage 3: Initiative versus Guilt.   During this period (2 to 6 years), children must be given an opportunity to *test* their capabilities. Erikson believes that initiative is the "willingness to undertake, plan, and attack a task for the sake of being active."[3] This is an exciting period when children begin to test their skills and, at times, to challenge authority. During this critical period, children begin to develop formative skills and concepts that will lead them toward higher levels of thinking. On the other hand, guilt occurs when children feel *unsupported* and *unchallenged* by their environment. They will begin to doubt themselves when they do not experience positive reinforcement or acknowledgment and when they fail to exert initiative.

Application to Child Care. In order for children to develop confidence, they need reinforcement from the important people in their lives. They must be free to explore and observe in order to develop self-awareness and competency. By interacting with people, children begin to develop a sense of identity. As they discover their world, children seek role models for *reassurance* and *reinforcement.* These are the people who help the child believe in himself. A child who is confident will exercise initiative. When children do not receive positive messages from their surrounding human environment and when they are not accepted by parents, adults, and friends, they will lose confidence in themselves and in others.

A child with initiative has a built-in sense of responsibility. She is a role model and a budding leader. She becomes a teacher's helper by natural selection because she is reliable and responsible. This is a child who is helpful to others; who can quickly locate a missing mitten and button a jacket. Her take-charge attitude is pleasing and unpretentious. She comforts children when they are sick or hurt, cares for younger children on fieldtrips, and carries the bag of snacks on and off the bus without complaining. She holds hands, listens, and respects authority. Unfortunately, she is not a typical day care child.

A child acquires initiative when she is encouraged to take responsibility and to believe in herself at an early age. The qualities she exhibits at four were becoming evident at three. The child was encouraged to be patient, to take turns, to develop self-control, to do her best, and to help others do their best. Responsibility can be trained at an early age *if* teachers reinforce its importance to young children.

Teachers are often agitated about the unwillingness of children to exercise responsibility. Coaxing and cajoling doesn't always work when children have an antiwork, negative mindset. For these children there's always an excuse for not picking up and there's always someone else to point a finger at for not doing his or her fair share. Some children will go to the extreme of not playing in order to avoid work. Their attitudes are unmistakably negative. Moving the clock forward to second or third grade, these are the same children who storm into day care, slam backpacks on tables, and start the afternoon complaining about too much work. When behaviors are instilled early on in day care environments, children do not need to be reminded about their responsibilities. When everyone does his or her fair share, it is truly difficult to distinguish work from play. Usually, when teachers are initiators, children display *initiative*. A teacher who cheerfully models cooperative behavior by sharing in pickup time will quickly have a following.

Initiative involves taking risks. A child should be able to anticipate and accept failure on her journey toward self-mastery. She should be willing to risk the toppling effect of an unstable building when she places one more block on the top. The last block on a wobbly, vertical structure is a breath-holder even for a child who can handle upsetting consequences. The less mature child might get angry or throw a block when she sees her building destroyed; the more mature child would probably pick up the pieces and start all over again. In the more positive mindset, the child is becoming *self-actualized* (increasing awareness and competency); he has *instinctively* accepted that the *process* is more important than outcome. Initiative will develop when caregivers:

- Avoid setting up roadblocks to self-development by discouraging making decisions and taking risks.
- Avoid making children so dependent that they cannot assert their independence.
- Avoid overprotecting children through negative feedback: "You see, I told you not to climb on the bars; now you've fallen and dirtied your clothes . . . next time you'll listen to me!"
- Encourage children to become efficient, enterprising members of a group (forming clubs, engaging in community activities).
- Encourage children to become self-starters and self-managers so they can function independently and competently in any situation.
- Allow time, space, and flexible time for children to fully engage in classroom activities.
- Praise their quality time and their positive efforts toward socialization and good citizenship.

Stage 4: Industry versus Inferiority.   During this period (6 to 12 years), children are beginning to see the relationship between *doing* a job and feeling good or not good about the outcome. They are moving into a less defined world that offers more choices and opportunities. Children begin to feel more competitive and goal-oriented. They begin to display initiative toward their schoolwork. They are learning about values, responsibility, and rules of conduct. The opposite of industry, inferiority, occurs when children feel unimportant and unaccepted. No longer self-directed, an unhappy child becomes unmotivated. She is reluctant to try new experiences because she is fearful of outcomes. She avoids people who make her feel uncomfortable, preferring to be an onlooker rather than an active participant.

Application to Child Care. An industrious child *applies* herself to a task-at-hand with perseverance and pride. She pays attention and knows how to allocate her time in order to complete a task and is not easily diverted or distracted. The amount of effort a child puts into tasks and the precision with which she performs these tasks tells a lot about the child. A little child painstakingly pastes one piece of paper onto another. With equal care, a school-age child glues together a model airplane, carefully wiping off excess glue as he strives for perfection. At both levels, a learner is occupied in productive work that requires patience and perseverance. Both children would be well served by reinforcement. A "good job" comment by the teacher symbolizes appreciation and recognition to a child. To help the child *internalize* the satisfaction, a teacher's comment might be: "You must really be proud of yourself for doing such a good job today." More than likely this brief but positive interaction will motivate a child to continue pleasing her teacher and satisfying herself.

There are some children who appear to be natural taskmasters; they apply their preference for order at work and at play. Blankets are meticulously arranged around dolls, homework is carefully organized and executed, shoes are always tied, and clothing in place. For most children, however, industry needs *training* and *reinforcement* from the beginning. If children are expected to be industrious, they will soon tire of escape mechanisms: "I can't." "My mother doesn't care if I don't do my homework." "I'm too tired, I'll do it later." Teachers can cultivate incentive by helping children recognize the importance of taking responsibility and becoming positive members of a group. . . . The little red hen worked very hard to make bread but her children were not very cooperative . . . and what happened? Lazy chickens and lazy children don't always get to enjoy the good things in life! Industry will develop when caregivers:

- Help children develop confidence and self-belief.
- Present tasks that are within the range of capability and avoid giving children too many steps and too many instructions.
- Make agreements with children regarding classroom chores and responsibilities.
- Have children evaluate outcomes and participate in decision making.
- Plan activities that encourage children to organize and implement classroom and community projects.
- Develop strategies for positive reinforcement.
- Develop a buddy system with child helping child—tutoring, peer support groups.
- Provide materials and activities to encourage self-development and resourcefulness—magazines and books, board games, community visitors and leaders with whom children want to identify.
- Reward children for good works (small but important symbols of appreciation like ice cream floats, handmade bookmarks, a trip to a park, a pencil, an "I had a great day," a ribbon).
- Teach children self-pride so they can say "I did a good job" with more frequency.
- Work with parents for cross-bonding, emphasizing the importance of recognizing and rewarding industriousness and initiative.

The Work of Lawrence Kohlberg

Lawrence Kohlberg (1927–1987) is recognized for his work in moral development. Expanding on Jean Piaget's work, Kohlberg conceived of moral reasoning as taking place in six sequential stages. The first two, moral reasoning and moral independence, are quite similar to those developed by Piaget; the next four represent more sophisticated levels of moral thought found in adolescents and adults. At the earliest level of moral reasoning, the child accepts rules as givens—rules come from adult authority figures; they are unchanging and not to be challenged. As the young child's thinking matures, he begins to adapt rules to fit his needs exercising moral independence. He interprets rules according to his own perceptions and experience. The way an individual reasons through a dilemma determines his level of emotional maturity. In Kohlberg's schema, each stage is qualitatively distinct, building on knowledge and understandings from previous stages.[4]

Understanding and Interpreting Kohlberg's Stages

Premoral Levels.   During the first two stages, referred to by Kohlberg as the "premoral levels," children abide by externally imposed rules categorized by right and wrong responses to their behavior. Their actions and reactions reflect their desire to avoid what is unpleasant (punishment), to serve their own needs and interests, and to please adults. They see rules as unchanging and having a reality of their own.

Conventional Levels.   The next two stages, referred to as the "conventional levels," reflect children's need to conform to social norms. Children can take the perspective of others and begin to think through the consequences of actions. There is a moral code from which to operate that is determined by a conventional social order. The child is gaining moral independence but still demonstrates compliance and respect for moral truths.

Principled Levels.   In the final stages, "principled levels," moral values reside in principles and standards that can be shared. The dominant motives are a sense of obligation to a social contract and the belief in universal principles. Children become attuned to societal values and expectations.[5]

Application to Child Care

Young children incline toward self-satisfying, pleasure-seeking behavior that is often *imitative* in nature. Rules of behavior can confuse children if they are not consistently applied and enforced. When children observe unkind and inappropriate behavior among peers, they begin to *challenge* the values they are practicing in classrooms. They observe how peers avoid punishment by stretching or distorting the truth. As they begin to identify with a group, they learn their own messages about personal conduct—messages that may undermine family values and affect children's character development.

As children mature, they can understand the difference between appropriate and inappropriate behavior. They are able to make moral judgments: "It is wrong to disobey the rules." "She didn't mean to do it, it was an accident." Sometimes, truth can be distorted by what a child wants to believe or by what a friend wants her to believe. Children need help in sorting out their feelings, in responding to personal and moral dilemmas, and in understanding the nature and consequences of making choices.

Moral training has traditionally been a family-centered responsibility whereby children are raised according to certain codes and principles that are passed from one generation to another. The church, synagogue, and school counselors also have served as exemplary conduits for guiding children toward a moral consciousness. No longer is moral training identified exclusively with home and religious training. Given that there has been a change in family structures and in family relationships, moral development is increasingly perceived as a *shared* responsibility between families and childrearing systems.

There is a growing sense that, in its efforts to protect diversity, the United States has neglected training in commonly accepted universal values that affect conduct and define our obligations as citizens. These values might include respect for human dignity, the cultivation of personal character, and the exercise of responsible citizenship.[6]

Most caregivers would agree that child care training should include moral training, but they are not certain how to define moral training. When working with young children, it is best to generalize commonly accepted values in words that children can identify with: "Children should be kind to all living things, they should be good friends, they should be good helpers, they should always tell the truth, and they should respect adults, friends and their environment."

On a deeper level, caregivers are called on to discuss moral issues that cannot be comfortably communicated to young children. Many, if not most teachers, feel inadequate and unprepared to discuss commonplace issues such as street violence, unwed mothers, child abuse, drugs, divorce. Before discussing moral issues that do not fall under accepted family values but appear to be important at a given time, teachers need to consult with parents so that there are no misunderstandings about what topics are to be discussed and how to present them. In cases where parents appear irresponsible or unconcerned, teachers may have to assume a greater responsibility for moral training. On issues where parents hold strong convictions, however, avoid or delay discussing them until an agreement is reached on the approach to use.

A value-conscious environment will help children clarify their feelings and attitudes in prosocial ways. There are many ways—through drama, music, movement, or by rereading favorite storybooks that encourage children to make observations about characters—teachers can create a moral climate for children. Should Goldilocks have helped herself to the three bears' breakfast and left a broken chair on the floor? What would have happened if she'd knocked on the door and had been invited to have breakfast with the bears? What would have happened if she'd waited for the bears and told the truth about the chair? A nurturing program will encourage children to develop strong moral values. They can learn to make healthy choices with regard to their own conduct when caregivers:

- Encourage young children to make healthy, appropriate choices.
- Encourage children to anticipate consequences before making choices.
- Help children understand cause-and-effect relationships.
- Help children develop internal codes of conduct that will develop strong character.
- Encourage manners and practical life training.
- Select literature to foster moral development.

- Provide opportunities for children to extend their services to others less fortunate or handicapped.
- Help children cope with feelings of failure and inadequacy.
- Help them release negative feelings and understand that everyone experiences doubt, frustration, and anger at times.
- Give children freedom to discover and express themselves.
- Help children develop social consciousness and compassion toward all living things.

The Work of James L. Hymes, Jr., and Daniel A. Prescott

In recent years, much of the work of educators James Hymes and Daniel Prescott has been devoted to continuing and expanding the child development point of view. Their focus on mental health and *affective* learning has strongly influenced contemporary education. Prescott believes that an emotional climate that affirms children through loving relationships is the key to wholesome, healthy development. He describes the value of living in a loving environment:

- Being loved can afford any human being a much needed basic security;
- Being loved makes it possible to learn to love oneself and others;
- Being loved and loving others facilitates belonging in groups;
- Being loved and loving in return facilitates identification with parents, relatives, teachers, and peers by which the culture is internalized more readily and organizing attitudes and values are established easily;
- Being loved and loving facilitate adjustment to situations that involve strong unpleasant emotions.[7]

Application to Child Care

There are many opportunities to communicate caring feelings to children in environments that nurture individuality and self-esteem. Children may be affirmed through direct contact and guidance. Training children to care for themselves and others is a loving message. Promoting the conditions conducive to their growth and development is a loving message. Helping them to extend their potential and to reach for new heights is a loving message. Letting children know relationships are *not conditional on behavior or performance* but grounded in love, even when people do not see one another, may indeed be the most important message one can give a child.

A loving environment is a nurturing environment. In his candidly refreshing book, *Teaching the Child Under Six,* Hymes (1989) expresses this message:

Today's young children are headed toward an increasingly interdependent world. The speed of transportation, the ease of communication, the interlacing of economies, the ever-present threat of universal destruction make this world one shrinking planet, one tight family of man. For children's self-protection, the capacity to care for others must be nurtured—for people we know, for people we have never seen; for people like us, for people very different, for people near at hand and for those far out of sight. This sense of caring must be nurtured just as much for our children's self-fulfillment, so that they can grow into the deepest potential of their humanity.[8]

COGNITIVE DEVELOPMENT

Cognition is the process by which children acquire knowledge. Knowledge occurs naturally as a child actively constructs, interprets, and transforms his environment. At the early childhood level, knowledge consists of concrete information and a growing awareness of one's surrounding physical and human environment. A child acquires knowledge by the quality of verbal interactions with adults and by direct observation. A theory that views knowledge as an *active interactional process* between the child and the environment would prioritize activities that fully engage the child. Such activities might include those that encourage questioning, problem solving, and self-regulated learning.

A young child acquires knowledge as she interacts with and manipulates physical objects, gradually comprehending why and how things work. An older child consolidates and extends her base of concrete operations through tasks and skills that require inquiry, experimentation, reasoning, problem solving, and critical thinking. A curriculum that values children's thinking does not limit or stifle opportunities for self-discovery that may have the potential for higher levels of awareness and understanding. A child's best tools are her own *need to know* and her own *desire for mastery*.

Even though stages differ qualitatively, *development is a continuous process*. The child is always growing, from the early stage of one phase to the later phase of the same stage and from one stage to the next. He absorbs and modifies information in order to accommodate new learning. He reasons as he experiments and makes choices as he plays: This will work, this will not work. He makes predictions and observes consequences. A flower dies when it is not watered, a child gets hungry in mid-afternoon if he doesn't eat his lunch. He tests himself and his sense of boundaries as he creates, makes changes, and moves forward. It is through testing, guidance, and by applying reason, that a child constructs his own base of knowledge. In the process, the child experiences insight (the sudden perception of new relationships) and motivation (the desire to acquire more knowledge).

Cognitive theorists believe that learning is the result of an individual's attempt to understand and to master his world. The way a person perceives and experiences the world influences what he will learn. What a child learns is related to *what* he has learned, to *how* he processes new information, and to the *quality* of his experiences. The quality and appropriateness of early childhood environments will strongly influence a child's ability to learn. John Dewey's (1938) pedagogical principles illustrate how important environments are to the educative process:

A primary responsibility of educators is that they not only be aware of the general principle of the shaping of actual experience by environing conditions, but that they also recognize in the concrete what surroundings are conducive to having experiences that lead to growth. Above all, they should know how to utilize the surroundings, physical and social, that exist so as to extract from them all that they have to contribute to building up experiences that are worthwhile.[9]

The Work of Jean Piaget

Jean Piaget (1896–1980), a major force in developmental psychology, began investigating children's thinking in the 1920s. It was not until the 1960s, however, that his work received major recognition in the United States. During a long and prolific life, Piaget investigated and grappled with *cognitive* processes from infancy through adulthood. His theories have produced both praise and speculation among contemporary educators, but as a theoretical framework for cognitive development, his work is unparalleled in depth and scope. Even into his eighties, this remarkable man was still continuing and expanding his extraordinary work.

According to Piaget, a person's cognitive abilities progress in four sequential stages. Each stage is invariant (in a fixed order) representing a different organization of knowledge and experience but critically linked to the preceding stage. Continuity of mental growth is assured as each structure "results from the preceding one, integrating it as a subordinate structure, and prepares for the subsequent one, into which it is sooner or later itself integrated."[10] As the child forms new cognitive structures he is able to think at higher levels. Each stage represents a different organization of experience, information, and knowledge.

For Piaget, the child develops intelligence as he spontaneously acts on and experiments with his physical world. Though the stages are constant, a child's learning is influenced by developmental factors such as maturation, social interaction, experience with objects, symbolic thought, language, and moral judgment. Along with these factors, it is necessary to consider the factor of *equilibrium*—a fundamental aspect of growth and development.[11]

In Piaget's developmental schema, children naturally progress from concrete levels of operations to more abstract, complex levels of operations. They draw on and reconstruct prior learning in order to reach new levels of maturation and understanding. In the process of acquiring knowledge, the mind is constantly *active*. Through the process of *assimilation* children internally absorb information that is continually being processed in an external environment. As a child continues to think, he *accommodates* new information to his ever-expanding base of knowledge. In the process, the child seeks *equilibration*—a sense of balance and harmony between his internal and external world. Piaget's insistence on the active role children play in their own learning is best characterized by a *child-centered* learning environment.

Understanding and Interpreting Piaget's Stages

The Sensorimotor Stage (0 to 2 years):   Piaget used the term *egocentricism* to describe infancy and young childhood. For infants, this is the inability to distinguish between the self and the external world; for a toddler it is the inability to see the world from another's perspective; in both instances, the "I" is the dominant motivating force. The child's understanding of his world is initially limited by what he experiences: by human contact, by his surrounding environment, and by sensory experiences. During the first months of life, the baby's movements are uncoordinated and his actions are spontaneous. Within a few months, the growing child learns to coordinate movements by reaching for objects or turning to look for the source of a sound. By further integrating sensorimotor information, the infant begins to discover the various properties of objects.[12]

When the child begins to crawl or walk, he becomes more and more fascinated with manipulating objects. As he satisfies one interest, he moves on to another—to what he can put in his mouth, bang around, grab, or throw. Though his movements are awkward and his behavior still appears unfocused, his intentions are quite clear; he wants what he wants! He is coordinating what he has learned with what he wants or with what is already familiar. He goes to a door and reaches for the handle that will open the door. He carries a shoe and puts it near a foot. He pulls glasses off his caregiver and attempts to replace them. To Piaget, the young child is demonstrating the beginnings of intelligence and problem solving by actively experiencing and experimenting with his environment.

The significant development during this stage is what Piaget refers to as *object permanence* which occurs at around 8 or 9 months. This is a higher level of operation by which a child can understand that objects and familiar people can exist *apart* from himself. He senses that even though he cannot see a familiar object, it is present. For a two-year-old, this means that a teddy bear may not be in his chair but it can be found somewhere else in the room. The rudiments of thought and memory are gradually developing.

Application to Child Care. The growing child operates primarily in a *sensorimotor* world of concrete objects. Central to this world is her dependency on primary adult figures. She enjoys exploring her world and imitating increasingly complex movements and sounds. She begins to coordinate body movements, sounds and language. If she is introduced to favorite songs, such as "Ring Around the Rosie," she will need little prompting to go into her act—turning around, making beginning sounds, and even falling down. (For a little child the best part of a song is a surprise ending that is accompanied by unexpected movement.)

Learning cannot be separated from a child's physical and human needs and from his basic desire to explore. The young child develops *self-awareness* as he touches, makes observations, and reacts to the people who occupy his space and who satisfy his needs. The young child's primary modes for learning are through self-initiated experiences that satisfy his curiosity, and through adult–child interactions that satisfy his need for comfort, affection, and attention. Learning, for the young child, is experiential, active, and dynamic. His relatively small world is a huge repository for hands-on experiences. The role of the adult or teacher is to guide him safely, securely, and confidently toward competency.

Learning takes place as the child discovers on his own, and as he *interacts* with his environment. In order to make discoveries, children need an unhurried, tension-free environment. They need many hands-on experiences such as riding on trucks, playing on mats, and digging in the dirt. Young children are very curious—a new object on a science table will immediately attract attention and curiosity. A bird's feather may become a focal point for a group experience—examining the feather under a microscope, identifying its source (a bird), going on a bird-watching trip, making a nest for a window sill. Adults provide stimulation, challenge and support by selecting activities, materials, and experiences that will enhance learning.

The Preoperational Stage (2 to 7 years).   Around age two, the child begins to develop *symbolic thought*—"the use of mental images and words to represent actions and entire events that are not present."[13] He is beginning to internalize experiences and to think about people and objects that are not present. He makes pictures that resemble familiar and important objects: the sun, a flower, a boat, or a plane. Children's thinking processes are still inflexible and limited to momentary experience, the most pervasive characteristic of this age being *preoperational egocentrism.* Piaget believed that children are unable to take the point of view of others which causes them to interpret the world from their own impressions.[14]

Preoperational children are *perception bound:* They are deceived by the appearance of objects based on their limited perception. Two glasses of equal amounts of water may be perceived as quantitatively different by a young child if one glass is tall and thin while the other is short and wide. Piaget referred to this operation as *conservation.* Nor did Piaget think preschool children were capable of *reversibility*—a logical operation that enables a child to reason a problem through and reverse direction. Accordingly, a young child could not make transformations by using reasoning; his thinking, though logical, consisted of disconnected facts and contradictions.[15]

Application to Child Care. Children learn through play. Play enables children to make connections and extend conceptual understandings. A child's play world often represents his real world. The child incorporates features and memories of his experiences into play schemes. He uses objects symbolically: two blocks may become a plane, a vertical block may become an air traffic control tower. As children play imaginatively, they *recreate* their world in their own terms, applying logic, thinking, and problem solving to the task at hand.

Children can begin to understand the concept of change at the preoperational level. By observation and experience they learn that some things remain constant (a stationary object) while other things, like seasons and weather, change. They can explain ways that people and nature adjust and adapt to changing seasons, and they can activate change themselves: making ice from water, applesauce from apples, a snake from play dough. As a young child experiments with objects and art experiences, her perceptual field widens. She begins to *discriminate* among shapes and textures, to *classify* by common attributes, and to *perceive* spatial relationships.

During the preoperational stage, the preschool child is beginning to think about actions and perceive consequences. He begins to use problem solving as a way of managing his world. Language becomes an increasingly useful tool for communicating needs and ideas. Language enables a child to translate thoughts into words: to negotiate, to clarify, and to question. It helps him to develop the social skills that will enable him to decenter—to take the perspective of others. Through language production a child learns how to negotiate and how to express his thoughts. He becomes aware that if he chooses the right words, he can influence outcomes.

A child-centered program will maximize opportunities for children to make observations and discoveries through *self-initiated learning*. At the early childhood level, play is the primary medium for learning. Children construct as they play, they learn social skills as they play, and they develop thinking and reasoning powers as they play. Play encourages children to make connections and to try new combinations. As they play, children naturally begin to sort and arrange objects. Sometimes they have a plan and sometimes a plan grows from an activity. As they play with toys, children become aware of spatial dimensions—when things don't fit, adjustments must be made.

A child-centered program also will provide children with many opportunities for socializing with peers. Children enjoy sharing experiences. If, for example, the bird feather became a topic of interest for group circle, the teacher might read a story about a little bird that gave away his golden wings to help others (*Tico and the Golden Wings* by Leo Lionni). To extend understanding, the children may write bird stories, make real bird feeders, and visit the birdhouse at the zoo.

The Concrete Operational Stage (7 to 11 years). Piaget viewed this stage as a turning point when children's thinking begins to resemble adult thinking. The basic characteristics of this stage is that children recognize the logical stability of the world, the concepts of transformation and conservation, and the fact that changes can be reversed.[16] The growing child begins to apply reason, to solve problems, and to predict outcomes. She is interested in acquiring and applying new information to her cognitive structure. New ways of thinking enable the growing child to understand cause-and-effect relationships and to *think conceptually*. Though the child still operates on a concrete level, she is developing perception as she adapts to a more challenging world.

Application to Child Care. The growing child is becoming more and more *self-reliant* and *knowledgeable*. She uses reflection and reason to direct her actions and to influence her decision making. She is curious to discover why things work and motivated toward self-directed learning. Influenced by what she observes and experiences, the child continues a building-block process of applying new learning to previously acquired knowledge.

A quality school-age program should provide many opportunities for children to develop cognitive skills and critical thinking. Learning centers are as important at school-age levels as they are at preschool levels. If education is viewed as a continuous process, children need to occupy their time constructively throughout the day. They need to be both *physically and mentally active* in school and center environments. A center may encourage constructive play or play/work by setting up a table game center, a play center, a project/discovery center, an arts center, and a den for reading or homework.

The Work of Jerome Bruner

Whereas John Dewey and Jean Piaget saw the child as qualitatively different from the adult, Jerome Bruner viewed the child as a little scholar. Children, he believed, are capable of mastering subject matter at a far younger age than traditionally acknowledged if material is presented in its simplest form. Bruner's *spiral curriculum* theory became the backbone of the discipline-centered curriculum reforms of the 1960s. The theory is based on the model of the learner who is capable of thinking by means of a process of *inquiry–discovery*.[17] Bruner believed that a massive transfer of knowledge can take place when children are given the opportunity to apply new understandings to previously learned material. The basic tool for gaining knowledge and insight is language. This process of inquiry and discovery is based on the scientific method.

Understanding and Interpreting Bruner's Stages

Enactive.   At the first level, children learn by doing, by observation, and by reacting to what others do.

Iconic.   At the second level, children begin to form images of objects.

Symbolic.   In the third stage, children represent their world through the use of symbols.[18]

Progression of Learning.   In his learning-through-discovery approach, Bruner believed that learning proceeds *inductively* from simple to complex levels of understanding. The basic tool for learning is language. As children learn to apply basic knowledge, they can perceive several possibilities at one time. An idea can become a catalyst for higher levels of development. If, for example, children are learning about animal homes, a teacher may begin by introducing a simple one-to-one problem-solving activity (draw a line from the animal to its home). As children gain more information about animal homes, they begin to identify animals with specific settings: an alligator with a swampy area, a deer with a woods, a whale with a large body of water. They are making generalizations and building concepts about the unique patterns and characteristics of animals—understandings that go way beyond a teacher's first lesson. Within a short period of time, they may be able to make their own animal/home book, identifying pictorially where animals live and the structure and materials of their homes.

Bruner's theory reorganized curriculums across grades. By simplifying fundamental subject matter and challenging children to think and solve problems, children were able to absorb and master complex forms of learning at far younger ages than previously believed possible.[19]

Application to Child Care. In a discovery environment, children should be exposed to information and ideas through simple, yet challenging experiences that generate thinking. The simplest project can become a catalyst for concept building. Number concepts, such as more, less, equal, unequal, can become a focus for a science discovery center. Learning a letter "B" can become an opportunity for expanded learning throughout the week: making a *b*irdhouse and a *b*ird's nest from natural materials, planting *b*ulbs, making *b*inoculars for a *b*ird-watching hike, making a big *b*ook on *b*locks, *b*aking a big cake with *b*lue candles to celebrate "B" day. A culminating project may be a "B" word list that incorporates all of these experiences. With ideas and information provided, in part, by a teacher, children can proceed on their own using the scientific method to gain mastery. With basic information, they can plan and design their own projects. A simple task such as introducing letter "B" has become a learning experience that far exceeds the initial experience.

The Work of Lev S. Vygotsky

Of Russian background, Lev S. Vygotsky was a contemporary of Jean Piaget. In 1962, his book, *Thought and Language,* was translated into English. Vygotsky believed that knowledge is created by society and transmitted to individuals by society. Individuals vary in the way they respond to various kinds of cultural stimuli. When development is perceived as socially induced, major cultural changes, such as television, computers, and fads, tend to affect the way people perceive the world and themselves.[20]

Increasingly, the premise that all mental functions have social origins has gained credibility among contemporary child psychologists and educators. In order to understand the psychology of childhood, one has to understand the pervasive impact society has on human growth and development, even at the earliest stages of life. Young children who have had group experiences at a young age will be socialized early on. They have been defining their personality and developing their own sense of identity as they interact with peers and supervising adults throughout most of their waking hours. Their world is not just one of family, but of group, community, and all of the impressionable experiences that influence behavior. The quality of an environment is clearly a powerful influence on developing personalities.

Understanding and Interpreting Vygotsky's Theories

A Social Interactional Theory.   Like Bruner, Vygotsky differed with Piaget about the importance of language to child development. Piaget believed that language patterns of the young child were primarily self-centered and immature due to the fact that the child lacked the capacity for meaningful communication. A child's monologues and utterances were not seen as significant indicators of mental awareness or development. In contrast, Vygotsky believed that language developed from social exchanges between a child and another person. Early monologues or babbles (referred to as private speech) were seen as meaningful functions in a child's quest to understand and relate to the immediate world.

Adult Guidance.   Whereas Piaget stressed the importance of peer interaction to language development, Vygotsky emphasized the importance of adult guidance in facilitating communication and comprehension. His term, *zone of proximal development,* was identified as a level of learning in the young child that required adult assistance.[21] The underlying premise was that tasks within this zone are too difficult for a child to handle alone. Under adult guidance, a child can perform better when he has direction and monitoring before he begins a task. As a child becomes adept at understanding and processing tasks, he requires less and less instruction. He is increasingly able to direct and self-regulate his learning.

Application to Child Care. With regard to group learning, a teacher can initiate inquiry and problem solving by structuring an experience in a creative way. For example, if children are making a bird's nest, a teacher might attempt to keep their focus by planning a nature walk to gather materials for the project. She gives each child a small bag to discourage children from gathering large objects, such as stones or debris, that are not related to the project at hand. By structuring and restricting choices, the teacher is promoting concentration, memory, and concept development. As they gather materials, children are *thinking* about what they need, the kinds of materials they want to work with, and the probable shape and size of the nest. Some may begin to think in terms of a specific nest for a specific bird. To expand the experience, a teacher may want to introduce children to various kinds of birds, their building styles, and nesting habits.

With regard to working with children in task-related areas, when a teacher explains the purpose of an activity, she is helping children to begin the activity. She is providing useful information that will facilitate understanding. When teachers provide a setting for learning, they are encouraging children to develop good work habits: to pay attention, follow directions, concentrate, and apply one's self to a task at hand. Under proper guidance, children gradually become less dependent on teachers and better able to work independently. By helping a child to self-start, a teacher is helping a child to *accelerate* the learning process and to *gain confidence* in her ability to complete a task. When a child experiences fewer obstacles, she has more incentive to direct her own learning.

Although most activities at early childhood levels should not be teacher-directed, *teacher-initiated learning* is acceptable as long as it does not overshadow children's need for independent, self-initiated learning. There are some circumstances, however, that do require direct teacher intervention. Students who are slow learners, easily distracted, in poor health, or who have emotional problems need help in applying themselves to a task and in completing it. Young children with physical deficits, such as poor motor control or visual perception deficits, will need direct assistance in cutting and pasting. Teachers who work directly with children on a one-to-one basis must always encourage, praise, and reinforce children's work regardless of the outcome.

School-age children in child care environments require some degree of overseeing or monitoring on a fairly regular basis. There are a number of unmotivated children who have poor attitudes or work habits, and children who have to be reminded about their homework or about an uncompleted project. In any adult/child relationship, children should not become dependent on adults to do their work for them. Adults should help children to *organize* their materials and their time and to *interpret* their task. As quickly as possible, they should encourage children to work independently. By letting children know what is expected and by reaffirming their efforts, children will be less likely to avoid taking responsibility for their own work.

By setting up clear guidelines at the beginning of the year (on the first day), a tone will be set for the whole year. A positive, productive work/play climate will require less and less of a teacher's personal time. Children will begin to help each other, they will become self-reliant and considerate members of a group. Teachers will have more time to interact with children on a personal basis that is not task-oriented and supervisory.

A DEVELOPMENTAL–INTERACTION APPROACH

This approach may best be described as an open, integrated concept of learning in which development is seen as a dynamic interplay between the learner and the environment. It is basically the "total child" operating within the "total environment."

Every child has a uniquely endowed personality with the *potential* to develop and function as a caring and competent human being. In the maturation process, a child's internal world of thought is in constant interplay with her external world of experience. *Affective* and *cognitive* factors influence a child's behavior and development. The interaction that takes place between a child and her environment may be growth-enhancing or growth-restricting. A growth-enhancing environment recognizes the vital interplay that takes place between a learner and her environment by setting up conditions that encourage positive and constructive interaction such as involving children in community projects and in projects that take them beyond their immediate environment.

When children experience themselves as unique and capable learners, they begin to conduct themselves like caring and responsible members of a group. In an environmental-interaction approach, children are both *shaping,* and *shaped by,* their surrounding world. Cognitive and affective domains are interrelated and reinforcing. Jean Piaget wrote: "There is no behavior pattern, however intellectual, which does not involve affective factors as motives. . . . The two aspects, affective and cognitive, are in the same time inseparable and irreducible."[22]

The Work of John Dewey

The developmental–interaction approach is personified by the turn-of-the-century writings of philosopher and theorist John Dewey. Dewey's panacea for educational reform envisaged an active learner working in harmony with his environment. Dewey's key hypothesis was that life itself, particularly the occupations that serve social needs, should be the focus of a curriculum. A second hypothesis is that freedom of expression is a necessary condition for growth but that such expression must be guided by a teacher. In this context, Dewey perceived freedom and open *learning as a means* to intellectual development and not as ends in themselves.[23] Dewey believed that the child and the school were a unit—organically connected and inter-supportive. Denouncing traditional approaches that prevented a child from experiencing active learning, Dewey conceived of a classroom as "a microcosm of democracy in which children are active participants and learning encompasses moral as well as intellectual goals."[24]

In progressive schools, children are given ample opportunities to engage in scientific thinking. A worthwhile activity is one that gives children a chance to test and evaluate their own work through problem solving. In this respect, the child, endowed with natural resources, is seen as central to the educative process. An active learner, he views school as intellectually stimulating and challenging. He develops skills and competencies in practical life tasks, in reasoning skills, and in social skills. Dewey's theories are identified with the open classroom, learn-by-doing approach referred to as progressive education.

> I believe that the school is primarily a social institution. Education being a social process, the school is simply that form of community life in which all those agencies are concentrated that will be most effective in bringing the child to share in the inherited resources of the race, and to use his own powers for social ends. Education, therefore, is a process of living and not a preparation for future living. The school must represent life, life as real and vital to the child as that which he carries home, in the neighborhood, or on the playground.[25]

Application to Child Care. In today's society, educational reformers are increasingly looking to Dewey's classroom as a model for the future. They are recommending a *developmentally appropriate approach* that encourages child-initiated learning, individualized learning, multicultural curriculums, learning centers, open classrooms, cooperative interaction among peers, group projects, and the scientific method. These changes are being recommended for children from birth through eight years of age. Of equal concern to reformers is moral training. Educators and adults, concerned about the lack of moral training that children exhibit, are recommending a social consciousness that is similar to Dewey's ideal society. Children are now being encouraged to identify with and participate in their larger community.

Child care centers are *miniature societies*—small versions of a bigger world that has common interests, needs, and points of view. In a miniature society, children *learn* by doing and by acting on their physical environment *in cooperative ways.* Children are affectively, cognitively, and socially connected to peers by shared experiences and common goals. Each child contributes something unique and special to his or her center/society. Children seek companionship and support from one another in a play/work environment that is challenging, nurturing, and growth-enhancing. In an open, organized classroom, the child and the environment are one unit.

The Work of Uri Bronfenbrenner

Uri Bronfenbrenner is credited with developing an ecological model of child development that, in many ways, complements and expands Dewey's interactional model. An ecological model emphasizes the interconnection between a child and society. Bronfenbrenner's model begins with the child, extends to: a *microsystem* consisting of family, school, day care center, peers, neighborhood play area, church, and health services; an *exosystem* of extended family and community services consisting of neighbors, legal and social services, family friends, schools, and workplace; and finally a *macrosystem* that encompasses attitudes and ideologies of the culture at large.[26]

Application to Child Care. In this context, child care is seen as a *dynamic, interactional* system of shared responsibility in the raising and nurturing of young children. Bronfenbrenner emphasizes the importance of community support for working parents that includes paid maternity and paternity leave, sick leave, as well as support for unemployed and disadvantaged families who feel isolated from the exosystem.[27] When a *system functions* at all levels of society, it will function *for children,* too. There will be more cross-generational participation in promoting a quality environment for children and staff. A system of shared responsibility provides an excellent role model for young children in child care environments who need to see themselves as not only important in their own right but as vital members of a larger society.

A developmental–interactional approach should begin at an operational level in a child care center. A miniature community is one that extends itself to all of its members: children, staff, and parents. It is connected to a larger community with equal interests and concerns. A program designed for children will generate its own sense of family. Everyone will become an integral and important member of a group. Barbara Biber and Edna Shapiro recognize the potential inherent in a developmental–interactional approach:

> It is a basic tenet of the developmental–interactional approach that the growth and cognitive functions—acquiring and ordering information, judging, reasoning, problem solving, using systems of symbols—cannot be separated from the growth of personal and interpersonal processes—the development of self-esteem and a sense of identity, internalization of impulse control, capacity for autonomous response, relatedness to other people. The interdependence of these developmental processes is the *sine qua non* of the developmental–interactional approach.[28]

SUMMARY

Children's development is integrally connected with their attitudes, training, perceptions, and environmental experiences. In a growth-enhancing environment that provides a myriad of creative opportunities for self-development and social development, children naturally flourish.

In a child-centered environment that encourages children to be inventive and industrious learners, children are eager to connect with peers. Language and thinking are natural accompaniments of a cooperative society (a miniature community). The beginning of social consciousness occurs when children share cooperative experiences that promote good feelings and goodwill. If, as educators, we believe that children emulate the values they are consistently surrounded by, we must begin to turn our attention to the "program" component of child care: How can we translate what we know about child development into a workable program for the contemporary young child in a child care environment?

A progressive system of education provides an appropriate model from which to develop a child care curriculum because it incorporates the basic premises of child development with the basic needs of child care.

NOTES

1. Sue Bredekamp, ed., "NAEYC Position Statement," in *Developmentally Appropriate Practices in Early Childhood Programs Serving Children from Birth through Age Eight.* (Washington, DC: NAEYC, 1987), pp. 1–2.

2. As cited in L. Hoffman, S. Paris, E. Hall, and R. Schell *Developmental Psychology Today*, 5th ed. (New York: Random House, 1988), pp. 31–35.

3. Erik E. Erikson, *Childhood and Society*, 2d ed. (New York: W. W. Norton, 1963), p. 255.

4. As cited in Zick Rubin and Elton B. McNeil, *The Psychology of Being Human*, 3d ed. (New York: Harper & Row, 1981), pp. 321–25.

5. Hoffman, *Developmental Psychology Today*, 302–304.

6. *Beyond Rhetoric: A New American Agenda for Children and Families* (Washington, DC: National Commission on Children, 1991), p. 346.

7. Daniel A. Prescott, "The Role of Love in Preschool Education," in Margaret Rasmussen, ed., *Readings from Childhood Education* (Wheaton, MD: ACEI, 1966), pp. 59–60.

8. James L. Hymes, Jr., *Teaching The Child Under Six*, 3d ed. (West Greenwich, RI: Consortium Publishing, 1989), p. 66.

9. John Dewey, *Experience and Education* (New York: Collier Books, 1938), p. 40.

10. As cited in Evelyn Weber, *Ideas Influencing Early Childhood Education* (New York: Teachers College Press, 1984), p. 160.

11. As cited in James D. Quisenberry, E. Anne Eddows, and Sandra L. Robinson, eds., *Readings from Childhood Education* (Wheaton, MD: ACEI, 1991), p. 19.

12. Rubin and McNeil, *The Psychology of Being Human*, pp. 372–75.

13. George E. Forman, *The Child's Construction of Knowledge* (Washington, DC: NAEYC, 1983), p. 73.

14. Laura E. Berk, *Child Development* (Boston: Allyn and Bacon, 1989), p. 238.

15. Ibid., pp. 238–39.

16. Anita E. Woolfolk and Lorraine M. Nicholich, *Educational Psychology for Teachers* (Englewood Cliffs, NJ: Prentice-Hall, 1980), p. 58.

17. Daniel Tanner and Laurel Tanner, *Curriculum Development* (New York: Macmillan, 1975), p. 121.

18. Woolfolk, and Nicholich, *Educational Psychology for Teachers* p. 66.

19. Ibid., pp. 209–12.

20. Hoffman, et al., *Developmental Psychology Today*, pp. 43–45.

21. Ibid., p. 44.

22. As cited in Weber, *Ideas*, p. 168.

23. Tanner and Tanner, *Curriculum Development*, p. 237.

24. Berk, *Child Development*, p. 678.

25. Ronald Gross, ed., *The Teacher and the Taught* (New York: Dell, 1963), p. 144.

26. C. B. Knopp, and J. B. Krakow, eds., *The Child: Development in a Social Context* (Reading, MA: Addison-Wesley, 1982), p. 648. Cited in Berk, *Child Development*, p. 22.

27. Berk, *Child Development*, p. 23.

28. As cited in Weber, *Ideas*, p. 186.

RESOURCES

For Affective Development

Biber, B. *Early Education and Psychological Development*. New Haven: Yale University Press, 1984.

Bredekamp, S., ed. *Developmentally Appropriate Practice in Early Childhood Programs Serving Children from Birth Through Age Eight*. Washington, DC: NAEYC, 1987.

Bruner, J. *Toward a Theory of Instruction*. New York: W. W. Norton, 1966.

Dewey, John. *Experience and Education*. New York: Macmillan, 1976.

Dworetzky, J. P. *Introduction to Child Development*, 3d ed. New York: West, 1987.

Elkind, D. *A Sympathetic Understanding of the Child: Birth to Sixteen*. Boston: Allyn and Bacon, 1974.

———. *Child Development and Education*. New York: Oxford University Press, 1976.

Furth, H., and H. Wachs. *Thinking Goes to School: Piaget's Theory in Practice*. New York: Oxford University Press, 1974.

Inhelder, B., and J. Piaget. *The Growth of Logical Thinking from Childhood to Adolescence*. New York: Basic Books, 1973.

Maslow, A. H. *Motivation and Personality* 2d ed. New York: Harper & Row, 1970.

McClellan, James E. *Philosophy of Education*. Englewood Cliffs, NJ: Prentice-Hall, 1976.

Mussen, P. H., J. J. Conger, and J. Kagan. *Essentials of Child Development and Personality*. New York: Harper & Row, 1980.

Piaget, J. *The Origins of Intelligence*. New York: International Universities Press, 1952.

Spodek, B. *Teaching Practices: Re-examining Assumptions*. Washington, DC: NAEYC, 1977.

Vygotsky, L. S. *Mind in Society: The Development of Psychological Processes*. Cambridge, MA: Harvard University Press, 1978.

Wadsworth, B. J. *Piaget for the Classroom Teacher*. New York: Longman, 1978.

For Cognitive Development

Berk, L. E. *Child Development*. Boston: Allyn and Bacon, 1989.

Dewey, John. *Experience and Education*. New York: Collier Books, 1938.

———. *How We Think*. Boston: Heath, 1910.

Elkind, David. *A Sympathetic Understanding of the Child: Birth to Sixteen*. Boston: Allyn and Bacon, 1974.

Forman, G. E., and D. S. Kuschner. *The Child's Construction of Knowledge: Piaget For Teaching Children*. Washington, DC: NAEYC, 1983.

Hoffman, L., S. Paris, E. Hall, and R. Schell. *Developmental Psychology Today*, 5th ed. New York: Random House, 1988.

Piaget, J., and Barbel Inhelder. *The Psychology of the Child*. New York: Harper & Row, 1981.

Rubin, Z., and E. B. McNeil. *The Psychology of Being Human*. New York: Harper & Row, 1981.

Webber, Evelyn. *Ideas Influencing Early Childhood Education: A Theoretical Analysis*. New York: Teacher's College, 1984.

Woolfolk, A. E., and L. M. Nicholich. *Educational Psychology for Teachers*. Englewood Cliffs, NJ: Prentice-Hall, 1980.

Every time we teach a child something, we keep him
from inventing it himself. On the other hand, that which
we allow him to discover will remain with him forever.
                                        — *Jean Piaget*

9

THE CHILD

CHARACTERISTICS AND NEEDS OF CHILDHOOD

Development occurs in a number of different ways in the maturation process. At birth, the child already is endowed with basic characteristics that will influence his growth. As the child matures, his development is affected by his physical and human environment. The quality of his *experiences* and of the people who surround him *strongly influence* his development. Development tends to occur in stages that are basic to childhood regardless of environs, i.e., children crawl before they walk and progress from simple to complex functions. Life circumstances also affect development in significant and less predictable ways, i.e., poverty restricts development because children are not getting their basic needs met. Within these parameters, children progress at their own rate and in their own way. Development cannot be hurried, nor can it be defined exclusively by ages and stages, particularly given the diverse backgrounds that typify a pluralistic society. Most of all, development evolves in ways that cannot be readily observed or anticipated. It is directly influenced by external factors in the environment and society, but in large part, it is an *internalized* process unique to each individual.

Those who work with young children would probably agree that within this broad definition of development, there are common characteristics and needs that are basic to childhood.

Children are . . .

- always adapting to an increasingly complex environment.
- active, often spontaneous, in their work and play.
- initiators and architects of their play world.
- flexible, creative thinkers.
- curious and inventive.

- by nature: empathetic and caring, innocent and loving, self-centered, and sensitive and vulnerable.
- resourceful problem solvers.
- forming habits and values that will influence and direct their lives.
- interested in people and in developing friendships.
- physically oriented.
- engaged by concrete things and tasks.
- interested in discovery.
- drawn to play.
- attracted to sensory stimuli.
- oriented to music and movement.
- stimulated by books.
- users of language.
- imaginative and expressive.
- not bound by time and space.
- immersed in the here and now.
- ever expanding their perceptions and understandings about how and why things work.

Children need . . .
- to feel in control of their environment.
- consistency and trust in relationships.
- loving, authentic relationships.
- interaction with important adults in their lives.
- to observe and learn from adult role models.
- a sense of balance and routine in their lives.
- praise and guidance from adults.
- limitations and appropriately administered discipline.
- a healthy balance of freedom and structure.
- freedom to: play without interruption; make choices; express themselves; and test their environment, themselves, and others to discover their potential.
- training in: self-management and self-care, foundational skills, social skills, and human relationships.
- outlets for creativity and self-expression.
- to develop:
  - understanding and concepts through integrated learning experiences;
  - their own resources;
  - talents and interests;
  - initiative;
  - competencies in many areas;
  - self-control;
  - good work habits;
  - good citizenship; and
  - a global, multicultural perspective.

- to discover and interact with their natural environment.
- to experience their own indoor and outdoor play world.
- to take responsibility for their environment.
- to become:
  - responsible, caring members of society;
  - self-directed and self-disciplined;
  - problem solvers and critical thinkers.

- to take the perspective of others.
- to experience the wonders and innocence of childhood.
- to be surrounded by people who care about them and who want to participate in their upbringing.
- to value and treasure every day, as so aptly put in *Everychild's Everyday:*

> *I find a little silence*
> *in the day*
> *To spend alone*
> *In the quiet*
> *I catch the day and see*
> *What I can make of it.*
> *I plumb my imagination*
> *To make more of what I have*
> *To give my child.*
> *I want our times together*
> *to be joyful and relaxed,*
> *Spontaneous*
> *And alive.*

A PROFILE OF THE YOUNG CHILD IN CHILD CARE

An Active Discoverer

The young child needs to touch and manipulate everything within reach. She will become fascinated and even fixated by common objects: a dry leaf, a piece of cellophane, a toilet bowl, a light switch, a cricket, and a multitude of tiny objects. She is a whirlwind of activity—climbing, running, patting, pulling, pushing, and jumping, tasting, smelling, listening, looking, and sometimes, crying. As the child explores and interacts with the people and objects in her environment, she develops awareness and confidence. She learns by doing, by *discovering*, and by experimenting with objects. Not everything works, not everything fits, and not everything is easy. It is through struggle and some risk-taking that children gain control of their environment.

An Explorer

Through exploration, the child begins to assimilate and order his physical world. He finds objects that go together, he rearranges these objects, and he tests ideas. His ideas do not always coincide with his buddy's ideas—sometimes it takes a strong push or pinch to make a point or solve a problem. The explorer soon finds out, however, that this behavior will not sustain friendship or attract new friends. The adaptable child learns the art of persuasion and accommodation, as well as the power of reconciliation. Though easily frustrated, the emotional young child is quick to recover his sense of balance. Once again, the child seeks guidance and support from a teacher friend. She comforts and counsels him when he feels frustrated. She encourages him to try again, praising him for his accomplishments and for his near accomplishments: "You almost made it, didn't you? I bet you'll make it tomorrow."

The curious child thrives in an environment that encourages investigation and active learning. Children develop an adventurous spirit by becoming imaginative, inventive players. An environment speaks to children—it welcomes them to play in cozy, creatively arranged activity areas that are, for the most part, off limits to adults. Children need areas for imaginary play: huts, caves, castles, forts, or tents. They need centers for imagination and discovery that stimulate exploration and open space for physical play. They need digging equipment, riding equipment, and climbing equipment. They need things they can move around as they create play themes; they need backpacks, binoculars, and compasses for hiking; kits and tools for exploring nature; and they need maps of their backyards and places to bury treasures. They also need to venture beyond their immediate environment to visit duck ponds, nature centers, and parks.

To a young child who delights in the ordinary, a walk around the block is a big adventure filled with novelty and wonder. Children need to *stretch* their bodies to reach new physical heights: climbing, balancing, skipping, hopping, running, and jumping—energy and movement are the beats of childhood. The growing-up child shows considerable initiative as he moves across handbars and finds new tricks to perform on a tumbling mat. He enjoys the pleasure of accomplishment for its own sake, but he also enjoys the favorable comments he receives from others. He needs praise and reinforcement when trying new activities but also needs to be reminded to exercise caution. The physical energy of the young child at play knows no bounds. Rest is tolerated but usually unwelcome. Rest time is particularly difficult unless, of course, a friend is nearby.

A Taskmaster

The child has a natural need to manipulate and master his world. His goal-seeking behavior requires endless amounts of physical energy and patience. Simple tasks like putting on a shoe or a mitten are major undertakings for the young child. Loading and unloading a lunch box, handling bathroom needs, or organizing a cubby are not easy tasks for little fingers. Children who are given time and encouragement to complete simple operations do not feel frustrated or bored by routine tasks—they enjoy play/work and, most important, it is through daily contact with familiar objects that children become *competent taskmasters*. These chores are far more important to the growth and development of a young child than instructing them in academic readiness skills.

By the time a child is between four and five years of age, he has mastered many of the basic routines involved in self-management. He is stimulated to learn and ready for more complex levels of operation. He already knows how to count to ten—now he is experimenting with number concepts in his everyday world. Though still at a basic level, he has little difficulty sorting, grouping, and arranging items in patterns. Similarly, he already knows many of his letters and some familiar words—now he is experimenting with printing them in his own way. He no longer listens quietly to a story; he thinks about the story as the plot unfolds and identifies with its characters and its message. At this level of mental functioning, the child is *processing* and using knowledge—he is *exploring* his own capabilities.

A Learner

Learning is a dynamic child-centered process. The child is *central* to the process. The teacher is a *guide;* she promotes learning by exposing children to ideas and by organizing activities that reinforce and build on their level of knowledge and awareness. She may present, point out, ask questions and help children organize and extend their thinking; but the teacher should avoid making statements, giving children answers, or interrupting their thought processes. Most of the time, a learning child will want to express her thoughts and ideas as they occur. Group conversations should reflect the natural flow of children's language and thinking. A child who has to wait her turn or raise her hand will probably forget what she had intended to share. A teacher can encourage courtesy and taking turns without placing unnecessary obstacles in the way of self-expression. As the child continues to develop mental competencies, she will be better able to hold on to ideas, and to wait her turn.

With each new experience the child continues to acquire knowledge and mastery. She can understand *cause-and-effect* relationships—a balloon pops when it gets too much air, and she can make logical assumptions—a lion can't find his tail because he is sitting on it, a flower needs water when it hangs its head, a caterpillar eats to get fat before it sleeps to become a butterfly.

Learning experiences often are presented in group circles. These are informal gatherings that take place in a designated area. Children sit on carpet squares or an area rug around their teacher. Group circles provide a way for teachers to develop social interaction, language skills, and thinking skills. They are sometimes organized around a theme, a creative activity, or a specific learning experience (e.g., a science experiment); other times they are spontaneous get-togethers with no particular theme in mind (children's favorites). A teacher may, for example, place an interesting object or tiny animal on a rug and wait for responsive interaction. By engaging interest, she is shifting the focus of the group from herself to the children. Group circles are difficult to manage because children vary in their communication ability, developmental level, and behavioral maturity. Often a small number of children tends to monopolize group circles. These children probably have good language skills and self-esteem and are further reinforced by the attention they receive. Other children may feel shy and intimidated in group gatherings—they are less reinforced by group experiences.

The time of day, the temperament of children, and the activity presented also influence group outcomes. A skillful teacher will know how to conduct a group experience to maximize child participation. She will not try to take on more than she (and her children) can handle. She will bring out less verbal children by inviting participation: "I think Mary knows how to take care of plants; her mommy told me she has her very own garden at home." Mary will probably smile, nod her head, and maybe even say a few words. By the end of a semester, Mary may be speaking in sentences. A skillful teacher will *limit* her objectives and her time frame when she is conducting a circle for an entire group. In smaller gatherings, a teacher will *extend* her objectives and her time frame to encourage participation. When children interact in small groups, e.g., half the class, they are far more attentive to what is going on and far less intimidated by peers. There are more opportunities for hands-on experiences and for freedom of movement.

A Language Maker

Language is an empowering tool for a young child. Children listen to one another intently and somehow manage to communicate the near-words that constitute early language development. Children love language in all of its forms: listening to language, making conversation, experimenting with sounds, and mastering the elements of speech—i.e., discriminating sounds, recognizing words, using sentences, asking questions, writing. They use language to express their thoughts and to communicate with one another. In the second and third years of life, children's ability to communicate dramatically increases. An open, play-oriented environment promotes language by supporting language. In play and in group experiences, children use language as a medium for communication and for peer acceptance. In its natural form, *language is an extension* of the child. If a child cannot find a word, he invents or makes up a word. Children become language users as they build on language experiences. They begin to organize their thoughts into sentences. They become fascinated with books and with the pleasure they bring. Young readers get to choose a book, turn its pages, look at illustrations, figure out words, recall favorite parts, and sometimes, they get to read with a teacher. To a young child, the process of selecting, opening, and "reading" a book is totally absorbing and exciting.

Experiences with language should abound in early childhood classrooms— nursery rhymes, finger plays, music, flannel board tales, poetry, picture books, dramatic play, and nonsense verse. An environment rich in language encourages children to use their own language and involves them in language activities. When children get to talk, they learn to *listen,* to *think,* and to *recall.* Group language experiences enable young children to integrate speech, thought processes, and body movements. When a teacher leads a finger play, children can hardly wait to point their finger at a naughty monkey: "No more monkeys jumping on my bed." Favorite books are read and reread until the child discovers another book. Favorite stories may be tucked away and worn away, but like *The Velveteen Rabbit,* they are never forgotten. Language is rooted in *familiar* experiences that generate feelings of joy and wonder in young learners.

A Creator

Creative expression can be a never-ending source of satisfaction for a young child. She delights in the process and in her natural, unedited productions. She creates when she plays with blocks, when she arranges a play center, and when she assembles a collage of dried flowers and lace doilies. She creates when she makes pictures, when she arranges clothes on a doll, and when she arranges a tea set on a table.

In order for a child to be creative with everyday experiences, she must instinctively feel that her environment is *creative.* A teacher who endorses and encourages a creative environment does not get concerned about spills or messes. She does not scold a child, and she does not punish a child by making her clean up her mess. A child who feels that she has done something wrong is not learning anything from a teacher's directive: "I told you to be more careful; get a sponge and clean up the mess immediately." A sensitive teacher will keep a bucket of water close by and clean up herself without drawing attention to the child, or, she may ask the child to help her clean up at the end of the project. In a positive mindset, children love to clean with a sponge and water; it is play/work for them.

Once materials are organized and children are wardrobed with good-sized smocks, the teacher need not interfere with the creative process. Children create according to their perception of their world, using materials in their own way. There should be ample time to complete tasks and to clean up before changing activities.

Teachers should make time to sincerely recognize children's artwork but need not lavish them with praise (children already feel good about their work). They should recognize neat, carefully painted pictures and those that are hastily painted, noticing special things about children's artwork: "I like the pink flowers so much. I wish I could pick them, put them in a vase, and keep them forever!" She encourages children to be inventive: "Would you like to see what happens when we mix red and white, green and yellow, black and white?" "What can we call this color . . . it's not red, it's not black, it's not green." She encourages children to try ideas—to design and create using many textures, mediums, and materials. In self-challenging activities that enable a child to feel in control, the child and the process are one. The child creates as the child experiments with materials. Unlike the school-age child, the young child tends not to be concerned about finished products. He is absorbed in using materials in inventive ways. In the untrained eyes of the child, everything is beautiful—especially his own work. It is an adult who introduces self-doubt: "Why don't you add a little yellow to your picture? I think it would make it prettier, don't you?"

A Person Who Delights in the Ordinary

A day flows naturally and comfortably for children when there is not too much stimulation. Children are already stimulated by the variety of people and colors that surround their day. In his delightful book, *Frederick*, Leo Lionni captures the natural glow of childhood. As other field mice busily prepare for winter, Frederick spends his time storing the rays of the sun, the colors of fall, and writing verse. Though not a practical mouse, Frederick is special in his own way. When food becomes scarce, it is Frederick who entertains his friends through the long days of winter. It is Frederick who gives them hope when their food supply is running out.

A teacher who recognizes children's delight in the ordinary does not rush them through early childhood. She will give them time to absorb their environment in their own way. She will find opportunities to capture special moments every day. Children may become sky watchers, bird watchers, pond lovers, and elves in a forest. They may follow an ant or a worm to its destination, catch the wind, fly like a butterfly, or wonder about a robin's journey southward or a seagull's preference for a cold, windy wintery day. They may wonder why some leaves fall, why puddles disappear, why little roly-poly creatures hide under logs, why spiders keep creating new webs, and why rainbows appear after rain. An ordinary world becomes quite extraordinary for children when they can *see, touch,* and *investigate* their natural world. When children are given time for quiet observations, they are gathering experiences that will continue to shape their personalities.

A Homebody

Children respond to environments in unique ways. Young children become personally attached to a classroom. A friendly, cozy atmosphere helps children feel comfortable and secure. A room should contain many soft colors that are interrupted occasionally with bold, bright colors and eye-catching objects—a bright area rug, a colorful flowering plant, an orange tree, a teddy bear in a rocking chair, windchimes, and window ornaments. Children enjoy looking at familiar pictures and photographs and they love looking at their own artwork. They enjoy experiences of discovery like matching textures, pouring water from one container to another, or looking through a magnifying glass at objects they have gathered: a dead bug, a piece of glass, a rock, a leaf. They enjoy quiet moments, soft lights, and music. They love new things and old things, and they particularly love surprises.

Children especially enjoy a room that invites play. They respond favorably to a room that is organized around activity centers. Still concrete-bound, children tend to see objects in relation to other objects. They perceive common attributes among play objects and their purpose. They realize that a paint center functions differently from a block center, a housekeeping unit functions differently from a listening center, and that a table area is used for sit-down finger and hand activities like eating or pasting. As they play in centers, children intrinsically develop organizational, discriminatory skills.

Within a familiar organizational framework, children love to use open play areas and to move objects from one place to another. They love to try new arrangements adding and subtracting items as they play. At the end of each play period, however, they enjoy seeing the familiar restored. This constant, repetitive process of playing, making choices, picking up, and restoring an environment, only to take it apart again, is fundamental to their learning. Through repeated actions, children gain self-confidence and mastery over their environment.

A Member of a Group

Children are natural friends. They enjoy and learn from one another. They like parallel play, close enough to enjoy companionship yet not too close to get in one another's way. As children mature, they seek playmates. They enjoy the closeness of dramatic play and of circle time. Even though a two-year-old cannot sit but a few minutes, she enjoys coming together with an adult friend. Group time provides opportunities for children to greet one another, to share, and to make observations and choices about their play world. Ideally, young children should experience several small group teacher/child gatherings throughout the day. During these brief intervals, a teacher can observe basic skill levels and language development. Through communication with a teacher, children gain knowledge about people, their environment, and themselves.

As the child nears the latter stages of preschool development (four to five years of age), she can participate in group activities for longer periods of time. She has increased her attention span and language usage and is curious about learning and about playmates. She enjoys experiencing herself in a group context, selecting words to express ideas that she is eager to share. Sometimes these ideas will enliven and reinforce a subject being discussed; oftentimes they will not. Given a young child's limited attention span, distractions may end a circle quickly. Within minutes, a conversation may be disrupted by a sneeze, a bug, or an unusual noise. Children, who love distractions almost as much as they love the last line in a favorite finger play, will quickly assert initiative. Through sound and movement one child can trigger a disruptive group reaction. The teacher has temporarily lost control.

A preschool teacher must plan her circles carefully, be ready for the unexpected, and be flexible. She must know when she has lost her audience and when it is time to make a transition. Despite the unpredictability of group *interactions,* they are important teaching aids and *invaluable* to children's overall development. A skillful teacher will maximize opportunities for group learning by engaging children's interest. When children are active learners, they tend to become absorbed in a teacher-initiated experience and less likely to wander off the subject. Some ideas for group participation might include the following range of themes.

> *Language Development:* "Today it is raining, let's sing our rainy day song . . . Do you think it's a good day to read about the mushroom in the rain? A mushroom is something like an umbrella, isn't it? Who can remember what happens to mushrooms when it rains? Do you remember all the friends who came to sit under the mushroom on that rainy day? Who are they? What happened when it stopped raining?"

> *Social Awareness:* "Did you know Matthew has a new puppy? Can you tell us what its name is, Matthew? Can you use your hand to show us how big your puppy is? What does your puppy eat? Do you think you can bring him to school?"

> *Discrimination Skills:* "If you listen carefully, you will hear many different sounds. What are some of the sounds you can hear, Jenny? Let's take a listening walk today. What do you think you'll hear? Should we take our tape recorder? Do you think we'll frighten the cricket? We certainly don't want to do that! How can we be absolutely quiet listeners so that we don't disturb nature's little creatures?"

> *Recall:* "Who can remember what Hansel had in his pocket? Do you think the birds ate all the bread crumbs? Who else would eat bread crumbs? Do you remember our trip to the duck pond? What did we feed the ducks? That's right—birds and ducks like bread. What kind of bread do you like? Where does bread come from?"

> *Manners:* "I think we are forgetting our manners. Is it hard to hear when people are shouting? What happens when two people talk at once? Do you think it's a good idea to take turns? Can anyone think of a time when everyone uses their voices at once? Good thinking—when we sing and when we play games outside. Would you like to play a whisper game? Let's pass a message around the circle and see if we can remember the words?"

Beginning each day with a welcoming circle will set a positive, friendly tone for the day. A circle *anchors* a day for a child; it provides a sense of routine and organization. A brief circle at the end of a session provides a sense of continuity and closure.

A Growing Child

Clinging to childhood, but challenged by growing up, a preschool child can be *unpredictable* and *changeable*. This is a volatile, high-energy period of development. One day a child wants to be a baby, thumb in mouth. Another day she is industriously washing tables, being the big sister in dramatic play, asserting her will, and probably sounding very much like her mother. Boundaries are opening and a child is claiming her right to independence and autonomy. In the process, a child is constantly testing relationships and her own powers. She is self-centered and often disagreeable when she wants her way. For the growing-up child, however, frowns become smiles within minutes. A child who can express feelings without hurting others is on her way to maturation. It is important to *acknowledge children as they really are,* not as adults think they should be. There is no pattern for a perfect child; a quiet child may not be a good child and a quiet, controlled classroom may not be a healthy classroom. Children need an environment that does not stifle initiative, self-direction, or active learning. They also need a sense of harmony and routine. A child-centered classroom encourages active child-initiated experiences in a prepared, organized environment.

Gradually, a child builds confidence, and with confidence, self-esteem. She learns how to negotiate and when to compromise. Sensitive to peer relationships, she releases some of her self-centeredness for group acceptance. She becomes a cooperative partner in the games that are played; sometimes a winner, sometimes a loser, but nearly always a friend. In the process, she is discovering something about leadership although she doesn't really understand what it means. What she does understand is that children are attracted by her and make her feel special. She begins to use her sense of importance to extend leadership—she volunteers to be the teacher's messenger or an arbitrator in playmates' disputes. She is quickly chosen as a lead character in play plots: a queen, a mother, a fairy godmother, a strong, but gentle lion. Watching a child at play provides a momentary glimpse of the child grown up. The patterns of childhood continue into the future; leadership is developed during the early years.

A Role-player

Pretend play peaks during the latter stages of early childhood. Children are extremely creative and expressive. Dramatic play is a primary channel for expressive development. Children will cooperate during dramatic episodes even if it means compromising or giving up a position. More than anything, they want to be accepted by playmates. Pretend play stretches imaginations and expands creative thinking. Children vacillate between fantasy and reality; they discuss and solve problems and quickly transform into the characters they have chosen for themselves. As plots grow, dramatic play becomes more directed and absorbing. In reality, children are acting out their present while practicing for a grown-up world. They become the people with whom they are familiar or with whom they identify, interpreting the world through their own vision.

One of the most important things an adult can do for children is to give them the *time* and *space* to express themselves. In a positive, supportive environment, self-expression generates self-awareness and self-knowledge. Children get to experience themselves through fantasy and real-life role models. In the child's play world, however, the distinction between make believe and real is not readily discernible. Characters and objects are immediately transformed by innovative role-playing children. Identities change as plots develop and as children move more deeply into a play motif.

A PROFILE OF THE SCHOOL-AGE CHILD
IN CHILD CARE

A Maturing Child

Young school-age children enter child care during a transitional period that places them somewhere between childhood and growing up. The child is changing inside and outside. Bodies are changing and boys and girls are becoming interested in one another. Outward growth is not typically balanced by inner growth causing children to feel off-center and somewhat vulnerable. The growing child manifests *conflicting* moods and emotions that may or may not be visible or understood. Much of what a child is feeling is kept inside until he feels confident that he can reveal himself without embarrassment. Uncertain about his own identity, a six- or seven-year-old finds security in the companionship of playmates.

A Time of Confusion

The growing child's world is changing from one of play and occasional work to one of work and occasional play. Gone is the freedom of nursery school days and the constant presence of nurturing adults. In primary school there are more responsibilities, more expectations, more demands, and less assistance. Play is scheduled into daily activities and structured around physical development that often places children in competitive positions. Spontaneous play is no longer possible for a child unless it can fit into recess or after-school hours. Recess is too short for serious, creative play and after-school hours are no longer under a child's control. Children are programmed into after-school activities that reduce freedom and restrict choices. For most children of working parents, structured, group-centered activities have become substitutes for independent, spontaneous play. In large groups of twenty or more children, a teacher is reluctant to give children freedom—it is easier to say no than to worry about their safety.

Yet the six-year-old is only one year older than a five-year-old. He recognizes that growing up entails some giving up, but he cannot be expected to adjust readily to the dramatic transitions taking place at this critical crossroad in childhood. Elementary school can be a big adjustment for a little child of five or six. The need to experience childhood and the desire to conform to social standards create anxieties and confusion for many young children. The passage is eased by an after-school environment that recognizes the importance of *integrating the two worlds* for a child—an environment that protects and nourishes childhood by softening harsh transitions and an environment that supports children's individual and social needs.

A Need for Companionship

The growing-up child still needs adult support but doesn't know how to express or satisfy the need. She is reluctant to demonstrate affection because she doesn't want to be labeled by peers. The desire to be independent and the need for companionship moves a child toward peers. Peers become an extension of self for many children. They influence behavior in both subtle and direct ways. Observing and listening to agemates causes a child to assess herself. More often than not, a child will imitate negative behavior. She makes adjustments that make her fit in. If she is grounded in values that contradict such behavior, the child will go through a sorting out process until she reaches a state of equilibrium that will eventually accommodate both worlds. She may, for example, attempt to influence a playmate's behavior or she may avoid situations that she knows would be unacceptable to those whom she loves—her family and her teachers.

Conversely, a child who is not guided by values may become vulnerable in peer interactions. Seeking peer approval, he may gradually change his behavior over a period of time. He may ignore or talk back to an adult who was once a good friend because that is the "cool" thing to do. He may avoid responsibility and become negative about his schoolwork and about center projects. A teacher begins to symbolize restriction and a child care center, an unwanted home.

An adult working with school-age children will find that it takes longer to develop and sustain relationships than with younger children. Projects can be beautifully planned yet snubbed by children who prefer doing nothing. An "I don't want to do anything" attitude can discourage teachers who don't understand that it will take time to win children over—to get them to say "Yes, I want to do it." Boys typically have more difficulty adjusting to child care than girls. Girls continue to identify with a predominantly female staff, enjoying their attention and interests. Boys, who are extremely physical at this stage, want freedom to play without rules and regulations and without adult monitoring. They do not want to be restricted or made to feel babyish. They especially enjoy male supervisors who can play rough and tumble with them in sports and challenge them in games. A school-age director needs to develop a program that addresses the needs and interests of both sexes, and one that gives children emotional support while recognizing their need for independence. Educator, Barbara Biber writes:

> In order to supply the child with the kind of psychological support which he needs, it is necessary that adults take his drive for independence for what it is really—the first steps in the difficult job of constructing one's own personality. The child still needs, together with his freedom to grow away from grownups, the confidence that they will stand by.[1]

A Need for Close Friends

Young elementary-age children are very sociable. Relationships are constantly examined and adjusted by young playmates. Leadership roles are implicitly and explicitly defined. Instinctively children move toward friends whom they find attractive and fun to be with. Once chosen, they quickly become best friends. Best friends act alike, think alike, dress alike, and quickly tire of one another. Close friendships create problems for the children who are not included in an inner circle. They promote an "in" or "out" mindset. Children who do not fit a peer's role model are often teased or ignored. Children can be very hard on one another especially if a child appears physically "different." Children also can be unkind and exclusive in their play patterns especially when they have peer support and reinforcement. When children bond in less than healthy ways, their behavior changes. They antagonize, control, and place unfair restrictions on unwanted playmates—i.e., only boys or only girls can join. To qualify for admission to a "club," children may have to compromise their standards of behavior. They may have to become equally exclusive. Conversely, activity clubs, set up jointly by teachers and children, are growth-enhancing in that they are open to all children.

A child care teacher must be attentive to the kinds of play that close friends are engaging in and monitor and intervene as necessary. Because friends tend to speak for each other, children cannot always be trusted to act appropriately; they may want to go off by themselves, or they may take chances that put them at risk.

A Need for Cooperative Interaction

Group activities should not induce or encourage competition. Any activity that a child participates in should promote cooperation, commitment, and a desire for completion, i.e., children should be discouraged from disrupting or giving up a project they have invested time in. By emphasizing cooperative interaction and good work from the beginning, a teacher will establish standards that children will find difficult to challenge. Children should understand that if they elect to put on a talent show, they have to apply themselves to the responsibility at hand. They have to be willing to extend themselves for their project. Once a project gets under way, commitment is rarely a problem. Young children are natural entertainers— they love the process and are somewhat more interested in the outcome (the finished product) than are younger children. The older children get, the more they evaluate themselves and their productions and the more competitive they become. In any event, a teacher is needed to keep children on track during the process, to motivate, to praise and, most important, to provide direction.

A Need to Take Risks

Children need challenging activities that develop skills and make them feel successful. To get in touch with their capabilities, children must experience some degree of risk-taking. Taking risks requires an environment that encourages initiative and reinforcement. In planning and equipping children's activity centers for age-appropriate play, safety is a primary consideration. Even in child-safe environments, however, children have accidents. Testing bodies and endurance, showing off, feeling confident, six- and seven-year-olds have difficulty anticipating outcomes. A teacher's role is to supervise without being obtrusive. Preventive measures might include: cautioning children, standing near children, redirecting dangerous play, and periodically reviewing guidelines for playground safety.

A Need for a Balanced Day

A school-age environment should provide opportunities for recreation, enrichment, and quiet activities. A balanced program will be responsive to the needs and moods of children at various times in a day. Children are understandably tired at the end of a long schoolday. The energy they bring into a center is deceptive. In reality, children are physically burdened with backpacks and emotionally burdened with the trials and tribulations of their day. Unfortunately, there is no place for releasing pent-up energy during the transition from a school to a center environment. Confined and unchanneled energy causes children to appear overly stimulated and, at times, irritable and impatient. A brief, sincere welcome, a nutritious, plentiful snack, and lots of fresh air can quickly restore spirits and change attitudes.

After outdoor play, children should be able to make appropriate choices in scheduling the remainder of their afternoon. The way children choose to spend time reflects their level of maturation, interests, and personal needs. Some children will go directly to a homework table, some will hang around, and others will immediately engage in focused play with peers; play-loving children usually know what they want to play with and how important it is to get there first. There always will be a large number of children (usually boys) who elect to continue outdoor play.

Indoor activities may include: block play, dramatic play, board games, carpentry, art projects, or specialized activities for small groups. Outdoor play may include: bar-work on a climbing apparatus, skating, jumping rope, shooting baskets, throwing a ball, or engaging in team sports. Most playgrounds are set up for specific types of play. There will be an area for active, vigorous play, for digging and exploration, for developing large-motor skills, and for contained, game-oriented play. A designated game area (usually a hard surface) is ideal for basketball, volleyball, wheel toys, four-square and hopscotch, tether ball, and roller skating.

Because play is the preferred way to spend after-school time, a great deal of consideration should be given to the quality and range of play experiences available to children. Children should have ample opportunity to create their own play experiences through cooperative interaction and independent initiatives.

Children also need some structure in their afternoon activities. Teachers need not participate in activities unless invited by children, but they should always have materials and ideas available for children to use freely. Projects, themes, arts and crafts, clubs, and interest centers are some of the ways a teacher and her students can creatively plan and structure daily activities. Few of these projects or activities will be completed in one day so space will be needed to store children's play/work.

A critical need at any age level is quiet, uninterrupted reflective time. Children must be in touch with their thoughts, their feelings, and their fantasies. They need time to think about their day before it is over. By scheduling *personal time* into a school-age program, a teacher is promoting mental health.

A Need to Practice Autonomy

All school-age children need to practice independence and self-management. Maturing children in the eight- to ten-year range want to be treated like young adolescents. They prefer not to have adults around when they socialize. They want to go outside by themselves, wander and play in halls, ride their bikes to child care, and visit a friend after school without permission. They want good snacks that are not always healthy. Above all, they do not want to be compared to younger children or labeled as day care children (meaning they can't take care of themselves).

Unfortunately, freedom of movement is seen as a risk in many child care environments, particularly those in large, open schools or community centers. Children's need for independence, however, can be met in other, more realistic ways. Teachers of school-age children can make a center look less institutional by designing cozy, contained areas for small group gatherings. They can set up Ping-Pong tables in hallways and let children do homework outside of a classroom in areas that are in sight of classrooms—e.g., under stairwells or in small auxiliary rooms that open onto a larger classroom. They can let children assist in planning a program and in selecting equipment and materials. They can take small numbers of children into the community—for grocery shopping, to toy stores, to libraries, and to parks.

The teachers can encourage children to participate in recreational activities outside of a center, finding ways to transport them safely between the two environments. They can hire high-school students of both sexes to play with children. They can hire senior citizens of both sexes to set up and direct activity clubs; these adults often come from diverse backgrounds and bring interesting talents and personalities to a center. Children can make root beer floats and order pizza (like real kids). Teachers can extend freedom by trusting children to go reasonably safe distances on their own—a bathroom, a locker, or back and forth to outdoor play.

Despite their craving for independence, maturing children continue to need the company of caring adults. They need to be made aware of their vulnerabilities as well as their strengths. They need counseling in interpersonal relations, in handling family relationships, in ordering and prioritizing their life, in caring for their bodies, in defining their values, and in practicing safe play and personal conduct. They need adult friends to communicate about all facets of growing up. Adults working with school-age children quickly feel the need to take refresher courses, to read sports pages, and to become familiar with the trends, fashions, and issues that influence their students.

The Importance of Adult Leadership

The school-age child literally grows up before one's eyes. It is extremely satisfying to participate in this growing up process. There are many crisis moments and there are many warm moments that endear children to adults and that bind relationships. Children perceive teachers whom they are especially fond of as friends for life. They are included in or invited to many key events in a child's life—recitals, family events, and graduations. An adult becomes an integral part of school-age experiences that undergird and strengthen a child's life. She sees a child through the trials and tribulations of growing up: loose teeth and braces, report cards, hero worship, tummy aches, nail polish, high periods and low periods. For a child entering middle childhood, a provider is something like a mom and it is not unusual for children to mistakenly call teachers "mom." Children in out-of-home environments look to adult caregivers for emotional support and for friendship.

A teacher must be sensitive to the developmental changes that influence behavior, attitudes, and appearance. Feeling somewhat uncertain about the face and body reflected in the mirror each morning, children may become compulsive about their appearance. Fads, cults, and styles may dominate their thinking. Hero worship is reflected on notebooks, on T-shirts, and on posters. Personalities shift to accommodate the latest interests, fads, and moods. With growing up comes giving up—the innocent look of childhood has given way to awkward, often outrageous preteen behavior. Yet, on occasion, children will slip back to favorite childhood games. A ten-year-old, tiring of board games, may wander over to a block center and begin to construct something he recalls making years ago.

A teacher also must understand the nature and needs of children as they mature. An eight- or ten-year-old has remarkable talents and can function quite well without adult intervention. He can become so absorbed in a project or a game that he is unaware of surrounding distractions. If he is an industrious and responsible taskmaster, he will do his homework on site, applying himself to a task at hand. He knows the difference between getting a job done and getting a job done well. Goal-oriented, he takes pride in his accomplishments and in the pleasure derived from adult and peer recognition. He is gradually becoming a role model himself.

The Importance of a Strong Foundation

The growing child is becoming a part of a broad social system that demands more from her than earlier environments did. She now views herself in relation to others—to what peers are doing, to what turns them on, and to what displeases them. As a child sifts through environmental influences, she hopefully will reaffirm her unique personality and values. As she becomes self-affirmed, a growing child's interests will turn outward toward the larger world. Its concerns will become her concerns. When a child identifies with the larger world, she becomes aware of the inter-connectedness of human relationships and needs. One of the best rewards a child care provider receives is the knowledge that a child will leave a center with a strong foundation, a sense of self, and a commitment to the larger world.

A CHILD-CENTERED ENVIRONMENT

A child-centered environment must instill in children a foundation for *lifelong learning* that enables them to function effectively and efficiently as individuals and as members of society. Foundations are established during the formative years of development. Attitudes also are established in early environments. A child's natural quest for knowledge is influenced by his total surroundings: the attitude of adults, the philosophy and objectives of a program, the atmosphere and design of an environment, the activities and materials that stimulate curiosity, the mood and feeling that prevail throughout the day, the continued presence of love. Things to consider for a child-centered environment are described below.

An Emphasis on Personal Growth

A child is an individual *before* he is a member of a group. He comes to an environment with a unique personality that distinguishes him from others. He exhibits distinct patterns of behavioral, creative, and mental functioning. His disposition influences his choices and his attitude. The inner child unfolds in a childrearing environment that maximizes opportunities for self-expression and personal growth. Quiet moments provide children important outlets for fantasy, daydreaming, and time alone.

If a child does not have a sense of identity by the time he enters elementary school, he will not feel confident about his ability to interact successfully. Stressful encounters will be magnified and coping skills less evident. Feelings of failure that began in the formative years will inhibit a child's later development. Children do not catch up or make up for early childhood deficiencies without continued intervention. A child without a sense of self will have difficulty making choices and decisions. Lacking in self-esteem, he will doubt his ability to function competitively in the larger world.

When a child is recognized as a special and unique member of a group, he will develop self-confidence and self-esteem. As the child continues to gain a positive self-image, he will be ready to move toward self-competency. Essential to maturation is the child's *recognition* that *he* is responsible for the way *he* chooses to conduct himself, manage his life, and accomplish his goals. A teacher can guide a child toward maturity but she cannot always be present to shield him from the risks and demands of growing up. A child must learn to function *both* independently and cooperatively. A good teacher will extend support without stifling initiative, recognizing that ultimately the child must believe in and exercise his own capabilities.

Self-care

Children come to child care centers at different levels—some need training in self-care, and some need reinforcement in already learned self-care skills. They need to understand from both parents and teachers how poor habits and inappropriate choices affect a person's health and well-being. An essential part of early training is to caution children about inappropriate, unhealthy behavior without unduly alarming them. They need to be cautioned about talking to strangers but not to the extent that they are afraid to respond to friendship. Despite very real concerns, we do not want children to view the world as a threatening and unsafe place.

Social Development

Children acquire positive social skills through positive, unstressful interaction. They need to experience being a friend before they can extend friendship to others. Being a friend is not always easy for a young child. Friendship requires a willingness to cooperate and an ability to compromise. Ultimately, children must manage for themselves in the social arena. They need appropriate amounts of adult guidance while they are learning to adjust to a group setting but not to the degree that a dependent relationship develops. Social skills develop slowly but surely in an atmosphere that is noncompetitive, value-centered, and child-centered. Children must become more and more *aware of the interdependent* nature of their community. They must use the lessons of early childhood to become fully functioning human beings.

Mental Growth

Children need to develop thinking skills in order to become functioning, capable members of a community. They need practice in communicating their thoughts, in debating issues, and in organizing knowledge. They need to connect ideas in order to formulate new ideas. A child-centered program will provide many outlets for divergent thinking and creative problem solving. It will provide opportunities for children to participate in projects that are purposeful and relevant to their level of interest and understanding. Planned activities should always be enriched by materials and follow-up activities that expand thinking and motivate the learner. Teachers are responsible for extending learning *beyond* the immediate environment.

Freedom to Grow

Each child must be given appropriate amounts of freedom to learn and discover, to question and challenge, and to practice and perfect talents. Continued exposure to quality experiences and to special caring adults will establish a framework for a happy, creative, and productive life. In a child-centered environment, adults need to:

- Be attentive to personal needs and growth patterns;
- Set the stage for later learning by encouraging children to learn how to learn;
- Encourage the development of good skills and positive attitudes;
- Give children honest and consistent messages;
- Provide opportunities for children to express creativity and develop self-confidence;
- Establish a nurturing environment that fosters compassion for all living things;
- Give children freedom to develop their competencies and talents and to experience the satisfaction that accomplishment brings;

- Provide personal time for children throughout the day;
- Encourage children to experience their total environment: to discover new things, to investigate their surroundings;
- Train children in practical life skills that can become useful adult skills:
- Help children to distinguish between positive growth-enhancing and negative growth-inhibiting behavior;
- Develop and design environments that are relevant, purposeful, and broadening to children;
- Provide opportunities for children to discover their ability to generate ideas;
- Bring families, community, and center closer together;
- Protect and nurture a child's childhood.

When a good teacher is in a truly child-centered environment, there is great reward and satisfaction—even amidst the stressful challenges and confusion. The moments of wonder in working with children are expressed in this poem from *Everychild's Everyday:*

> *You renew*
> *Me*
> *When I really look at you*
> *Really respond*
> *You renew me*
> *When I forget all else*
> *But the amazing*
> *Unfolding of*
> *You*
> *I am renewed.*

A CHILD-CENTERED CURRICULUM

A child-centered curriculum that is appropriate for all age levels and environments should include four primary components that in combination, meet children's total needs for play, learning, self-expression, and nurturing.

Play

When children play, they acquire self-sufficiency and mastery. They become inventive, resourceful, and self-reliant. They define and accomplish their objectives when they can play without interruption for long periods of time. If they cannot find something that fits their play scheme, they substitute and improvise with objects at hand. The systematic play strategies children use as they interact with materials are linked to creative and cognitive development. The absorption and intensity that characterizes children at play reveals an insatiable need for self-direction and exploration. Whether their play is solitary or social, children work through ideas and express feelings as they play. They transfer their ideas onto an environmental drawing board—a mound of dirt, a sandbox, an arts and crafts table, a block center, a dramatic play center.

Motivated by a desire to interact with materials, children direct and control their play projects. They design and create interesting combinations of pretend plots, organize, evaluate, and make changes. The process may take only a few minutes—a child absorbed in her own thing does not stop for lunch. Although spontaneous play is process oriented, children tend to want to complete their projects. Serious play requires planning, concentration, determination, and when playmates are involved, cooperation. Children tend to repeat play themes that hold their attention; they enjoy seeing familiar constructs or dramatizations from a new perspective and they enjoy recreating routine themes.

The function that *play* serves in child development can be both pleasureful and therapeutic. Children are happy when they play—they smile frequently and move with confidence. When children play, they release anxieties because they focus more on the project and playmates than on themselves. As they play, *children reveal themselves*. They act out feelings, attitudes, and real-life themes that may need to surface. Spontaneous play facilitates mental health. It uses energy in productive ways. Everything a child creates involves body movement and control, be it modeling clay, painting, pretend play, moving objects in a play yard, collecting play items, pounding wood, or building free-standing objects. When a child is physically and mentally absorbed in something he likes, he loses his sense of time and place.

Play generates happiness. For a happy child, life is a playground filled with objects and people that attract and motivate natural curiosity. A child moves at her own pace as she discovers how to function in a strange and wonderful world. There is no written curriculum that can possibly do justice to the wonders at work within the child and no adult who can fully comprehend the magnitude of development taking place within the child in a relatively short span of time. In the hands of a child, something commonplace becomes a small wonder: a stone, a bug, a wild flower. Play engages children permitting them time to grow, to think, and to let their thoughts wander through the *fields of discovery*.

Learning

In challenging, creative environments, learning is not separated from the child or treated as isolated tasks. It is ongoing and all-inclusive. The learning child is a curious child who questions and learns through active, self-initiated channels. On a less abstract level, learning skills are integrated into a child's full day through direct and indirect experiences that stimulate thinking and develop competency. In an open learning environment, children perceive relationships as they connect ideas to concrete experiences. A teaching unit on transportation is extended to include large-motor play, an art project, a cooking experience (cookies shaped like little autos), and a language experience, thereby enabling children to participate in a whole learning experience.

For example, a group of children may take a seeing walk in their backyard, noticing specific features that identify their play environment—equipment, grass areas, trees and shrubs, extended surroundings. They record their visual concepts on paper, drawing what is important to them. They talk about and compare the items and features they remember. They begin to see a difference between a natural and a man-made environment. They talk about caring for nature and caring for property. Later the same day, children may take another seeing walk, this time making a picture of their school. Shapes, colors, and materials are identified, windows counted, and friends added. A hands-on, sensory experience may even motivate children to write a story about their backyard.

A skillful teacher knows how to direct and extend the learning processes that are already at work within the child. She encourages investigation, questioning, and reasoning. She generates ideas and concepts through natural, spontaneous dialogue. A teacher encourages children to discover things for themselves.

Self-expression

When children are encouraged to express themselves, they sharpen their senses and expand their level of awareness. They interpret the world as they paint, paste, build, and engage in dramatic play. They use their eyes to study intricacies, their bodies to experience pleasures, their hands to explore and investigate features and thereby construct a base of knowledge from personal, hands-on experiences. A child, for example, may paint a butterfly after observing its movements outside. She reproduces the features that stood out in her memory. She remembers its design and the shape of its wings. She adds flowers and personal touches to the picture—a picture that is uniquely hers.

Through a variety of mediums, children continue to develop and explore their creativity. They connect feelings and ideas through *sensory experiences* that help them to communicate with their environment. They use their imagination to become the characters they are portraying, finding words, props, and apparel to authenticate their role-playing. Children who express themselves creatively begin to see the world from a more sensitive perspective. They take notice of little things that are not usually apparent. They become extremely attentive to their environment—its changes, its people, its rhythm, and its potential.

Nurturing

When children are exposed to a nurturing environment, they develop attitudes that foster trusting relationships and good character. As in any family structure, child care relationships are built on open communication and cooperation. The teacher, like the parent, establishes and cultivates a climate conducive to growth and to learning. She encourages responsibility to one's self and to one's group. She helps children to become culturally conscious and sensitive to the diversity that surrounds them. She provides materials that strengthen children's backgrounds and identities. By developing core values, the teacher is encouraging lifelong habits that will enable children to function as competent and caring adults.

There are many ways to provide nurturing in a classroom. One important way is through books. Books are pathways to enlightenment and self-discovery. Literature is one of the most important gifts we can share with, and pass on, to children. Books are a part of a nation's literary tradition and heritage. Through books young children move beyond immediate experience into infinite gardens of knowledge and inspiration. Every idea we wish to communicate to children may be found in a book. Every picture we wish to paint for children may be found in a book. Every feeling we wish to convey to children is symbolized in storybook characters. Literature enables children to connect to a world of ideas and possibilities: to dream, to laugh, and to hope.

Nurturing is the *bridge* between what a child accomplishes and how he feels about his accomplishment. Without nurturing, an organism languishes; the flower and the child begin to tire and development is stifled.

For a happy child, gardens can grow even without watering cans. When given the opportunity to fully experience, the child will cultivate seeds of wisdom. In a child-centered program, adults will:

- Help children acquire knowledge and develop literacy skills;
- Help children develop basic skills that promote self-management and competency;
- Help children develop capabilities in mental, physical, and social areas;
- Encourage children to appreciate the fine arts and their cultural heritage;
- Encourage children to become active, competent learners;
- Encourage children to develop their creative talents;
- Encourage children to become nurturing young adults through early childhood experiences that generate individual and social values.

WORKING WITH CHILDREN

Teaching Methods

The preferred method for working with children in any setting is one of *guided discovery* through which teachers introduce ideas, inspire awareness, generate a sense of inquiry, and motivate children to extend their learning. In open, play-oriented environments, teachers are more facilitative than instructional. Their primary objective is to develop a cognitive, creative, and attitudinal *foundation* that will enable children to function as capable, competent, and caring human beings. The specific roles that characterize child-centered teaching may be described as those of an *initiator*, a *partner*, and an *observer*.

An Initiator

In this role, teachers extend learning opportunities by interacting with children in small groups or in a group circle. Teachers initiate when they plan a unit, organize skills and activities for children's enjoyment, and work with small groups of children to encourage or facilitate developmental skills. Teacher-initiated experiences are especially critical at the early stages of development when skills and concepts are forming and when children have more need of adult guidance. Objectives for teaching with an initiator method are to:

- Practice and extend basic foundational skills;
- Help children integrate learning experiences;
- Stimulate interest in learning;
- Develop thinking and language skills;
- Develop listening and recall skills;
- Help children become sensitive to their physical world through sensory experiences;
- Encourage eye–hand coordination;
- Help children organize and consolidate information;
- Promote talents and interests;
- Assist children in specific areas of development;
- Get to know children as whole persons;
- Assess children and communicate their progress to parents.

A Partner

In this role, teachers interact with children as friends and role models. Teachers are partners with children whenever they spend personal time enriching their lives or sharing experiences. During these periods, teachers are facilitative, nondirective and nonjudgmental in the way they converse and interact with children. Often, they are next to a child, saying little but adding comfort, guidance, and support to a child at play. Teachers also may use this concept of partnership to redirect or change inappropriate behavior. If a teacher is skilled at problem solving and behavior management, she can use personal time to initiate conversation that helps children identify and work through problems. Objectives for teaching with a partner method are to:

- Get to know children by spending quality time with them throughout the day;
- Help children develop self-control;
- Help children cope with problems and develop prosocial behavior patterns;
- Personalize and individualize relationships so that children can feel secure and confident in their environment;
- Work independently with children who have special physical or emotional needs.
- Comfort and help children through their adjustment process;
- Share and help develop children's interests and skills;

- Support and enhance children's creativity;
- Help children connect a center to a home and a teacher to a parent.

An Observer

In this role, teachers are noninterventionist unless children need attention or assistance. Reasonable limits and expectations already have been set by adults and children. Children understand and, for the most part, respect agreements. The environment has been designed for independent play, exploration, self-management, and safety. Children are encouraged to use their time constructively and to be attentive to one another's needs. Even though there is minimal interaction, staff is always attentive to where children are and what they are doing. Objectives for teaching with an observer method are to:

- Encourage children to make choices and anticipate consequences;
- Encourage children to solve their own problems;
- Encourage children to interact with peers for an extended period of time;
- Help children develop self-control and autonomy;
- Encourage children to develop responsibility for their actions;
- Encourage creative expression;
- Encourage children to develop communication skills;
- Encourage original thinking and creativity.

MANAGING CHILDREN

Preventing Misbehavior

A well-designed and managed program prevents misbehavior by: limiting the number of children in a classroom; having adequate staff; limiting the number of transitions in a day; discouraging competition; having enough for children to do; providing a balanced, integrated day; being attentive to children's needs for outdoor play, good nutrition, and good health practices; encouraging children to express feelings, and be empathetic; supporting children's choices; encouraging children's interests; opening time frames to maximize independent play; and developing and discussing rules of conduct. (See Sample 9–1.)

If teachers and staff members model appropriate behavior and consistently reinforce the standards that are operative in a given environment, children will understand and, most of the time, accept limits. Limits can be reinforced by posting and reviewing agreements for behavior in the classroom, on the playground, and on fieldtrips. Children accept rules of conduct that are presented at the beginning of a child care experience. It is imperative that teachers at all levels agree on the *manner* and *methods* of discipline so children have consistency throughout their child care experience. If bad language is not permitted at the age of three, it should not be permitted at the age of four. By agreeing on fundamental behavioral guidelines, a staff will know how to deal with problems as they occur

SAMPLE 9–1   A Child-Centered Approach for Handling Behavioral Problems at School-Age Levels

1. State problem:	Student/teacher discuss the stated problem in open, respectful, trusting manner
Purpose:	To encourage a child to verbalize a problem without anxiety or fear of reprimand
2. State feelings:	Student self-examines and expresses feelings; teacher counsels
Purpose:	To help a child come to a position of understanding and forgiveness
3. Solve problem:	Student/teacher discuss alternative ways to solve problem
Purpose:	To help a child find appropriate ways to solve a problem
4. My intentions:	Student selects a method of solving the problem and makes a written agreement with himself or herself
Purpose:	To help a child come to a position of acceptance and responsibility
5. What have I learned?	Student talks, teacher listens and reinforces child's agreement
Purpose:	To help a child bring the problem and feelings to closure
6. Follow-through:	Student and teacher agree to meet periodically to continue the self-examination process
Purpose:	To help a child sustain positive behavior and feelings toward self and others

NOTE: This approach may be modified for preschool-age children.

and will undoubtedly experience fewer problems. Positive expressions like: "kindness, cooperation, friendship, good job, I'm proud of you," should be used repeatedly in a learning and play context. Through direct and indirect repetition, appropriate behavior practices will be absorbed and practiced by children.

The purpose of setting disciplinary guidelines is to enable children to develop *internal* control mechanisms that foster growth and promote societal values. Children must be trained in basic rules of conduct (see Sample 9–2) before they are expected to follow general rules of conduct. As they progress in development, children will be exposed to increasingly higher levels of human interaction. In the process of developing an understanding about how social systems operate effectively, children will learn to replace physical or verbal aggressiveness with acceptable modes of interaction. They will not only learn the *consequences* of their actions but begin to *internalize* information in ways that generate feelings of empathy and compassion.

SAMPLE 9–2   Rules of Classroom Conduct for School-Age Levels

In this center children are expected to:
1. Be courteous
2. Be respectful
3. Have good manners
4. Be kind to one another
5. Make wise choices
6. Be responsible members of a group
7. Be good self-managers

If there is a problem:
1. Teachers talk with children.
2. Teachers talk with parents.
3. Children may not be able to remain in this center, if the problem continues. This would make children, parents, and staff unhappy.

Please help by being a positive member of this team.

_____

(Student signature)

NOTE: This agreement can be modified and simplified for preschool-age children.

Dealing with Misbehavior

Children should not be spanked, threatened, or mistreated in any way by adults. They should not be punished by isolation (removing a child from a group for an extended period of time), ridicule (reprimanding children in front of peers), or deprivation (taking a snack away). Continuing patterns of misbehavior should be recorded and communicated to parents so there is agreement on how to discipline children. A parent must not only be consulted but must be *required* to share with a center's staff the responsibility of managing their child's behavior. There is no single method for dealing with children's stress and anger. There are *five* strategies that, if used consistently and carefully, will soothe and mollify upset children as they begin a healing process.

The first strategy is to develop a system of *positive reinforcement.* Children should be given positive feedback when they are expressing sympathy and cooperating with others. Teachers can reward children for good behavior in small but personalized ways. A teacher may hold a hand, slip a special smiling face on a picture, or whisper something a child wants to hear—gestures that make a little child feel important and good. Teachers can use puppets or other dramatic conveyers to emphasize or reinforce a message: "I am your friend. Will you be my friend?" She can also use a nurturing curriculum to make children socially cognizant and more sensitive to the needs of one another (see Part V).

The second strategy is one of *prevention*. A teacher who knows a child knows what triggers and escalates anger, i.e., sharing favorite toys, interruptions, irritating peers. By redirecting a child before a crisis occurs, the teacher will help restore a child's sense of control and balance. By understanding the nature and needs of each child, a teacher will use appropriate intervention strategies. Some children need more direction than others. They can't handle long periods of free play, they can't make choices, and they can't interact effectively with peers. These children need considerable student/teacher partnering before they can become self-directed and trustworthy. Some children like to test rules of behavior through argumentation or aggressive behavior. By reminding children about classroom rules that pertain to respect, the teacher will discourage a challenging child.

Finding constructive ways to manage behavior before an incident escalates into a dramatic encounter is a teacher's challenge. An important first step is to *notice*, rather than to *ignore*, behavior. If a teacher senses an argument or fight brewing, she should make her presence known and, if necessary, immediately step in to redirect or stop unkind behavior. Children should always be spoken to *privately* at the time of an incident. A child's misbehavior should never become the object of group attention. By ignoring unacceptable behavior, a teacher is giving a child the *wrong* message—she is basically affirming his unacceptable behavior. The child, in turn, feels confused and unsatisfied, the problem is not going away, it is worsening. He reacts by continuing the behavior that is giving him attention, albeit negative attention. His friends are watching and implicitly labeling him "a bad boy." When a teacher deals with behavior at the moment of crisis (as difficult as this may be), she is making a statement that "I care, this is not acceptable." Eventually, the child will stop testing and begin to believe in and trust his environment.

A third strategy is to *obtain information*. Often, a child does not know what she has done wrong, or, truly believes in her own innocence. Distinguishing an *accuser* from an *aggressor* may become a challenge for a teacher who did not witness the incident or who is not clear what precipitated the incident. Both children feel wronged and probably both are crying. Neither wants to accept blame. Before discussing an incident with a child, a teacher might try to obtain information from peers who witnessed the altercation. An impartial teacher will listen to both sides, make suggestions, and help children find a solution and reconcile their differences.

If a child is clearly the aggressor, a teacher will speak firmly and look for ways to resolve the problem without unnecessarily hurting a child's sense of dignity. When a child understands that he cannot conduct himself in ways that harm or offend others, he will take responsibility for his actions, finding acceptable, less aggressive ways to solve problems. A child must, in essence, forgive himself before he can *honestly* say "I'm sorry." He must feel the need to restore a harmonious relationship with the child he has hurt. This may be done in indirect ways: by holding hands on the way to a bathroom, sharing a favorite toy, or sharing a lunch treat. These follow-up acts of kindness are extremely important to a child's emotional growth. They are far more important than a mechanical, "I'm sorry," prompted by a harried teacher.

A fourth strategy is to *remain objective*. The maturation process is never without dips and curves. For whatever causes, children go through behavioral fluctuations. A teacher who overreacts to a child's change in behavior needs to take time to self-assess and reflect. She should look at her relationship with the child, think about possible causes and ways to change or redirect negative behavior. She should not ignore the behavior, nor should she exaggerate the behavior—she simply needs to put it into *perspective*.

A fifth strategy is to *ask for help*. When, over a reasonable period of time, standard procedures are no longer effective, a teacher knows that it is time to ask for help. It is not unusual for children in child care environments to have multiple problems that are not easily resolved by behavior management techniques. A dysfunctioning child will probably require professional intervention within a controlled environment.

Intervention Techniques

The most beneficial way of handling a child who is having a temper tantrum or a serious fight with a peer is to remove the child from the setting for a reflective cool-down period that is *not punitive* but *restorative*. A drink of water, a walk outside, or a conversation with a teacher will help a child gain control. An extra pair of hands to handle emergencies, such as sickness, accidents, and behavioral problems, is essential in child care environments.

With some training, senior citizens can become perfect assistants. Unlike teachers who have a group to consider, senior citizens have the time to sit with children and to comfort them in their times of need. An alternative to a senior citizen is a secretary or office helper who is willing to sit with a child for a few minutes until she can gain control and reenter her group.

The time that is spent handling behavioral problems in child care environments must be an essential part of program planning. Daily activity plans must allow ample time for teacher/student interactions, and an environment must have additional staff to assist a teacher in handling behavior problems. It is far more important for children to feel secure and happy than it is for them to finish projects. Projects eventually get thrown out; a child's *memories last forever*.

A Discipline Policy

Most state regulations require child care centers to disseminate a discipline policy for parental review. A policy might read:

> In keeping with the Center's philosophy, children are expected to exercise self-control, respectful attitudes, concern for others, and appropriate behavioral patterns. When problems arise, children are spoken to in a firm but supportive fashion, and are encouraged to express feelings and to acknowledge their responsibility for an incident. After a quiet, reflective interval, children will be given the opportunity to resume their play or, if necessary, asked to select a

quiet place where they can reflect on their behavior. If inappropriate behavioral patterns continue, parents are notified and asked to work in partnership with the Center on their child's behalf. At this time, a behavior modification plan will be agreed on and implemented. A child who continues to demonstrate aggressive or unhealthy behavioral patterns may need specialized help that cannot be provided at this Center.

A Shared Responsibility

What is not recognized in child care centers is that poorly trained teachers may be contributing to children's misbehavior. A center that meets developmentally appropriate criteria and hires teachers who are skilled in behavior management should not be overly burdened with behavioral problems. Skillful teachers establish a foundation of values that encourage children to respect people and property at the very beginning stages of development. They encourage good manners and kindness and discourage lying or taking things without asking permission. Teachers encourage forgiveness and discourage negative thinking. They handle behavioral problems with care and attentiveness to the feelings and needs of children, understanding that children, by nature, want to please. They will not label children or minimize their problems.

If an environment does not model *cooperation* and *empathy,* it is teachers who must assume responsibility for this neglect and its consequences. A center that is *pro-child,* affirms the importance of early training. Advice to teachers about controlling children's behavior might include:

- Talk and interact with them as often as possible;
- Be attentive to their dispositions and personalities;
- Be attentive to their vulnerabilities—to circumstances that make them feel different and inadequate;
- Record, assess, and understand their behavior;
- Support their growth and development;
- Advocate for them;
- Extend yourself for them;
- Acknowledge responsibility for the way they grow, develop, and receive and transmit information;
- Affirm and support behavior that reveals and acknowledges their movement toward social growth and notice the little gestures that often go unnoticed;
- Include parents in a center/child relationship.

SCHEDULING A DAY

A daily activity schedule should consider the total needs of children (see Figure 9–1). It should not be focused on activities but on children, reflecting the age, interests, backgrounds, and abilities of an individual group. There should be ample

FIGURE 9–1 **A Daily Activity Schedule**

Early-Childhood Level

8:00–9:00 AM	Independent play—a daily project is set up for children's enjoyment, e.g., an art activity, a science/math activity.
9:00–9:30 AM	Opening group time—children greet, share, discuss plans for the day, and engage in a brief learning activity, e.g., a theme-related activity, a language activity, a science experiment, a creative movement or music activity.
9:30–10:00 AM	Outdoor play—children play independently, play circle games, or share a group experience
10:00–10:15 AM	Transition—bathroom, snack.
10:15–11:00 AM	Independent play in activity centers—teacher-initiated play/work projects are also set up, e.g. a cooking or art project, a creative writing or science/math project, a practical task
11:00–11:30 AM	Transition to quiet activity, e.g., reading a story, artwork, playing a group game
11:30–12:30 PM	Lunch and transition to rest—children may go outside before rest
12:30–3:00 PM	Rest and transition to afternoon activities
3:00–4:00 PM	Snack, outdoor play, or indoor large-motor play
4:00 PM–pick-up	Independent play—a teacher-initiated play/work project is set up; a specialist may visit on a weekly basis; children may enjoy a short film or a carefully selected television program one or two days per week

School-Age Level

7:00–8:30 AM	Greeting, quiet activities—activities are set up on tables or in an art center; children may do homework or play games with playmates
3:00–4:15 PM	Transition from public school to child care center—greeting, discuss activity options, plan activities, snack, outdoor play (independent and group activities are offered)
4:15–4:45 PM	Homework or quiet play time—children choose activities
4:45 PM–pick-up	Independent play—a teacher-initiated play/work project is set up; children may attend special classes, clubs, or enjoy a carefully selected film or television program once or twice a week during this time frame

time for: basic routines, scheduled events, skill-building, the unexpected, self-initiated learning, transitions, behavioral episodes, special activities, play, and most important, being with children. The best way to plan a day is to avoid overplanning. By opening time frames, children will be able to complete their projects and to make transitions without frustration.

SCHEDULING A WEEK

A weekly activity frame provides information about content areas and special events (see Figure 9–2). It encourages parents to reinforce children's activities in the home. It *integrates* activities and themes in ways that enhance the natural flow

FIGURE 9–2 A Weekly Activity Frame

Age Level: Four Year Olds
Unit: "Animals"
Theme: "Pets"

Activities	Monday	Tuesday	Wednesday	Thursday	Friday
Circle:	Greeting Planning			⟶	Pet Show
Theme Projects:	Start book on pets	Finish book: make a cover	Visit a pet store; buy mice	Learn about mice	Make a shoe box home for mice
Language Experiences:	Introduce letter "M" (for mice)	Play "Hide the Animal"	Read/Discuss "Pet Show"	Identify animal sounds	Game:"Guess what animal I am?"
Math/Science Experiences:	Make a bar graph of favorite pets	Create a pet with shapes	Play pet bingo	Sort pet objects and name them	Make animal cookies
The Arts: Music Art Movement Drama	Make an animal puppet	Act out "The Three Little Kittens"; make mittens	Read and act out "Frederick." Talk about feelings	Music: Theme-related	Creative movement/ woodworking
Circle:	Review	Review	Review	Review	Film

Theme Objectives:
1. To learn about animals that are classified as pets.
2. To gain knowledge about caring for pets.
3. To compare domestic animals to wild animals.
4. To make a book about "Our Favorite Pet."
5. To visit a pet store and purchase a classroom pet.
6. To learn about animal characteristics and needs.
7. To make homes for pets using shoe boxes to construct with.
8. To introduce literature that relates to pets.
9. To compare pets to human beings: How are we alike and how are we different?

Special Activity:
Parents are invited to watch "Alice in Wonderland" with us this Friday.

of learning. It provides an organizational framework for educational objectives and activities and also provides a method for evaluating a program. Without a plan, a teacher cannot fairly assess children or her own performance. A weekly activity frame also provides an important communication channel to parents, enabling them to support, reinforce, and participate in their child's center life.

A MONTHLY CALENDAR

A monthly calendar provides an overall framework for ongoing activities and events planned for a given month, e.g., language-experience stories on Wednesdays, a science experiment on Thursdays, a hot lunch on Mondays. Space permitting, a monthly calendar also will include special events, routine reminders, seasonal plans, birthdays or holiday activities, and so on. (See Figures 9–3 and 9–4.)

ASSESSING CHILDREN'S PROGRESS

The purpose of assessing children's progress is to understand and evaluate their growth patterns and development. The most careful way to *assess* children's progress is by observing children in their *total environment* on a *daily* basis. Equally important is recording children's behavioral and developmental progress on an as-needed basis. Teachers are advised to document children's progress by keeping anecdotal (brief) records on child-related concerns and areas of general development. Documentation might include behavioral, developmental, or social areas. A teacher observes a child's behavioral patterns and his physiological make-up, temperament, disposition, and personality and notes his family background and prior experiences. She observes a child's developmental characteristics: interests and talents; ability; distinguishing features; skills—physical, language, and listening skills; sensory development; thinking, recall, and discrimination skills; number concepts, reasoning, and problem-solving ability; expressive skills; and self- and task-management skills. She observes a child's social skills—ability to communicate and cooperate with peers on a fairly sustained basis.

By being aware of each child's activities and interactions throughout the day and by spending personal time with a child, a skillful teacher will not need to record everything that happens in the course of a day. An excessive preoccupation with recordkeeping may cause children to be unfairly or prematurely labeled. It also may take a teacher's time away from children and shift a classroom atmosphere from one of open-learning to closed-learning. A teacher must use discretion in what and when she records about her children. Some items should be noted at the time of occurrence, e.g., unusual changes in behavior, confidential information, developmental milestones, a specific developmental concern, accidents, or contagious illnesses. Areas of general progress, however, such as basic skill, eye-hand coordination, physical or behavioral development, can be recorded cumulatively rather than daily.

FIGURE 9–3 A Monthly Calendar

Age Level: Unit: Month:	Monday	Tuesday	Wednesday	Thursday	Friday
Week of:	Introduce theme ↓ Math/ Science ↓ Art	Language Discovery theme ↓ Drama	Special activity in the Arts ↓ A Field-trip	Language activity ↓ Story-telling ↓ Music	Theme project ↓ Cooking ↓ Film ↓ Cleaning
Week of:	Introduce theme ↓ Math/ Science ↓ Art	Language activity ↓ Theme-related	Special activity in the Arts ↓ Drama	Language activity ↓ Theme-related	Theme project ↓ Cooking ↓ Music ↓ Cleaning
Week of:	Introduce theme ↓ Math/ Science ↓ Art	Language activity: Word friends ↓ Music ↓ Art	Special activity in the Arts ↓ Outdoors	Language activity: Word friends ↓ Drama	Theme project ↓ Cooking ↓ Film ↓ Cleaning
Week of:	Introduce theme ↓ Math/ Science ↓ Art	Language Discovery Theme ↓ Movement ↓ Film	Special activity in the Arts ↓ Drama	Language activity ↓ Story-telling ↓ Movement	Theme project ↓ Cooking ↓ Music ↓ Cleaning

Special Activities:

Comments:

Classroom News:

Books to Read:

Friends of the Week:

FIGURE 9–4 Sample Calendar

GHCCC

Session: _4 – 5 Year Olds_

Teachers: _____

Calendar for
DECEMBER

Monday	Tuesday	Wednesday	Thursday	Friday
31 Winter is coming; walk and chart observations	**1** Language Experience "The Littlest Tree": Picture and verse.	**2** What do we know about water? Water cycle/ wordchart	**3** Continue discussion; make rain inside a jar ✎ Word: that	**4** Sharing: Read <u>Frederick</u> Interpret/ Language Experience
7 Children may select winter art projects: Letter "I" for ice/igloo	**8** What do we know about ice? A "cold" number book	**9** What do we know about weather? Make a thermometer	**10** Continue: Make a weather wheel for winter Begin H&G ———	**11** Sharing: Make a snowman book
14 The concept of "migration"; start a feeding tray/continue through winter	**15** Identify birds who migrate and those who remain behind	**16** The concept of "hibernation", make a forest mural for H&G	**17** How "people" prepare for winter; make a giving tree ✎ Word: he/she	**18** Make Ginger- bread holiday houses; practice for H&G
21 ...Setting the Stage	**22** ...The Production 1:00 P.M.	**23** A special gift for the animals	**24** Closed	**25** Closed
28 GHCCC Open for	**29** Day Care only ———	**30**	**31** ⟶	Happy New Year

Themes: WINTER BRINGS CHANGES: WHAT IS HAPPENING?
1. Landscape changes: Observations
2. Weather changes: Experiments, observations, discussions
3. Animal changes: Migration, hibernation; discussions and activities
4. People changes: Meeting needs; winter activities; contributing socks, mittens, scarves, or hats to a holiday Giving Tree (ages one through six)

Special Events and Fieldtrips:
The children are dramatizing "Hansel and Gretel" on Tuesday, 12/22. Parents and friends are invited. Time: 1:00 P.M.

Ongoing Activities:
Ms. Katherine provides music on Fridays; Ms. Dana, movement on Mondays Language experience, phonics, feather words; begin animal vowel strips "A"; review and use numbers 1 through 8; practice working with sets, patterns, and number concepts; theme-related literature.

Parent Participation: We would appreciate the following items by December 14th:
1. A small milk carton for a Gingerbread house.
2. Items for our Giving Tree.
3. Candy for our play. (Children will be assigned one or two items.)

✎ Feather word: A high-frequency word common in early readers.

There should be a developmental checklist on file for every child. A checklist is filled out before a parent conference and again at the end of the year. It provides a composite profile on a child's progress in cognitive, attitudinal, social, and creative areas of development. For a sample developmental checklist, see Appendix B.

SUMMARY

A primary purpose of all child care environments is to establish a foundation for experiencing a quality life that *begins* with the child, *extends* to the surrounding environment, and *expands* to the larger environment. In the maturation process, a child moves toward self-affirmation. She internalizes truths and develops the skills and competencies that will enhance her life. A child gradually becomes less dependent on adults and peers and more self-reliant. She knows who she is and what she is capable of doing. She doesn't need a sticker or a gold star for completing her tasks. She is not a perfect child by any means, but she is aware of her strengths and to some degree, of her limitations.

A child is interested in developing her talents but understands that not everything is easy, not every day is perfect. By developing her capabilities, she is developing her capacity for decision making, patience, and self-care. In the process, she is gaining self-direction and confidence. Someday she may become a ballerina, a teacher, a scientist, or a rock singer but for now she is where she is—a little child experiencing her world through eyes that see beauty, friendship, and possibility.

A child care center must walk a fine line between *caring* for children and *encouraging* them to care for themselves. Adults cannot shelter children from the experience of growing up, but they can guide their progress and nurture their development to the extent that they can become self-sufficient and productive human beings.

NOTE

1. Barbara Biber, "The Five to Eights and How They Grow," in *Readings from Childhood Education,* ed. Margaret Rasmussen (Wheaton, MD: 1966), p. 73.

RESOURCES

The Developing Child Series (Cambridge, MA: Harvard University Press):
Child Abuse, by Ruth Kempe and C. Henry Kempe
Children Drawing, by Jacqueline Goodnow
Children's Friendships, by Zick Rubin
Children's Talk, by Catherine Garvey
Daycare, by Alison Clarke-Stewart
Distress and Comfort, by Judy Dunn
Early Language, by Peter A. de Villiers and Jill G. de Villiers
Early Literature, by Joan B. McLane and Gillian D. McNamee
Learning Disabilities: A Psychological Perspective, by Sylvia Farnham-Diggory
The Perceptual World of the Child, by T. G. R. Bower

The National Education Association Early Childhood Series (Washington, DC: National Education Association):
Activity-Oriented Classrooms, by Milly Cowles and Jerry Aldridge
Behavior Management in K–6 Classrooms
Cooperative Learning in the Early Childhood Classroom, by Harvey C. Foyle, Lawrence Lyman, Sandra A. Thies
Developmentally Appropriate Teaching in Early Childhood, by Dominic F. Gullo
Educationally Appropriate Kindergarten Practices, ed. Bernard Spodek
Learning Centers for Child-Centered Classrooms, by Janice Pattillo and Elizabeth Vaughan
Multicultural Education in Early Childhood Classrooms, ed. Edwina Battle Vold
Parent-Teacher Conferencing in Early Childhood Education, by S. Dianne Lawler
Perspectives on Early Childhood Education, ed. David Elkind
Play's Place in Public Education for Young Children, ed. Victoria Jean Dimidjian
Problem Solving in the Early Childhood Classroom, by Joan Britz and Norma Richard

Multicultural Education in Early Childhood Classrooms, ed. Edwina Battle Vold

Early Childhood Education Series, ed. Millie Almy (New York: Teachers College, Columbia University):
Island of Childhood: Education in the Special World of Nursery School, by Elinor Fitch Griffen
The Joy of Movement in Early Childhood, by Sandra R. Curtis
Diversity in the Classroom: A Multicultural Approach to the Education of Young Children, by Frances E. Kendall
Making Day Care Better: Training, Evaluation, and the Process of Change, eds. James T. Greenman and Robert. W. Fuqua
Ideas Influencing Early Childhood Education: A Theoretical Analysis, by Evelyn Weber
Young Children Reinvent Arithmetic: Implications of Piaget's Theory, by Constance K. Kamii

For Further Information

Bender, Judith, Elder Schuyler-Hass and Charles H. Flatter. *Half a Childhood: Time for School-Age Child Care*. Nashville, TN: School Age Notes, 1984.

Bentzen, Warren R. *Seeing Young Children: A Guide to Observing and Recording Behavior*. Albany, NY: Delmar Publishers, 1985.

Bos, Beverly. *Before the Basics: Creating Conversations with Children*. Roseville, CA: Turn the Page Press (203 Baldwin Street, 95678), 1987.

Brenner, A. *Helping Children Cope with Stress*. Lexington, MA: D. C. Heath, 1984.

Dodge, Diane T., Amy L. Dombro, and Derry G. Koralek. *Caring for Infants and Toddlers*, Vols. I and II. Washington, DC: Teaching Strategies, Inc., 1991.

Greenberg, Polly. *Character Development: Encouraging Self-Esteem and Self-Discipline in Infants, Toddlers, and Two-Year-Olds*. Washington, DC: NAEYC, 1991.

Honig, A. S. "Research in Review. Prosocial Development in Children." *Young Children,* 37(5) 51–52.

Honig, A. S. "High Quality Infant/Toddler Care: Issues and Dilemmas." *Young Children* 41(1), 40–46.

Hymes, James L., Jr. *Teaching the Child Under Six,* 3d ed. West Greenwich, RI: Consortium Publishing, 1989.

McCracken, Janet Brown, ed. *Reducing Stress in Young Children's Lives,* Washington, DC: NAEYC, 1986.

Mitchell, Grace. *A Very Practical Guide to Discipline with Young Children,* Chelsea, MA: Telshare Publishing, Inc., 1982.

Mitchell, Judy, David, and Anne, eds. *Explorations with Young Children: A Curriculum Guide from the Bank Street College of Educa-tion.* Mt. Rainier, MD: Gryphon House, 1992.

"Project Home Safe." In *Developmentally Appropriate Practice in School-Age Care Programs,* eds. Kay M. Albrecht and Margaret C. Plantz, Alexandria, VA: Project Home Safe (1555 King Street, 22314), 1991.

Rutter, M. "Stress, Coping, and Development: Some Issues and Questions." In *Stress, Coping and Development in Children,* eds. N. Carmezy and M. Rutter. New York: McGraw-Hill, 1983.

Stonehouse, Anne. *Trusting Toddlers.* St. Paul, MN: Toys 'n Things Press, 1990.

Wilson, LaVisa, C. (College of Education, Auburn University). *Infants and Toddlers: Curriculum and Teaching,* 2d ed. Albany, NY: Delmar, 1990.

Some children may have innate ability that is identified early as "gifted," but all children hold the potential for becoming competent, caring, and artistically creative human beings.

P A R T   V

A CURRICULUM GUIDE:
A "PLAN" MODEL

"Play" is a small word, only four letters long. Children may be playing when they manipulate objects, climb walls, or tumble in autumn leaves. Yet philosophers debate its meaning, researchers study its forms and functions, and teachers ponder its place in the curriculum. In play, children solve self-imposed problems. Some are social and some are material; some are imitative and some are original. Even though researchers distinguish particular forms—functional play, pretend play, and games—one form often blends into another.
— Greta G. Fein

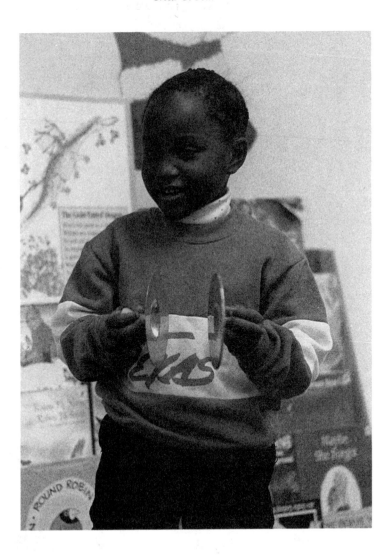

10

COMPONENT ONE: PLAY

No one has to persuade children about the value of play. When a parent asks a young child "What did you do in school today?" the child readily responds, "I played." The parent may be looking for a more substantive response but for the child this message has considerable meaning. It means he had a happy day, but he can't explain why; it means he was occupied, but he can't recall how; it means that he made discoveries, but he doesn't understand that they have already been internalized. He does know he wants more of whatever "it" is.

Play is a child's way of meeting, greeting, responding to, and mastering his world. It symbolizes pleasureful and purposeful activities that are natural and necessary to growing up; activities that involve movement, manipulation, initiative, experimentation, problem solving, anticipation, satisfaction, and most important, a desire for continuation—for more of whatever it is that engrosses and pleases a child. An appropriate definition for play might be that . . . *play is childhood.* It is at once all the emotions, needs, desires, and possibilities inherent in childhood.

Something so intrinsic and natural to childhood cannot be readily understood by parents or by educators who often interpret play as recreational or nonproductive. How often has a teacher or a parent admonished. "When you finish your work, you can play." With such contradictions, how can a director explain to her staff that play is the *common denominator* that integrates and gives meaning to childhood experiences? How can she explain to a parent that play is a *critical* dimension of learning at early childhood levels? How can she set up a play environment that is constructive as well as creative? How will she assess play from a child's perspective? from a teaching perspective? Can she trust her instincts and knowledge enough to make play a primary component of her curriculum? Can she support her beliefs when she is confronted by challenging parents?

By its very nature, play allows a child to feel successful and in control. Wherever there are objects to manipulate and space to explore, children will spontaneously gather. Motivated by their own energy and curiosity, children *envelop* a play space. Each play experience has its own special meaning to a child. Unlike teacher--initiated experiences, play does not have to begin with objectives or end with goals. It is intrinsically motivated, self-generating, and ongoing. It may or may not begin with a plan, and it may or may not end with a finished product. It is under the child's direction and control; therefore, like the child, it is *difficult* to assess and impossible to measure.

Play is active and self-absorbing. A child may play alone or she may invite peers into her play world. As she plays, the child uses physical and creative energy to construct or dramatize a play theme. The process involves initiative, planning, problem solving, and when peers are involved, cooperation.

At times, play can be a *less active* but equally absorbing experience. A little girl chooses to play in a discovery center. She becomes fascinated by a mother mouse and her new litter of ten babies. The child begins to identify with the mother: busy, protective, alert. Every now and then the little girl stops watching the mother and attempts to count the babies. When her finger gets too close to the mouse heap, mother mouse gets upset and flitters around. Sensing the mother's anxiety, the sensitive child momentarily backs away. After a while, she continues her vigil, watching in quiet fascination. She'll remember the experience later that day. She will recall details that suggest her level of concentration; patterns of behavior, the mother's attentiveness to her babies, the size of the babies. The child has had a *personal* and *pleasant* experience that has significantly enriched her life.

Play enables children to interact in positive, meaningful ways that connect and bond child to child. When the little girl tires of her mouse vigil, she shifts her attention to playmates. Joining friends in a housekeeping center, the child redirects her focus to a dramatic play theme already in progress. In a brief period of time, the whole *gamut* of human relations may be dramatized by the child/actor—a child/mother scolds a peer/kitten for spilling milk on a clean floor. A child/father reminds a peer/child to get busy and stop fussing. Two little ponies in an open field frolic and giggle unabashedly in a secure world of make-believe that is momentarily unaffected by right and wrong, yes and no, and the many conflicting messages of childhood.

Play enables children to *define* and *express* themselves. When children role-play, they pretend to be something or someone that has particular meaning to them, adding their own impressions to their characterizations. The fairy is good or bad depending on the child's perception and feeling about fairies. As children engage in dramatic play, they make rules to fit an occasion. They employ strategies that *sustain* play and *reinforce* their perceptions of how things ought to be. They decide how a plot is to be structured and carried out. If necessary, they promote and defend their feelings by using language *inventively* and *imaginatively*. In the process of role-playing, children become skillful at negotiating and manipulating a theme in order to maintain their position. They learn to listen and relate to conversation. They learn to use language, an important dimension of dramatic play. They become socially adept, because friends are part of their play world. They become resourceful because, without impromptu props and inventiveness, a play theme may not progress.

Play requires *preparation* and *innovativeness.* Children need to gather materials and make decisions about the use of space and the friends who will occupy it. Children will spend a great deal of time setting up a play theme. Preparing for dramatic play can become a *consummate* undertaking requiring considerable fore-thought and organization. Selecting a theme, assigning roles, and choosing props requires agreement among the players. (Children don't think of play items as props—they create an environment by using things that connote an image and impression that is very real to them.) In play themes, children move from background to foreground as they test their play powers. Play validates childhood as a time to:

- Express, to act on and to engage in unconditional fantasy;
- Enjoy all of the wonders and challenges of childhood;
- Try on and try out being "me";
- Find out about others;
- Take risks, reach out, and experience autonomy even if things don't always work and even if people don't always cooperate;
- Be free from external rules;
- Investigate and discover;
- Be autonomous;
- Make choices and exercise decision making;
- Open imagination and thinking, stretch boundaries, and claim one's self as a unique and special person.

WHAT IS PLAY?

Playful behavior is identified with *voluntary, self-generated* entertainment that holds the attention of a young child. Although at the initial stages of pretend play, children appear unfocused and disorganized, in reality they are *preparing* for play. They are play/working as they gather and define a play theme. Young children do not distinguish between play and work. Most of their efforts require busy, indus-trious work and attention to a task at hand. A child works when he connects tracks, when he peals apples, and when he moves large blocks from one area to another. He works at negotiating roles and on making agreements that clarify the rules of play at the moment of decision making.

If play is a child's work, a definition of play should include the concept of *play/ work.* When children perceive themselves as both *players* and *taskmasters* (getting the job done), they do not need incentives. It is only when work is construed as unpleasant or unwanted that children develop negative connotations and attitudes. According to Catherine Garvey, play has the following characteristics:

1. Play is pleasurable, enjoyable. Even when not actually accompanied by signs of mirth, it is still positively valued by the player.
2. Play has no extrinsic goals. Its motivations are intrinsic and serve no other objectives. In fact, it is more an enjoyment of means than an effort devoted to some particular end. In utilitarian terms, it is inherently unproductive.
3. Play is spontaneous and voluntary. It is not obligatory but is freely chosen by the player.
4. Play involves some active engagement on the part of the player.
5. Play has certain relations to what is not play.[1]

The last characteristic of play, Garvey notes, is the most intriguing and challenging one. The similarities between play and nonplay activities, i.e., interrupting play by chasing someone or making fun of someone, make it virtually impossible to arrive at a working definition of play. Similarly, Brian Sutton-Smith talks about the *salutary* nature of solitary play: a pleasureful dimension of play that may be more wholesome than social play, a form of play that does not fit into standard categories.[2] For example, a child who exhibits quiet pleasure while spending time alone is expressing an *inner* dimension of herself that is at once fulfilling and growth-enhancing.

PLAY PATTERNS

Children tend to progress from *simple* levels of sensori-motor, object-centered play to *complex* levels of fantasy, imagination-centered play. The development of play corresponds to children's physical, maturational, and experiential levels of development. Most researchers agree with Jean Piaget's classification of play as incorporating increasingly complex levels of interaction; practice (sensorimotor), constructive, symbolic, and games-with-rules.[3] In contemporary environments, these categories will be adjusted to reflect present-day childhood experiences, maturation levels, and preferences.

Practice (Early) Play

A child at the beginning stages of play (ages one to two) is learning about his world through direct contact. He is learning the fundamentals of play by manipulating objects and repeating actions. He runs around the room, stops to observe something, and moves quickly on to something else. Moments of observation lengthen as children begin to *investigate* and *manipulate* objects. They gradually become familiar with names, shapes, properties, and textures. They begin to *discriminate,* grouping like objects together.

A two-year-old carries a cardboard block, enjoying its bigness. He finds another cardboard block, putting one down and stacking the other on top. Two lead to three—the construct takes on a shape that pleases the child. He goes back for more blocks. At some point, he may run a toy car through an opening in the block arrangement. The opening becomes a tunnel. Blocks have now become objects for *extended,* more interesting modes of play. Piaget refers to this functional level of exploratory play as practice play.[4] It is motivated by a child's *innate curiosity* and *need to manipulate* and *master objects.* What the child sees, he wants. At this *self-centered,* self-preoccupied level of development, cooperative play is not critical to a child's play space and play needs. Children act and react *spontaneously* because their level of thinking, of perceiving cause-and-effect relationships, is still at a basic level.

When young children play, they are not concerned with goals' there is no rehearsed script and no "practice makes perfect" reminders. There is, however, *a need to identify with and control* the surrounding play space. This requires freedom of movement *within* safe boundaries and interesting toys to manipulate, to climb on, and to pull or push around. It also requires open space for physical movement and alert adults to monitor children's active and unpredictable play patterns.

As observation and awareness levels increase, the young child becomes intrigued with the size and function of familiar household objects. A broom, a brush, or a hair roller becomes the focus of attention. Initially, a little girl imitates her mom: sweeping the kitchen floor, brushing and curling her doll's hair. Gradually, the objects take on an *extended,* more symbolic meaning. They become objects of pretend play. As the young child continues to expand her imagination, she is *empowered* by the possibilities inherent in *symbolic play:* the use of familiar objects to represent something else.

Parallel Play

Children enjoy observing and imitating the actions of peers at play—filling, dumping, and endlessly arranging and rearranging objects within reach. At some point, an observing child becomes a *participating* child. He is fascinated by the activity and wants to get into the act—by adding something to a simple construct, he makes bigger piles and gains peer approval. This, however, is still a relatively immature level of interaction that occurs spontaneously and is not readily sustained. Young children have short attention spans and even less patience. They do not share easily and they do not like to be pushed around. Nor can they be counted on to sustain moments of cooperative behavior.

The developmental level of most young children precludes meaningful relationships with playmates. There are, however, young children who can interact effectively with peers. These are children who are acclimated and socially adjusted to groups at early ages. A young two-year-old, for example, can call a friend by name, follow a friend around, learn minimal rules of play and enjoy feelings of friendship. She is already in the process of practicing moral standards that have been taught by families and teachers. She can, for example, show empathy when a peer is hurt and even give up a treasured toy—at least for a little while. She is learning about appropriate and inappropriate behavior through experiential exchanges with playmates. She instinctively knows that more can be gained through cooperation than through physical encounters. There are clearly social advantages to early group experiences that use constructive play as a *means* for *social* and *moral* development. Therefore, a teacher should not be limited by a parallel play mindset (a two-year-old simply cannot play cooperatively) when her children clearly demonstrate interest in playmates and in pro-social behavior.

Children are very impressionable and often will act the way they are expected to act. If a teacher *promotes* and *models* cooperation, children can become sociable and surprisingly empathetic toward peers at a very young age. If a teacher models and practices love and kindness, children will move closer together, enjoying the warmth of friendship. This is a wonderful way to begin an out-of-home child-care experience. Moreover, it is an *essential* pathway toward social consciousness and a multinational identity.

Associative, Cooperative Play

As children invent stories and imaginary games and as they become more adept with language, children become less dependent on objects for satisfaction and more attracted to peers. The pretend skits that children begin to act out at a very simple level are enhanced by the presence and interaction with playmates. As children experience cooperative interaction, they are learning social skills naturally. Early peer play requires some degree of reciprocity and cooperation. Children need to communicate their ideas effectively enough to hold playmate's attention; they begin to use language expressively and persuasively.

> As pretense becomes more social, its structural characteristics become more differentiated. Children discuss the activities they and others will enact. Their role characterizations are richly detailed, although not always enacted. In their themes, the possible and the impossible are juxtaposed, with each receiving its due. . . .[5]

Children's pretend play peaks around the ages of four and five years. They become more and more sophisticated in the way they apply themselves to a task at hand, particularly in their inventive use of language, objects, and props. As children engage in higher levels of fantasy (around six or seven years of age), they depend less on objects and use language and body movements to represent an absent prop.[6]

The pretend play of preschool children in child care centers may be categorized generally as constructive play (playing with blocks and manipulatives) or dramatic play (role-playing in a dramatic play center). Most activities fall in one of these categories.

Constructive Play

A favorite activity of preschool children is constructing with blocks and manipulatives. Some children enjoy playing alone during constructive play but most tend to play in partnership with peers. A construct (assembling parts) is an elaborate undertaking for a child. He must make decisions, experiment with space and with design. Sometimes a child will have a plan before he starts building, but more often a construct grows under a child's control and imagination. As a project expands, imagination expands. Lincoln logs are used as a rocket launcher, a paper towel roll as the body of a spaceship, and marbles symbolize shooting stars.

Children who engage in cooperative play are increasingly aware of what each one can contribute to a pretend theme. They are willing to listen to ideas and to adjust their play themes to accommodate others. When children plan and play cooperatively, they generally experience a successful outcome. Within moments a freestanding object becomes a launching pad for dramatic play—a spaceship is airborne, props are added; a cube becomes food for the astronauts; and a yellow bristle block becomes a light beam that guides the ship while in flight.

Dramatic Play

When children play together in a pretend mode, they are engaging in dramatic play. By changing costumes, children change their identity; a frog prince becomes a growling, hungry lion, a swan becomes a princess. Children borrow ideas for role-playing from real-life experiences, cultural trends, television, literature, and from peers. In dramatic play, girls tend to favor nurturing roles: mothers, grandmothers, or little purring kittens. Boys tend to favor action roles that often involve larger-than-life figures and rough-and-tumble play. If they agree to be animals, boys would probably choose one that symbolizes strength and dominance such as a lion or a panther. Role preferences, however, are becoming less discernible in contemporary learning environments and should be discretely discouraged in early childhood environments. In contemporary child care settings, dramatic play centers are arranged to attract boys and block centers are arranged to attract girls. The choice of play areas, however, is determined not by the teacher, but by the child's interests.

The toys and novelty items that a teacher selects for dramatic play will influence children's play choices. One study indicated that significantly higher themes and richer fantasy were elicited by minimally structured materials at kindergarten through second grade levels than were elicited by highly structured toys.[7] Minimally structured toys might include drawing paper, paints, play-dough, wooden blocks, cardboard cartons, pipe cleaners, rag dolls, and costumes. Highly structured toys might include "plastic molds or cutters for use with play-dough, a service station, a metal dollhouse, Barbie dolls, G.I. Joe [figures], and specific outfits for them—a nurse's uniform, a bride's dress, an army uniform, and an astronaut's suit."[8] In another study, four- and five-year-old children were observed using a toy phone, puppets, and stuffed animals more often in social pretend play than such items as puzzles, Legos, small blocks, and coloring materials.[9]

To function independently in dramatic play, children need to become self-managers and industrious participants. Unrehearsed dramatic play demands language facility, a point of view (I think, or, why don't we), planning, and cooperation. Children must be able to communicate well enough to interact with peers and must have reached a level of maturity that enables them to function independently for long periods of time. Anxious to play, children recognize that they must *reconcile* differences and reach accommodation or they will lose their friends to an activity across the room. A play theme may be inspired by a favorite fairy tale, by a favorite television show or movie, by a field trip, or by a holiday such as Halloween. It may be a reenactment of typical family situations—a child gets sick and goes to the doctor, a mother and daughter dress for the theatre, a husband and wife go shopping or fishing, and, of course, everybody goes to the supermarket. Often children will replay the same theme over and over, changing roles to add variety.

Children become amazingly facile in dramatic play. They button, snap, and improvise with aplomb. They combine objects that are functionally related (cups and saucers) and transform objects into inventive combinations that have meaning only to the child at play (a carpet square becomes a sailboat). For the imaginative child at play, *what is real is pretend and what is pretend is real.* As inanimate objects take on new meaning, children's imaginations soar. Noise levels increase to reflect play themes (children can't play in quiet voices). From time to time, communication becomes argumentative and challenging. In pretend play, children have to stand up for themselves—there is no one to solve their problems, but they instinctively know there is always someone to take their place. A child in the background may be an eager and ready understudy.

Prancing in high heels, pushing a stroller, and carrying a shopping bag require agility as well as imagination. Children extend themselves to "fill the shoes they are wearing." Friends become an extended version of self as the child moves from "me" to "we." Children's dramatizations are not unlike real-life drama. One of the reasons dramatic play is so valuable to children's development is because they get to practice being grown up. They get to express themselves *without inhibition* and *constraints.* They experience *being free* and *independent,* and they love their sense of importance.

Sociodramatic Play

Dramatic play becomes sociodramatic when children engage in cooperative theme building. To engage in higher levels of pretend play, children must have some awareness of plot structure and narrative development. They must be able to reconstruct experiences in order to use language to express ideas and characterizations. They must be able to *negotiate* with one another to determine the progression of a plot or theme. As children communicate through cooperative interaction, they develop extensive language facility. They react to each experience internally as they formulate ideas (speech-to-self) and externally as they select or invent words to express their thoughts (oral language). In his impressive research on learning, Vygotsky emphasized language as a cognitive-social tool developed through both private speech and oral communication.[10] Language serves a definite purpose in dramatic play. It facilitates comprehension, communication, and self-confidence. At its best (gaining a peer's attention and approval), it allows a child to feel successful.

In sociodramatic play, children draw from a wide variety of resources and interests. They must be able to engage in thematic fantasy play (enter into a pretend play space), role-play (I am Beauty.), make believe with playmates (I know! You be the Beast) and with objects (This can be your magic ring.), reenact remembered experiences, use language, engage in symbolic substitution (a pipe cleaner becomes a magic ring), and persist in role-playing so a plot can be played out without a great deal of disruption or confusion.[11]

Some researchers believe children should be trained in sociodramatic play. Extensive research conducted by Sara Smilansky (1990) supports the importance of teaching children how to play. She believes that pretend play can be promoted by training and exposure to direct experiences such as a teacher participating in dramatic play, or by exposing children to experiences that facilitate role-playing. Smilansky's findings indicate that adult participation is particularly effective when working with underprivileged, environmentally impoverished children. In her pioneering research with Israeli children in 1968, Smilansky found that socially disadvantaged children rarely exhibited social pretend play because, unlike in middle-class homes, such play was not modeled or encouraged by adults.[12] As important as these findings are, they must be kept in perspective. Children will often stop playing or become inhibited when an adult is present or intervening in a child's space.

Games with Rules

As children engage in higher levels of thinking (ages 6 to 11) and as they become more socially cognizant, they enjoy playing games that are skill oriented and physically challenging as well as competitive in nature. When children engage in competitive play, they are building intellectual, social, and personal skills. They are strategizing and learning to think logically in order to win a game or win others to their position. Competitive play may be challenging and enjoyable, but in excess, it can become unhealthy for children who identify themselves as winners or losers. Children who measure their popularity by success in competitive peer play are frequently disappointed by outcomes. They rarely can be satisfied when winning means holding on to one's position and losing means adjusting to an ego-deflating situation (I didn't win, I never win!).

A major developmental task of this age is the internalization of conscience and an increasing awareness of moral conduct and codes that regulate behavior.[13] Fairness and following rules become an *absolute* condition for participating in group games and for being expelled from group games. Teachers in child-care environments find it beneficial to encourage school-age children toward cooperative play with fewer rules as a way of encouraging pro-social behavior and avoiding altercations. They also look for alternative ways for children to develop and practice affective behavior rather than competitive, goal-oriented behavior—forming community or service-oriented clubs; tutoring peers; collecting and distributing food; scout groups; forming a drama club, a tutoring club or a "friends of the community" club.

THE ROLE OF COMPETITION IN CHILDREN'S PLAY

At early childhood levels, competition is a difficult issue for educators to grapple with. Competition is a *natural* part of living, learning, and working together. Cooperative play becomes contentious when children compete for the same toy, when they push and pinch to be first in line, and when they manipulate board games so they win. In every group, there are children who demonstrate aggressive, argumentative behavior, particularly when they are playing with minimal or inadequate supervision. When a situation works against these children—when they are challenged or don't get their way, they often become sullen, negative, or even hostile toward peers and adults. Lacking objectivity and unable to take the perspective of others, these children are easily frustrated and, from the teacher's perspective, frustrating to work with. As time goes on, an aggressively competitive child is not a favorite playmate and not readily accepted by a group.

Unhealthy competition at early childhood levels is not compatible with a cooperative interaction approach to teaching and learning. It can best be discouraged by training young children in pro-social behavior at the earliest levels of development when values and attitudes are shaping. It also can be discouraged by: selecting toys that nurture children; prohibiting negative influences such as violent, aggressive, or adult-oriented television programs; playing directly with aggressive children in ways that model appropriate behavior; avoiding practices that promote negative behavior such as requiring children to stand in line, sit at a table, or sit in circle for long periods of time; avoiding activities that generate competitiveness such as board games or winner/loser outdoor games; encouraging children toward choices; offering enough toys and materials to encourage cooperative play; and by working in partnership with parents.

At school-age levels, competition is generally accepted as a fact of life. Some forms of competition are construed as unattractive while others are respected. Demanding, controlling children who define themselves by their accomplishments are not pleasant to be around. On the other hand, children who train to excel in a skill or a sport or in positive leadership roles are respected as are children who strive for good grades, and especially those who have to work for them.

Competition tends to devalue creative, original thinking (important dimensions of play/work and self-expression). Competitive children are often into stereotypical attention-getting modes of behavior that define activities and peers as acceptable or unacceptable, i.e., "Drama is sissy," "Jazz is for girls," or "Why do you want to play with her?" With set-in attitudes and biases, children become intolerant toward anything (or anyone) that does not fit their model. During the elementary school years, when peer identification is at its height, these children not only command a following but become even more opinionated and empowering because of their new-found popularity. They no longer have to compete for attention: They have become role models. They are leaders who should not, but do, command attention and respect.

A center can model and reinforce healthy, growth-enhancing competition in a school-age group by hiring staff who have the qualities we are seeking in children—individuals who can counsel, challenge, and influence children's attitudes and behaviors.

DEVELOPMENTAL ADVANTAGES OF A PLAY CURRICULUM

Play and Cognition

Pretend play symbolizes a gradual change in a child's thinking processes from concrete operations to abstract levels of reasoning. To make the transition from simple stages of pretend play to more elaborate forms of pretend play, a child must be able to consolidate knowledge and replicate (or reproduce) reality. She must have acquired a mental image of the appearance and function of objects in order to find substitutes. A child demonstrates mental growth when she combs a doll's hair with an object that represents a comb, pushes a block and pretends it is a car, or pours pretend tea into a small cup. She is recalling objects, their functions and using them imaginatively.

A child's play patterns tend to correspond with her level of mental functioning, experience, and awareness. A young child benefits from the use of familiar objects in pretend play. When a two-year-old is given a realistic cup and toy horse to play with, she has little difficulty getting into a pretend mode. If a less realistic object is substituted for one of the objects, pretense drops slightly. If less realistic substitutes are provided, pretense decreases markedly. For a more mature child, however, there is less need to use realistic objects in play. The child can recreate familiar images from memory by using (or not using) the unrealistic objects at hand.[14]

From playing with familiar objects, such as a toy telephone, or tea cups, children begin to expand their play patterns into more complex arrangements (making a space station with Tinkertoys). In the process, they plan, organize, improvise, manipulate, assemble, and solve problems—"I need a longer stick, you need a spoke . . . here, you give me yours and I'll give you mine." They become enterprising and goal-oriented when an idea begins to develop into a project. Children who begin to expand their creative play are motivated by their own initiative, curiosity, sense of autonomy, and sense of accomplishment.

At a more advanced stage of development, children no longer need concrete objects to trigger imagination. They can symbolize their identification of objects by gesturing; the child waves a pretend wand or waves his arms rhythmically to symbolize flying. They are engaging in mental playfulness.

Play stimulates mental development. It is particularly important during the early years when children's language and thinking processes are developing.

Through exploration and imaginative play, children form impressions and under-standings about their world. Mental playfulness generates a desire for continued learning. In her book, *Ideas Influencing Early Childhood Education,* Evelyn Weber writes:

> Play is a child's way of making sense out of the world. The child's active manipulation of objects, his repeated activity with people and things, leads to a growing awareness that objects have properties, and that they can be viewed along different dimensions. Through continual use of materials—lifting, sort-ing, arranging, building—the child comes to note similarities and differences, to work out his own imagery.[15]

Play and Creativity

When children play spontaneously, they are creating from new perspectives and new levels of awareness. Sometimes, a child at play will reenact real-life experi-ences and interests; a doll is a baby brother or sister, a stuffed animal a real pet, steps an escalator, a box a car. Other times, a child will create plots that are highly original and not readily identifiable. They will reenact favorite stories, such as Cinderella and Peter Pan, changing story lines, adding characters, and embellish-ing plots with childlike fantasy and humor. As children mature in their play, their levels of thinking and imagination become more elaborate, more abstract, and more skillful.

Children bring their individuality to every play experience. Within minutes, children at play can create something from nothing using odds and ends in resourceful and innovative ways. The level of intensity that generates creative play suggests a need not only to express but to control and transform an environment. Nothing is fixed in creative play; children constantly sort through and select items while they set up a play scene.

Divergent (open-ended) thinking is identified with creativity. Flexible original thinking automatically accompanies spontaneous play. A child absorbed in play uses improvisation and forethought to accomplish immediate goals. Concerns (something that doesn't fit or match a child's expectation) necessitate problem solving and creative solutions. A child at play must clothe and equip herself according to the character she is playing; she must find a way to fasten oversized garments, to negotiate for an item she needs, and to manage her role within a very short time. While she is busy at her tasks, her playmates are also scurrying for favorite dress-ups. A frenetic atmosphere prevails when children get ready for dramatic play.

Preparing for dramatic play is an all-consuming, challenging experience for a young child. A setting must correspond to a theme. With few materials available, a child must be inventive in the way she selects and arranges play objects. When setting a table, a child will use what is available and create the rest. A small basket filled with acorns, "borrowed" from a science center, becomes a centerpiece. The child hurriedly makes place mats and places dolls in appropriate sitting arrangements. Some objects are realistic and some bear only a slight resemblance to known objects. Her thinking is open-ended; a sense of freedom and excitement enables the child to think and act intuitively, to become her character.

Children use their senses imaginatively and inventively as they play. Sensory awareness is essential to the creative process. As they pretend play, children taste, smell, and listen. Dinner is served, coffee is poured, and the baby is crying for a bottle. They select from dress-up fabrics that please and attract them—feathers, lace, fur, leather, velvet. They become familiar with textures as they physically interact with materials.

Sensory stimulation through pretend play is equally important to school-age children. Children who rarely get to experience their artistic culture or to express feelings of creativity are missing a vital dimension of child development. They are unwilling or unable to express themselves in novel and original ways that enhance their development. Unchallenged by literature and the arts, these children experience a cultural vacuum and a personal loss that may never be filled.

Elliot Eisner asserts that by neglecting the arts in American education, we are depriving children of sensory experiences that are vital to intellectual and creative development. "Sensory forms of representation found in such activities as poetry, the visual arts, music, and dance can provide the conceptual basis for meaning that will be represented later in the oral and written language codes."[16]

Play and Personal Development

Watching a young child engaged in pretend play is like watching a home movie that is filled with little vignettes of movement and expression passing before one's eyes too fast to be absorbed. Energetic whirlwind movements, emotive chatter, and a wonderful sense of aliveness radiates from children's play.

The child at play is expressing an inner world; a real, unedited script that portrays the child/actor. Where do children get their scripts? Mostly, children act out what they have experienced and what they are familiar with. When children play, they can cause things to happen or change things. They can express moods and emotions that are inside, feelings that suddenly may be triggered by play. Expression is a form of release especially when it comes spontaneously from the child at play.

Play promotes confidence and self-validation. A child is better able to express her ideas and feelings in nonthreatening pro-social settings than in group-controlled settings. She can practice and validate the standards of behavior that are expected in her real world. She can care for a kitten, rock a baby to sleep, iron a scarf, and set a table with an unlikely combination of food. She can schedule an appointment, make a shopping list, clean the house, and make dinner before going to the office. She can become a homemaker, a career woman, and if she wants to, she can turn herself into a fairy godmother. Everything is possible during dramatic play when children are free to be themselves and express themselves in a pretend world.

Playful people are able to find fulfilling interests and hobbies throughout their lifetimes. They are self-motivated and rarely bored. This is borne out when, at the age eighty, a woman gathers tiny shells or pine cones, imagining an arrangement that reflects her nature and continuing desire to create. The fingers may not be as nimble as they once were but the imagination is still in full gear. Originality and imagination are shaped in childhood. Creativity challenges a person to move beyond conventional levels of thought, to open and travel the corridors that lead to a fulfilling life.

Play and Social Development

Pretend play promotes social interaction. As children observe peers at play, they are attracted by feelings of companionship. A child pulls a friend in a wagon all the way to Disneyland. Other children are patiently waiting to get on board. Pretend tickets are passed out and gas is needed. The adventure grows. The lead child derives pleasure from the attention he is getting from peers and his sense of importance. He works harder, exerting more and more physical energy.

Nearby, two friends are swinging side-by-side looking for interesting cloud images. Some clouds look like huge, threatening animals while others look like peaceful, soft pillows. The two friends feel a sense of intimacy that is like sharing a secret.

As children progress in cooperative play experiences, they become inventive. A small rug may become a magic carpet and a scarf a distant mountain top, hand-painted by little gnomes. As children mature, they are less bound by gender and are willing to try multiple roles in dramatizations. In creative environments that support imaginative play, children are less inhibited in their choice of roles and characters—they are willing to step beyond stereotypical casting that makes a flower a girl or a tree a boy. Less bound by conventionality, a boy may become an Annie and a girl a Peter Pan.

Maturation affects the quality of children's pretend play. Children who are socially mature are capable of sustained levels of play. Little, if any, teacher intervention is required when children are playing positively and cooperatively. Without cooperation, however, feelings get hurt. In some instances, a teacher may need to intervene on a child's behalf. She may have to help children get a plot underway, and she may have to oversee its progress until children are able to sustain cooperative play.

Play and Movement

Children at play are extremely active, developing muscle control, refining motor skills, practicing eye–hand coordination. Through movement, they recognize

> . . . their position in space, their relationship to the space around them, and the relationship between three-dimensional and two-dimensional space. They develop a sense of laterality (two-sidedness) and dominance (one side is the

dominant side) and kinesthesia (knowing the location of a part of the body in relation to space and other external stimuli). They refine other skills such as large- and small-muscle control, eye–hand coordination, and the increasing ability to change the focus of eyes from near to far or from far to near.[17]

As children play, they become aware of themselves in relation to their physical environment. They use their bodies resourcefully to claim their play space and, if necessary, to change their play space. They become skillful and adept at negotiating space and managing themselves in many different settings—a small loft, a large activity center. Teachers who allow children to make choices and move freely within their environment are promoting both mental and physical development. Early childhood educator, Clare Cherry writes:

> Children's entire orientation to the world develops through movement. Through play, their understanding of the world is enhanced. Wholesome play involves movement of all kinds. It provokes the reception of accompanying sensory information and brings about an awareness of feelings and thoughts. Every action of a child at play relates to learning, self-image, self-awareness, and self-esteem.[18]

Large- and small-motor play releases energy, develops coordination, and empowers children with a sense of accomplishment. A simple trike ride or a walk on a balance beam engenders both skill and imagination in children. A child uses his hands to assemble manipulatives, to hammer a nail into wood, to pound dough, to play a drum, and to finger paint. He uses his imagination to transform a simple activity into a creative experience. For the child at play, motor skills are rarely divided into small- and large-motor categories. The child who is in constant motion uses his total body when he plays. In order to master movement and skills, he needs both defined and open play parameters.

Specific motor skills can best be developed through teacher-initiated activities such as tumbling, cutting and pasting, bar work, rhythm and movement activities, follow-me games, and so on. The frequency and range of physical activities children are exposed to will affect their large- and small-motor development. The manner in which teachers initiate and present activities will influence a child's degree of participation. (See Table 10–1.)

Play and Special Needs

Play can facilitate confidence and self-esteem in children with special needs. The therapeutic and self-affirming aspects of play provide unique learners a secure environment that is self-paced and extremely reinforcing. Children with an emotional, social, or physical impairment require individualized attention before they can be mainstreamed into a normal day-care environment, and they will need special consideration thereafter. Teachers must be sensitive to developmental differences through nurturing exchanges.

TABLE 10-1 Play: From Infancy to Age Five

Age	General Development	Social Play	Physical Play	Cognitive Play	Age-appropriate Toys	What You Can Do
Infants to 18 Months	■ Major advancements in physical development (walking) ■ Major developments in language (talking) ■ Is learning about the world, especially through taste and sight	■ Plays alone and with no regard to other babies ■ Laughs during play ■ Enjoys looking at self in mirror ■ Peek-a-boo and pat-a-cake are favorite games	■ Baby is gaining control of body: crawling, standing, trying to walk ■ Follows the movements of objects with eyes ■ Hits, holds, and drops objects ■ Baby is exploring her environment	■ Baby repeats banging and sucking movements ■ Imitates sounds and facial expressions ■ Learning characteristics of toys ■ Baby plays with one toy at a time and can control it	■ Rattles and mobiles ■ Bars to hold onto when learning to walk ■ Pots to bang ■ Mirrors ■ Water toys and soft blocks (with holes) ■ Light ball between 8" and 24" in diameter ■ Plastic containers	■ Give baby lots of crawling room ■ Spend time playing with baby ■ Provide different types of sensory stimulation ■ Facilitate baby's self-awareness with mirror and peek-a-boo games
18 Months to 3 Years	■ This age group is *very* curious ■ Walking is a new means of independence and a great way to explore everything ■ Experimentation with the joys of language—especially the word *no* ■ Temper tantrums	*Parallel play:* ■ Children play with similar toys—like pails in the sand—but don't interact while playing ■ Play on their own ■ Will not share toys ■ May take toys from others	■ Stands, walks, and turns pages of a book ■ Uses large and small muscles ■ Kicks and rolls a ball, pulls a wagon, and rides a small trike or big wheels ■ Chases other children	*Functional play:* ■ Child's play is thought through—ordering, gathering, and dumping objects/materials ■ Children use *more* than one toy at a time ■ Trying out new roles and situations through fantasy play ■ Pretend themes	■ Balls ■ Books with cloth pages ■ Toy phones ■ Wagons ■ Beads to thread ■ Unit blocks ■ Play corner and simple play props	■ Encourage children to play together ■ Allow children to make *choices* about what they wish to play with ■ Provide lots of small and gross motor toys ■ Encourage children to play out fantasies

Age	Social/Emotional	Play Type	Physical/Motor	Materials	Teacher Strategies
3 to 4 Years	■ Like to please adults ■ Very independent and begin to assert independence ■ Still some tantrums and the need to say "no!" ■ Interested in other children	■ *Associative play:* Children play together, talk to each other while playing, and engage in a common play activity ■ Play intentions are still different ■ Sharing is still a difficult behavior	■ Children like to balance and tiptoe ■ Love moving to music rhythmically ■ Climbing steps and small ladders ■ Kicking a ball, and catching a large ball are favorite activities ■ Jumping is fun	■ *Constructive play:* The child builds structures ■ Uses materials such as blocks, paints, and clay to make things ■ Children engage in pretend play—taking on the role of a familiar person such as mom or dad	■ Dress-up props of familiar people for dramatic play ■ Unit blocks, duplo blocks, and snap blocks ■ Balance beams and slide and ladder structures ■ Play-dough, crayons, sand ■ Dolls	■ Encourage children to experiment with creative materials ■ Allow children to make choices ■ Encourage and support fantasy play ■ Allow lots of physical activity
4 to 5 Years	■ Ask lots of questions ■ Children at this age are extremely egocentric—they view things only from *their* perspective ■ Imaginary friends are big with this age group ■ Very active; often destructive	■ *Cooperative play:* Children play with others and can wait their turn ■ Three or more children play together ■ Sharing is a common behavior ■ Children may have a common play goal	■ Enjoy chasing games and obstacle courses ■ Ride small bikes with training wheels ■ Can button shirts and tie shoes ■ Skip, hop, run, skip rope, and do puzzles	■ Involvement in constructive play more than 50 percent of the time ■ Role-playing is based on more complex and less familiar people and situations (often based on fiction such as superheroes, ghosts, etc.) ■ Complex structures are built (blocks, clay)	■ Blocks, Legos, sand, water, and wood work ■ A bike with training wheels and scooters ■ Climbing structures ■ Fantasy play props ■ Tape recorders and muscial instruments ■ Puzzles and dolls	■ Use props and stories to encourage fantasy play ■ Avoid sex-role stereotyping in fantasy play ■ Help children share and take turns ■ Provide choices rather than "you must"

Source: From PRE-K TODAY, Issues from 1987 and 1988. Copyright © 1987, 1988 by Scholastic Inc. Reprinted by permission of Scholastic Inc. All rights reserved.

A reinforcing, play-oriented environment will benefit *all* children. Nothing is more soothing than a sandbox, a water table, or an easel set up with fresh, inviting paints. Nothing is more reinforcing than children feeling accepted and loved as they are. In a nonthreatening atmosphere, children cease to look on one another as different. If anything, children will extend themselves to protect playmates whom they perceive as vulnerable and less able to perform age-level tasks.

HOW TEACHERS CULTIVATE PLAY

Observing Children's Play

Even though there is great potential for learning through play, a teacher must avoid the tendency to "teach" children at play by intruding unnecessarily on children's play, by structuring environments, or by monitoring outcomes. Reasons for intervention might include: helping children organize a play theme, stepping in when a situation gets out of hand, or helping a child with limited-play skills feel comfortable in a play group. At two to three years old, children need considerable guidance and reinforcement during free-play experiences. Even though young children need help in making choices, adults should encourage independence and decision making. At four to five years old, children perceive play as primarily a socially and self-motivated experience that does not require the same degree of adult guidance, although reinforcement and praise are always important. J. Schic-kedanz cautions teachers about overinvolvement in dramatic play:

> Adults who are sensitive partners in children's play never stay involved for long, unless children truly need them to fill a role that sustains the play. While playing, we must allow children to take the lead in directing the play. The play must fulfill the children's purposes, not our preconceived notions of what we think should be taught.[19]

Acculturating Children Through Play

Teachers should promote a "one world, many friends" concept that children can imitate in play experiences. The way a child talks to dolls, animals, or friends reveals a great deal about the child and her earlier experiences. Without emphasizing differences, teachers should sensitize children to special needs as a universal given; we all have special needs but some of us need a little more help and attention than others: Some of us don't have enough to eat, some of us don't have a place to sleep, some of us don't have clothes, some of us can't speak, some of us can't walk, and some of us don't have a mommy or a daddy. How can we help one another? Yes, by being a friend. How could we help a child in a wheel chair? a child on crutches? a child who drools? a child wearing a helmet to protect his head? How could we help a child who has trouble sitting still or who can't understand our language . . . a child who has no one to play with? When a child can project her personality and feelings toward others who are in some way different, she is experiencing empathy.

Creating a Play Environment

Teachers should provide structured and unstructured materials for children to increase their interest in play centers. They should add items that inspire imagination and sensual pleasure: scarves, feathers, soft items, curiosity items, and unusual items. Teachers should also change the themes in activity centers from time to time so that children can experience many different materials.

Teachers should provide interesting activity centers for children's enjoyment. There should be several activities to choose from: arts and crafts, painting, modeling, water play, sand play, dramatic play, block play. Teachers should permit children freedom to manipulate their environment. They should permit children to move and rearrange objects that enhance a play theme. Art and science items, books and puzzles, blocks, musical instruments, a tape recorder, and real animals can become important additions to a dramatic play center. If children are responsible for returning each item to "its spot," a teacher can be flexible in the degree of freedom she extends to children during a play experience.

Activity centers must grow with children's interests if they are to extend imaginations. A family of ducks may be added to a water table and a picture of a farm scene hung nearby. A block center can be enhanced by a mural, a train set, or by photographs of children at play. Boxes may be added to dramatic play centers and a tape recorder to a listening center. Something new or something unique will always attract the young child. Children's imaginations will grow when teachers show imagination. (See Table 10–2.)

Promoting Dramatic Play

Teachers should promote dramatic play by providing a creatively rich environment that offers children many opportunities to vary and extend their play themes. Visuals, interesting items, and prop boxes will motivate and enhance children's play. Photographs of ballet shoes, a theatrical mask, a child fishing, or a seasonal theme will stimulate imaginations as will concrete items such as a typewriter, real clothes (for both sexes), and real food boxes. Prop boxes (boxes that contain realistic and imaginative items that are theme-related) that depict familiar experiences for children are wonderful additions to dramatic play in all activity centers. Children love to explore prop boxes that are set up to enhance play themes such as a bank, a farm, an animal hospital, a pet store, a paint store, a hair salon, or a restaurant. A picture of a ballerina, a pair of ballet shoes, an umbrella, a pair of workman's boots, an attaché case, and an interesting quilt will stimulate imagination in a dramatic play center.

TABLE 10–2 Gross-motor Development: From Infancy to Age Five

Physical Development (Ages are approximate.)	Activities that Support Gross-motor Development	Environments that Support Gross-motor Development
Infants to 18-month-olds	Infants to 18-month-olds	Infants to 18-month-olds need:
■ Roll over (3 months)	■ Make noise with a rattle so infant must turn entire body	■ Soft surfaces to cushion frequent falls
■ Lift head and chest (5 months)	■ Encourage infant to stack small foam blocks	■ Large, free, safe surfaces to encourage crawling
■ Sit supported (5 months)	■ Encourage infant to fill container with many objects	■ Mirrors and stimulating safe toys
■ Crawl forward or backward (8 months)	■ Provide social reinforcement to infant's efforts to raise head, roll over, crawl, etc.	■ Mats to crawl and roll on
■ Fill and empty containers (9 months)	■ Spend lots of time playing with infant	■ Hand holds and bars to assist in standing and walking
■ Stand by flexing knees (12 months)	■ Let child get what he or she needs; don't bring everything to the child	■ Foam rubber shapes: cubes, rolls, and ramps
■ Walk alone (13 months)		■ Toys to sit on and move; push-pull toys
■ Walk backward a few steps (18 months)		■ Light balls, 8 to 24 inches in diameter
18-month- to 3-year-olds	18-month- to 3-year-olds	18-month- to 3-year-olds need:
■ Walk up and down stairs	■ Roll balls back and forth	■ Low climbing structures with ramps, steps, and tunnels
■ Jump off one step	■ Provide opportunities for kicking	■ Large balls: plastic, rubber, and foam
■ Throw objects, including balls	■ Provide tape or a chalk line to follow	■ Lots of indoor space
■ Stand on one foot	■ Provide obstacle courses including tunnels and stairs	■ Foam and gym mats; a rocking boat
■ Climb up steps and slide down a slide	■ Provide space and encouragement for lots of running	■ Doll wagons and wheelbarrows
■ Run without falling (2 years)	■ Provide ramps for children to walk and run up and down	■ Foam blocks, ramps, and cylinders
■ Pull wagons	■ Take short walking fieldtrips	■ Cardboard or plastic blocks
■ Kick a ball and catch a large ball (3 years)	■ Play follow the leader to music	■ Safe outdoor playground space

3- to 4-year-olds
- Walk in a straight line without watching feet
- Walk backward
- Run smoothly, avoiding objects
- Stop suddenly and turn sharp corners
- Jump in place; balance on one foot for a few seconds
- Pedal a tricycle with some control
- Climb stairs without holding rails
- Climb jungle gyms

4- to 5-year-olds
- Make U-turns with tricycles
- Catch balls thrown from five feet
- Jump down three or four steps
- Jump rope; hop on one foot
- Have good balance on balance beam
- Hammer nails into wood
- Somersault and roll; pump swings
- Catch a small ball with hands

3- to 4-year-olds
- Play noncompetitive circle games
- Take fieldtrips to parks, nature walks, and hikes
- Play creative movement games to music
- Throw and catch balls and beanbags
- Build and explore obstacle courses together
- Have plenty of free play outside; offer tricycle riding and wagon pulling

4- to 5-year-olds
- Take fieldtrips to parks, greenways, and hiking areas
- Throw and catch large and small balls
- Encourage kicking balls, tumbling, and somersaulting
- Do creative movement activities
- Skip rope as a group and individually
- Do woodworking activities
- Encourage building with boards and hollow and unit blocks
- Provide free play on playground that includes climbing and riding tricycle

3- to 4-year-olds need:
- Wooden blocks: hollow, unit, and nesting (wood is essential)
- Balls: small and large; plastic, rubber, and foam
- Beanbags and tumbling mats
- Tricycles, scooters, and wagons
- Large art brushes for pretending
- Outdoor playground with climbing structures, swings (including swivel swings), balance beams, slides, and tricycle paths
- Indoor gross-motor climbing structures

4- to 5-year-olds need:
- Woodworking bench
- Wooden blocks: hollow, unit, and nesting (wood is critical)
- Balls of different sizes and materials
- Indoor wheeled toys: trucks, tractors, etc.
- Skip ropes, beanbags
- Stacking blocks for outside
- Tumbling mats and foam ramps
- Large, well-equipped playground space
- Tricycles

Source: From PRE—K TODAY, Issues from 1987 and 1988. Copyright © 1987, 1988 by Scholastic Inc. Reprinted by permission of Scholastic Inc. All rights reserved.

Promoting Physical Play

Teachers should provide opportunities for both large- and small-motor development throughout the day. Classrooms should be set up to include trucks, trikes, pull toys, and wooden steps, as well as blocks and small manipulatives. School-age children should have daily opportunities to engage in outdoor sports and large-motor activities as well as indoor recreation that includes table games and free-standing games such as Ping-Pong, bowling, soccer, field hockey, and badminton. Children should have a variety of experiences in creative movement and gymnastics as well (exercise, mat work, dance).

Cultivating Language and Thinking

Creative play enhances communication and thinking skills. Without interfering with the natural flow of language and thinking that accompanies children's natural interactions, teachers can, at appropriate times, encourage these skills. They can encourage language and thinking out-of-doors through music, movement, games, and exploration. Children can chant and dance to nature's rhythm instruments (striking rocks, sticks, or nuts together) and make sand shakers, pod whistles, grass horns). They can make up songs as they swing; they can make up games on a see-saw (naming animals, birds, flowers, vegetables, classmates—staying in an up position until they respond). Teachers can make letters and words in the sand or dirt; they can make observations on nature walks noting and recording insects and tiny animals at play (making tunnels, crawling, flying, jumping, resting, digging, carrying, weaving, singing).

Teachers also can encourage language and thinking during indoor play, using rhyming words as children tumble, go on "Name me" walks (teacher touches object and child names object), and invent new words to familiar childhood tunes. They can encourage children to write their own verse using inventive spelling. They can ask children thought-provoking questions at the end of a session: "What was your favorite activity today?" "I noticed you were Red Riding Hood . . . what were you gathering in the woods?" "Did you visit grandmother's house? . . . was she feeling better? . . . What did you bring her?" "Lucky grandma! . . . Did you remember to lock the door?" A culminating circle after play sessions enables children to retell or recount some (but not all) of their experience.

Becoming a Playful, Creative Person

Teachers must value creativity to promote originality in children. They must look at books in a different way; not only as appealing stories but as catalysts for creative thinking and pretend play. They also must look at music, poetry, drama, and the arts from a teacher/learner artistic perspective: "How can I incorporate these wonderful ideas in my classroom so that children can extend their experiences and their imaginations?"

INTEGRATING PLAY
INTO A CURRICULUM

A play curriculum should promote an atmosphere of: enjoyment, enrichment, expression, and imagination. Teachers can integrate play into a curriculum by:

   1.   Visualizing how basic skills and concepts can be taught through play.

   2.   Selecting themes and units that promote creative play and imagination: a unit on families can be integrated into a drama center through toys and props that show families at work and at play; a unit on community helpers can be integrated into a drama center by setting up themes that interest children (a post office, a firehouse, a library, a hospital, a school); a unit on farm animals can be integrated in a drama center by adding a farm, miniature animals, and other accessories; a unit on Woodland Indians can be integrated into a drama center by making a "long house" out of cardboard boxes, by creating an authentic Indian village, by providing props that depict a farming and hunting community, by setting up an arts and crafts center that includes stitchery, rugmaking, stringing beads, making jewelry, and making authentic Indian food.

   3.   Changing play toys and areas of interest in activity centers to highlight seasons, holidays, and special themes and events.

   4.   Having a specialized teacher in movement or drama visit a class on a weekly basis.

   5.   Developing techniques for simple classroom presentations that encourage children to select parts, to interpret characters, and to speak spontaneously— creating a production that is something like a familiar story or fable.

   6.   Planning fieldtrips to reinforce children's interests: a trip to a zoo, to a nature center, to a firehouse.

   7.   Creating novel play spaces that correspond with classroom themes: a log cabin, an igloo, a cave, a tree house.

   8.   Approaching all learning projects from a play/work perspective that encourages:

   –   Imagination and creativity;
   –   Self-awareness;
   –   Self-expression;
   –   Self-appreciation;
   –   Decision making and risk-taking;
   –   Autonomy and initiative in making choices;
   –   Expressive language;
   –   Social sensitivity;
   –   Divergent, flexible thinking;
   –   Autonomy and independent thinking;
   –   A sense of self-mastery and self-worth;
   –   A creative disposition.

ASSESSING CHILDREN'S PLAY

Teachers should make informal observations about children's play world and play experiences:

- What type of play does the child spend most of his time doing?
- What areas of play seem to make the child uncomfortable?
- Does the child appear to be happy and in control most of the time?
- Can she solve problems and make decisions most of the time?
- Can he take the perspective of others?
- Is the child demonstrating responsibility and initiative?
- Is the child developing healthy values and attitudes?
- Does the child use appropriate behavior and language while playing?
- Is the child communicating effectively with peers?
- Is the child developing social skills?
- Can the child perform basic tasks that are important to a play experience?
- Does he demonstrate organization and attention to a task-at-hand?
- Can he play constructively for a reasonable period of time?
- Are there areas that suggest concern?

ACTIVITIES

Because play is primarily self-directed and self-motivated, teacher-initiated activities should be purposeful and creatively presented. When teachers work with children in groups, the focus of play should be primarily on large-motor development (creative movement, gymnastics, and skill-building games), on small-motor development (making a mural, assembling a collage for a hallway, gardening or cooking, playing musical instruments), or expressive language experiences (group dramas). (See Table 10–3 for more detail.)

Examples of Fine-motor Activities

For Young Children

1. Acting out finger plays—finger plays are rhyming nonsense verses that coordinate language and sensory development, e.g., "I'm a Little Teapot," "The Wheels on the Bus," "This Little Frog Broke His Toe," "Two Little Blackbirds," "Open Shut Them," "Johnny Hammers with One Hammer," "Two Little Eyes that Open and Close."

2. Playing follow-me games—wiggle fingers, wiggle toes, wiggle nose, wiggle ears, open and clasp hands, open mouths wide, make funny faces, blink eyes, wink, curl up tight, stand on tiptoes, be raindrops, be rainbows stretching across the sky, be a buzzing bee, be a fly on your nose. Now pretend you're a bean bag—put it on your knee, on your tummy, on your foot, on your head; now pass it to a friend—careful don't let it fall!

3. Using musical instruments—children may tap to music or to rhythms initiated by a teacher; drums, sticks, tambourines, triangles, and bells are favorite instruments of young children.

4. Making group murals or seasonal art projects—children can gather leaves and paste them on a large piece of colored paper; children make a collage using scissors, glue, paste-on objects; children finger paint a mural.

5. Assembling a miniature construct—children can build a gas station, an airport, a farm, a pond in a cardboard box setting; or they can make a birdhouse using a hammer and nails.

6. Cleaning up day—children can sponge tables, clean windows, sort toys, wash doll clothes and hang them to dry, wash trikes.

7. Cooking—children can wash and cut vegetables, knead and roll dough.

8. Doing-a-good-job day—children practice hanging up or putting on their coats, buttoning and snapping, brushing their teeth, setting a table.

9. Writing a note to a friend—children write and mail a "happy note" to a friend.

10. Using-your-five-senses day—children are given one item, such as an orange, to experience: they feel it, peel it, smell it, squeeze it and listen as it drops into a glass, and, if there is anything left, eat it.

For School-Age Children

1. Design and make: a terrarium, an airport, a dollhouse, a model city, a wildlife sanctuary, a new food, a metro system, an outdoor restaurant, a building for the twenty-first century, a classroom, a playground, a best friend, a car, a sandwich. Use odds and ends, arts and crafts, and imagination to construct each project.

2. Assemble arts and crafts kits that reinforce interests: wall-hangings, hook rugs, embroidery, knitting, model airplanes and boats, parachutes, rockets, space ships, and bird houses.

3. Carve animals and fish using soft wood and acrylic paints.

4. Make soap sculptures.

5. Cook for fun, using favorite and inventive recipes; make a cookbook as a culminating experience.

6. Design and decorate a school-age den: paint the walls and decorate with hand-made objects.

7. Create original games.

8. Paint and sketch outdoor life; make a portfolio of personal drawings.

9. Take (or make) interesting pictures and frame them.

TABLE 10-3 Physical Development: From Infancy to Age Five

Age	Developmental Milestones	Large-muscle Development	Small-muscle Development	Sensory Development	Creative Movement	Relaxation
Infants to 18 months	*Large muscles* ■ Rolls over (3 months) ■ Sits unassisted (9 months) ■ Creeps forward (9 months) ■ Walks alone (13 months) *Small muscles* ■ Reaches for toys (6 months) ■ Fills and empties containers (9 months) ■ Feeds self (6–9 months)	■ Put a toy just beyond baby's reach to stimulate mobility ■ Provide large safe areas for exploring ■ Provide push-pull toys ■ Provide climbing structures, bouncy swings, and ride-on toys for toddlers	■ Provide rattles, squeeze toys, and cradle gyms for infants to swipe at and grab ■ Provide stacking and nesting toys, pans with lids, and a pounding bench for older infants ■ Play pat-a-cake ■ Provide small plastic blocks and balls	■ Provide textured toys for mouthing and teething ■ For water play: provide cans with holes, plastic containers, and bath toys: place baby walker in shallow puddle ■ Attach mirrors to cribs ■ Provide food experiences for tasting and smearing	■ Carry child while dancing to music and pat out rhythm on child's back ■ Playfully roll child into different positions for fun ■ Show children ways their bodies can move as you talk about them	■ Help babies relax by rocking, cuddling, and singing to them ■ Stroke or rub babies' backs while singing softly to them ■ Help babies relax with soft rhythmical music or the burring sound of a fan
18 months to 3 years	*Large muscles* ■ Climbs up and slides down low equipment; climbs stairs (19 months) ■ Jumps and runs (20–21 months) ■ Kicks ball (24 months) *Small muscles* ■ Scribbles with crayons (18 months) ■ Uses scissors (3 years)	■ Provide climbing gym, moderate slides, swings (no pumping), and tricycles ■ Provide bouncy mattresses for jumping ■ Provide balls for kicking and rolling ■ Encourage older children to march to music	■ Provide markers and crayons for scribbling ■ Allow plenty of time for easel and finger painting ■ Provide simple puzzles with frames ■ Provide containers with twist-off/on tops ■ Encourage sandbox play (spooning and filling)	■ Provide manipulative materials like dough and clay ■ Set up beginning cooking experiences; allow time for tasting, smelling, and feeling ■ Substitute cornmeal or seeds in sand table ■ Allow for water play	■ Use props and dress-ups to encourage movement ■ Have children dance like a bear, hop like a bird, etc. ■ Ask, "How little can you make yourself?" ■ Have children ride rocking horses to music (vary tempo): two horses together are fun	■ Provide soothing activities such as swinging or rocking in chair ■ Allow for water and sand play ■ Stroke or rub children's backs at naptime

Age	Developmental characteristics					
3 to 4 years	*Large muscles* ■ Climbs readily ■ Runs, hops, and kicks ■ Steers and pedals trike ■ Balances briefly on one foot *Small muscles* ■ Buttons and zips with help; uses tools ■ Catches and tosses balls	■ Provide swings, slides, and climbing gyms ■ Plan balancing activities (rim of tire, edge of sidewalk, etc.) ■ Throw beanbags at large target ■ Kick a still or slow-moving ball ■ Bounce large/small balls	■ Allow time for large and small block play ■ Use woodworking, cooking, and art materials ■ String beads ■ Provide puzzles and other manipulatives ■ Let children practice self-dressing	■ Finger painting with scents or textures added ■ Compare sound containers for those that match ■ Step in tubs of different textures (feathers, styrofoam, pea gravel) ■ Spin around (to feel dizzy sensation)	■ Have children creat/move through obstacle course ■ Shaking activities (shake like a wet dog, a salt shaker, a sheet) ■ Move in response to music; vary tempo ■ Jump on mattress to music; march	■ Shake arms and legs loosely like limp puppet ■ Provide quiet corner or child-sized bed in housekeeping corner ■ Flop down when music stops
4 to 5 years	*Large muscles* ■ Can hop but not skip ■ May pump self on swing ■ Catches both large and small balls ■ Balances self on beams *Small muscles* ■ Can copy a few letters ■ Hammers nails in wood ■ Can cut with scissors	■ Allow for free, joyful running and leaping ■ Provide trikes and scooters ■ Offer intricate obstacle courses ■ Encourage cooperative large-muscle play (giving rides in wagon, pretend games on climbing gym)	■ Provide puzzles with more pieces and large un-framed jigsaw puzzles ■ Block play (building elaborate structures) ■ Hit balloons with paddles ■ Provide practice cutting with scissors on curved lines	■ Use senses to sort materials by touch, taste, sound, etc. ■ Match flowers or scents ■ Have children guess who they're touching (with eyes closed) ■ Substitute snow in water table; play as it melts ■ Identify sounds on tape	■ Have children propose ways to use parachute ■ Inspire movement with questions: "How would you walk in deep snow? On ice? In honey? How could you cross the room if you couldn't use your feet?" ■ Provide props to enhance movements	■ Have children "tense up" and "let go" ■ Have children pretend to be frozen—then melted—ice cream, or a plate of cooked spaghetti ■ Have children imagine peaceful scenes, such as floating on a cloud, to relax

Source: From PRE—K TODAY, Issues from 1987 and 1988. Copyright © 1987, 1988 by Scholastic Inc. Reprinted by permission of Scholastic Inc. All rights reserved.

Examples of Large-motor Activities

For Young Children

1. Acting out nursery rhymes—e.g., "Jack and Jill," "Little Miss Muffet," "Jack Be Nimble," "Hey Diddle, Diddle."

2. Playing group games—e.g., "Dog, Dog," "Duck, Duck, Goose," "London Bridge," "The Farmer in the Dell," "Freeze Tag," "Red Rover," "A Tisket, A Tasket," "Go In and Out the Circle," "Giant Steps," "Musical Chairs (or Carpet Squares)."

3. Creative play on a mat—e.g., "Guess What I Am," "Be . . . a slithering snake, a kangaroo with a heavy pocket, a fat frog, a slow turtle, a swinging monkey, a grinning crocodile, a jack-in-the-box, a ballerina, a tight-rope walker, a magician, an old man with a cane, a frightened rabbit, a storm, a swan, a kitchen appliance.

4. Creative play on a parallel bar, a balance beam, wooden steps, or a stage. Be a circus performer, a gymnast, an amphibian.

5. Creative movement activities using records, musical instruments, or songs (libraries are good resources for children's records).

6. Acting out favorite stories that require gross-motor actions such as "Three Billy Goats Gruff."

7. Using hoops or tires for spatial awareness—children go around, over, through, in and out using one foot, using both hands and feet, going forward, going backward.

8. Cleaning-up-our-backyard day—children gather and rake leaves, wash windows, and clean out a storage shed.

9. Doing gymnastics—children do log rolls and forward rolls (supervised by a teacher), crawl, move in different directions, jump, hop, skip, gallop in place, play Simon Says.

For School-Age Children

1. Large-motor games and activities—e.g., four square, tennis, basketball, soccer, tag games, dodge ball, badminton, scoop ball, nerf balls, parachutes, ring toss, bowling, soft balls and bats, twister, hopscotch, hoops, jump rope and streamer contests.

2. Gymnastic—aerobics, tumbling, bar work.

3. Recreational outings—camping, hiking, cleaning the environment, playing in the park, skating, bowling, swimming, miniature golf, walking to a high school to watch football practice, jogging on the track before the practice begins.

4. Classes in creative movement, jazz, and other types of dance.

NOTES

1. Catherine Garvey, *Play* (Cambridge, MA: Harvard University Press, 1990), p. 4.

2. Brian Sutton-Smith, "Play Research: State of the Art," in *When Children Play,* eds. Joe L. Frost and Sylvia Sunderlin (Wheaton, MD: ACEI, 1985), p. 13.

3. Nancy E. Curry, "Four- and Five-year-olds: Intuitive, Imaginative Players, in *Play's Place in Public Education for Young Children,* ed. Victoria Jean Dimidjian (Washington, DC: National Education Association, 1992), p. 39.

4. S. Rogers Cosby, and Janet K. Sawyers, *Play in the Lives of Children* (Washington, DC: NAEYC, 1988), pp. 12–13.

5. Greta G. Fein and Shirley S. Schwartz, "The Social Coordination of Pretense in Preschool Children," in *Reviews of Research, Vol. 4,* eds. Greta Fein and Mary Rivkin. (Washington, DC: NAEYC, 1986), p. 101.

6. Anthony D. Pellegrini and Jana Dressden, "Play in School? Yes, We're Serious," in *Play's Place in Public Education for Young Children,* ed. Victoria Dimidjian (Washington, DC: National Education Association, 1992), p. 21.

7. Mary Ann Pulaski, "Toys and Imaginative Play," in *The Child's World of Make-Believe,* ed. Jerome L. Singer (New York: Academic Press, 1973), pp. 74–103.

8. Dorothy G. Singer and Jerome L. Singer, *The House of Make-Believe: Play and the Developing Imagination* (Cambridge, MA: Harvard University Press, 1990), p. 84.

9. Jennifer A. Connolly, Anna B. Doyle, and Erica Reznick, "Social Pretend Play and Social Interaction in Preschoolers," *Journal of Applied Developmental Psychology* 9 (1988): 301–13.

10. Laura E. Berk, *Child Development* (Boston: Allyn and Bacon, 1989), p. 256.

11. Rosalyn Saltz and Eli Saltz, "Pretend Play Training and Its Outcome," in *The Young Child at Play,* eds. Greta Fein and Mary Rivkin (Washington, DC: NAEYC, 1986), pp. 156–161.

12. Ibid., 157–58.

13. Sara H. Arnaud, "Play Themes and Processes in Seven- and Eight-year-olds," in *Play's Place in Public Education for Young Children,* p. 65.

14. Greta G. Fein, "Pretend Play: New Perspectives," in *Curriculum Planning For Young Children* (Washington, DC: NAEYC, 1982), p. 23.

15. Evelyn Weber, *Ideas Influencing Early Childhood Education,* (New York: Teachers College Press, 1984), p. 208.

16. As cited in Dr. Richard Sinatra, "The Arts as a Vehicle for Thinking," *Early Years* 16(7) (March 1986): 56.

17. Clare Cherry, *Creative Play for the Developing Child,* (Belmont, CA: David S. Lake Publishers, 1976), pp. 14–15.

18. Ibid., p. 52.

19. As cited in Carol Vukelich, "Where's the Paper, Literacy During Dramatic Play," *Childhood Education* 66(4) (Summer 1990): 209.

RESOURCES

Cherry, Clare. *Creative Play for the Developing Child.* Belmont, CA: David S. Lake Publishers, 1976.

Claycomb, Patty. *Love the Earth: Exploring Environmental Activities for Young Children.* Livonia, MI: Partner Press, 1991 (distributed by Gryphon House, Mt. Rainier, MD).

Dickson, Lori S., and Lisa W. Wamsley. *Teaching Through Creative Play.* Colorado Springs, CO: As They Grow, Inc., 1988.

Dimidjian, Victoria Jean, ed. *Play Place in Public Education for Young Children.* Washington, DC: National Education Association, 1992.

Fein, Greta, and Mary Rivkin, eds. *The Young Child at Play: Reviews of Research,* vol 4. Washington, DC: NAEYC, 1986.

Frost, Joe L., and Sylvia Sunderlin, eds. *When Children Play.* Wheaton, MD: AECI, 1985.

Garvey, Catherine. *Play: The Developing Child Series.* Cambridge, MA: Harvard University Press, 1990.

Heidemann, S., and D. Hewitt. *Pathways to Play: Developing Play Skills in Young Children.* Mt. Rainier, MD: Gryphen House, 1992.

Luvmour, Sambhava and Josette. *Everyone Wins!* Philadelphia, PA: New Society Publishers, 1990.

McKee, Judy Spitler, ed. *Play: Working Partner of Growth.* Wheaton, MD: ACEI, 1986.

Miller, Karen. *Things to Do with Toddlers and Twos.* Chelsea, MA: Telshare Publishing, 1984.

Provenzo, Eugene F., Jr., and Arlene Brett. *The Complete Block Book.* Syracuse, NY: Syracuse University Press, 1983.

Rogers, Cosby S., and Janet K. Sawyers. *Play in the Lives of Children.* Washington, DC: NAEYC, 1988.

Singer, Dorothy G., and Jerome L. *The House of Make-Believe: Children's Play and the Developing Imagination.* Cambridge, MA: Harvard University Press, 1990.

Sisson, Edith A. *Nature with Children of All Ages* (The Massachusetts Audubon Society). Boston, MA: Prentice-Hall, 1982.

Sullivan, Molly. *Movement Exploration for Young Children.* Washington, DC: NAEYC, 1982.

Wassermann, Selma. "Serious Play in the Classroom," *Childhood Education* 68(3) (Spring 1992): 133–39.

Contemporary research confirms the view that young children learn most effectively when they are engaged in interaction rather than in merely receptive or passive activities. Young children should be interacting with adults, materials, and their surroundings in ways which help them make sense of their own experience and environment. They should be investigating and observing aspects of their environment worth learning about, and recording their findings and observations through talk, paintings, and drawings. Interaction that arises in the course of such activities provides a context for much social and cognitive learning.

— *Lillian G. Katz*

11

COMPONENT TWO: LEARNING

THE PREMISE

Learning is a cumulative process through which individuals acquire knowledge, skills, and attitudes. Children acquire knowledge *incidentally* and *directly* as they interact with an environment. They gain knowledge *internally* through mental processes and *externally* through their physical and social environment. Knowledge and concepts are acquired gradually through process skills that include reasoning, thinking, and problem solving. Innate curiosity and basic needs propel a young child to find out about his immediate world through exploration, experimentation (trial and error), manipulation, and sensory experiences. Through direct experience, a child assimilates, organizes, and clarifies knowledge gained. He is motivated by an innate desire to control and master, by his learning environment, and by his social environment.

As children continue to gain knowledge, they are increasingly interested in their surrounding world. As their interests expand, their thinking expands. As they begin to see themselves in relation to others, they want to do more and learn more. Specific skills (increments of learning) are developed through training, practice, and motivation. Children learn to read and to write, to play a piano, and to master a handstand. They also continue to gain information on a higher level by developing concepts (organizing and categorizing information) and by expanding their knowledge (exercising, reflection, reasoning, problem solving). The degree of success a child experiences as she progresses through levels of learning will affect her attitude and motivation. A person who feels good about herself and her accomplishments will view learning as a *lifelong* process—a pursuit that reaffirms and gives meaning to experiences. The time to cultivate and nurture learning is in early childhood.

A primary goal of teachers in child care environments is to *nurture* and *train* children to become responsive and responsible adults—the kinds of people who can use their resources to fulfill their aspirations and to benefit others. These qualities are planted in the early years. What are the attributes we would like to see transmitted into adulthood and how do they relate to learning? Early childhood educator and author, Peter A. Bergson, defines the skills that create an ideal adult as:

1. The ability to make reasoned choices and decisions to enhance individual goals as well as society's interests.
2. The ability to look at problems from different perspectives, to make new connections, and to develop fresh solutions to old problems.
3. The ability to think clearly and to speak without fear of criticism.
4. The motivation to observe the world as it is, to question and to challenge, to explore, to speculate, and to invent.
5. A positive sense of self that is able to nurture others.
6. The ability to use resources at hand to solve daily problems and create new opportunities.
7. The willingness to use natural resources prudently to build toward our collective survival.[1]

CREATING A LEARNING ENVIRONMENT

If we accept learning as primarily an *interactional, cumulative* process between a child and an environment, then we must assume that a child's experiences will significantly influence the quality and rate of his learning. If a child experiences early success in most aspects of his development, he will continue to build his base of knowledge. A child experiences success through active and positive contact with his *physical* and *human* environment. A parent and a teacher play *primary* roles in a child's development. Without adults to help him interpret, organize, and order his world, a child has less opportunity to develop his potential. It is the adult who designs an environment so that it is conducive to learning, and it is the adult who encourages a child toward competency. In order to accomplish and master tasks, the child must take risks and on occasion, experience failure. He needs to understand that not everything is easy and that not everything is hard; that slowly, with patience, he will arrive at a *healthy balance* between the two. A caring adult will help a child deal with obstacles, frustrations, and disappointments. She will praise his progress and his near-progress. She will encourage him to try again, to go further, to break through self-imposed boundaries. It is through *interpersonal* relationships with adults that a child discovers more about himself.

The qualities described by Bergson are rooted in an open, *idea-centered* environment: one that encourages children to think and apply reason to their play/work. To test their environment (and themselves), children must feel inwardly confident and trusting. They must believe that the people who surround them support them—that they won't change the messages children have already put into practice. Children's development requires, above all, continuity and stability. A change in an environment can cause a decline in momentum, create confusion, and alter a child's perception of learning.

These are some of the *characteristics of a learning environment*. It supports:

- Using the scientific method—observing, experimenting, questioning, thinking, communicating, testing, problem solving, integrating, and expanding knowledge.
- Learning through interaction with one's total environment.
- Learning by discovery and by guided activities.
- Developing thinking skills.
- Developing basic foundational skills.
- Developing concepts.
- Encouraging self-initiated learning.
- Encouraging cooperative learning.
- Using one's natural world as a catalyst for learning.
- Promoting an idea- and activity-centered classroom.
- Designing a program that integrates knowledge and stimulates thinking.
- Promoting an environment that encourages dialogue through reasoning and creative thinking.

HOW TEACHERS CULTIVATE LEARNING

Through Play

Self-initiated

Children learn skills through spontaneous play that promotes curiosity, exploration, and active learning. In the early years, children's learning is primarily influenced by the quality of their play environment. When children play, they learn *incidentally* as they interact with objects, materials, and playmates. They experiment with ideas and objects in imaginative and thoughtful ways. As they process information, they make discoveries and predictions.

In a block center, a child observes the effect of varying heights of an inclined plane on the speed and distance of objects (small vehicles). He has constructed a ramp by stacking square blocks and elevating a block to facilitate movement. By raising the ramp (adding one more block), he discovers he can change the velocity. He also discovers that heavy objects move more slowly than lighter objects. Another child may use flannel shapes to create an imaginary story. She experiments with the arrangement of shapes until she creates a pattern that pleases her. Still another child may ask a teacher to assist her in making a balance scale. Together they discuss the idea and the materials needed to construct the project. The child decides to use a string and a piece of wood as the fulcrum and two small plastic containers glued together as weights. The teacher continues to support the child's initiative by suggesting that they find items to test out the scale: acorns, plastic spoons, block cubes, buttons. Lawrence Frank describes the process at work *within* the child as:

A conception of play that recognizes the significance of autonomous, self-directed learning and active exploration and manipulation of the actual world gives a promising approach to the wholesome development of children. . . . It is a way to translate into the education of children our long-cherished, enduring goal values, a belief in the worth of the individual personalities, and a genuine respect for the dignity and integrity of the children.[2]

A child who can function effectively on his own is developing competency through *internal controls*. He understands that freedom connotes responsibility and self-management. Because he is self-motivated the child can play for a long period of time and is not easily distracted by surrounding activities; he has his own play agenda. As he plays, he is processing and assimilating ideas to add to his growing repertoire of knowledge.

Cooperative

Children also learn through cooperative play. When children interact with peers at play or in group activities, they extend their interest, curiosity, and ideas. They develop greater levels of awareness and sensitivity to the interplay and importance of human interaction and resourcefulness. They become more tolerant and patient in order to sustain and deepen friendships. Best friendships do not just happen— they progress through mutual accommodation and support. As children develop social skills, they broaden their cultural base and cognitive awareness. As they listen, observe, and identify with peers, they become sensitive to a wider, more complex world—a world far beyond a block center or a language center. Through an interchange of ideas, children incorporate new thinking on to accepted practices. They extend their base of knowledge to incorporate new information and attitudes. Developing positive social skills and relationships is invaluable to the learning process, especially when children are exposed to a diverse, multicultural environment. As children begin to identify with others, they make adjustments in their patterns of thinking and behavior. They begin to see value in discussing and valuing the ideas and thoughts of others. Cooperative play extends and enriches experiences. An autonomous child will balance what she sees or hears with what she knows. The child understands that she still has the capacity to make choices and to exercise her autonomy. Influenced by peers, however, in a pro-social, value-conscious environment, she can now make decisions from a broader level of understanding.

Through Quality Environmental Experiences

Promoting Learning

A quality environment promotes learning by providing active, hands-on experiences, interesting activity centers, competent leadership, and opportunities for creative thinking. It is the adult who *sets the stage* for learning and who *guides* the child through the learning process. Guidance is not teaching; it is a *process* that generates self-directed learning and higher levels of awareness. In the process, a teacher extends learning by providing opportunities and an environment that promote thinking and problem solving. In an atmosphere that values self-initiated learning, children are given time to complete tasks. Children develop thinking skills when they are able to extend and apply their knowledge in both practical and inventive ways. A child needs to understand the consequences of not buttoning a coat on a cold day and she needs to learn to outfox the fox by finding the shortest route to grandmother's house!

Promoting Problem Solving

Finding out how to do things and solving problems are the tasks of childhood. A classroom must be organized and arranged to maximize problem solving through hands-on experiences. In a prepared, child-centered environment, children develop organizational skills that help them channel and direct their thinking. They apply themselves to a task, making decisions as they work; they set goals and self-evaluate. They take responsibility for outcomes when they are *in charge of* and committed to a task. What could I have done differently? How do I feel about this grade? What are the consequences? How important is it to organize materials, to set goals, and to self-evaluate—to accept responsibility?

Encouraging Thinking

In a learning environment, children are challenged to question and to make predictions. Do you think it will rain today? I wonder what will happen if we mix these colors together? Something has been changed in this room; can anyone guess what is different? What story would you like to listen to? As children learn to become competent and capable thinkers, they learn to respect the opinions of others, to question and evaluate information, and to discover new ways of thinking.

Promoting Organization

A carefully designed learning environment will offer a child sufficient choices to stimulate curiosity and imaginative play through individual and group experiences. It will define spaces and activities so that children can play independently. Children react to how a center looks and feels. The more personalized and interesting a center looks to a child, the more she will want to explore it. As children play independently, they learn to identify objects by their placement and attributes: a magnifying glass is located in a science center, a record is in a listening center, and a book is in a media center. When children perceive order, they connect objects with a specific environment that complements their function. They understand that objects have properties and purposes. A creative child will move objects and use them innovatively at play but will continue to perceive them as members of a unit commonly called "activity centers," i.e., a block center, a manipulative play center, an arts center.

By Training Children to Think

"Thinking," according to John Barell of New Jersey's Montclair State College, "is a process of searching for and creating meaning involving the mind's creations—symbols, metaphors, analogies—in an attempt to establish relationships between the world of particulars and the ideas and concepts that give them structure."[3] At the early stages of development, a prelude to thinking is *awareness*. When children develop awareness, they begin to discriminate and reason. Teaching for awareness is *more important* than teaching for basic skill development. Most children learn skills naturally but they may not develop thinking and reasoning without *external* stimuli and training. To teach for awareness is to *challenge* children to think and to communicate their thoughts. An environment that challenges children to think and to find their own answers is *extending* the learning process by leaps and bounds.

Barbara Z. Presseisen's model of essential thinking skills identifies "levels of thinking as: *qualification* (finding unique characteristics), *classification* (determining common qualities), *relationships* (detecting regular operations), *transformation* (relating known to unknown, creating new meanings), and *causation* (establishing cause and effect, interpretation, prediction; forecasting)."[4]

Examples of the first level (qualification) might include identifying parts of a body, shapes, or familiar objects. Games such as "What Is Missing?" that require children to identify missing parts (a squirrel's tail or whiskers on a mouse) will stimulate thinking. Examples of the second level (classification) might include sorting, sets, or comparisons. Children might sort blocks by color and size; they may classify food, musical instruments, or play objects by sorting and placement. They would need to understand the common characteristics and use of objects before they can classify them. Examples of the third level (relationships) might include activities that promote sequencing, patterning (part to whole), and discrimination. A child might put sequence cards in order (the apple, making a pie, oven, eating), order beads by their color pattern (what comes next), or identify objects that don't go together.

The fourth level (transformation) involves recognizing analogies and developing concepts. Examples of this level might include children playing word games that show relationships between objects that are physically different but are identified with one another (root is to tree as bottle is to baby, as hat is to head); or developing generalizations by categorizing objects found in the water, on land, and in the air. Examples of the fifth level (causation) may include predicting the aftermath of a hurricane or discussing the effects of ocean currents and tides on shorelines and sea life.

Children enjoy brainstorming as a channel for communication and thoughtful dialogue. Children who express themselves openly are responsive to the thoughts of others. They can discuss the pros and cons of changing a room, of implementing a behavior policy, or of selecting one fieldtrip instead of another. The object of brainstorming is to reach *consensus* through open dialogue. It is a healthy way for children to express their ideas and feelings without being intimidated or criticized.

By Encouraging Critical Thinking

Children use higher levels of thinking when they begin to connect ideas, to analyze, and to resolve discrepancies. Higher levels of thinking in early childhood include: reflection, asking questions, making generalizations (a child belongs to a human family; a cat belongs to an animal family), expanding ideas (making a chart of probable members in each category), extending learning (comparing how families live to how animals live). As children begin to challenge assumptions, they no longer accept simple explanations as truisms. They sift through information, applying their own logic and insight to their base of knowledge. If children are able to exercise their thinking in a social context, their ideas become more fluent and less predictable or conventional.

As children challenge each other in open dialogue, they learn strategies that activate thinking capabilities. ". . . It doesn't go that way, I can show you how it goes." They enjoy analyzing a problem from several perspectives: "Why don't we make one go this way and one go that way?" They become enthusiastic language users, selecting words to fit the occasion: "My daddy took me to a car wash. I felt trapped but excited. I wondered, if the equipment ever breaks down, would the whole system stop working at once?" To persuade others, a child must have an idea, be able to express the idea, and motivate his listener.

School-age children in child care may practice critical thinking by forming a debate club. They may use newspaper articles or timely issues as catalysts for discussions and follow-up activities. A teacher might offer to assist them in formulating procedures: a format, a protocol, time frames, and scoring. A system for evaluation also would have to be considered. As an incentive, a teacher may arrange for her children to attend community planning board sessions, mock trials, political debates, or public forums. By direct experience, children will become aware of the power of language and expression. They will quickly become critics—"She made her point. She was not prepared. I wouldn't vote for her because . . ."

There are many opportunities to encourage critical thinking among school-age children. They can be encouraged to read and evaluate good books. They can explore topics that can be researched and discussed in class. Children can be exposed to games and activities that stimulate thinking: concentration, attribute, and memory games; crossword puzzles, word finds, chalkboard games such as "hang man"; group games such as "twenty questions"; or imaginative games (think of all the things that a tire could be used for). Every activity should be looked at from its inherent potential for developing thinking and language skills. With few materials, children can create models for parks, for cities, for bridges, for sports centers, and for bird sanctuaries. By planning, problem solving, inventing, and applying knowledge to a project at hand, children's time while at a child care center can become productive and extremely fulfilling.

By Encouraging Problem Solving

Problem solving is *central* to the thinking processes. In order to identify and deal with a problem, children need time to formulate and test ideas. An environment that limits children's options by not providing challenging activities is inhibiting learning. Materials to stimulate thinking include items like a magnifying glass, containers, a sieve, a water table, charts, notebooks, markers, a thermometer, terrariums, growing things, simple machines, a balance scale, discrimination cards, sensory materials, a hammer and nails, string, and blocks of wood.

Children are natural problem solvers while they play. They define a problem by *trial and error*—moving and changing things until there is an acceptable fit. If a car is too large to go through a block tunnel, a child must find a smaller car or make a wider tunnel. If a baby doll is too big for a carriage, a child will have to find another vehicle (a wheelbarrow, a wagon, a shopping cart). When children realize there is a problem, they look at options and think about solutions. They develop a *plan* and carry out their plan. In the process, they become resourceful and capable learners.

As children mature, they begin to experiment with problem solving from a social perspective. A great deal of children's time is spent developing and affirming relationships. Interpersonal relationships require different and, in many ways, more demanding levels of communication. Children must learn to accommodate others by adjusting their attitudes and patterns of behavior. Relationships require active listening and *de-centering* (taking the perspective of others). Some children lack the maturity required for meaningful sustained interaction. Their perceptions are influenced or distorted by what they have experienced. Reciprocity in social relationships comes slowly for children who are not trained and reinforced in cooperative play at an early age.

Children solve problems by making choices. They think through alternatives and give up something when they make a choice. Children can begin making choices at an early age. They can choose whether they want to swing forward or backward, and whether they want to slide sitting up, lying down, or on their tummies. They can choose a swing mate or a see-saw mate; they can select digging objects for a sandbox and the songs they choose to sing as they play. Children can choose a snack (I would like raisins, I'd rather not have juice), select their clothes (choices should be limited), their books, their outings, their lunch, and many of their activities.

By giving children choices on a basic operational level, teachers are preparing them for problem solving on a more complex level. A child who must decide whether to play indoors with one friend or outdoors with another friend has a difficult choice to make. What she would like to do is to persuade both friends to play indoors. Because this is not an option, the child must make a difficult decision. How she resolves the problem will affect her attitude, and her self-confidence. John Dewey viewed thinking and problem solving as inter-connected aspects of a child's total development. He defined the process as:

1. Becoming aware of a problem (someone else is using the hammer that I want);
2. Clarifying and defining the problem (what must I do to solve the problem? I can't connect the wings to the body without that hammer);
3. Searching for facts and formulating a hypothesis (if I use something equally strong like a block or a pan, I can complete the task);
4. Evaluating proposed solutions (the block is stronger than the pan but is it as strong as the hammer?);
5. Experimental verification (it works, I got the nail in!).[5]

By Promoting Decision Making

When a child makes a decision, she determines the best response among alternatives that are available to her. Before making a decision, a child must think about consequences. An overweight child must think about choosing ice cream instead of nonfat yogurt. Another child must think about the consequences of not inviting a friend to a birthday party or letting a friend down. Decision making can create conflict and stress in children, especially when they are not clear about alternatives or are uncertain about their ability to make appropriate decisions. Often children make decisions adults are not comfortable with. Consequently, a decision may become so diluted by parental influence that children feel confused ("You can go it if you want to, but I think you're making a mistake.")

Children need to be given fewer options until they are better able to make appropriate choices (choose between two garments rather than selecting from a closet full of clothes). Decision making also can be taught by giving children the opportunity to exercise judgment. Would you wear a sweater on a cold day? Why or why not? Would you pick shiny shoes if you were playing on bars? What might happen? Do you think Janie should have crossed the street by herself? Why or why not? What information do we have about Janie before we make a judgment—i.e., how old is Janie, is she allowed to cross streets, did she cross at a corner, how busy is the street, was she cautious? Children soon understand that some choices are easy and fun (like choosing a flavor of ice cream) and others are not so easy (like solving a problem). If parents and teachers *guide* children in decision-making strategies, children will feel autonomous without feeling frustrated or confused. Gradually children will solve their own problems because they have the resources and the confidence to make decisions. Educator Barry K. Byer has identified the skills involved in decision making as:

- Defining the goal;
- Identifying obstacles to achieving the goal;
- Identifying alternatives;
- Analyzing alternatives;

- Ranking alternatives;
- Choosing the best alternative.[6]

Clearly decision making is a complex skill that children need to begin to learn in the formative years.

By Being Flexible and Creative Thinkers

A creative person is an imaginative, inventive person. *Creativity* is identified with fluency (producing many ideas), flexibility (producing unusual ideas), originality (producing unique ideas), and elaboration (adding detail to the ideas).[7] Creative thinking is generated in a *process-oriented environment* that encourages self-expression. A child who is not hurried through an activity is able to connect ideas and to think about the various choices and combinations that may be used in its development. He is practicing divergent thinking when he can look at his project from several perspectives and points of view. As he progresses in a task, he will naturally make changes and evaluate his work. A child will be enterprising and imaginative in the way he applies himself to a task at hand. A child who thinks creatively will use ideas in innovative ways. Peter Bergson identifies flexible, creative thinking as the:

- Ability to change;
- Ability to look at ideas and situations from different perspectives;
- Ability to make connections among apparently unrelated ideas;
- Ability to think about an idea, take a piece of it, and shape it into a novel solution;
- Willingness to experiment and take risks without being preoccupied with other people's opinions;
- Ability to create new combinations of objects and ideas;
- Willingness to question assumptions and to reach past their apparent boundaries.[8]

By Developing Concepts

Concepts are a collection of experiences or ideas that contain common attributes. They naturally evolve in an integrated, idea-centered curriculum. As children play, they gather, analyze, and process information. They identify attributes as they organize, sort, and store familiar items. Children label items by the words that describe and identify their characteristics. Gradually they begin to sift through and organize data in terms of meaning and association. Children develop concepts through direct experiences that encourage them to connect ideas. An integrated environment extends the ideas that eventually become concepts. For example, a child develops a concept of water by direct experience (playing in water), by experimenting (with evaporation, water vapor, condensation, and precipitation), and by integrating knowledge (playing in a stream). She will soon learn to distinguish a pond from a river, a river from an ocean, and the kinds of life that inhabit each environment.

A good way to develop concepts is to organize a learning activity around a theme such as food. Under the broad category of food, children can begin to develop an understanding of the basic food groups: meat and meat alternatives, vegetables and fruits, breads and cereals, and dairy products. They can talk about healthy eating habits, the nutritional value of food, and how food arrives at a supermarket and can culminate the activity by making a concept web (see Figure 11–1).

By Developing Perception

Perception is a sense of awareness that causes children to react or respond to an environment in a personal way. Children derive meaning from experiences that stimulate their senses. They develop impressions or understandings from their total surroundings—smells, textures, appearance, and activities. Children's awareness can be increased by providing a large variety of experiences inside and outside of the classroom. Children develop insight through daily hands-on experiences that capture and hold their attention. They begin to distinguish between indoor and outdoor play, and they begin to identify certain activities with moods and feelings: playtime, resttime, and snacktime.

FIGURE 11–1 Concept Web for "Foods We Eat"

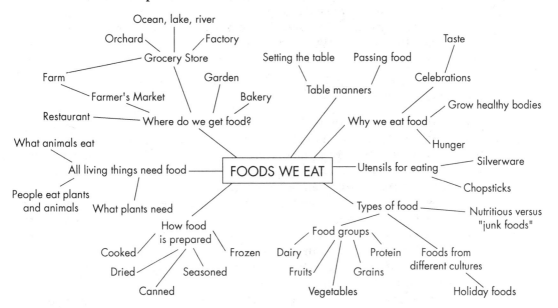

Source: From *Educationally Appropriate Kindergarten Practices,* copyright 1991, National Education Association. Reprinted with permission.

Awareness is centered in sensory experiences; the more children can touch, taste, smell, listen to, and ingest, the more sensitive they will become to the nuances that create and define an environment. Awareness leads to discovery, to self-understanding, and to creative thinking. Teachers should point out or suggest ideas to children at appropriate times, but they should encourage children to extract their own meaning from each experience. Young children need ongoing exposure to visual, auditory, and tactile stimuli. They need to look, to listen, and to touch as much as possible. School-age children benefit from sensory experiences that inspire curiosity and generate imagination. They need to move, to try being someone else, to try new ways of doing things, and to open their minds to creative thought.

By Making Discoveries

Children need both spontaneous and directed experiences in order to stretch their imaginations and develop competencies. Education is more than the acquisition of knowledge; it is learning how knowledge can be used. As much as possible, children should use their intuitive reflective resources through self-initiated activities. For example, a child may save a pumpkin seed to plant outdoors; he may bury it in a dry, shallow hole and remember to put a little stone nearby so he can find it again. He'll water the plant for a few days but after a while, the child will forget about it until one day he happens to see a green sprout in the vicinity of the pumpkin seed. The sprout may be a summer weed, but to the child, it will trigger a memory of the pumpkin seed planted a long time ago. The child has made a discovery. When he later reads a story about a pumpkin vine, he will identify with the experience with the slimy seed in a moist hand, the feeling of dirt, and the excitement of a fall day. Anytime a child gets an idea or recalls an idea, he needs to be encouraged and recognized as an inventive, original thinker.

By Stretching Minds

Children also need exposure to ideas and materials that will trigger thinking processes and communication skills. At times, a teacher will assume the role of initiator. On these occasions, she will introduce ideas and stimulate the learner to reason and make observations. Children might plant seeds (and experiment with placement), make shadows (and observe what happens to a shadow as it moves away from the light), examine a puddle (and chart its gradual disappearance), experience the wind (by blowing on a milkweed pod), or study the social patterns of ants (by observing and recording the activities of an ant colony). Or, a teacher may initiate conversation with a child who is sailing a paper boat in a basin of water: "I see your paper boat is floating in the water. I wonder what would happen if you put three marbles in your boat. What about six marbles?" If the child demonstrates interest in the teacher's inquiry, she would test the marbles and observe for herself what happens. The teacher may gather other materials to experiment with, pointing out that some things float and some things sink: "I wonder why?" In the process of discovering, the child may expand a concept by making a larger boat. By providing incentives for children to act on and try out interactions, they will become motivated to learn.

A LANGUAGE CURRICULUM
FOR EARLY CHILDHOOD

Oral Language

Young children need daily, ongoing opportunities to develop and practice communication skills. A language program for young children should include these basic components: speaking (oral language), listening, writing, and reading. In addition, a language program for young children should be enriched by units and themes.

Children learn to speak primarily by imitating and observing the people in their environment. In an open, supportive environment, children acquire language skills naturally as they interact with and observe others. In an article, "The Teacher's Role in Helping Young Children Develop Language Competence," Ilse Mattick supports a developmental interaction approach rather than an instructional approach—an approach that views language as closely integrated with all facets of a child's development. She points out that:

- Even the most quiet child is capable of using language unless there is a physical handicap;
- The teacher plays a significant role in fostering language development, particularly with children who have limited language capability;
- Language development does not mean only language production, it also means language comprehension.
- Children will use language at an early age such as two years when there is something to communicate;
- A varied and rich language program stresses quality over quantity.[9]

An early childhood program must provide many opportunities for children to use language, to listen to language, to develop comprehension, and to recall previously learned information. An informal environment that encourages children to communicate openly and confidently accelerates language usage and comprehension.

By practicing and extending verbal abilities, children develop confidence in their ability to communicate. When children play with peers, they are extremely attentive to what is being said. Children discover not only that they can communicate with words but that they can make friends with words. They are quick to perceive that words elicit favorable responses (and sometimes negative responses). As they hear and interact with language, children extend their awareness of words, word sounds, and syntax (the arrangement of words in a sentence).

Books stimulate oral language development. Children learn language as they hear language. Little children need constant exposure to books from the moment they are born. They need to be read to individually and in groups, and they need to read alone in a special area designated for reading books. Young children should have cloth or vinyl books for personal reading so that teachers don't have to be concerned about care. Teacher-made, laminated books are also good starter books for children. These books have the advantage of reinforcing a curriculum by focusing on specific learning areas that are familiar to children (colors, shapes, families, baby animals). Children ages four and five should have access to early readers that emphasize whole language.

At early childhood levels a book is judged by its pictures. Illustrations are keynotes to children's enjoyment. Because children have a limited reading ability, they use pictures to provide clues about the story's content. As children become familiar with a story, they will want to read it over and over again. Books can be wordless, written for beginning readers, or can have complicated narratives that require concentration and discussion. They can have interesting plots that capture imagination, a message, or a moral; and they can provide opportunities for children to make discoveries—a little worm is hiding in the crack of an apple or a wind is creeping around a corner looking for things to get in to.

It is important for teachers to remember that many children come to centers with limited language backgrounds. Children use language patterns modeled from home environments that may be language unique. Peers may react negatively to children who express themselves in unusual dialects—who appear to be different. Language deficient children will not develop fluency in English if they feel excluded or embarrassed by their communication skills. A reinforcing approach is to accept children's language as it is without imposing corrective suggestions. Gradually, as children are exposed to others' language patterns, they will adjust their patterns to accommodate to the environment. They will become bilingual. Oral language may be developed by:

- Reading and telling stories;
- Using puppets and role-playing as catalysts for language;
- Reciting nursery rhymes, doing finger plays, and singing;
- Encouraging language production during group circles;
- Promoting language awareness through literary and personal experiences;
- Providing an atmosphere that stimulates oral language;
- Respecting children's natural language.

Listening

Listening is an important component of language acquisition. When children are not talking, they are listening to the sounds of their environment—processing and attending to the myriad of stimuli that surround them. Young children need to be trained to become attentive listeners. Good listening will help comprehension and recall. It also will facilitate sensory awareness and creative development. All children should have a listening, language center to encourage independent experiences. Storytelling, records, and tapes are excellent vehicles for auditory discrimination and language development. Teachers will find that children vary considerably in their listening skills and tolerance. Some sounds are hard to make, some pleasing, some are harsh, and some are extremely objectionable. Some children can tolerate high noise levels while others cannot function effectively in loud settings.

Children's needs will be met if a teacher is sensitive to noise levels and intervenes when children are getting too boisterous during indoor play. She also can encourage children to become courteous listeners during circle and to speak one at a time. A calm environment helps children organize thoughts and feel secure. A loud environment creates fatigue and confusion. Listening skills may be developed through creative experiences that stimulate children's curiosity and desire to learn by:

- Training children to discriminate among sounds;
- Training children to follow directions;
- Training children in auditory memory skills;
- Asking questions and assessing recall;
- Helping children develop their attention spans;
- Encouraging children to develop good listening habits;
- Providing listening experiences during group activities and outdoor play.

Writing

Writing, reading, and listening experiences seem to develop almost simultaneously for the young child. Children typically hear, see, read, and write in no particular order. One child might suddenly print a familiar letter or word and another might suddenly identify a word meaning. Paintings and art projects are natural places for children to begin making letters and words; they usually ask teachers how to make letters or how to spell words. Letter models, puzzles, games, and adult encouragement will enable children to build language from basic to more complex levels.

Children also may enjoy personal word banks (card files of favorite or familiar words), sentence strips (simple sentences written on paper), journals (books that children can write in), writing their own books (original stories), and special projects (writing cards, invitations, and thank-you notes).

Children especially like to read and write as they play. A child may make stick drawings in the dirt (and label the characters), make words in the sand, and doodle with words on a moist windowpane. As the child plays with letter or word configurations, he develops eye–hand coordination and perceptual discrimination. A letter *A* begins on its side, moves to an upside-down position, and eventually lands on its feet. A teacher should respect the inner expressions and feelings of children's nonverbal language by not repeatedly asking them to explain or identify their creations in "written-down talk." As children write, they gradually realize the relationship between the written and spoken words. A teacher can encourage children's writing by:

- Providing children with manipulatives and activities that promote fine-motor skills;
- Encouraging children to express themselves through writing;
- Supporting children's natural writing;
- Reading back to children what they have written;
- Providing a language-rich environment.

Early Reading

Children who are exposed to a variety of language experiences in an enriching environment will develop a strong foundation for reading. A child-centered program doesn't promise that children will learn to read. It encourages reading by providing children a variety of books at different skill levels and by individualizing a reading program. In this context, children read at their own paces and in their own time. Language specialist Dolores Durkin points out the importance of early exposure and training:

> A set of common features that characterizes young children who are early readers has emerged from the literature. Early readers enjoyed learning to read so much that they persisted in seeking answers to their questions about written language—questions about the sounds of letters, spelling, writing, etc. They tended to come from literate homes in which books abounded, adults read, and someone was available to read to them and to answer their questions about reading.[10]

An early reading program begins with simple word recognition. Children learn words that have meaning, that relate to a familiar or desirable experience. A teacher might, for example, label items in activity centers. Children will soon imitate by making another set of word cards or eventually by replacing their teacher's words with their own version. A teacher may also introduce key words by reading charts (and emphasizing familiar words) that relate to classroom themes and activities and by rereading familiar books that encourage children to participate.

At a five-year level of development, some teachers might want to introduce children to high-frequency words (words that often appear in early reading experiences) through creative language experiences. Unlike key words—familiar words that children can identify with an object, high-frequency words are not easy to recognize or recall, e.g., "have," "the," "in," "is," "yes," "no," "they," "what," "when," "go," "on," "come," "here," "to," "and," "he," "she," "you."

A "kangaroo word game" is an example of a creative way to introduce high-frequency words. A large kangaroo carries words in her pocket for children to take home in their pockets. They must return them (and read them) the next day so kangaroo's pocket is always full of words. At the end of the year, the children make their own kangaroo filled with pocket words to practice over the summer.

Children also will want to experiment with printing and reading in activity centers. With a little prompting, they will print key words in journals and begin to print simple sentences. When they reach this stage of interest, they will become fascinated with pencil sharpeners and with how words are spelled. A busy teacher will find time to help children sharpen pencils (a very difficult motor task) and respond to children's curiosity about spelling. She will carefully enunciate each letter of a word and hope for the best. Even though children cannot remember all the letters in order, when they concentrate (as they often do), they will come pretty close. The results are wonderful—interestingly shaped letters, randomly placed but close enough to make something like a word. A child is satisfied that he has written something important and that the teacher can direct her attention elsewhere.

By exposing children to familiar words in natural ways, teachers are promoting the reading process. As teachers introduce children to simple books and as children develop language competency, they will discover:

- A book is read from left to right, from the top to the bottom of a page, and from beginning to end.
- A book contains a story with characters, with whom the reader may identify.
- A story generates feelings and attitudes in a reader.
- Authors and illustrators express ideas in many different genres such as folktales, fairy tales, rhyming verse, narratives, and wordless books.
- Setting, characters, and plot are important to understanding stories.
- There are many ways to develop characters and many ways to develop themes.
- Authors and illustrators have personalities and distinctive ways of writing and drawing.
- Reading is fun and books are companions.

A Reading Method: Language Experience

A language experience activity (LEA) method recognizes children's own language as a catalyst for learning to read and write. The LEA method uses whole language as a natural approach to reading and writing. Children perceive a reading experience that comes from their own words as written-down talk. Their words are the content for a personal story; their illustrations, the pictures.

Whole language is less a method than a philosophy of becoming familiar with a sentence that a child can identify with through experience. Psycholinguist Ken Goodman is an advocate of the "whole language" concept. He places a strong emphasis on functional, oral language experiences and reading aloud as a means of encouraging students to use their language knowledge to make sensible predictions in constructing the meaning of text.[11] In his "top-down" model, Goodman begins with a whole text (a story) so that students can experience its fullest meaning. After hearing or reading a story as a whole, students focus on the parts (a sentence, words, and letters). In this way, a teacher has helped a child to learn skills contextually by adding meaning to an experience. Reading in this context becomes a thinking process—a catalyst for continued learning.

To adapt this concept to a beginning language-experience program, a teacher begins with an experience (e.g., a discussion, a film, a story, or a field trip), adds meaning to the experience by having children make a picture about the experience and dictates (teacher prints children's words) a story about the picture/experience. Because young children are primarily visual learners and love to draw, art is a natural catalyst for an LEA project.

Whenever possible, children should be encouraged to write their own story, or to underline words they recognize. Paper for language experiences has unlined space for pictures and lines for dictation or for inventive writing. Children have difficulty staying on the lines (if they are writing) but eventually learn to scale down their letters, adding more and more words to a page.

When stories are finished, children can read back their own words to a teacher or to a classmate. Some children may want to extend a writing project by adding key words (words that have been underlined) to a personal word bank or a journal. When language experience activities are accepted and enjoyed by children, they can be extended into cooperative "group" books that relate to a shared experience or a theme. At the end of a theme, each child contributes *one* page to a book which is then coordinated by a teacher. She reproduces each page, asks one or two children to make a cover and asks children to color their book (they typically color their own picture first and their best friend's second). The "reproduced" book has a picture story from each classmate.

Another way to make a group book is to integrate original picture stories into one book that may be checked out and shared with parents (laminate the covers). The advantage of making a single group book is that it can be quickly assembled, it is totally original (each child's contribution is authentic), and it can be reread by children and eventually becomes a "classic" early reader in a classroom.

A whole language approach enables children to:

- Connect reading and writing.
- Become personally involved in a reading experience.
- Use art as a catalyst for creating picture stories.
- Gain immediate satisfaction by seeing their own words in print.
- Experience several reading-related processes before a project is complete.
- Follow-up and reinforce early reading activities.
- Develop a personal library in their classroom.

Phonics

Both whole language (seeing and reading words as units) and phonics (discriminating the sounds of words) are important components of language acquisition. Children typically print letters before they print words. They are exposed to sounds through a myriad of early childhood experiences: rhyming verses, finger plays, music, literature, poetry, sensory experiences. As children develop language proficiency, they recognize that sounds combine to make words and words combine to make sentences. A program that exposes children to the *whole* process of language acquisition, by not excluding phonics, is recognizing the natural evolution of language in the total development of the child. A critical dimension of early childhood training is to maintain a *natural* rhythm and method when teaching and training young children in any aspect of development. At early childhood levels, teaching is training through awareness and exposure; it is not rote, superficial, or unnatural training. Children learn in different ways at different rates, and at different times, but eventually, through competent and creative teaching, they do learn!

Children love to play with letters just as they love to play with words. They enjoy: magnetic letters, sandpaper letters, tracing letters, flannel letters and objects, letter printing or stamping, inventive printing, markers, fat pencils, and lots of hand-me-down computer paper to practice their developing skills. Exposing children to phonics will:

- Facilitate reading and language competency;
- Sharpen sensory perceptions and discrimination skills;
- Reinforce children's natural progression in acquiring language;
- Enhance appreciation for music and literature;
- Encourage good listening habits.

An early reading program should emphasize oral language and language-rich experiences that integrate and reinforce a *total* learning environment. Early reading should not be considered an instructional activity but an area of children's development that can be enriched by training, usage, and exploration. Language is developed by:

- Reading stories that evoke curiosity, imagination, identification, and sensitivity;
- Encouraging original writing;
- Providing opportunities for language experiences;
- Emphasizing a *total* language approach;
- Reinforcing word recognition through labeling, visual clues, games and activities, and art projects;
- Helping children make connections between speaking, writing, and reading;
- Helping children realize that "a library" is a "friend."

Philosopher and educator Bruno Bettelheim, a proponent of the whole word approach, addresses the importance of teaching reading as a joyful experience:

If the child did not know it before, it will soon be impressed on him that of all school learning, nothing compares in importance with reading; it is of unparalleled significance. This is why how it is taught is so important; the way in which learning to read is experienced by the child will determine how he will view learning in general, how he will conceive of himself as a learner and even as a person.[12]

Developing Language Through Units and Themes

Units

An effective way to develop language and learning competency is through theme-building. A theme is organized around a specific topic such as "A Trip to the Park," or a broad topic such as "Transportation." Language development is greatly enhanced by extended themes that are presented and reinforced over a period of time (two to four weeks). An extended theme is often referred to as a "unit" (see Sample 11–1). If a teacher plans a unit on "Transportation," she might introduce the concept at circle time, using books and visuals to generate interest. Over a period of weeks the unit might be broken into various themes: kinds of transportation, a transportation mural, a ride on a metro or on a bus, making a train from cardboard boxes, making theme-related alphabet books, and perhaps, designing a car of the future. Unit topics might include:

1. My community	10. Transportation
2. All about me	11. Communication
3. Families	12. The solar system
4. Animals	13. Current events
5. Pond life	14. Famous artists
6. Insects	15. Interesting places
7. Food and nutrition	16. Where people live and work
8. Seasons	17. Circus life
9. My five senses	18. Community leaders

SAMPLE 11–1   A Format for Language Units

During the period _____ to _____, I plan to present a unit on

_____.

1. A brief description of the unit
2. Main objectives
3. Themes or subtopics
4. Procedures and materials
5. New words
6. Integrated activities
7. Complementary literature and other resources
8. Special events and culminating experiences
9. Evaluation

Literary Themes

Books provide an excellent channel for building language themes. A teacher many read or tell a story as a catalyst for a follow-up activity using drama, movement, music, and special projects as a means for enhancing and dramatizing the story (see Sample 11–2). A literary theme should take place within one time frame. For examples of a language unit and a story theme, see Appendix B.

Cultivating a Language-rich Environment

To develop a strong language foundation, children need appropriate amounts of direction and training in *all* facets of communication. Experiences should be *child-centered* (the child selects language activities and partners), one-on-one (the child and the teacher work/play together in language areas), small group experiences (the teacher and a small group of children work/play together in language areas), or whole group experiences (the teacher organizes and presents language activities and projects to a group). In every setting, a teacher should guide and encourage children's natural desire to learn by: providing materials that attract children and enhance learning, personalizing learning so that it matches children's interests meets their needs, and stretches their potential. (See Table 11–1.)

Age-Level Activity Guidelines: Two- to Three-year-olds

- Provide language enrichment activities that include repeated exposure to nursery rhymes, fairy tales, imaginative picture books, puppetry, finger plays, familiar songs, beginning drama, storytelling, and poetic verse.
- Introduce children to letters and sounds in creative, playlike ways that promote physical movement, good listening, and discrimination.
- Provide listening activities that include nature outings, sound games, playing musical instruments, listening to stories, records and tapes in a listening center, listening for discrimination and recall.
- Label items and make picture word charts so that children become familiar with words. Have children dictate words that express their pictures and art projects. Record children's language as it is spoken.

SAMPLE 11–2   A Format for Literary Themes

1. Name and author of book
2. Objectives—why did you select this book?
3. Method—how will the main idea be presented?
4. Materials—what props or visuals will be used?
5. Outcome—what did children derive from the experience?

TABLE 11-1

Age	General Development	Ways to Encourage Language
Infants to 18 months	■ Cries and uses body movements to communicate ■ Vocalizes with cooing (three months) ■ Babbles (6 months) ■ Gestures to express needs ■ Acquires pacing and rhythm of adult language ■ Responds to spoken cues—waves bye-bye ■ Uses one-word sentences having different meanings ■ Vocalizes less while learning to walk	■ Use nonverbal communication: expressive sounds, gestures, smiles, clapping, tone of voice, facial expressions ■ Converse during caretaking routines of feeding, bathing, and dressing as well as during playtime ■ Talk purposely, slowly, clearly. Use short, simple sentences, naming objects that interest the child ■ Parallel talk: Describe what the child is seeing, hearing, thinking, and doing as the action is happening ■ Self-talk: Describe to the child what you are doing, hearing, seeing, as you are doing it
18 to 24 months	■ Uses two-word sentences—"go car," "up play" ■ Depends on intonation and gesture ■ Points and/or names objects in pictures ■ Responds to many words (receptive language), though he can not speak them (expressive language)	■ Share stories about concrete objects, people, and situations in his life ■ Stop and listen to child's verbalizations, even if unintelligible ■ Ask questions requiring a choice (e.g., "Do you want a bath with the rubber duck or the horsie?") ■ Provide outings and shared experiences to the store, zoo, park, and library ■ Play folk tunes, nursery rhymes, and marches
2 to 3 years	■ Generalizes—apple is a ball; all four-legged animals are dogs ■ Uses pronouns "me" and "mine" ■ Uses "no" ■ Enjoys imitating and mimicking nursery rhymes ■ Acquires past, possessive, plurals, prepositions ■ Obvious increase in communication behavior and interest in language ■ Large jump in vocabulary growth ■ Fifty percent correct in articulation	■ Discuss daily events before, during, and after they occur. ■ Even if not coherent, stop and listen to child's verbalizations ■ Read stories that involve the children in finishing a rhyme or giving a different ending to a story ■ *Tell* stories, freeing child from looking at pictures and bringing him closer to the power of words ■ Give labels to children's expressed emotions (e.g. "You're feeling sad that the paper tore") ■ Collect pictures from magazines showing action to encourage use of verbs
3 to 4 years	■ Communicates needs and questions: who, what, where, why ■ Dysfluency (hesitates and/or repeats whole words or phrases)	■ For dysfluency: Be patient, wait, do not interrupt; slow down your speech; be matter-of-fact; do not pressure child to speak before strangers.

TABLE 11–1   *Continued*

Age	General Development	Ways to Encourage Language
3 to 4 years *(cont'd)*	■ 3–4 word sentences; 400–900 word vocabulary ■ Responds to directional commands, "beside," and "under" ■ Responds to two active commands; "give me your plate and sit down" ■ Knows parts of songs; retells familiar stories ■ Rapidly acquiring the rules of grammar, using adjectives, verbs, and pronouns	(Most children outgrow this stage without professional help) ■ Use open-ended sentences requiring more than one word for an answer (e.g., "Tell me what your dog looks like") ■ Provide language experiences rich in rhyme, repetition, fantasy, humor, and exaggeration ■ Encourage children to dictate stories about themselves, their families, friends, pets, and the things they do
4 to 5 years	■ Uses irregular noun and verb forms ■ Talks with adults on adult level in 4–8 word sentences ■ A great talker, asks many questions ■ Uses silly and profane language to experiment and shock ■ Giggles over nonsense words ■ Makes similar speech adjustments as adults when speaking to a younger child ■ Tells longer stories ■ Asks what words mean ■ Recounts in sequence the events of the day	■ Provide opportunities for children to act out favorite stories ■ Create group discussions about a class problem to solve, a decision to make, activities to plan ■ Set aside a listening center with records of children's poetry and stories ■ Plan weekly themes and have children bring in objects that relate to the theme. Display and discuss objects ■ Drum patterns: Children can repeat the sound pattern by clapping hands or stamping feet

Source: From PRE—K TODAY, Issues from 1987 and 1988. Copyright © 1987, 1988 by Scholastic Inc. Reprinted by permission of Scholastic Inc. All rights reserved.

Age-Level Activity Guidelines: Four- to Five-year-olds

- Expand oral language and listening skills.
- Encourage children to identify sounds, to write inventively, and to begin reading familiar words.
- Practice letter and sound familiarity through creative, informal experiences.
- Make original group books, individual books, and encourage children to borrow library books from a media center to read with teachers and parents.
- Expand literary experiences to include a variety of literary genre (poetry, wordless books, folktales, and books that stimulate thinking as well as creativity.
- Encourage children to keep a journal for pictures, letters, words, and sentences.
- Encourage children to keep a word bank.
- Design picture/word charts and projects that facilitate language development—e.g., a current events bulletin board, an activity chart, a weather chart,

a "Star of the Week" chart, and picture/word projects that accompany units and discovery themes.

A SCIENCE/MATH CURRICULUM FOR EARLY CHILDHOOD

The Scientific Method

There are many commonalities between science and math that suggest the wisdom of a combined approach, particularly at the early childhood level. Both disciplines require basic process and thinking skills that are developed through the scientific method. Both are enhanced by a *discovery method* of teaching and learning. An early childhood program can successfully integrate the two by setting up centers that are integrally connected by materials, methods, and tasks. A child will use science functions when he plants an indoor garden and math functions when he charts its growth.

In a discovery environment, the child is an active explorer, seeking experiences that attract his attention and extend his thinking. A child's laboratory for learning is any space that absorbs and challenges a child; a child's learning field is as wide as his opportunities and interests. Children are born with an instinct to explore and discover why, and how, things work. To develop in-depth understandings about their natural and physical world, they must practice the skills that are basic to the scientific process. To become young scientists, children must have experiences and activities that enlighten and challenge their minds and that test their capabilities.

Observation and Investigation

When children make observations, they are focusing and concentrating on an activity that holds their interest. They are noticing physical characteristics, texture, shape, function, and prospects for play. Nature's gifts that often go unnoticed by adults are treasures to children. A child observes with acumen. She finds that tiny seeds, shells, and rocks are fascinating items to feel, observe, and play with. She uses them in imaginative ways that challenge her teachers. Ideally, a child should have an opportunity to extend his learning beyond the playground through follow-up activities in a discovery center (observing a snail shell under a magnifying glass).

A teacher can instill a child with the desire to learn by arousing interest in experimentation. She may open a lima bean, talk about the purpose of its embryo, experiment with germination, and with its uses. She may bring in seashells for a child to examine, pointing out how ocean tides and currents change shells and shorelines. A teacher may encourage a child to start a personal rock collection; the child may begin by categorizing and labeling rocks. In the process, the child begins to understand how some rocks come from volcanic eruptions (igneous rocks such as granite) and some from erosion (sedimentary rocks such as limestone). The teacher encourages the child *to question* and *to extend knowledge beyond* the classroom. She shares the child's interest with parents, suggesting ideas for follow-up activities (visiting a nature center, a quarry, or any water environment), hoping that a child's interest will become a parent's interest.

Sorting and Classifying Information

When children classify items, they collect and organize by attributes and by items that naturally go together. Math and science skills are integrated when children compare and contrast, group, count, solve problems, and as they interact with materials and objects. Children begin to see math and science as a *whole* integrated discovery process. They arrange objects from nature by making sets (a collection of objects with similar or identical characteristics) arranged in a discovery box.

Children use math and science skills as they compare a set of three acorns to a set of five pinecones using words like more, less, equal, and unequal. They discuss the concept of quantity and decide how many acorns are needed to make the sets equivalent. A curious child soon learns that a set with the same elements is equal while a set with the same number of members, but not with the same members, is equivalent. They extend their knowledge by matching (making the part equal) and labeling sets of leaves and by creating empty sets (by removing all the objects). They match numbers to objects and they can look for sets in their classroom: tools, dishes, musical instruments, markers, coins. Through first-hand experiences, children are investigating, ordering, comparing and contrasting, making observations, extending learning, and, most important, adding new materials to their science/math discovery centers.

Testing and Predicting

When children experiment with materials and objects they naturally begin to problem solve. They want to figure out how much water to put on a plant, how to measure temperature, how to be certain all the eggs are turned in an incubator every day, and how to determine what leaves to avoid touching on a nature outing. To solve problems, they must gather information and formulate a hypothesis (if I do this, then this will happen). By observing different kinds of clouds and climatic conditions, a child can predict rain. By mixing colors, a child can predict a new color; by freezing water, a child can predict its change in volume and shape. By experimenting with vibration, a child can produce sounds and predict sound volume (loose strings vibrate at a lower frequency than tight strings).

Documenting and Recording Data

Assisted by a teacher, young children can record and chart discoveries that take place in one day or over a period of time. A simple method of recordkeeping might include a date, a purpose, a process, findings, and illustrations. School-age children can record by synthesizing an experience with their classmates in written form. "Today we learned about fossils. A fossil is something that is dug out of the earth like a leaf print or an animal print that has been preserved in a stone. Fossils tell us about life on earth many, many years ago. Today we made a print of a fern in clay that looked like a fossil. Tomorrow we will dig for fossils in our backyard." Children can record the growth of seeds or plants by measuring and observing changes. Simple picture graphs that compare findings or visual experiences can be displayed in a discovery center (leaves, wild flowers, worms, insects, birds). "Today's Observations: 2 cardinals, 1 robin, and 1 bluejay." "These are the leaves we found today: 6 oak leaves, 4 maple leaves, and 2 magnolia leaves."

Developing Concepts

As children broaden their base of understanding and knowledge, they begin to make generalizations. Concepts develop as children proceed from concrete to abstract thinking. They are able to distinguish between living and nonliving objects and their natural and physical world. They can identify animals, plants, and insects as well as concepts of energy, astronomy, and weather. They are able to perceive life as cyclical and changing and begin to understand the interrelationships between organisms and their environments. They begin to perceive water not just as a drink or a puddle but as a vital life-sustaining element that is all-encompassing. They begin to perceive themselves in relation to their whole environment, identifying themselves as important actors in the continuance and preservation of the environment.

Evaluating One's Progress

By evaluating outcomes, children discover better ways of doing things and become more demanding of themselves. If an experiment doesn't work, a teacher can help a child to understand why. The scientific process is, by its very nature, an open-ended system that challenges children to try things. Trial-and-error learning that promotes critical thinking can begin at a very simple level of making choices and observing and by experiencing consequences. A child who can learn from mistakes is well on her way to being a self-sufficient, able learner.

Thinking in Terms of an Ecosystem

The concept of an endangered ecosystem is no stranger to today's child. Through on-site media coverage, children grasp the significance of an oil spill, especially on wildlife. Through documentaries, they learn about endangered species, acid rain, and the effect of pollutants on the environment. As they learn about the close relationship of all forms of life, they begin to perceive their world as interdependent. In her book, *Science With Young Children,* Bess-Gene Holt describes an ecosystem concept:

> An ecosystem is a community of living things interacting with each other and with their nonliving environment. An ecosystem includes energy, food, living organisms, and such factors as light/darkness, water/dryness, air, temperature, the swell of the land, or currents of water. It may be an ecosystem on or under the land, in the ocean, or in fresh water. You and children share one. You sometimes experience others: the park, the vacant lot, the downtown area, the suburbs, the farmer's fields, the mountains, the deserts, the forests, etc.[13]

An ecosystem approach connects a curriculum and an environment in significant ways. As children mature, they become aware of the environmental factors that influence the space they live in—how the sea alters the land and how land vegetation influences the survival of species. They become more sensitive to seasons, to weather and to environmental forces that affect life. Children read and respond to issues that describe how communities adjust to falling trees, floods, power outages, dry summers and cold, snowy winters. They begin to look beyond an event to its consequences; to its impact on a total environment. They begin to perceive science as a natural and necessary way of life. Children see how humans affect environments, and they begin to realize that it takes a community of people working together to preserve and conserve resources.

Young children will begin to develop environmental awareness if teachers have the background and skills to communicate ways that children can effect change. Through specific projects that are community-based or nationally identified, children can experience their environment from an interdependent cause-and-effect perspective. Through guided experiences, children will begin to understand that life is cyclical—season to season, seed to flower, tadpole to frog, caterpillar to butterfly, baby to man, and life to death.

Through environmental awareness, a child can develop a sensitivity for life in its many and varied forms. For a young child a spider-watching experience may begin with a simple observation—a child watching a spider spinning a web. The child can record an experience with only limited understanding or she can continue to *build on* her experience. A curious child may continue to watch the spider meticulously form its web-house, finding it hard to imagine how something so inexplicably beautiful can come from a tiny creature that is somewhere between insect and animal. The purpose is to entrap, but by understanding the relationship between the web and the spider's survival, the child can deal with the experience in a mature and positive way. A follow-up reading as sensitive as *Charlotte's Web*, by E. B. White, will further a child's understanding and compassion for all living things.

An ecosystem framework that incorporates problem solving and scientific inquiry will challenge children to discover more about their world. A child may find a fern or a cactus plant and attempt to replicate its environment. What conditions are conducive to growth—what kind of soil is needed, how much sunlight, how much water? How many eggs does a queen bee lay? Who takes a queen bee's place in a beehive? What happens to butterflies that don't migrate? How can animals sustain life during periods of hibernation? As children become agile thinkers, they exhibit flexibility and curiosity. They no longer accept simple responses or unsatisfactory answers. They value the interplay of ideas and the challenge of questioning.

Children become original thinkers in a discovery environment. A piece of bark with interesting markings may become a "fossil" for a science table and an unusual, round rock, a "dinosaur egg." Children are profoundly influenced by the quality of their experiences. When experiences permit them "to find out" through the investigatory process and when they begin to apply divergent thinking to their tasks, children use reason in their everyday tasks.

Units and Discovery Themes

Units

A teacher can develop a science and math curriculum using a unit approach. Each unit can be broken down to meet the developmental and interest level of the learner. By tailoring units to age levels, teachers can use the same topics year after year, encouraging children to accumulate knowledge. The subjects in Sample 11–3 may be developed for group presentation in early childhood environments.

For a young child who cannot process a great deal of information at once, a science unit should focus on immediate experiences organized around a familiar theme. For example, a chicken-hatching project may include several subthemes that are relevant and interesting to children. The teacher may plan a trip to a hatchery, storytelling experiences, art projects, and group discussions about caring for chickens. Ongoing activities will be centralized in a discovery center. Materials and activities may include: an incubator, books about chickens, feathers, a magnifying glass, pictures of a hatchery or a farm, flannel board activities that relate to the unit, original pictures made by children, a picture word chart, and a calendar to mark and count the days until the hatching. If a duck egg is included in the hatching, a teacher could expand her unit by simultaneously adding more items and extending thematic experiences (feeding ducks in a pond, learning duck songs and finger plays, reading Hans Christian Anderson's *Ugly Duckling*). As the eggs begin to hatch, the teacher may have the children compare the birth process of the two types of eggs. She may have children record the final data—how many eggs were hatched, what differences were noted, and what conclusions were made? During the first few days of caring for the new animals, the children may enjoy observing or discussing the differences between the duck and the chickens: their size, their interactions with one another, and so on. The children may or may not enjoy a culminating fieldtrip—returning the chickens and the duck to a farm.

SAMPLE 11–3   Topics for Science and Math Units

1. Growth and Change	8. Air and Space
2. My Natural World*	9. Wind
3. My Five Senses	10. Magnets
4. Foods and Measurement	11. Sound
5. Health and Nutrition	12. Light and Energy
6. Water and Sand	13. Simple Machines
7. The Weather Cycle	14. Conservation

*The natural world is a favorite topic in child care centers because many children can experience nature firsthand. All environments have characteristics unique to a setting that are fascinating to study. A unit may be selected from the following topics: animals, plants, insects and spiders, amphibians, seasons, ecology, food, and geology.

Discovery Themes

A discovery theme is presented in one day. A theme presented and completed in one experience enables children to process learning from a part to a whole perspective. They feel a sense of closure, of having completed an experience. When presenting a unified theme, a teacher generally proceeds from concrete to abstract levels. She identifies and presents a theme that will absorb and challenge each child using several mediums to "capture" her young audience, e.g., visuals, hands-on experiences, real objects, films, tapes (see Sample 11–4). She may, for example, give each child a bean to open and investigate and a bean to plant. She may then "capture imagination" by telling the story of *Jack and the Beanstalk*. Suggestions for theme topics are:

A rainbow	A rock
A balloon	An acorn
A worm	A blade of grass
A caterpillar	A flower
A cloud	A pumpkin
A feather	A shell

For examples of a unit and discovery themes, see Appendix B.

A Discovery Center

A discovery center is designed to integrate math and science activities for independent, child-initiated exploration (see next section). Each component should be set up on a separate but adjoining shelf so that children can identify each area in concrete terms while perceiving and experiencing the symbiotic relationship between science and math. The center can be described as a "thinking" center where children can explore and find out, mixing math and science materials and concepts in exciting ways.

For Science.   Science items should be arranged and labeled neatly and attractively on a wide shelf or table. They may include plants; terrariums; collections from nature; small animals such as mice, gerbils, horseshoe crabs or larger animals such as a guinea pig or a rabbit. Items such as magnets, prisms, magnifying glasses, and

---

SAMPLE 11–4   A Format for a Discovery Theme

1. An idea—why did you select this theme?
2. Main objectives—what are you hoping to accomplish?
3. Materials—how will the main idea be presented?
4. Extended activities—how will you supplement learning?
5. New words
6. Evaluation

---

fossils also should be included. Science materials should be changed periodically so that children can feel motivated to explore. Picture charts, seasonal pictures, and graphs made by children should be displayed in the center. Books and magazines should be neatly placed on a shelf. A center also should have paper, pencils, rulers, and journals available for children to make notes or keep records. A key word bank also is recommended. As children learn new science words, they should be written down and illustrated.

For Math.   Hands-on math activities should be located in an adjoining unit in a discovery center. A teacher may use this center to encourage children to participate in projects that are math-related: making a map of a neighborhood, redesigning a classroom, creating an adventure playground (using a diorama model or a sketch book for developing the concept), making simple pictures or bar graphs with children (the number and kinds of pets children have, favorite desserts, favorite sports, kinds of homes, and so on). Items should be carefully selected and age appropriate. They may include puzzles, games, manipulative, shape, number and discrimination activities, matching games, a balance scale, rulers.

Cultivating a Discovery Environment

Teachers who have a spirit of adventure and a desire to develop a quality science/ math program will have little difficulty cultivating a discovery environment. Making an environment into a mini-laboratory can be as exciting as developing a dramatic play center. Science is so basic and integral to children's experiences that teachers will find ideas for activities and displays that far exceed the dimensions of a discovery center. Recognizing the correlation between discovery learning and ample resources, a teacher will have to be selective in choosing materials and themes for her discovery center. She will need to expand her plans to include outdoor experiences and fieldtrips.

Teachers and children enjoy discovering together. Teachers get as enthusiastic as children when an experiment works or when there is a moment of insight shared by a group. Together, teachers and children can make a rainbow, a chemical garden, a water cycle, or measure temperature. They can make volcanoes, experiment with shadows, make a pulley, experiment with vibration, and make windchimes for their backyard. They can plant gardens or go on bird-watching walks, scouting for animals, and wandering in streams; they can help squirrels gather nuts, explore ponds and have adventures in their own backyards. They can measure earth worms, make dandelion chains, and find out if plants give off water vapor. They can gather and identify leaves, plant seedlings, and figure out why weeds grow so prolifically. When children hear the words "adventure walk," they will feel anticipation and excitement and dash for their equipment: a box containing a compass, a trowel, a flashlight, some plastic cups with lids, a pad and pencil, a mini first-aid kit, and a discovery bag for odds and ends that don't fit into pockets. These experiences *are* the scientific method in action.

LEARNING AT SCHOOL-AGE LEVELS

A Project Approach

Every center should have a list of potential projects and accompanying resources to encourage children toward extended learning. The list might include: community-based projects such as planting flowers and shrubs in front of public schools, special interest projects such as a national or international event that has potential for a science theme, an environmental study such as the effect of erosion on a salt marsh or barrier island, constructing models or simple machines, writing a book or a play, or a nurturing project such as entertaining senior citizens one Friday each month.

Children should participate in selecting and developing interest-based projects (for a format, see Sample 11–5). They can use brainstorming methods to make decisions, to solve problems, and to reach a consensus. Brainstorming allows children to see things in different and unusual ways—to stretch their imaginations. If, for example, children elect to learn about the patterns and life cycles of insects, a teacher might initiate thinking by asking why some insects are considered useful such as bees, and others, like fleas and flies, are considered harmful. Questions such as the right to life may cause children to reflect on their behavior and attitude toward insects. Every discussion can be examined from a creative thinking, interactional perspective to raise children's awareness of the meaning and purpose of life for all living things. For an example of a school-age project, see Appendix B.

Cultivating Learning at School-Age Levels

Teachers can encourage school-age children in their learning process by:

- Encouraging fluency: children should be encouraged to think, to question, and to find their own answers.
- Promoting a language-rich environment that uses children's own language as a catalyst for comprehension, communication, and language fluency.

SAMPLE 11–5   A Format for School-Age Projects

1. Project Design:
2. Estimated Time Frame:
3. Materials Needed:
4. Main Objectives:
5. Classroom Activities:
6. Community Activities:
7. A Culminating Activity:
8. Resources:
9. Evaluation:

- Encouraging flexibility: children should be encouraged toward reflective thinking and original ideas.
- Encouraging children to exercise imagination: to think of new solutions, different endings, and from time to time, to be somewhat outrageous.
- Encouraging children to stay on task.
- Encouraging children to think inventively and creatively.
- Encouraging children to solve problems and anticipate consequences.
- Stimulating discovery through first-hand experiences.
- Encouraging and providing opportunities for individual interests and talents to develop.
- Encouraging scientific thinking: what if, why, suppose, let's find out.
- Providing an inquiry, discovery-oriented environment that connects outdoor and indoor experiences.

CUMULATIVE OBJECTIVES

A child-centered learning environment will encourage all children to:

- Become young explorers and researchers.
- Learn by doing.
- Become critical listeners and thinkers.
- Develop discrimination skills.
- Predict events and anticipate outcomes.
- Question and think.
- Communicate fully and develop confidence in language.
- Develop originality through self-expression.
- Experiment with creativity.
- Make connections between language and thinking.
- Make connections between science and math.
- Develop an awareness of the inter-connectedness of knowledge and experience.
- Appreciate and value one's human and physical environment.

ASSESSING CHILDREN'S LEARNING

Teachers should make informal observations as children play in activity centers, share in teacher-initiated activities, and engage in group experiences.

- Am I encouraging children to think divergently?
- Do I encourage them to seek alternative solutions and to solve problems?
- Are my objectives broad enough to include creative thinking as an approach to learning?

- Are children exercising initiative, independence, and self-management in their attitude toward learning?
- Is my language program meeting the developmental level of my students?
- Am I encouraging children to develop foundational skills in math and science?
- Have I integrated my curriculum in ways that are meaningful and exciting to young learners?
- What resources can be added to my curriculum and to my classroom?
- How can I make better use of parent's interests and talents in forwarding my program?
- Am I achieving a healthy balance between teacher-initiated activities and child-initiated activities?

Group Activities for Early Childhood:

1. *A reading tree:* Children bring in a tree branch from out-of-doors and decorate it with key words or with words that relate to a theme (fall: leaves, rake, red, yellow, squirrel, nuts), the words may be printed on color paper shaped in patterns such as leaves, flowers, hearts, snowmen, apples, pumpkins.

2. *A class word bank:* Children (or teacher) print key words on 3" × 5" index cards, provide a picture clue on the reverse side; cards can be categorized by subject and put in a file box or in large envelopes.

3. *Original books:* A classroom book should relate to a special event or theme—when each child has contributed a page, the teacher can bind the book, have children make/create a cover design, and a title (books should be laminated for wear and tear).

4. *Original teacher books* that children can illustrate and learn to read.

5. *Flannel board stories:* Children can create stories themselves—they can think of a theme, make the characters (from cardboard), add a velcro backing, make a flannel board (using heavy cardboard), and enjoy their own creations.

6. *Mail a letter:* Children can compose a letter each week to someone special—each child can contribute a comment and make a picture. After the teacher addresses the letter, the children can add stamps and mail it. (These can be thank-you letters, which are important to value training.)

7. *Friend of the week:* Each week a child can select and honor one classroom friend. They can make a book about the child and her playmates, write special comments on a star (I like the way Barbara plays ball, and so on), help a teacher organize a "Barbara bulletin board" with family pictures and children's drawings; and they can plan a special event for Barbara—put on a puppet show, read a book, or make her favorite cookies.

8. *Circle Games:*

Telephone: A message is passed quietly around the circle and the last child in the circle repeats the message out loud.

Matching Items: Teacher distributes picture card sets of animals and their homes. Children need to find a match before the drum beats.

Sharing: Children bring something special from home, put it in a bag, give clues, and classmates guess what the object is.

Planning: Plan a special day each month—color day, pick-your-own clothes day, pet day, senior citizen, or grandparent day. Children get to make choices and love the anticipation that precedes a special day.

Learning Letters: A four-year-old can practice letters by sound. A teacher introduces children to one letter per week. On letter day a child brings a novelty item from home that begins with the letter sound and classmates have to guess what the item is. The children make a letter snack (banana bread), a letter project (a bear puppet), and enjoy a related story (*Goldilocks and the Three Bears*).

Making Changes: The teacher may change the sequence of a story, the characters, or the ending and observe reactions (children also can be asked to change the ending of a familiar story), e.g., Goldilocks broke papa bear's chair; Red Riding Hood met a bear on her way to grandpa's house.

Tall Tales: A story is begun in circle and grows bigger and bigger as it is passed around.

Finishing Sentences: The teacher provides a message and the child, the ending— A zebra lives . . . A monkey eats . . . A bee makes . . . A mailman . . . A forest ranger . . .

Rhyme in Time: A teacher sings or tells a rhyming sentence or verse and the children continue—I met a man, his name was . . . That big fish, lived in a little _____.

Polly or Pete Parrot: The teacher whispers a message to a child (touch something hard, something cold, something yellow)—the child (Polly) must fly to items whispered, touch them and fly back home without forgetting the message.

Seeing Patterns: The teacher makes a pattern on a flannel board with objects, e.g., a square and a triangle—following the pattern the child must add the next shape (the task can become more challenging by making more difficult patterns, e.g., three squares, two triangles, and one circle).

Sequencing: The teacher asks children "What comes first, picking apples, baking a pie, or planting an apple tree?"

Discrimination: The teacher draws a picture on chart paper—the children must guess what is missing on the objects drawn by adding the missing object, e.g., a house without shutters, a bus without a door, a face without a nose.

What's Wrong: The teacher shows children picture cards of objects that belong to a set and adds something that does not belong (e.g., a hammer, a nail, a banana, or a bird, a nest, a bee, an egg)—the child responds appropriately.

Take Away: The teacher lines up colored blocks—children look, hide their eyes, and the teacher takes away one or two blocks. The children must guess which blocks were taken away.

Observing: The teacher makes changes on a child's garments outside the classroom—when teacher and child return, a classmate must guess what has been changed (sleeve rolled up, shoes reversed, glasses removed, hairclip removed).

Who Am I? A child hides behind a screen, sings "Do You Know the Muffin Man?"; one friend comes up and knocks on the door which prompts the child to sing. The friend must guess who is behind the screen.

Guess What's Inside? The teacher fills a bag with a familiar item (clothespin, a brush, a toothpick, a fork), and each child gets a turn to feel and name the object.

What Could This Be? The teacher brings an object to circle (a scarf, a tennis racket, a clothespin, a rolling pin, or a bar of soap) and children must think of all the ways the object could be used. (The teacher can write down the responses to show children how imaginative they are.)

We're Going on a . . . : The teacher tells children where they are going and children have to think about what they will bring on their trip (on a bear hunt, a rock climb, a trip to the moon).

What Am I? Children act out being an animal or an object and their classmates must guess what they are. Children may give a clue—I have wings or I like milkweed pods, or I hum and live in a meadow in a tiny nest.

Hide and Seek: The teacher hides something, gives clues, and makes an approximate map of the location—children must find the item or items.

Books that Promote Learning at Early Childhood Levels

Anno, M. *Anno's Counting House* (number concepts)

Barton, Byron. *Airplanes, Boats, Trains, Trucks, Machines That Work* (concepts)

Becker, J. *Seven Little Rabbits* (counting)

Briggs, R. *The Snowman* (prediction)

Burningham, John. *Mr. Grumpy's Outing* (sequence, counting)

Broekel, R. *Your Five Senses* (perception)

Carle, E. *The Grouchy Ladybug* (time and size)

Carle, E. *The Very Busy Spider* (concentration, design)

Carle, E. *The Very Hungry Caterpillar* (sequence)

Crews, D. *We Read A To Z* (letter names, recognition)

Crother, R. *The Most Amazing Hide-and-Seek Counting Book* (pop-up counting)

de Paola, Tomie. *Strega Nona* (prediction)

Flack, Marjorie. *The Story About Ping* (cause, effect)

Kellog, S. *Chicken Little* (sequence, prediction)

Kroll, S. *The Biggest Pumpkin Ever* (size relationships, divergent thinking)

Liberty, G. *First Book of Human Senses* (perception)

Lionni, L. *Inch by Inch* (thinking, problem solving)

Miller, B. *Alphabet Word* (letters and sounds)

Mostel, Z., and G. Mendoza. *Sesame Street Book of Opposites* (demonstrates meanings of antonyms)

Reiss, J. *Colors* (the many shades of colors)

Scheffer, V. *The Seeing Eye* (perception: texture, color, form)

Schwartz, D. *How Much Is a Million?* (speculation)

Steig, W. *Sylvester and the Magic Pebble* (time changes)

Tafuri, N. *Have You Seen My Duckling?* (observation)

Turkle, B. *Deep in the Forest* (counting, groupings)

Yektai, N. *Bears in Pairs* (rhyming number concepts)

Ziefert, H., and A. Lobel. *Where's the Guinea Pig?* (curiosity, problem solving)

NOTES

1. Susan D. Shilcock and Peter A. Bergson, *Open Connections: The Other Basics* (Bryn Mawr, PA: Open Connections, 1980), p. 5.

2. As cited in Joan Moyer, et al., "The Child-Centered Kindergarten," *Childhood Education* 63(4) (Wheaton, MD: ACEI, April 1987): 238.

3. Ruth Duskin Feldman, "What Are Thinking Skills?" *Instructor* XCV(8) (April 1986): 35.

4. Barbara Z. Presseisen, *Thinking Skills Through the Curriculum* (Bloomington, IN: Pi Lambda Theta, Inc., 1987), 14.

5. John Dewey, *How We Think* (Boston: Heath, 1910).

6. Barry K. Beyer, What's in a Skill?: Defining the Skills We Teach," *Social Science Record* 21 (1984): 19.

7. Anne Schreiber, "Fire Up Those Brain Cells," *Instructor* 98(3) (October 1988): 63.

8. Shilcock, and Bergson, *Open Connections*, p. 11.

9. Ilse Mattick, "The Teacher's Role in Helping Young Children Develop Language Competence," in *Language in Early Childhood Programs,* ed. Courtney B. Cazden (Washington, DC: NAEYC, 1981), pp. 83–88.

10. As cited in Ida Santos Stewart, "Kindergarten Reading Curriculum," *Childhood Education* 61(5) (Wheaton, MD: ACEI, May/June 1985): 357.

11. As cited in Irene C. Fountas and Irene L. Hannigan, "Making Sense of Whole Language: The Pursuit of Informed Teaching," *Childhood Education* 65(3) (Wheaton, MD: ACEI, Spring 1989): 134–35.

12. Bruno Bettelheim and Karen Zelan, *On Learning to Read.* (New York: Vintage Books, 1982), p. 5.

13. Bess-Gene Holt, *Science with Young Children* (Washington, DC: NAEYC, 1977), p. 110.

RESOURCES

For Language and Thinking

Althouse, Rosemary, and Cecil Main. *Science Experiences for Young Children.* New York: Teachers College Press, 1975.

Bender, Judith, et al. *Half a Childhood: Time for School-Age Care.* Nashville, TN: School Age Notes, 1984.

Brown, Janet F., ed., *Curriculum Planning for Young Children.* Washington, DC: NAEYC, 1982.

Cazden, Courtney B., ed., *Language in Early Childhood Education.* Washington, DC: NAEYC, 1981.

Charlesworth, Rosalind, and Deanna J. Randeloff. *Experiences in Math for Young Children.* Albany, NY: Delmar, 1991.

Gilbert, LaBritta. *I Can Do It! I Can Do It!: 135 Successful Independent Learning Activities.* Mt. Rainier, MD: Gryphon House, 1984.

Honig, Alice S. *Playtime Learning Games for Young Children.* Syracuse, NY: Syracuse University Press, 1982.

Kamii, Constance, and Rheta DeVries. *Group Games in Early Education.* Washington, DC: NAEYC, 1981.

Kamii, Constance. *Numbers in Preschool and Kindergarten.* Washington, DC: NAEYC, 1988.

Lind, Karen K. *Exploring Science in Early Childhood.* Albany, NY: Delmar, 1991.

Levenson, Elaine. *Teaching Children about Science.* Englewood Cliffs, NJ: Prentice-Hall, 1985.

Lorton, Mary Baratta. *Workjobs.* Reading, MA: Addison-Wesley, 1972.

Neugebauer, Bonnie, ed. *The Wonder of It: Exploring How the World Works.* Redmond, WA: Exchange Press, 1989.

Petrash, Carol. *Earthways: Simple Environmental Activities for Young Children.* Mount Rainier, MD: Gryphon House, 1989.

Presseisen, Barbara Z. *Thinking Skills.* Bloomington, IN: Pi Lambda Theta, Inc., 1987.

Raines, Shirley C., and Robert J. Canady. *Story Stretchers: Activities to Expand Children's Favorite Books.* Mt. Rainier, MD: Gryphon House, 1989.

———. *More Story Stretchers.* Mt. Rainier, MD: Gryphon House, 1991.

Redleaf, Rhoda, *Teachables II: Homemade Toys that Teach.* Mt. Rainier, MD: Toys 'n Things Press, 1987.

Rockwill, Robert E., Robert A. Williams, and Elizabeth A. Sherwood. *Everybody Has a Body: Science from Head to Toe.* Mt. Rainier, MD: Gryphon House, 1989.

Sawyer, Walter, and Diana E. Comer. *Growing Up with Literature.* Albany, NY: Delmar, 1991.

Schickedanz, Judith A. *More Than the ABC's.* Washington, DC: NAEYC, 1986.

Seefeldt, Carol, and Nita Barbour. *Early Childhood Education: An Introduction,* 2d ed. New York: Macmillan, 1990.

Shilcock, Susan D., and Peter A. Bergson. *Open Connections: The Other Basics.* Bryn Mawr, PA: Open Connections, Inc., 1980.

Sisson, Edith A. *Nature with Children of All Ages.* New York: Prentice Hall Press, 1982.

Sisson, Linda G. *A School-Age Program Guide for Directors.* Nashville, TN: School-Age Notes, 1990.

The Smithsonian Institution. *Science Activity Book.* New York: Galison Books, 1987.

———. *More Science Activities.* New York: Galison Books, 1988.

Spodek, Bernard, ed. *Educationally Appropriate Kindergarten Practices.* Washington, DC: National Education Association, 1991.

Sprung, Barbara, Merle Froschl, and Patricia B. Campbell. *What Will Happen If . . .* New York: Educational Equity Concepts, 1987 (distributed by Gryphon House, Mt. Rainier, MD).

Williams, Robert A., et al. *Mudpies to Magnets: A Preschool Science Curriculum.* Mt. Rainier: MD: Gryphon House, 1987.

———. *More Mudpies to Magnets.* Mt. Rainier: MD: Gryphon House, 1990.

I am convinced that the quality of our individual lives and the quality of our society are directly related to the quality of our artistic life. We need the arts as the key to the higher order of things—our cultural heritage, our gift of expression, our creative faculty, our sense of beauty.

— John D. Rockefeller

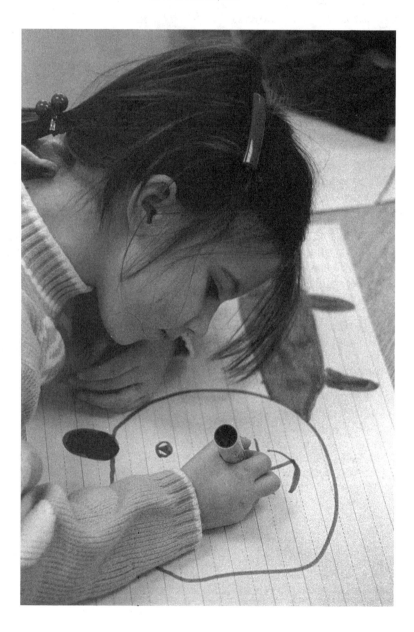

12

COMPONENT THREE:
THE ARTS

THE PREMISE

A child care program that cultivates the arts in early childhood is cultivating the creative process. The creative process is vital to early childhood because it feeds and nurtures all facets of human development—play, learning, physical, social, moral, and emotional. Self-expression is an *integral* part of children's daily ongoing, experiences. A child who is encouraged to invent and experiment with ideas and materials in activity centers or at an art easel is expressing himself creatively. What teachers fail to realize is that a child who is role-playing is not just pretending and a child who is painting is not just dabbling. Each child is expressing in a different way something about himself: his perception, his experiences, his personality, his interests, his needs. A child who is absorbed in an art form does not require outside stimulation; he is centered within himself. The creating child is making important connections between his internal and external worlds. He can make puppets talk using his own words. He can paint and produce language to express his artwork. He can use his body to become something or someone that stirs his imagination.

An experience is satisfying and pleasurable when it is self-generated and fail-free. A picture grows before a child's eyes, a picture that is somehow connected to the brush he is holding and the paint he is using. A child's artwork is the child and his canvas, his entire environment. Art should never be limited to an art center or to a dramatic play center. Art is inside and outside of a center and implicit in every learning experience; it is whatever a child decides to play with or think about or imagine; something that is an extension of himself. A child needs to experience many forms of art to satisfy his curiosity and his need for self-expression. When a child tires of building castles in the sand, he will look for another way to express himself. He might carry little cups of water back and forth from a water fountain to a dirt pile, excited by the texture, look, and feel of wet dirt. He doesn't perceive (like adults) that dirt is dirty; he views it as a stimulating texture with enormous possibilities. A child doesn't understand why he can't play in mud; he views it as a totally natural part of his natural world. Nor does he understand that rocks or sticks can be dangerous when they are natural "playmates" that trigger pretend play.

When a child engages in the arts, he is a creator. He is producing an authentic art form that has intrinsic meaning for him. As such, the child becomes a meaning-maker absorbed in a pleasing experience that he can control. He will find ways to prolong something that he likes. He will add sticks and rocks to a mud construct and paint over a painting. He will make a mess and be oblivious to its consequences. Art is integral to play and play is integral to art. Both are integral to the child.

A child engaged in the creative arts demonstrates awareness, imagination, and autonomy. Awareness comes from experiences that *stimulate* the senses. Multisensory experiences are excellent catalysts for the creative arts. The more a child can observe, interact with and respond to her total environment, the freer she will become to express herself through the arts. Imagination is generated by the act of creating. It can be cultivated by teachers and it can be promoted in an environment that has aesthetic appeal and creative tools to draw on. Autonomy is the child at play/work. The arts, like play, is child-initiated and a relatively free form of expression. A child who is free to express is not inhibited by artificial barriers that stifle his creativity.

In an environment that cultivates originality, children's original productions are respected and valued. Children vary in their interests and are therefore selective in the way they express themselves. Some children may be extremely adept at constructing with blocks but disinterested, and therefore less developed, in artwork. If the meaning of art can be expanded to include anything a child creates, it will include all of the arts—the visual arts and the expressive arts. And, all children will become creative artists.

In a child-centered environment, children are free to experiment with many expressive mediums. Through cumulative experiences, a child develops a creative attitude. With each personal experience, she becomes more confident and more expressive. A child who carefully selects flowers for a bouquet is expressing an art form; a child who is playing with a doll or with a pretend friend is expressing an art form; a child involved in dramatic play is expressing an art form; a child playing and singing with musical instruments is expressing an art form. Creativity is any experience that satisfies and holds a child's attention. It is the child at play/work.

When the child is expressing himself authentically, a creative experience originates and ends with the child. Children's authentic productions are always unique. No two paintings look alike, no two dramatizations are executed in the same way. Art is not patterns or copywork; it flows naturally from the child's imagination and expressive language. A child's productions reflect their creator—an ever-changing, ever-growing and highly inquisitive young child. There is no gallery painting and no dramatic script that can ever be as authentic, as original, and quite as delightful as a child's original productions.

Through creative expression, imagination abounds. Children can become tiny insects and huge birds on a musical fantasy trip. They can feel and experience their environment in new and exciting ways. They communicate with their bodies, their minds, and their spirits. Through creative experiences, a child *expresses* what he already knows, *experiences* what he needs to find out, and *experiments* with the unknown. He is able to find extraordinary meaning in ordinary everyday objects and experiences.

DEFINING THE ARTS

In a position paper, "The Child's Right to the Expressive Arts," the ACEI (1990) has defined the arts as music, art, drama, dance, and writing stating that:

- Every child has a right to opportunities for imaginative expression;
- Educating the child's imagination is education for the future;
- The educated imagination is the key to equity and intercultural understanding;
- Children's creative productivity is qualitatively different from adults';
- Creative expression should permeate the entire curriculum;
- Imagination is the key to artistry in teaching and excellence in our schools;
- We must refashion our schools for the twenty-first century.[1]

INTEGRATING THE ARTS INTO A TOTAL CURRICULUM

In child care environments, a definition of the arts should be extended to include all creative constructs or experiences that occur as a child interacts with his environment. From a programmatic perspective, if art is to permeate the curriculum, it must be a primary component in program development. It must be seen as a *bridge* that connects all areas of a curriculum in meaningful and relevant ways that can be understood by children and appreciated by a teacher. No longer confined to an arts and crafts table, art is perceived as *integral* to all play centers and to all learning experiences.

An arts-based curriculum will perceive learning from a different, somewhat less conventional frame of reference than traditional programs. It will be less time bound and less structured. It will redefine the arts from a child-directed perspective, taking into account children's creative instincts. It will develop program objectives that acknowledge the importance of originality, resourcefulness, inventiveness, and independence to a child's development. The objectives will affirm and reinforce characteristics[2] of a creative person, defined by Leon Burton and Kathy Kuroda as:

Interest in ideas and meanings
Eagerness to explore the environment because of a need to know
Willingness to risk the unknown
Openness to new experiences, ideas
High tolerance of ambiguity
Interest in personal expression
Preference for complexity
Persistence in examining
Sensitivity to problems
Spontaneity
Curiosity
Playfulness
Flexibility
Independence
Intuitiveness

A creative program will integrate the arts and learning. A science center is enhanced by an aesthetically arranged group of materials that invite exploration. If children are studying woodland Indians, for example, there might be a large wooden bowl filled with real vegetables and nuts for children to smell, feel, and sort on a science table. The parts of a piece of corn may be labeled and defined. The teacher and children might add a long house (made from a milk carton) and a wigwam (made from clay and covered with bark) to the science display. The teacher will include white potatos, red potatos, and sweet potatos in any combination and encourage children to note differences. Leaf prints and pressings will be hung on a wall nearby. Each week a new artifact will be added: moccasins, a totem pole, jewelry, dolls, tools, an animal print mold, bark, baskets, an Indian alphabet, Native American music, and musical instruments. The science table will become an arts-in-education project that is close to authentic and clearly hands-on learning.

Through ongoing, multisensory experiences in a discovery center, children get to experiment with different textures (smooth, soft, rough), with smells (vinegar, vanilla, pepper, garlic, lemon, cinnamon), with environmental stimulants (charts, plants, growing things, animals, soft cushions), and with eye-appealing activities that encourage creative thinking and exploration (geoboards, tangrams, cubes, terrariums, sorting trays, water experiments). The feeling and look of a science center that abounds with art forms, colors, and textures will be recreated by children in their own artwork.

Virtually all science and math skills can be presented artistically in a child's natural play setting. Similarly, a social studies unit can be presented through arts and crafts, visuals, literature, and hands-on experiences that are a natural and pleasurable function of play. A language-experience story often begins with a child's artwork. Cooking experiences become aesthetic and sensory delights when presented creatively. A teacher who is aware of the relationship between the arts and learning will design and develop her program from a creative perspective. She might, for example, think of ways that basic skills can be creatively introduced to children. A skill theme may become a truly exciting experience if it is presented in a dynamic and meaningful way, if a simple fact becomes a stimulating concept when expressed through the arts. Every time a teacher considers a learning objective, she should think about ways it can be integrated into an expressive, self-generating experience.

HOW TEACHERS CULTIVATE THE ARTS

By Observation

A teacher can serve an important role in cultivating visual, sensual, and kinesthetic awareness by drawing children's attention to the aesthetic and physical world that surrounds them. A teacher may take children on daily "seeing walks," encouraging them to look, listen, touch, and notice things. She can point out little things like the delicate green color of a praying mantis and big things like a helicopter twirling around interrupting the tranquility of a sky-scape.

A teacher can take children on a "shape walk," pointing out various shapes in a natural environment, having children sketch what they see, compare what they find, and identify common characteristics. She can take children on a "feeling walk," pointing out the textures (and smells) of nature and collecting interesting things for observation, like worms, mollusks, anthropods, and tiny creatures. (Live creatures should be returned to their natural environments in relatively good health after visiting with children.) She can take children on a "space walk," observing how distance changes one's perspective, noticing how space moves around and through freestanding objects, asking children to sketch a one-dimensional and perhaps, a two- or three-dimensional picture. She can take children on a "body awareness" experience that encourages freedom of movement—playing with balls and balloons; swinging; running up hills; rolling down hills; dancing with scarves; moving in, out, and around hoops; crossing pretend streams (on a balance beam) and pretend oceans (on a nesting bridge); blowing and chasing bubbles; flying kites and following birds in flight. She can take children on a "surprise walk," a walk that is done so quietly that not even the birds hear; a walk that is meant for finding special treasures (hidden by a treasured teacher). First-hand experiences that extend perceptions help a child identify and interpret the physical world.

Through observation, a child becomes more knowledgeable about space and his own place in space. He notices large, imposing buildings and small clusters of houses. He notices big things and little things. A child notices things that often go unnoticed to the casual, uninterested observer.

By Valuing Originality

Creativity must be understood and reinforced by teachers if it is to flourish in children. A teacher who interferes with the artistic process or who identifies a ditto as artwork may, unknowingly, destroy it. She is replacing children's original artwork with a reproduction (something that is produced by adults). An obedient child will follow directions and eventually tire of a teacher-directed project while an independent child will say "I don't want to" more often than not. What she really means is that the teacher is expecting something from her that she is not interested in doing. If a child is required to at least begin an art project, the teacher will undoubtedly complete the project for the child. Under adult monitoring, a child will soon lose interest in art as an expressive outlet, choosing drama or blocks for creative play.

A method that invalidates children's authentic artwork is not in keeping with the principles of child-centered learning. It is depriving a child of the right to give her own meaning to an experience; it is taking away her right to choose how and what she will create. A cut-out turkey with colored feathers neatly arranged by teachers may look cute, but in reality, it is a distorted impression of the subject. A child visiting a farm will not see a turkey with a perfect tail in erect posture. She will see a straggly, hardly colorful, rather unfriendly bird that spends most of its time with its head down looking for food. Parents may not be particularly impressed with the results of child-initiated artwork, but if they are informed about the value of an authentic experience, they will be more inclined to praise what comes home, no matter how it looks!

By Praising and Encouraging Children's Artwork

Adults can cultivate the arts by affirming children's self-expression. Children receive messages by the way a teacher communicates and responds to authentic artwork. A teacher who throws artwork away because it is too messy or is reluctant to hang artwork on a wall because it does not fit into her visual scheme is not supporting creative expression. Similarly, a teacher who touches up artwork or who instructs or directs projects is giving a child a message that her work is not acceptable.

A teacher who is able to step back and observe a happy child engrossed in artwork is cultivating creativity. As she studies a child at work and observes her productions, she will see the child from a different perspective. She will notice that the child creates with unique blends of color, shapes, and imagination. At appropriate times, a teacher may inquire about a painting or a picture, encouraging a child to share its meaning. By showing interest, she is communicating to a child that she appreciates and values her work.

By Selecting Appropriate Art Experiences

Appropriate art experiences should reflect children's levels of development and interests. In an informative and sensitively written book, *Early Childhood Art*, Barbara Herberholz describes the categories of experiences that may prove useful in developing an arts curriculum: visual and tactile perceptual encounters, production of art, aesthetic judgment and valuing of art, and heritage of art.[3]

Visual and Tactile Experiences

At early levels of development, these experiences are natural, ongoing activities that invite exploration such as painting at an easel, finger painting, experimenting with colors, cutting and pasting paper, sand and water play, coloring with large crayons, drawing on a blackboard with chalk, playing with play-dough, playing with textured fabrics that are in a feel box, reading picture books, planting seeds, caring for baby animals, taking "seeing" walks, and exploring one's play environment. They are important stimulants for children's creative instincts.

Production of Art

As children become more interested in the art process, they move from simple to more complex levels of production. They know what they need and they know how and where to obtain materials. They can design and complete a multistep art project without adult intervention. A child involved in an art project can work for extended periods of time without distraction. He has infinite patience for his work. As he works, he is *developing* an *awareness* of tactile and shape variations, of design and composition, of figure-ground orientation, of parts to a whole, of spatial awareness, and of balance. Encouragement always factors into children's continued interest in an activity. An art center must have a place to display artwork and a teacher who appreciates and understands children enough to display it, as is.

Aesthetic Judgment

It is very difficult to assess the artwork of children other than on its own terms. Although children should not judge one another's work they can develop aesthetic appreciation that will prepare them for aesthetic judgment as they near adulthood. In his book, *Art and the Creative Development of Young Children*, Robert Schirrmacher sensitively defines aesthetics:

> Aesthetics is the study of beauty; not the Hollywood view of glamour, but beauty in color, form, and design. In a time of mass production with little concern for effort and quality craftsmanship, the quest for beauty is difficult. Still, there is a human need to make sense out of and appreciate one's self and one's environment, just as there is a basic need to create.
>
> Beauty can be found in nature, in one's surroundings, and in everyday objects. Children can use their senses and their bodies in their pursuit of beauty. The eyes can visually explore art, the ears can listen to sounds and music. Three-dimensional artworks can be touched, scents can be smelled, foods can be tasted, and the body can respond through movement and dance. Young children can learn to appreciate and have beautiful experiences.[4]

Aesthetic appreciation is a gradual perceptual skill that is linked to experience. When children experience live entertainment, they naturally become art critics. Sometimes they cannot explain why they didn't like something, but often, with some questioning from a teacher, they can become quite verbal about their opinions. A teacher will promote aesthetic appreciation by challenging children's ability to think creatively. She might ask questions that pertain to plot development, character development, costumes, set designs, lighting, sound effects, the moral or meaning of a story, seating, interactions among the characters and the audience, the length of a production, and feelings generated by the experience.

Heritage of Art

As children mature, they can appreciate all forms of artistic expression through direct experiences with theatre and cultural activities, i.e., visiting art galleries, museums, photography exhibits, a sculpture garden, arts and crafts exhibits, a botanical garden, folk festivals. Child care centers can help children develop their heritage by introducing them to famous artists and their productions. They will become familiar with the various forms, styles, and periods of art. They will pick out a Rembrandt painting by its use of dramatic lighting and a Picasso by the placement of dissimilar shapes on a flat, one-dimensional surface. They will become familiar with schools of art and their characteristics: medieval and classical art, romantic art, neoclassical, impressionism, expressionism, cubism, and modern art. They will become familiar with themes and styles that are identified with certain artists, e.g., landscape, seascape, portrait, sculpture, still life, impressionism, geometric abstracts, splash paintings, and pop art.

STAGES OF ART

Scribble Stage

Young children progress in the arts much as they do in any other skill, from simple to complex levels. Most educators specializing in the arts agree that children's artwork tends to develop sequentially through various stages. Although chronological ages may vary, the sequence of stages tend to be fairly predictable.[5] Early artwork that appears between the ages of fifteen months to around three years reflects a child's developmental level. At this basic level, children's art resembles random scribbling. Early scribbles are primarily zig zags, curves, or spontaneously placed splashes that appear to have little meaning. One marking often fills up a whole piece of paper. As primitive as early art is, it represents a child's increasing level of awareness and coordination.

As children develop eye–hand skills, scribbles become more controlled and recognizable—circles, loops, and intricate swirls indicate the beginnings of representational art. Familiar objects begin to appear; creatures that resemble amoebae (tadpoles). By adding lines for arms or legs, the little creature becomes more humanlike. A child begins to identify his picture as a person when he adds dots for eyes, and if somewhat more perceptually advanced, clawlike fingers and toes. The child, who is very pleased with his accomplishment, identifies the picture as "mommy, daddy," or, never lacking in ego, "me." If the experience is positive, the child will ask to make another picture; this time with a marker (or two), or, with a Q-tip that can be dipped in paint, creating a whole new experience for the child.

Preschematic Stage

Between the ages of four and seven, children progress into a preschematic stage (also referred to as a pictorial stage). Children's pictures take on form and symbolic meaning (simple drawings begin to represent something or someone). The child has control over the direction and size of lines and has advanced in levels of motor control. Objects that are important to a child are the subjects of most early artwork. A circle with four legs is identified as a dog or a cat, a circle with a vertical base is identified as a tree, a dash of color on the ground is a flower. As a child's perception heightens, his pictures begin to fill more space and gradually convey a feeling of a balanced composition. A person once floating sideways in the air will be firmly placed on a grass line. Clouds and raindrops will be placed above the person and the composition may well be framed by a border.

By centering and reducing the size of primary objects, children discover there is more space to fill with birds, flowers, bugs, and raindrops. A child's paintings often reflect her current interests at a developmental stage such as dinosaurs and action figures. Familiar subjects such as family members, pets, homes, friends, and seasonal symbols (hearts and pumpkins) are fairly constant themes of the young painter.

Schematic Stage

Between the ages of seven and twelve, a child's artwork enters a schematic stage that reflects children's interest in their ever-expanding concrete world. Despite occasional escapes into fantasy, children like to depict a very detailed, precise world in their drawings. They become caught up with features, parts, and balance. Their artwork requires a great deal of organization, time, and thoughtfulness.

The way a child approaches artwork reflects his disposition, interests and developmental level (see Figure 12–1). Some children will meticulously arrange shapes according to some preconceived pattern while others prefer spontaneous bold strokes that may or may not develop into a recognizable form. Most children tend to experiment with both *free form* and *idea-centered* compositions especially if they are in a creative classroom.

VALUING THE ARTS

Art Is Learning

A creative child is a learning child. As children explore with materials, they become increasingly sensitive to their physical world and creative potential. They perceive differences in line, volume, colors, textures, and shapes. They observe the spatial placement of familiar scenes. The sandbox is next to the swings and the swings are in front of the hill. Space begins to take on *dimensionality* and *scale;* things that are close appear large, those at a distance, small. The sky appears to be an infinite,

FIGURE 12–1 Developmental Levels in Children's Art

Stage	Age Range	Motor Control	Purpose	Characteristics of Stage
Random/ disordered scribbling	1½ to 3 years (Toddlers)	Lacks good motor control and hand–eye coordination	Scribbles for pure physical sensation of movement	■ Lacks direction or purpose for marks ■ Does not mentally connect own movement to marks on page
Controlled scribbling	Young pre-schoolers	Improving motor control and hand–eye coordination	Scribbles with control	■ Explores and manipulates materials ■ Tries to discover what can be done—explores color, texture, tools, and techniques ■ Often repeats action ■ Makes marks with intention and not by chance
Basic forms	3 to 4 years	Has more developed motor control and hand–eye coordination	Enjoys mastery over line	■ Masters basic forms: circle, oval, line, rectangle, and square ■ Discovers connection between own movements and marks on page
Pictorial stage (first-drawings stage)	4 to 5 years and older	Has control over direction and size of line Has most advanced motor control and hand–eye coordination	Communicates with outside world through drawing Expresses personality and relationship to symbols drawn	■ Combines basic forms to create first symbols ■ Names drawings as a form of true communication

Source: From PRE—K TODAY, Issues from 1987 and 1988. Copyright © 1987, 1988 by Scholastic Inc. Reprinted by permission of Scholastic Inc. All rights reserved.

shapeless mass occasionally interrupted by bird forms, planes, and patterns of clouds moving through and around children's visual images.

As children experience themselves in an expressive environment, they clarify and expand meanings; they discover cause-and-effect relationships, the power of nonverbal communication, and the possibilities of using their own ideas. In that art is primarily a subjective, *internalized* experience, children are not so dependent on external reinforcement for gratification as they are in many social or content-oriented activities that make children feel like they have to perform.

When children are free to create, they apply divergent (flexible) thinking to their tasks. As ideas are generated, children *invest* in their production and become less concerned with outcomes. They become more fluent in producing and developing ideas. They adapt and modify their combinations until they feel satisfied. The personal satisfaction a child derives from an original production is enormous. They do not require external gratification. Self-directed children trust and follow their own ideas.

Art Is Barrier-free

An arts-in-education program encourages children to become imaginative and inventive producers. Children naturally transfer their impressions into their productions. A child who notices a sky will paint it with the same attention she gives to a landscape, noticing the shapes and movements of clouds, colors, and the sky. For a creative child, an interesting branch may become an object of classroom art decorated in its seasonal attire—a symbol of spring, fall, winter, and summer. Pinecones, a piece of driftwood, dried flowers are natural enhancers on a science table. Creative thinking is not bound to a project or an idea, nor is it apportioned at birth. Some children may have innate ability that is identified early as "gifted," but *all children hold* the *potential* for being culturally aware, competent, and artistically creative human beings.

Art Promotes Social/Emotional Development

An informal, relaxed atmosphere invites children's participation. A nonthreatening environment puts forth positive signals and feelings. Children naturally respond to activities that stimulate good feelings. All children profit from the freedom to express themselves. Joyful children experience more joy as they create. Troubled children release the tension that is holding them back or interfering with their self-esteem. In either situation, a child who is free to pound, to hammer, to splash, and to create is a happy child.

As the child develops self-confidence, he sifts, identifies, and expresses problems through vicarious experiences. As he expresses his feelings, he is able to let go of some of the fears that restrict his movement and limit his capabilities. He learns to trust his instincts and to experiment with his talents. As a child makes contact with his extended self, he gradually *affirms* his own potential and *enjoys* his own productions.

Creativity can be enhanced or stifled during the formative years. Creative opportunities often are lost in structured environments: a child doesn't get to make stick drawings in the dirt because sticks are prohibited, climb a tree because its too dangerous, or wear a ballet outfit in block play because it is not allowed. When a child's movements are unnecessarily restricted and challenged, she loses her inquisitiveness and imagination. Anxious to please, a child becomes a product of the conventional environment that surrounds her.

Early childhood is the time to foster original thinking through the expressive arts. Creative imagination peaks at four to five years old. Through acculturation, however, creative imagination declines at school-age levels. The challenge for early childhood teachers, therefore, is to stimulate . . . to keep alive children's natural desire to create so that as an *intrinsic* part of the child, it grows with the child.

IMPLEMENTING THE ARTS

The Visual Arts

Arts and Crafts

For the child younger than three years of age, table art should focus on tactile experiences and aesthetic enjoyment. Seated or standing at an art table, children might enjoy such activities as string painting (dipping string in paint and smearing it on a piece of paper); marble painting (rolling marbles dipped in paint on a piece of paper that is contained in a box); printing (dipping vegetables, shapes, or leaves in paint and stamping designs on plain paper); finger painting with paint, shaving cream, or whipped soap flakes; painting cardboard boxes; making handprints or footprints; or assembling and pasting (using various shapes and textures). For holidays or special events, teachers may want to initiate a special art project that can be enjoyed by children and parents: an apple or pinecone turkey, paper bag pumpkins, tissue paper ghosts, a simple puppet, dried flower arrangements, or holiday ornaments. As pleasing as these projects are, they should not be considered original productions unless the child controls the process. They should be labeled "crafts."

When a child reaches four or five years of age, she has a better concept of form and design and enjoys more extensive experiences at an art table. She is especially attracted by colorful, unusual materials and will delve into construction and assemblage with fervor. Children exercise choice and decision making in the materials they select and the compositions and constructs they design. Arts and crafts give children a chance to experience a multistep art project that requires attentiveness to one task. In addition to cognitive stimulus, a craft project also should provide many opportunities for experimentation and free association. Children should be able to make choices and to orchestrate their production without teacher interference. Some materials like foil, felt, glitter, and doilies are particularly eye-catching and appealing for a collage (an assemblage of materials arranged in random order on a plain piece of paper). Ideas to develop for arts and crafts are making:

- Holiday gingerbread houses;
- Mobiles;
- Wild flower arrangements and molding a vase;
- Corn meal and sand drawings (add powdered tempera paint to sand);
- String art;
- Designs by stitching on fabric;
- Wire sculptures;
- Baker's dough (1 cup flour, 1/2 cup water, food coloring);
- Oily dough (3 cups flour, 1 cup salt, 3 T oil, 1 cup water);
- Gadget junk art sculptures;
- Costumes and shirts by tie-dyeing;
- Prints (draw designs with pencil point on interesting surfaces such as styrofoam trays, cover with paint and press onto paper);
- Crayon-resist pictures (draw designs with crayons and paint surface of paper);
- Drawings out-of-doors with charcoal, feathers, or colored chalk;
- Objects from toilet paper rolls;
- Baby food jars colorful by layering with different colors of sand;
- Placemats with materials gathered or designed by children (should be laminated for continued use);
- Magnets made with cute eye-catching objects;
- Shoe box art themes;
- Alphabet or number art;
- Puppets (from socks, fruits and vegetables, paper bags, paper plates, peanut shells, tin cans);
- A puppet stage from a large cardboard box;
- Interesting variations on collages.

The act of gluing, organizing, and assembling artwork is far more important to the child than the finished project. A picture or creation eventually emerges—sometimes incredibly balanced and beautifully orchestrated and sometimes a potpourri of glue, drips, holes, and blending colors that have long since lost their distinctiveness. As the child works with mediums and materials, he becomes more aware of composition and design. He studies and selects from the various materials that surround him. He balances his composition by repeating designs and by arranging shapes in harmonious and sometimes bold, uneven patterns that add variety and interest to his design. He transforms ordinary shapes into extraordinary assemblages, into unique art forms.

The Teacher's Role. It is the teacher's responsibility to provide the materials and experiences that promote creative expression. An arts and crafts table/shelf should have a wide variety of materials for children to assemble and interact with: paper plates; styrofoam trays; paper bags; a scrap box containing material, tissue paper, newspaper cartoons, wrapping paper, flannel shapes, fabric, yarn and other visual delights; an odds and ends box containing gadgets, paste-ons and novel accessories; and, of course, play dough and modeling clay. By adding simple accessories to a paper bag such as buttons, yarn, and pipe cleaners, a child can create a hand puppet. By stuffing a bag with paper, she can make a cute little creature, adding feet, ears, hands, a tail, and a face. She can name the creature and write a story about it.

Some children who lack fine-motor control get frustrated with tedious tasks that are identified with finished products: stringing clay beads, sewing, or completing a diorama that has little meaning to a child. These children should not feel compelled to engage in a "creative activity" that is not creative for them. Art projects and experiences should be *choices* and not requirements for children. If a teacher has set up an art experience that requires more than an initial explanation, the project is probably too difficult for a child to understand and manage independently.

School-age children will spend endless hours with arts and crafts. They enjoy the challenging projects and interesting materials a good program provides, in large part, because they are able to transform and work with materials in their own way. They especially enjoy innovative projects such as making masks, candles, home decorations, marionettes, little creatures made with styrofoam or pom pom balls, collages, murals, mosaics, prints, corn husk dolls, embroidery, and stitchery. Children's artwork can peak when they are involved in group projects or dramatic productions. For many children, making scenery or costumes is as important as becoming a star.

Because school-age children are project oriented, they will need space for storing ongoing projects, a place that is away from other little hands. Projects such as woodworking, building models, weaving, hooking rugs, stitchery, and knitting are not usually finished in one day. Projects for holidays and for special events such as drying and arranging flowers, making candles, or working on a ceramic project will require careful handling before they can go home. It is important to children that their creations are cared for and appreciated by teachers.

Painting

At the early stages of artwork, children enjoy the pleasure derived from holding a crayon and scribbling on paper. Early scribble art strengthens children's small-muscle development, making them more agile in eye–hand coordination. The same strokes used in scribble art are used later when children begin to write. When young children are introduced to painting, they typically experience a three-step process: holding paint brush, dipping it in paint, and transferring the paint to a piece of paper. Often one or two strokes will satisfy a child's initial interest in painting. At the early stages of development, children should choose among primary colors: red, blue, or yellow. A large supply of white paint always should be on hand to soften and change color tones and to add excitement to a child's creative experience.

Like children's babbles, early painting experiences do not appear to say very much but they are a necessary part of a child's development. Through early art experiences the child becomes aware that he can make things happen; he can change things; he can create something. Somewhere between three and four years of age, random strokes evolve into lifelike objects. These early expressions of form gradually evolve into more realistic and recognizable objects and people: a house, the sun, an animal, a child, or a parent. A child paints what he sees, what is familiar to him, and what is important to him. Children typically use geometric shapes to symbolize people and objects and horizontal lines to identify the ground and the sky. There is little linear perspective and symmetry in their early productions. A child will often exaggerate important objects in a painting, e.g., a life-sized father or mother, a tiny new baby, an oversized pet.

As children develop coordination and a sense of composition, their paintings and drawings become enchanting expressions of childhood. When children are four or five years of age, their artwork begins to reveal perceptions and emerging personalities. Some children love bold, open strokes, others paint linear drawings that are meticulous in form and design. A girl, sensitive to patterns, may frame a painting with a border of alternating flowers and hearts. A boy, preoccupied with dinosaurs, may paint dinosaurs and huge eggs until the fixation is replaced by something else. As perceptions sharpen, paintings become more and more detailed. Figures are elongated when necks, feet, toes, arms, and fingers are added. Animals get tails and eye lashes; birds get long beaks, long legs, and worms in their mouths.

School-age children enjoy painting with many colors and mediums and in various settings. They enjoy mixing and blending colors and using a variety of materials: paints, payons, water colors, acrylics, oil, and chalk. Children enjoy sketching out-of-doors; coloring at a homework table or in a loft; and drawing on blackboards, on sidewalks, and in art centers. They love to decorate sets for plays and performances, making props and costumes from boxes, containers, kitchen and attic discards, and whatever else suits their fancy.

The Teacher's Role. Teachers should recognize the potential art holds for children by creating a child-centered, expressive environment. In a genuinely creative environment, children should be encouraged to construct with sand, mud, and dirt; arrange leaves, berries, and nutmeats in interesting patterns; finger paint with soap on doors and windows; make chalk pictures on sidewalks; and paint a building with water. By expanding the arts to include all hands-on, creative experiences, children will perceive art as an integral part of their natural world. They will become aware of design, composition, linear and horizontal dimensions, texture, form, shape, and materials. They will react strongly to pleasure-inducing experiences and be less attracted by adult-initiated experiences. In an arts environment, children should become acquainted with important artists and their works. A young child will enjoy looking at the primitive, childlike paintings of Grandma Moses, at a soft impressionist painting by Renoir, or at the bold angular lines of a Cézanne landscape.

A school-age child can become familiar with periods of art and famous artists: with classical painters such as Michelangelo, DaVinci, Raphael, and Rembrandt; with romantic painters such as Delacroix and Copley; with impressionist painters such as Renoir, Monet, Pissaro, and Manet; with post-impressionist painters such as Cézanne, Van Gogh, Gauguin, Matisse; and with contemporary painters such as Picasso, Léger, Chagall, Klee, and Kandinsky. Children can become familiar with (and think about) distinguishing techniques used by artists: El Greco's use of elongated figures, Cézanne's unfinished paintings, Vermeer's detailed, meticulous organization of objects, and Kandinsky's musical composition themes, and Rembrandt's use of light.

Children can recreate works of arts that hold special meaning. They can make dot paintings (pointillism), construct with two-dimensional shapes (cubism), and splatter paint (like Jackson Pollack). They can use cut-up comics, scraps of paper, and everyday household objects to create pop art. By visiting galleries, purchasing inexpensive prints, and borrowing reproductions from a local library, children can develop expertise and a lifelong interest in the arts.

Photography

An introduction to photography provides a visual experience that is quite different from artwork. Children should understand the difference between taking a picture and painting a picture. They should understand that unlike art (at least at the early stages), photography is a multistep process. Children must decide on a subject, position a camera, take a picture, and wait for its development. They may discover that through photography, an artist can capture detail, moods and emotions, and action. Through photographs children learn about their world and its people; children become less bound by the here and now. Some books are enhanced by this process while others rely on an artist's illustrations for visual effect.

Through photography children sharpen and expand their perceptual field. They can see things from a three-dimensional perspective—a friend, a play yard, and the sky. They can understand that what is in the forefront is larger than what is at a distance. Photography therefore requires decision making, problem solving, and experimentation. The child must decide what she wants in a picture and how to obtain her perceptual image.

The Teacher's Role.   By taking and looking at photographs, teachers can help children perceive photography as a unique art form. Photographs provide instant pleasure for young children. Albums that include family members, grandparents, teachers, and special events will facilitate continuity and bonding in young children's lives. Taking pictures of children at play and on fieldtrips will enrich an experience. Children will look at pictures of themselves and their friends over and over again; they love identifying family members and friends. Photographs personalize shared experiences and nurture self-esteem.

Children love cameras, but they need instruction before experimenting with real film. Simple, inexpensive cameras can launch school-age children into filmmaking. Disc and Polaroid cameras are intriguing playmates for children at beginning levels of photography. They can learn how to load film and how to identify the parts of a camera: the lens, the viewfinder, the shutter, and the film cartridge. They can approximate distance and consider the effects of light and atmosphere on their subjects. Older children can assist in operating a 16mm projector, in rewinding films, and in operating slide projectors. At an appropriate time, and with some tutoring, children can make their own films.

Woodworking

Children in child care environments love the challenge of woodworking. Woodworking provides an important emotional and physical outlet for children. Young children's experiences with woodworking should be limited to large blocks of wood, small light hammers, and large-head nails. A tree stump provides a wonderful base for hammering. In time, children can progress to independent projects with wood.

As children mature, they enjoy organizing, measuring, and coordinating constructs and enjoy using tools that perform specific functions. They soon discover that hammering nails into a block of wood or using a small saw to cut light wood is not easy. Nails bend and frustrate a young builder. Wood splits easily and is not always soft. The task of assembling a construct or a sculpture requires patience and perseverance. School-age children enjoy using more formidable tools such as drills, pliers, screwdrivers, a vise, and measuring devices. They enjoy sanding and varnishing wood. Children also enjoy using assorted materials such as hardware accessories, ice cream sticks, parts of games, buttons, packing materials, wire, string, rubber bands, and bottle caps as parts of their design.

The Teacher's Role. Teachers can encourage woodworking by arranging materials and tools so that they are accessible and inviting. Various sizes of soft wood and tools will challenge children to construct creative objects. Accessories will provide incentive and guidance in developing and shaping constructs. Pictures of buildings, bridges, railroad trestles, welders, and artisans may be displayed in a woodworking center. Certain individuals may be singled out for their contributions to the art of woodworking, such as architect Frank Lloyd Wright or sculptor Henry Moore. Children may enjoy seeing how space can be used dramatically in both architecture and in sculptures. Wright fused buildings into the natural settings; Moore used space to make figures stand out, creating a sense of vitality and permanence in their settings. By studying artworks, children are impressed by a great variety and individuality of the styles that have preoccupied artists. They learn that an artist works to perfect his style and his skills. Some works are impersonal and abstract, some convey explicit expressions of feelings and emotions, while others have a hidden meaning.

Creative Writing

For Young Children

At early childhood levels, creative writing is identified with the visual arts. Young children learn to read by associating words with pictures. Pictures illuminate meaning by helping a child make a connection between the visual and the literal arts. In an arts center, children often begin writing on their own. They imitate real books as they cut, assemble, and staple paper together for a story theme. Young children will make a book of sorts, marking each page with a simple stroke and an occasional picture. If asked, they will tell a story about their pictures. More advanced children will develop a story that resembles a real book. When children write spontaneously, they print words to describe pictures and they make pictures to describe words. At any level, there is considerable initiative and inventiveness in the way children organize, illustrate, and assemble original writings.

The Teacher's Role in Early Writing.   A teacher provides materials and ideas for children's original writings. She encourages practice writing in journals and more extensive group projects such as making "big books" (oversized books that are usually read to groups of children). Big books may be developed around a theme such as letter day. An *A* big book may have an apartment cover with children's faces at each window; a *B* big book may have a bear-shaped cover (Bobo the big brown or black bear); a *C* book may have a corn, cactus, or cake cover. Children then would write stories that correspond to the sound of the key letter. The stories are stapled inside the big book.

Writing projects can be individualized (each child makes a picture storybook), collective (each child contributes one picture story to a group book), or something in between (a teacher and her students write and illustrate a story together). Because big books can be cumbersome to work with and individual books are time-consuming, a teacher will want to participate in the process. In writing projects with school-age children, a teacher might make suggestions, edit, type, and assist in the overall production of a book.

The Teacher's Role in School-age Writing.   School-age children are prime for creative writing experiences. Every child care center should have a writing center for school-age children. This can be as simple as a table and shelf, or it can be a fully equipped center for creative writing—with space for a typewriter and/or a computer. Children can begin writing at an elementary level by making picture/ storybooks for young children. A good way to begin writing is to become reacquainted with children's literature. From the vantage point of maturity, a school-age child can renew interest in classical children's books or nursery rhymes to the extent he or she feels the urge to write in a similar genre.

By returning to early language experiences, children can bring back important creative memories. They can recapture the images, sounds, and sensations of their favorite nursery rhymes and reexperience their pleasure. In the words of Dylan Thomas,

> The first poems I knew were nursery rhymes, and before I could read them for myself I had come to love just the words of them; the words alone. What the words stood for, symbolized, or meant, was of very secondary importance. What mattered was the sound of them as I heard them for the first time on the lips of the remote and incomprehensible grown-ups who seemed, for some reason, to be living in my world.[6]

Perhaps a child's first experience with creative writing should not begin with children's literature at all but with listening to the beloved sounds of nursery lore that began way back in the beginning; the rhyming sounds of "Jack Be Nimble," "Old King Cole," "Bah, Bah, Black Sheep," and "Peter Peter Pumpkin Eater"—where the sound of *p* and the full, round shape of the pumpkin create an image that makes every reader want to crawl in a pumpkin shell and "be kept very well" forever.

As children discover the elements of writing, they soon notice that writers and illustrators have unique styles and characteristics that distinguish them from other writers and illustrators. This alone is an enlightening experience for a young writer who may find herself discussing Maurice Sendak or William Steig's literary style and appeal to young children. Attention will invariably turn to the child: What kinds of books are particularly pleasing to young children and why? A point of view will emerge.

Children soon will learn that writing is an art and that a book, even as simple as a picture book, takes concentration, skill, and a very serious commitment. As they practice writing, children will learn to appreciate the importance and placement of words to the progression of a story, the elements of a story (plot, character, form, and setting), and the appeal of a story.

Serious writers will implement what they have learned through theme-building techniques by jotting down ideas—What is the story about? Who are the main characters? What are they like? Where does the story take place? What form of writing will be used to develop the plot (narrative, poetic verse, wordless)? Is there a problem and if so how is it resolved? What is the climax? and of great importance in children's literature, What is the ending?

From theme-building, a child writer can begin to think in terms of layout (number of pages, illustrations, and a cover design). Some children may prefer to begin with an idea or a picture and develop the plot as a story evolves. Others will have a story theme in mind at the beginning of a project. Both free writing and story building should be encouraged at early stages of writing.

Similarly, school-age children can begin writing poetry by writing a book of verse for young children. Children can be introduced to poetry by rereading favorite poems of their not-so-distant early years. The poetry of Myra Cohn Livingston, John Ciardi, Joanne Ryder, Eve Merriam, and Shel Silverstein or Robert Louis Stevenson's *A Child's Garden of Verses* may help to reacquaint children with poetic verse. Children will discover that writing has a unique rhythm, quality, style, and pattern and that poetry can be free and it can be metrical. Children may, for example, enjoy writing haiku to create vivid and sensory images. Haiku is a Japanese form of verse consisting of three unrhymed lines; it represents two images: one an enduring condition such as changing seasons and the other a theme. What could be more charming than Myra Cohn Livingston's descriptive verse in haiku:

Even in summer,
bees have to work in their orange
and black striped sweaters.[7]

Children also may experiment with humorous verse:

> *My snowman has a cold today,*
> *He's sneezing and freezing and refuses to play,*
> *He wants to go south with the birds on the block,*
> *But he has no wings to follow the flock.*
>
> *I'll dress him in earmuffs, mittens, and socks,*
> *and give him a name like Mr. Tick Toc,*
> *I'll tell him a story and feed him hot tea,*
> *He'll soon be better to play with me!*

By reading poetry, children will become comfortable, if not enthralled, with the idea of writing poetry. As children discover poetry, they discover themselves. A poem, writes Lenore Sandel: "can sing with its own music of rhythm, it can paint a picture with words, it can tell a story, or it can say things to a person by bringing forth moods and emotions."[8]

When children are in the poetic or story-writing mode, a good way to help them organize their thinking is through clustering activities. In *Writing the Natural Way*, Gabriele Lusser Rico describes clustering as follows:

> To create a cluster, you begin with a nucleus word, circled, on a fresh page. Now you simply let go and begin to flow with any current of connections that come into your head.[9]

In clustering, words trigger related ideas that expand outward and connect until all associations are exhausted. Descriptive words like summer, rain, snow, dying, birth, grandmother, or food will immediately conjure images that can be put into words and expanded into creative writing. Writing becomes not only a free and creative experience but a self-organized process. (See Appendix B.)

Teachers should encourage children to critique their writings. A guideline for creative writing will be helpful for young, inexperienced writers; it might pose self-help questions: Did I say what I intended to say? Does my paragraph hold together? Have I used interesting adjectives? Have I used interesting images? Is the plot clear to the reader? Is there a climax or a high point in the story? How might I improve my writing? Have I asked a friend to critique my work? Should I "sleep on my ideas" and rethink my story tomorrow?

A Quiet Area

In order for children to write, they need a private area that is equipped for writing. Typewriters and a computer are wonderful tools for writing but are not always available to children. Traditional writing materials, i.e., a pencil and a piece of paper, are actually preferable at beginning writing levels. The physical environment strongly influences the creative process. A quiet area promotes concentration and reflection.

Music

The Value of Music

Music is an important dimension of creative development. At early childhood levels, play activities often are accompanied by music. Music is aesthetically calming and pleasing to a young child. A listening experience can stimulate a child and open up his creative instincts. It can get him in the mood for nonverbal communication and creative pursuits.

All children love to sing and listen to music. Music is a vital part of daily living because it produces joy and relaxation. Research on the social effects of music indicate that it has tremendous potential for associative play. Music has been found to:

- Sustain children's participation in group activity;
- Encourage their positive emotional arousal;
- Promote their readiness to participate in group activities and their acceptance of group recommendations;
- Promote trust and cooperation;
- Reduce anxiety.[10]

Children can enjoy music by playing instruments, singing, playing games, and quiet listening. Music, like art, can be integrated into all activities. It can be used in theme-building (to reinforce language and listening activities), in dramatizations (as an accompaniment to role-playing and plot-building), in language activities (look and listen records), in discovery centers (discriminating and identifying sounds by tone, sound, and by timbre, the source of the sound), during group circles (creative movement, counting songs by rhythms or singing phonics, e.g., "B" is for "Baby" . . . B, B, B), and in writing centers (to stimulate ideas). Music can be a specialized activity that focuses on instruments (a guitar, a piano, or an autoharp) and lyrics (folk songs, holiday songs, action songs, theme songs, and favorite songs). It also can be an authentic child-centered experience—putting on a musical talent show or a musical such as *Annie* or *Oliver.*

Music Develops Naturally

At the early stages of development, music and rhyming verses are virtually indistinguishable. A three-year-old hears rhythm when she recites finger plays and nursery rhymes. The songlike, lyrical patterns that are repeated in nursery rhymes are similar to children's first songs. In both instances, motor movement, voice inflection, repetition, and rhyming words are used. By imitating and repeating rhyming words, children are hearing the same melodic sounds and rhythmic beats (cadences) that are used in many songs: "This little froggy broke his toe; this little froggy went oh, oh, oh; this little froggy cried and was sad; this little froggy laughed and was glad; . . . but this little froggy was thoughtful and good and he hopped for the doctor's as fast as he could" (author unknown).

Children perform as they listen and chant—mimicking characters, memorizing words, and making appropriate movements (and faces). They listen for cues and favorite verses: ". . . And frightened Miss Muffet away! . . . Jack jump over the candle stick! . . . Just tip me over and pour me out!" They listen for discrimination and appreciation and they learn about the nuances and patterns of language. A teacher who can read with intonation, knows when to raise or lower her voice. She knows how to share the beauty and power of language with children.

As children mature they are able to expand their musical abilities through practice and training. In her exceptionally informative book, *Music in Our Lives: The Early Years,* Dorothy T. McDonald points out that:

- Musical sounds may be high or low in pitch.
- Melodies may move up or down by steps or skips.
- Many melodies move home to a tonal center that may be felt and identified; a satisfactory sense of completion results.
- Certain melodic phrases may be repeated in a song; such repetitions may be recognized and identified.[11]

At early childhood levels, a music experience should incorporate movement as well. Music and movement are enhanced by descriptive pictures (visuals). A teacher, for example, may present the Froggie finger play visually on a flannel board. The children sing the song while each one gets a turn to move a froggie on a flannel board. Four froggies may jump into a pond and the last one (everyone's favorite) may hop off the board on his way to the doctor. "Row, Row, Row Your Boat" is another example of a song that has potential for multi-body movements. Glen T. Dixon writes:

> For young children, experience in music and art can compensate for the pervasiveness of verbal interaction and abstract symbolism in the classroom, at an age when words and written symbols may have insufficient relevance to their own expression of ideas. Plastic, visual and aural media provide means for children to realize ideas that need not rely on verbal or numerical concepts stressed in other areas of the curriculum.[12]

The Teacher's Role in Music.   Teachers need to provide opportunities that stimulate children's interest in music. A child's early interest in music increases when he is encouraged to use instruments regularly. Instruments provide creative outlets for experimentation with sound and self-expression. Each instrument has a name, a shape, and an individual sound. By combining instruments and listening for directions, children can make an orchestra or a marching band. In a creative approach to making music, Emil and Celeste Richards describe everyday objects such as washboards, thimbles, glasses, funnels, plastic bottles, coffee cans, scraps of wood, coat hangers, and garbage cans that can be used to create musical instruments.[13]

Homemade instruments might include banjos, bells, drums, tambourines, sand blocks, sticks, triangles, and tuning pipes. As children invent and use their own instruments, they become aware of the elements of sound and the rhythmic patterns of music, melodies, and tempo. They choose favorite instruments for favorite songs. Some children develop an interest in playing a real instrument. School-age child care programs should consider offering interested children special classes in music such as group piano, guitar, electric ukuleles, or choral singing.

Movement and Drama

Creative Movement

Creative movement is a wonderful, expressive outlet for children in child care centers. Children can dance on their own or they can enjoy creative movement during group experiences. Initially, teachers may feel apprehensive about organizing a creative movement curriculum, but with the help of records and musical instruments, most teachers can move into a "dance motif" with little difficulty. Through movement, children can learn to follow directions, to develop listening skills and rhythm, to express feelings, to explore locomotion (how a body can move in space), to develop body coordination, and to project themselves into becoming something or someone else. They also can develop cooperative skills because movement requires cooperative interaction in the sharing of space.

Drama

Young children should not be expected to perform "on-stage" before an audience in a child care center unless a production is handled naturally and comfortably without a great deal of preparation and rehearsing. Children often feel insecure when they are put in the position of performing. If children are enrolled in special arts classes, they are more prepared for an audience and more confident about performing. A nice way to include parents in dramatic events is to invite them into a classroom to observe an impromptu dramatic experience—one that is performed without elaborate costumes or set decorations. Familiar stories such as "Billy Goat Gruff" or "Red Riding Hood" are perfect themes for classroom presentations. When children are familiar with a script and free to improvise, they will enjoy the experience more.

Through reenactments, children develop language fluency, a knowledge of plot development, and a sense of identity with the characters who tell the story. When language is open and free, children can be inventive and on occasion, outrageous. They can embellish a dramatic event with their creativity and humor.

School-age Drama.　School-age children love to engage in improvisational drama in their classroom, and they also enjoy putting together an "on-stage" presentation before a live audience. Unlike young children, school-age children are capable of piloting a production from beginning to end without a great deal of adult assistance. A five-year-old can follow a simple script reasonably well, while a six- or seven-year-old can orchestrate an entire production with some help and guidance from a teacher.

Large-scale productions should be prepared well in advance by children and teachers. Each child has a sense of her role and importance to a theatrical production. As part of the preparation, children should read scripts and choose roles they feel comfortable with. Every role, no matter how small, is important to a production.

A Teacher's Role in Movement and Drama

A teacher's guidance and support is always welcome. An adult can help children to organize a production so that it "appears" to hold together. Musicals tend to work well at school-age levels because children like to sing. Even a relatively serious drama, such as "Hansel and Gretal" or "Alice and Wonderland," will be enlivened and integrated by music. When words are forgotten and cues misread, music has a way of making a not-very-good production a natural success.

Teachers can serve as coaches; they can help children plan and design costumes; they can assist in set decoration; and they can soothe children who may feel opening-night jitters. They also can remind children that a dramatic production is a serious effort that should be given time and sincere effort. Children need to understand that anything worth doing is worth doing well. They need to invest themselves in their production.

After several child-produced efforts, a center may decide to offer special classes in the arts for children who are developing talents and interests in drama or other creative areas. Classes in dance, script writing, set design, creative dramatics, and puppetry will provide an important next step for a school-age arts program. Imaginative names for art classes such as "Back stage" or "Playworks" will also stimulate interest.

In order to attract children, classes in the arts should be presented innovatively in ways that appeal to both sexes. An indoor aerobics class, for example, may be presented as a creative movement class. A group piano class may offer opportunities for live performances with local bands. A drama class may highlight creative writing, staging, critiquing, and media production. A puppetry class may become a puppet theatre that performs at community events.

School-age children enjoy putting on plays for parents and friends, especially plays that they write and produce themselves. The emphasis should be "back stage" rather than "on stage." When children are not expected to memorize lines, they will become enthusiastic, natural performers. Most of the time should be spent on creating costumes and painting or making scenery and props. Young children love to be trees, nontalking cats, birds, or any little "pop-up" creatures that can be cleverly worked into a script.

Children who participate in dramatic productions come to realize that dramatic play is a powerful form of self-projection as well as expression. The Lion, the Tin Man, the Scarecrow, and Oz are seen from a new, more sympathetic perspective. Children select characters that hold personal meaning; characters that, for whatever reason, they want to identify with. As children role-play, they begin to affirm themselves; they sense that the stage is a safe place to become someone else for just a little while. The experience may strongly influence their lives as well as their feelings about themselves. Through drama, children are catapulted into a world that they can control, that demands something different from them, that has new meaning and tremendous possibilities.

OBJECTIVES FOR AN INTEGRATED ARTS CURRICULUM

A centerwide arts program will encourage children to:

* Become self-aware through self-expression;
* Use materials in creative and original ways;
* Focus on a task until satisfaction has been achieved;
* Develop flexible, process-oriented thinking;
* Solve problems as they arise;
* Develop autonomy and a strong sense of accomplishment;
* Express feelings and attitudes in creative ways;
* Become sensitive to the roles the arts play in human development;
* Extend and develop interests and talents;
* Explore an environment from a creative perspective;
* Feel confident in one's own abilities;
* Experience art from a cultural, multidimensional perspective;
* Develop an understanding of one's artistic tradition and cultural heritage;
* Perceive the arts as a process that is a catalyst for human development and creative thinking.

ASSESSING CHILDREN'S PRODUCTIONS

Teachers should be attentive to children's development in the arts by observing a child's:

* Eye–hand coordination skills;
* Developmental level;
* Use of materials and activities that interest her;
* Barriers to self-expression;
* Attention level;
* Ability to communicate verbally;
* Ability to communicate nonverbally;
* Ability to discriminate and draw inferences;
* Ability to work independently and stay on task;
* Ability to make choices and organize a project;
* Willingness to cooperate and engage in dramatic play;

- Interest in completing a dramatic production;
- Ability to interact socially with peers;
- Ability to be inventive and resourceful;
- Interest in being adventurous and innovative;
- Ability to think divergently and flexibly;
- Attitude toward the creative process.

GROUP ACTIVITIES

Improvisational Drama for Young Children

Teachers guide children in acting out a story using their own ideas and words to reenact the plot. Every child gets a turn and chooses a character or object to become. Simple props such as a chair or a basket will hold children's attention during the activity.

Improvisation Examples

Billy Goat Gruff by M. Brown.
Props: Wooden steps, a balance beam, or a nesting bridge
Follow-up: Grow fresh, juicy, green grass in a styrofoam cup; when the seeds sprout children can make a Billy Goat face on each cup and add cardboard horns.

The Three Little Pigs by The Brothers Grimm
Props: A cardboard house, cut-outs to symbolize straw, sticks, and bricks for a chimney.
Follow-up: They can make puppets out of felt and make the pigs talk.

Goldilocks and the Three Bears by The Grimm Brothers
Props: A housekeeping table set for three; one little bear in a highchair
Follow-up: Children can make a snack of porridge using instant oatmeal; they can invite a favorite stuffed animal to join them.

Hansel and Gretel by The Brothers Grimm
Props: Use masking tape to make a path through the woods; add a plant and a moon to the scene.
Follow-up: Children can make their own gingerbread house using milk cartons, graham crackers, meringue (to hold the parts together), and all kinds of good things to eat.

The Chalk Box Story by D. Freeman
Props: A large cardboard box colored in pastels that match the colors in the story; neck scarves that match the colors in the story for each child to wear.
Follow-up: Children can make wet chalk pictures; each child may be given a box of colored chalk and a pad to make their own original stories.

The Little Red Hen by P. Galdone

      Props: A bunch of wheat, and a loaf of French bread

Follow-up: Children can make their own bread.

The Little Engine That Could by W. Piper

      Props: Painted cardboard boxes in assorted sizes; add wheels.

Follow-up: Children can fill the boxes with special items and ride over the mountain.

Little Red Riding Hood by The Brothers Grimm

      Props: A red scarf, a basket, a bouquet of flowers.

Follow-up: Have children make a mural about the story and have them make cookies for their grandparents or for a special friend.

The Gunniwolf by W. Harper

      Props: An orange flower placed in a vase on a small table, a gunniwolf puppet made out of a paper bag.

Follow-up: Children can paint orange flowers to bring home to mother. They can re-tell the story using their gunniwolf puppets.

Additional Books for Dramatizations

Who's in Rabbit's House? by V. Ardema
Mooncake by F. Asch
Snow White and the Seven Dwarfs by The Brothers Grimm
The Very Hungry Caterpillar by E. Carl
Book of Nursery and Mother Goose Rhymes by de Angeli
Corduroy by D. Freeman
The Birthday Wish by C. Iwasaki
The Snowy Day by E. Keats
Chicken Little by S. Kellogg
The Teddy Bears' Picnic by J. Kennedy
Alexander and the Wind-Up Mouse by L. Lionni
Frederick by L. Lionni
Tico and the Golden Wings by L. Lionni
Mousekin's Golden House by E. Miller
The Tale of Peter Rabbit by B. Potter
Caps for Sale by E. Slobodkin
Mr. Rabbit and the Lovely Present by C. Zolotow

For Young Elementary-Age Children

The following circle warm-ups encourage imagination:

Let's pretend: Children act out being a skater, a wilting flower, a melting snowman, a storm, a pumpkin seed, an elf, an airplane landing, a hot-air balloon, a shooting star, Humpty Dumpty, The Mad Hatter, circus performers, the last leaf on a tree, a ball that is losing air.

Guess Who I Am? Children pantomime being an animal, an insect, a household gadget, or a color of the rainbow.

Once Upon a Story: One child starts a story and everyone adds to it.

Guess Who Is Coming to Dinner? Teacher whispers a guest's name to a child who must act out the character or object (an umbrella, a monkey, a hippopotamus, a ballerina, a rock star, a space man or woman, a friendly giant, a top, a mosquito, a spider).

A Story in a Box: A teacher fills a box with novelty items that have potential for storytelling (small animals, items for a magic show, a circus, or a birthday party). Children must create stories from the objects.

Imagination: Teachers share novelty objects with children who must think of creative uses for each item, such as an egg beater, a doorknob, a screen, a top hat.

Movement: Children move to a drum beat—stop, freeze, and have three seconds to become something that is called out by a teacher.

Follow the Leader: Children must follow their partners without laughing or making a sound.

Relaxation: Teacher guides children in relaxation techniques that allow them to free their bodies and their minds.

Three Guesses: Children are given an object (or a picture of an object) that is not seen by the group. A child has three chances to describe the item, without using body language to give clues. The group has to guess what the object is from the verbal description.

For More Mature School-Age Children

Create an "Arts Gallery": Display items may include pottery, samplers, sculptures, hooked rugs, woodcuts, masks, paintings, photographs of nature, theatrical costumes (a cane, ballet slippers, or a top hat), historic relics, and novelty items. Colored chalk and paper should be available for sketching.

Plan and Produce a Play or a Talent Show: Specialists from various artistic backgrounds can visit a center and provide workshop sessions for interested children.

Plan a Special Workshop in the Arts: Children may enjoy planning specialized workshops that enable them to make choices, develop interests and talents while inspiring creativity.

Create a Children's Theatre: Children can form a child care backstage theatre and perform for community groups and for parents.

Specialized Classes: Weekly sessions in piano, dance, gymnastics, pottery, photography, art, writing, cooking, and drama may be scheduled on an alternating basis. Specialized teachers should be hired to lead these groups.

Write Original Stories: Children can create their own books. A teacher may use objects or feelings to trigger imagination such as a kite, a fantasy voyage, or a trip to the desert. These storytelling themes may be described as "kite tales" or "creative voyages."

Creative theme-building topics might include:

One Day the Sun Forgot to Shine
When the Wind Blows
Inside My Box
Big and Small
A Puppet Named Pedro
Around the Corner
A Bird Who Couldn't Fly
Down by the River
Inside Out, Upside Down
A Rainy Day
Me and My Friend
If Alligators Were Little
There's a Bug in My Soup
What I Don't Want to Be When I Grow Up
The World's Best Sandwich
Jumbo, McPherson, and Me
Knock, Knock, Who's There?
The Big Splash

Poetry Themes

A teacher may use a "poetry in a pocket" theme to encourage children to write free verse. For "pocket poetry," children may select themes from the pocket of an apron. To facilitate writing, a catalyst message might read: "Poems tell stories, create moods, and express feelings. Sometimes they are funny, sometimes they make no sense at all, sometimes they are sad but whatever you say is never bad . . ." "Go for it!" Themes for pocket poetry may be:

I once met a man from Manchu
Under the rainbow
One wet day
If I could, I would
Drip, drop . . .
Under a mushroom . . .
A cricket named Picket
What is soft?
Two little snails named Mac and Pac
A forgetful frog
Waiting for Willy
A teeny, tiny town . . .
Did you ever?
The wind blew . . .

NOTES

1. Mary R. Jalongo, "The Child's Right to the Expressive Arts: Nurturing the Imagination as Well as the Intellect," *Childhood Education* 66(4) (Summer 1990): 195–200.

2. Leon Burton, and Kathy Kuroda, *Arts Play: Creative Activities in Art, Music, Dance, and Drama for Young Children* (Reading MA: Addison-Wesley, 1981), Introduction, ix.

3. Barbara Herberholz, *Early Childhood Art* (Dubuque, IA: William C. Brown Company, 1974), p. 2.

4. Robert Schirrmacher, *Art and Creative Development for Young Children.* (Albany, NY: Delmar), p. 115.

5. Lilia Lasky and Rose Mukerji, *Art: Basic for Young Children.* (Washington, DC: NAEYC, 1980), Developmental Chart, p. 12.

6. Dylan Thomas, "Notes on the Art of Poetry," *Modern Culture and the Arts,* eds., James B. Hall and Barry Ulanov (New York: McGraw-Hill, 1967).

7. Myra Cohn Livingston, *4-Way Stop* (New York: Atheneum, 1976), p. 14.

8. Lenore Sandel, "What Can a Poem Do?" *Childhood Education* 66(4) (Summer 1990): pp. 210, 211.

9. Gabriele Lusser Rico, *Writing the Natural Way* (New York: St. Martin's Press, 1983), p. 35.

10. Andrew Gunsberg, "Improvised Musical Play," *Childhood Education* 67(4) (Summer 1991): 223.

11. Dorothy T. McDonald, *Music in Our Lives: The Early Years* (Washington, DC: NAEYC, 1979), p. 25.

12. Glen T. Dixon and F. Graeme Chalmers, "The Expressive Arts in Education," *Childhood Education* 61(1) (Fall 1990): 12.

13. Emil and Celeste Richards, *Making Music around the Home and Yard* (New York: Award Music Co., 1972).

RESOURCES

Bayless, Kathleen M., and Marjorie E. Ramsey. *Music: A Way of Life for the Young Child,* 4th ed. New York: Macmillan, 1991.

Burton, Leon, and Kathy Kuroda. *Artsplay: Creative Activities in Art, Music, and Drama for Young Children.* Reading, MA: Addison-Wesley, 1981.

Cherry, Clare. *Creative Art for the Developing Child.* Belmont, CA: Fearon Publishers, 1972.

Colgin, Mary Lou. *One Potato, Two Potato, Three Potato, Four: 165 Chants for Children.* Mt. Rainier, MD: Gryphon House, 1988.

Foletta, Karen Haas, and Michele Cogley. *School-Age Ideas and Activities.* Nashville, TN: School Age Notes, 1990.

Herberholz, Barbara. *Early Childhood Art.* Dubuque, IA: William C. Brown Publishers, 1974.

Hoffman, S., and L. L. Lamme, eds. *Learning from the Inside Out: The Expressive Arts.* Wheaton, MD: ACEI, 1989.

Jennings, Coleman, ed. *Plays Children Love: A Treasury of Contemporary and Classic Plays for Children.* New York: St. Martin's Press, 1988.

Kelner, Lenore, Blank. *A Guide for Using Creative Drama in the Classroom.* Silver Spring, MD: InterAct, Inc., 1990.

Koch, Kenneth, and Kate Farrell. *Talking to the Sun: An Illustrated Anthology of Poems for Young People.* New York: The Metropolitan Museum of Art, 1989.

———. *Go In and Out the Window: An Illustrated Songbook for Young People,* 1989.

Kohl, MaryAnn F. *Good Earth Art: Environmental Art for Kids.* Bellingham, WA: Bright Ring Publishing, 1991 (distributed by Gryphon House, Mt. Rainier, MD).

Kohl, MaryAnn F. *Mudworks: Creative Clay,*

Dough, and Modeling Experiences, Bellingham, WA: Bright Ring Publishing, 1991 (distributed by Gryphon House, Mt. Rainier, MD).

Kohl, MaryAnn F. *Scribble Cookies and Other Independent Creative Art Experiences for Children.* Bellingham, WA: Bright Ring Publishing, 1991 (distributed by Gryphon House, Mt. Rainier, MD).

Lasky, L., and R. Mukerji. *Art: Basic for Young Children.* Washington, DC: NAEYC, 1980.

McDonald, Dorothy T. *Music in Our Lives: The Early Years.* Washington, DC: NAEYC, 1979.

Merriam, E. *Rainbow Writing.* New York: Atheneum, 1976.

Rico, Gabriele Lusser. *Writing the Natural Way.* New York: St. Martin's Press, 1983.

Shirrmacher, Robert. *Art and Creative Development for Young Children.* Albany, NY: Delmar Publishers, 1988.

Skeen, Patsy, et al. *Woodworking for Young Children.* Washington, DC: NAEYC, 1984.

Sullivan, Molly. *Movement Exploration for Young Children.* Washington, DC: NAEYC, 1982.

Tchudi, Susan and Stephen. *The Young Writer's Handbook.* New York: Scribner's, 1984.

For additional resources in "The Arts," see Appendix C.

*. . . I do not like the idea of the emphasis on infor-
mation acquisition and skills development without
comparable emphasis on play, on creativity, on learning
to work in groups. What I want for children is for them
to be able to grow and become the kinds of adults who
will be deeply and profoundly concerned for the future of
humankind—not only in their rhetoric, but in their day-
to-day behavior. I want them to be contributors to our
society, not just consumers. I want them to become
decent, loving and compassionate. Problem-solvers not
just problem-makers. . . . In spite of the fancy hardware
and sophisticated software we have, it is only the
human, growing teacher who can help us to reach these
person-oriented goals.*

— Selma Wassermann

13

COMPONENT FOUR: NURTURING

THE PREMISE

In order for children to become decent, loving, and compassionate human beings, a child care center must surround each child with a nurturing environment. Nurturing, as a concept, conjures feelings identified with *affective* learning: empathy, support, warmth, positive attitudes. For nurturing to be instated as a formal program component, it must be articulated in concrete terms; not only *we nurture children, but how we nurture children* in this center. A center nurtures children by giving serious consideration to social/emotional factors that influence a child's development and a classroom climate. Social/emotional factors interface at early childhood levels; each area is intricately connected to the other.

A primary objective in child care centers is to socialize children through *positive* and *meaningful interactions* to prepare them for entering and functioning in a larger society. This requires early training in areas of personal care, emotional well-being, safety, health and literature, social courtesies, moral and character development, and important practical life skills. The broader concept of nurturing can be reduced to manageable proportions in a child-centered environment. Specific content areas such as health, literature, and social studies are particularly fertile areas for curriculum development.

The most important way to nurture children in social development is to create a multicultural atmosphere that recognizes and respects all people. For many young children there is an unhealthy gap between home and center environments. Language, food, clothing, religious beliefs, and childrearing patterns may vary considerably from family to family, which creates confusion and insecurity for a child caught between two worlds. A multicultural program will encourage children to affirm their heritage while assimilating the American education experience. It will create a sense of democracy within a miniature, multinational community such as a child care center.

TRAINING CHILDREN

Training may be accomplished at early childhood levels by example and by instruction. Training requires intent, commitment, and follow-through. Before training children, teachers must first accept the fact that children cannot grow up with the skills and attitudes required to function fully and effectively in a society without strong guidance and direction during the early years. They then must accept their responsibility for training children in critical areas of early childhood development.

A good way to begin is to list the characteristics that one would most like to see in a democratic, miniature society. Words that come to mind are consideration, cooperation, respect, kindness, fair play, responsibility, honesty, patience, empathy, trust, good conduct, and an understanding of cultural and racial differences and similarities. *Children practice what they are taught and what they experience.* To become *affective* human beings, children must be given the opportunity to: exercise autonomy, practice cooperative play, use judgment, express love, express feelings, make decisions, feel in control, exercise leadership, take pride in their identity, overcome cultural differences, and develop empathy.

By Example

Training by example establishes a *humanistic* framework for a nurturing curriculum. Adults model the behavior they desire from children. Children view their teachers as respectful, caring adults who are trustworthy and dependable. They do not yell or express anger inappropriately, they do not favor one child, and they certainly know how to please children. They also view adults as real human beings with feelings and emotions who sometimes display anger or become upset.

Child-centered teachers view children as vulnerable and innocent. They want to protect them from a world that is at times hostile and unhealthy. Therefore, training is an important component of nurturing and child care. A teacher cannot remain passive when children are unkind, rude, or acting inappropriately toward others. She must let them know emphatically that certain kinds of behavior are not tolerated in her classroom. High on this list are cruelty, rudeness, discrimination, and unkindness.

A teacher will *model the special qualities* that led her into teaching: kindness, understanding, and firmness. With skillful strategies and attentiveness to children's behavior, a teacher promotes an affective environment. When a teacher exhibits firmness and assertiveness in appropriate ways, she is gaining children's respect. A firm voice is not a yelling or unpleasant voice. A misbehaving child is taken aside, spoken to, asked to explain the behavior, asked to think about the consequences of the behavior, and given an opportunity to change the behavior.

"What do you think you should do?" is a far more effective closure than "I want you to apologize," or "I'm going to tell your mother." Parents may need to be informed, but not in a way that makes a child feel threatened. When a teacher threatens to call parents, she is acknowledging that she cannot handle the problem by herself—either she is angry with the child, she's too busy to deal with the problem, or even worse, she has given up on the child.

Training by example requires forethought and attention. It is not enough to say the right words. A teacher must set a nurturing tone that becomes so natural to an environment that eventually the words and their meaning become self-evident. *Nurturing is built into a foundation;* it begins with a philosophy and is cultivated by the adults who are hired to teach and train young children. Children are nurtured in a total environment that creates a context for caring relationships. Educator Judith Leipzig writes:

> As educators of very young people who are in the midst of creating their selves and their futures, it is our responsibility to think about what kinds of raw materials we are providing them. Each child should have the support, the attention, and the experiences that will help that child grow to be a competent, well-rounded, and loving person—one who has a clear picture of his or her self, one who is able to cooperate and to work on her or his own, and one who is able to both give and receive support and nurturing. As teachers of infants and toddlers, we should be doing everything in our power to support the development of individuals who will be capable of leading rich and balanced lives.[1]

By Instruction

Teachers can train children by adopting an antibias, cooperative learning curriculum that prevents the spread of unacceptable behavioral and attitudinal patterns in early childhood classrooms. In a comprehensive and insightful book, *Anti-Bias Curriculum,* Louise Derman-Sparks and a task force of early childhood educators emphasize the importance of early training:

> Learning nonoppressive ways of interacting with differences requires more than introducing diversity into the classroom. It also requires gentle but active and firm guidance by adults. Unfortunately, many teachers and parents are uncertain about what to do when a preschooler exhibits biased behavior. All too often, uncertainty results in nonaction: "I was struck speechless," "I was afraid of saying or doing the wrong thing," "It made me so upset (angry), I couldn't do anything" are typical comments.
>
> Discriminatory acts are one form of aggressive behavior, as hurtful as physical aggression, and should be immediately and directly addressed. Teachers must become aware of any attitudes or feelings that prevent them from intervening in discriminatory interactions between children and practice appropriate techniques like role-playing.[2]

Role-playing

Teachers can train children in manners and good conduct through role-playing techniques of which puppetry is a favorite. Puppets can be presented in any color, shape, or form. They can be used to: discourage gender identification (boys are mean, girls are kind), discrimination, unhealthy peer identification, poor manners, unhealthy eating habits, poor hygiene, and improper speech. They can speak to a child who is feeling lonely, sad, or inadequate. They can speak to a child who has a stressful home situation. Mostly, teachers should let children talk vicariously through puppets: "I wonder what is troubling Ernie today; he looks a little sad?" "Do you think it's because he lost a button on his new jacket?" "No, then what could it be . . . ?"

Themes and Projects

Teachers can develop cultural awareness and understanding by planning themes or projects that invite nurturing. A unit on families or a unit on children around the world will expose children to a widening human experience—to one that reflects diversity in living patterns, in social patterns, and in cultural patterns. A social studies unit can provide unlimited opportunities for children to learn about the people and places that make up the world.

Literature

Teachers can help children understand right from wrong through literature. The wolf in *Little Red Riding Hood* or the fox in the *Gingerbread Man* are examples of favorite stories that clearly have moral implications. Stories that enable children to make observations and draw conclusions should be very carefully selected and presented. They should be stories children can identify with, enjoy, and learn from.

A Bilingual Language Program

A teacher can promote self-esteem by supporting an environmentally appropriate bilingual language program that reflects languages spoken by a fair number of students. Although English is appropriately considered the primary language in U.S. schools, many children experience an abrupt transition at times when they are particularly vulnerable. Children who do not speak English, or who speak limited English, can profit from a program that appropriately blends their native language(s) with English. By hearing their own language(s), children affirm their identities. A director can require teachers to keep a list of key words and phrases that are customarily used in all classrooms. When non-English speaking children are enrolled, parents can be asked to provide native language support to facilitate the child's adjustment. In environments that are primarily Spanish speaking, hiring bilingual teachers should be a priority.

Health, Safety, and Nutrition

Children in out-of-home environments depend on adults to gain knowledge about their bodies and about ways they can nourish and protect their bodies. It is the first responsibility of teachers to provide an environment that is physically and psychologically safe—one that makes a child feel secure and confident. Units on health, safety, and nutrition should be presented periodically and reinforced daily. Children should be informed about good eating habits, good grooming habits, and good living habits. They should be cautioned about environmental risks but encouraged to take risks that are important to their healthy development. They should be trained to care for themselves at an early age.

Learning through Parents

Children can learn a great deal about their classroom culture by observing and listening to visiting parents. When parents of various ethnic backgrounds are invited to visit a class, they should be encouraged to wear native garments, to bring artifacts or pictures that describe their country, and, of course, to bring in food for a tasting party. Children should be expected to show good manners and to ask questions. They should be expected to be polite when offered an unfamiliar food. Rather than "I hate that," or "I don't want any," they should be encouraged to take a little taste, or at least to say, "No thank you." The way children greet and interact with adult visitors tells a lot about a classroom, its leadership, and its objectives.

Writing and Reviewing Rules of Good Conduct

At early childhood levels rules of conduct should be simple in word and content:

> Be courteous.
> Be kind.
> Be a good friend.

At four or five years old, as well as school-age levels, children should participate in writing and in reading back their own rules. If behavior becomes unruly, a teacher may take a child over to the chart to remind him or her about this agreement.

Objectives for a Democratic Classroom

Teachers should encourage children to:

- Respect and support others;
- Learn to take turns;
- Be cooperative and courteous;
- Develop self-control;
- Think about right and wrong, good and bad, kind and unkind practices;
- Take the perspective of others;
- Recognize and respect differences;
- Become responsible members of their classroom and of their community.

When children are *expected to be responsible* members of a group, they will *respect freedom* and not abuse its privileges. They will learn to care for property, to cooperate with their friends, to take turns, and to have good manners. They will understand what they can and cannot do to feel successful about themselves and their environment. Understanding their limits, they will make appropriate choices. Socially conscious, they will support one another and respect one another's feelings. They will develop cooperative skills that will diminish aggressiveness or self-centeredness.

A teacher will create a community of caring. She will be ready to assist a child who is experiencing difficulty or frustration, but she also will encourage independent problem solving. In helping children develop socially, she will know when to step forward and when to remain in the background. In his book, *The Social Development of Young Children,* Charles A. Smith writes:

> Helping children learn social skills, such as making friends, is a troublesome effort for many adults. Ultimately, every child is alone in the social arena. We can stand by the sidelines and cheer their efforts, but they must be the ones to act. By becoming too involved in manipulating a social situation, we take the risk of alienating children from their peers. Yet, by doing absolutely nothing for them, we may contribute to their own confusion and sense of isolation. These two extremes can be avoided by becoming involved without being oppressive, and detached without being aloof.[3]

Encourage Community Identification

Children need to understand and connect with their larger social community. They cannot think of a center as a cocoon—a self-contained environment that opens at 7:00 A.M. and closes at 6:00 P.M. Children must be taught to appreciate their larger community by becoming actively involved in its affairs, its problems, and its projects. They should know the name of their county and city and be able to read maps and identify major streets and highways that connect people to places. Children should visit libraries, museums, hospitals, courthouses, state houses, and arts and crafts festivals. They should participate in ceremonies and march in parades; they should become responsible, caring citizens.

Promoting a Nurturing Environment

Too often expressions of unhappiness are ignored or trivialized by caregivers: "I don't know what's wrong with her, I couldn't find a minute to talk to her privately; I think she's just tired . . ." Perhaps this is the case, or perhaps the child has had a miserable experience that needs to be communicated to a caring adult. She may have been made fun of or intentionally left out of a game. A superficial reaction to stress glosses over problems that may be far more serious than meets the eye. Teachers of young children must become sensitive to changes in behavior and record unusual patterns observed over a period of time. They must bring their observations to a parent's attention at an appropriate time.

The *human environment* that surrounds the child is the *psychological core* of a child care program. It is from caring and sympathetic adults that children receive affirmation and support. A relationship between a child and an adult is critical to a child's emotional well-being.

Children's moods and feelings are usually up front for those who choose to notice. When we *stop noticing,* children *stop responding* and they *stop trying* to please. They become programmed to do what they are expected to do. Those who no longer protest become compliant, slowly becoming less responsive. Those who protest become caught up in power struggles that eventually break down relationships and deepen a child's sense of disharmony and alienation. Yet knowledgeable and caring adults often place unreasonable demands on children every day. Teachers become so caught up in routines and schedules that they fail to notice the children they are trying to help. It is unfair to expect a grumpy little three-year-old who is dressed for school by 6:30 in the morning to come into a circle at 8:00 with a happy face. It is unfair to expect a child awakened from a nap to hustle into the bathroom or a school-age child to be sociable at 3:00 in the afternoon without a few moments of transition: to breathe deeply.

A TEACHER'S ROLE IN PROMOTING AFFECTIVE DEVELOPMENT

A day care center must be perceived as a loving homelike environment where a child can feel secure. If teachers are too busy or too insensitive to target into a child's emotional needs, one of the most important functions of a child care center has been ignored. Teachers can promote emotional growth by using some or all of the growth-enhancing techniques described below.

Establish Feelings and Values in the Early Years

When children are nurtured in cooperative and pro-social play at an early age, they internalize attitudes and patterns of behavior. Ideally, an environment should not be bound by rules but by agreements. The more children are encouraged toward kindness, the more accepting they become. Children behave as they are conditioned to behave. They look to adults for clarification and direction. *Prejudice is bred,* it is not endemic to young children. They are not born with negative feelings toward others. In a nurturing classroom, children do not see differences. When children are open and loving they do not distinguish between black and white dolls, between Asians and Caucasians. When an environment appropriately *models equality and fairness,* children become considerate and caring. They understand that people are different in some ways and alike in others. They become sensitive to their human environment by expressing empathy and compassion, by reaching out to hold hands and to hug one another.

Not all environments are nurturing, however, and not all children are untainted in the way they regard others. Louise Dermon-Sparks points out that young children's "development is harmed by the impact of sexism, racism, and handicappism."[4] Some research indicates that children begin to see differences and act differently toward others at a very young age. By age two, they are learning the appropriate use of gender labels and color names—as applied to skin colors. By three (or earlier) they begin to notice gender and racial differences to the degree that they may exhibit "pre-prejudice toward others on the basis of gender, race, or being differently abled."[5] As children mature, they often become stereotyped in their attitudes and behavior. They judge people superficially: by what they wear, how they look, how much money they carry in their pockets, by what cars their parents drive, how many vacations are taken in one year, how many activities they participate in after school. Teachers must use both indirect and direct strategies to change inappropriate attitudes or behavior so that children who may not "fit in" are not "written off" by peers.

Counsel Children

Teachers must build personal time into their daily activities. Personal time requires personal space. An area set aside for children's personal use can be called a *den*, connoting *d*evelopment, *e*nrichment, and *n*urturing. This area can serve a dual purpose—it can be used for child-time (children play alone or with small groups of friends) or for teacher–child time (teacher and child visit together and, when appropriate, a teacher counsels a child who is unhappy or who has been misbehaving). Personal, meaningful interactions often will lead to problem solving or conflict resolution. Educator Susanne Wichert identifies the following steps that may be used in a counseling session targeted toward changing behavior:

- Calming and focusing;
- Turning attention to the parties concerned;
- Clarification/stating the problem;
- Bargaining/resolution/reconciliation;
- Affirmation.[6]

This method is effective for children in child care environments because it gives them time to cool down, to discuss a problem, to think of other ways a problem might have been handled, and to resolve the problem in ways that allow a child to regain emotional composure. If a teacher is counseling a child who is distressed, she should: comfort the child, encourage the child to share feelings, identify with the child—"I know how you are feeling . . . , I feel that way sometimes too"—and raise her self-esteem: "You have such a pretty smile, I wish you would smile more often."

Often a child will come to the realization that the perceived problem is really not the problem at all. A child may have been unusually distraught for other reasons: a new baby in the family, an angry parent, a sick grandparent. When a child has someone to talk with at a time of distress, she often will release her anxieties quickly. Children's problems are not usually so complex that with a little stroking and nurturing, they cannot be resolved. Sometimes, by minimizing a child's problem, a teacher is helping her put it in perspective: "Your teacher will understand that you forgot your homework" or "Charlie didn't mean to hurt you—he was trying to move a very heavy object." Sometimes, a more direct message should be given: "You have two choices—you can dry your tears and get on with your day or you can sit here and feel sorry for yourself—I know which one I would choose!"

Be Available for Conversation and Consultation
Teachers should set aside time to:

* Have a weekly visit with each child to share and discuss feelings, concerns, and happy times;
* Be available to assist a child during a crisis or upset at the time of occurrence;
* Consult frequently with parents;
* Observe and record children's behavior on a regular basis;
* Be attentive to changes in dispositions or behavior patterns;
* Report signs of dysfunction or unusual emotional stress to the director and to the parents;
* Consult a center's resource specialist in areas that suggest intervention;
* Keep an updated file on each child's progress;
* Provide opportunities for relaxation and stress reduction in a classroom.

Help Children Develop Self-control
Children gain self-control by understanding what is expected of them and by positively connecting with their environment. When a child feels secure about himself and his surroundings, he will conduct himself in an appropriate manner most of the time. The child who lacks self-control usually finds someone else like herself to pal around with. Children who lack control are emotionally immature. A child who explodes because she has too much work to do is exhibiting immature behavior. Teachers can support a child by initiating direct and honest communication. By helping a child to *self-examine,* the teacher is helping the child to change behavior. She might ask the child: "Why is homework important?" "Whose job is it?" "What happens if it doesn't get done?" "What do you think will make you feel better?" By pointing out that anger is consuming the energy that could be going into homework, the teacher is helping the child accept responsibility and *gain control.*

Help Children Gain Self-esteem
If children are withdrawn and fearful, they are undoubtedly lacking in self-esteem and confidence. They may not know how to make choices or to manage their time. They may experience failure in relationships and in their work. They may not know that they are cared for or loved. They are afraid to trust and unable to ventilate feelings because they fear rejection and a greater sense of loss. A person without an identity needs to build confidence slowly through relationships and experiences that engender success. *Love is central to the process.* There are many who believe that the ability to express and give love is the primary requisite for working with young children. Love should *never* be *conditional.* It should never be withheld

from a child because a child has misbehaved. A teacher must seize every opportunity to build a child's self-esteem by praising, supporting, and identifying with a
child's needs.

Help Children Develop Appropriate Behavior

Children misbehave frequently in day care centers. There is no one example; there
are many examples. Children's behavior, or more precisely their misbehavior, is
one of the most pervasive and troublesome aspects of working at a center. Children
can be deceptive and dishonest; they can be rude and hostile to those who are
central to their lives. In complex and changing family patterns, there is rarely a
simple explanation for negative behavior.

Children can be angry or negative even when they have been treated with
affection and love. Misbehaving children want attention for whatever reason.
They may not be getting quality time with parents; they may not feel very good
about themselves; they may be frustrated by various forms of dysfunction and may
have no place to ventilate their feelings. Lacking the wherewithal to find acceptable ways to express their frustrations, children find other ways to get approval.
Negative behavior prompts immediate satisfaction. By acting out what she is
feeling, the misbehaving child is getting attention (albeit the wrong kind) from
peers. She is, in effect, acting the way she feels others are treating her.

There are no magical formulas and no instructional guidelines that will address the many problems a teacher confronts in dealing with children's behavior.
There is no socioeconomic status that immunizes children from anger and aggressive behavior. Each human environment is unique and each teacher has her own
level of endurance. When lives get off-balance, there are consequences. Much of
the time a teacher uses intuition when responding to a misbehaving child. She
realizes that even under stress, she is still responsible for assisting a child in self-
growth and in reaffirming values.

Use a Self-monitoring Behavior Management Technique

At school-age levels, a child-centered, self-management plan may prove effective.
In this approach, a child and a teacher discuss a problem and the various ways it
can be resolved. The child decides on the period of time required to change the
behavior. He assesses his behavior and discusses his progress or setbacks with his
teacher. He keeps a chart or a diary to help in self-understanding, and he is asked to
share this evaluation with his teacher. In the interim, the child is restricted from
the activity or the friend (if this is the problem) until he feels ready to resume play
and a positive relationship. If a child has seriously violated codes of conduct, more
serious action may need to be taken. The child, for example, may be asked to
contribute a certain number of community service hours to a center—cleaning,
painting, picking up the grounds, washing trikes, or entertaining younger children
with a special art project. Parents should always be informed about the nature of
the problem and the manner of discipline in order to reinforce a center's efforts.

Be Attentive to Children's Mental and Physical Well-being

Unfortunately there are some areas of emotional support and understanding that cannot be tapped by nurturing teachers. More and more, children are victims of child abuse and negligence. Dr. Barbara J. Meddin, a child protection specialist, and Dr. Anita L. Rosen, a private consultant, define child abuse and/or neglect as ". . . any action or inaction that results in the harm or potential risk of harm to a child." This includes:

- Physical abuse (cuts, welts, bruises, burns);
- Sexual abuse (molestation, exploitation, intercourse);
- Physical neglect (medical or educational neglect; inadequate supervision, food, clothing, or shelter);
- Emotional abuse (actions that result in significant harm to the child's intellectual, emotional, or social development or functioning);
- Emotional neglect (inaction by the adult to meet the child's needs for nurture and support).

The signs or symptoms of child abuse are:

- Bruises or wounds in various stages of healing;
- Injuries on two or more places of the body;
- Injuries reported to be caused by falling but that do not include hands, knees, or forehead;
- Oval, immersion, doughnut-shaped imprint burns;
- Reluctance to leave school;
- Inappropriate dress for the weather;
- Discomfort when sitting;
- Sophisticated sexual knowledge or play;
- Radical behavior changes or regressive behavior;
- Child withdraws or watches adults;
- Child seems to expect abuse;
- Revealing discussions, stories, or drawings.[7]

Teachers need to watch for patterns of abuse and report observations and concerns to a director or administrator for immediate follow-up. In most states, a child welfare agency investigates each report and takes whatever action is necessary to protect the child.

Set Limits

Children tend to test limits in open, low-structure environments. They try things that would not be tolerated in highly structured environments. A child carries play dough around on a spoon until it crumbles into tiny pieces all over the floor, a child takes indoor blocks outdoors without permission, a child gives a portion of his lunch to a friend every day, a child wears a favorite dress-up all day because she doesn't want to risk giving it up, a child keeps little bugs in a cubbie. Teachers need to decide what is acceptable and what is not acceptable so that children understand specific boundaries in their play and play/work worlds.

Questions to Help Set Boundaries and Limitations

- Can children play superheroes indoors; can they use blocks and Tinkertoys as weapons?
- Can children carry equipment and materials from one activity center to another?
- Can they mix and use paints freely and without assistance?
- Can they add items to a water table?
- What language is acceptable and what is prohibited?
- How are children handled when they bite or hit?
- How are they handled when they have temper tantrums?
- Is there a restriction on the number of children in activity centers at one time?
- What are the rules for picking up; do children all pick up or do they pick up what they played with?
- Can children play outdoors in mud and dirt?
- Can they play with sticks and stones?
- How high can they swing; can they jump off?
- Can they go indoors for drinks without permission?
- Can they go to the bathroom or lockers without permission?
- Is there a dress code; no slippery shoes on climbing bars?
- Can children climb on fences; can they climb on a big old tree?

Make Agreements

In a play environment, teachers must always evaluate the quality of children's activities. Play is not always pure and innocent. An unhealthy or unacceptable mode of play is one that may physically or emotionally harm or hurt another child. Teachers need to make agreements and understandings with children regarding play rules. Agreements can be made regarding:

- Social relationships and attitudes;
- Classroom responsibilities;
- Activity center rules;
- Personal behavior;
- Care of equipment;
- Safety and health rules;
- Attitudes toward work and play;
- Understandings about values.

With reasonable review and a great deal of reinforcement, children will generally abide by their agreements.

Reduce Fatigue and Stress

A child-appropriate environment *generates good feelings* among children by reducing the elements that cause fatigue and stress. Activities and materials are matched to children's age levels, interests, and needs. There is a healthy balance between play, rest, and quiet activities. Environmental factors that affect behavior such as heat, light, and noise levels are closely monitored and adjusted when necessary. A great deal of attention also is given to health and nutritional factors that influence children's behavior. In her insightful book, *How to Generate Values in Young Children,* Susanne Wichert describes an ideal environment as one that would:

- Allow children to function with the maximum degree of independence. When children are able to do many things for themselves or with the help of another child, not only is there an enhancement of self-esteem and increased opportunity for altruistic behavior, but staff can spend less time on purely custodial tasks. Obviously, the teacher who is freed from these custodial tasks is better able to monitor for conflict and guide it to its resolution.
- Allow all persons in it to function at a low-stress level. A number of physical factors can influence stress level, among them noise level, visual clutter, use of color, and space/child ratio.
- Be as comfortable as possible for a variety of uses. Space in a preschool classroom should aid in establishing a strong link between the parent and the center. With that aim in mind, there should be a number of places where a parent and child can be together comfortably for a while. The parent's comfort and sense of trust is passed on to the child and has a direct influence on the child's ability to feel secure and to view the values expressed at the center as consistent with the values in the child's family. The space also should have a number of "retreats" for children or adults who need time alone during the day.[8]

Praise and Reinforce Children

Children like to please. If their gifts are appreciated, they will continue to give. The basically generous and loving nature of children overflows in an affective environment. Play dough is shaped into meatballs for a teacher's lunch, "I love you" messages are tucked discreetly into pockets, a yellow dandelion and a blade of grass become a bouquet of love from a child to an adult friend. In order for children to give love they need to feel accepted and worthy of love. Adults can instill a *sense of self-worth and importance* in children by acknowledging the little moments of each day when special time is needed or appreciated. Praise and reinforcement require so little effort. Teachers need only remind themselves from time to time how important it is to recognize and identify with children—to be sensitive to where they are coming from and what they need from adult friends.

Extend Love

In childrearing environments, it is unconscionable to consider caring for a child without extending love. Without love, potential fades. Young children need a great deal of physical contact and warmth. A hug or a gesture can give a child strong feelings of comfort and security throughout the day. When children experience love, they give back love. They are able to put themselves in the place of others and express sympathy. Eric Fromm drew a connection between loving others and love of ourselves: "The affirmation of one's own life, happiness, growth and freedom is rooted in one's capacity to love. . . . If an individual is able to love productively, he loves himself too. . . ."[9]

Extend Freedom

Young children need to experience freedom in order to develop independence and self-control. Children should not have to hold hands to walk to a bathroom or use whispered voices in public places. When a child is required to behave in a way that is restrictive and unnatural, he will break free at the first opportunity. A fieldtrip is the perfect place for a child to change the rules. Running freely, disregarding instructions, children will often behave the way they have been taught not to behave. Appropriate training for young children is not to inhibit behavior but to *encourage self-control.* A teacher who yells at children and threatens them with punishment does not gain self-respect. Each fieldtrip will become progressively worse. By continuing unworkable techniques, a teacher is basically punishing herself. Until she changes her position by expecting more from children, she will continue to lament her burden and drastically reduce her fieldtrips! A child who *receives and respects freedom,* over time, will view herself as a responsible, supportive member of a group.

Freedom is established by mutual agreement, by clear understandings, and by trusting the basically good instincts and nature of children. *Freedom is a process* that begins with early training. The young child is encouraged to make choices and entrusted with reasonable amounts of autonomy in decision making until he understands his responsibility for supporting relationships, honoring agreements, and building trust. The more cohesive a group, the more freedom children can and should be entrusted with. Children begin to feel a sense of community when they are part of a team. They are unlikely to disappoint one another or their adult friends if they have participated in establishing rules of conduct and if they have learned to recognize the privileges that accompany freedom.

Give Children the Right to Make Choices

There are many ways children exert independence. Children choose playmates and activities. They choose to eat or not to eat their sandwiches; they choose to paint or not to paint a picture. The more opportunities children have to make reasonable choices, the more socially adept they will become. When children make choices, they make commitments and accept the possibility of failure. They *assume accountability* for their choices. Nurturing teachers will not try to shield children from the consequences of their decisions unless the choice is clearly inappropriate or unsafe. Children, like adults, need to experience some disappointments in order to recognize and value achievement. When giving children choices, it is important to remember that it is the adult who holds the discretionary powers that guide children toward appropriate decision making. Sue Spayth Riley comments:

> I have observed that in raising children some parents think of decision making only in very lofty terms. For them, decisions are grandiose choices between earth-shaking alternatives and may be turned over to children only when they have reached the age of reason. It is quite true that earth-shaking moral decisions cannot and should not be presented to young children. The opportunity, however, to make decisions involving less significant options may be given to the very young. Practice in the process of choosing is a must, with the options being in keeping with the age and ability of each child. When children are given practice in choosing, the chances are good that they will develop decision-making ability, insight, flexibility, and the imagination to cope with the loftier choices to come later.[10]

Extend Empathy

Empathy is projecting one's self into sharing the thoughts and feelings of another. In an affective environment, teachers naturally express empathy because they are mentally and emotionally tuned in to each child. They are concerned about the development of the whole child: how the child looks, feels, develops, and expresses himself. They are informed about a child's history, present environment, and overall developmental level. Teachers are constantly evaluating children without a pencil and a pad. They know where children are coming from because they understand where children are at a given moment.

Getting to know a child from a whole-child perspective requires *communicating with all* the adults who attend to a child throughout the day. The child is not just turned over to another caregiver but to a teammate who shares equally in a child's well-being. An empathetic teacher recognizes the value of developing a close and caring relationship with parents and other primary adults who surround a child.

Provide a Secure and Happy Environment

An affective classroom is equipped for comfort, challenge, and investigation. There are busy corners and quiet centers, soft places for rest and lots of things to get little hands into. Some children paint, others parade around in grown-up clothes. Two friends are listening to records; another is pestering to become a part of the group. These little tête-à-têtes bind children together. Day care is like a big family filled with grabbing, teasing, moodiness, and hugging. At the baseline, however, there is always forgiveness and acceptance. Little children have an infinite capacity to forgive and forget—to live and to let live, to get on with the play world. Noted educator and writer Jim Greenman has made all educators aware of the importance of providing children and adults with soft, companionable environments:

A soft, responsive, physical environment reaches out to children. It helps children to feel more secure, enabling them to venture out and explore the world, much like homes provide the adults the haven from which they can face an often difficult and heartless world. The moments alone spaced out on a swing, rocking in a chair or a rocking horse, or kneading dough allow children to recharge.[11]

Provide Personal Space

Children identify with their classroom if they feel a sense of belonging—a place to call mine. Cubbies are important symbols of independence and possession to young children. They are places children can claim and control. Though not for leftover tuna sandwiches or dying insects, cubbies perform an important self-affirmation function for every child. What the child deems important is inevitably slipped into a cubby: a piece of glass, an acorn, a stick, a present from a friend, an invitation to a birthday party—all the important collectibles that have made up a child's day.

Encourage a Reverence for Life

In affective settings, there is a *reverence for all living things*. Children identify with nature and care about their environment. It is through nurturing insects, flowers, and animals that children develop a greater sense of unity with their surrounding world. A child who can relate to living things in positive ways will never be alienated or lonely. A primary way to generate compassionate feelings in young children is to give them pets. Professor Gladys F. Blue suggests that pet–person relationships are most relevant to a growing child because they provide:

- Love, attachment, and comfort;
- Sensorimotor and nonverbal learning;
- Responsibility, nurturance, and sense of competence;
- Learning about life, death, and grief;
- Therapeutic benefits to psychological and physical health;
- Nurturing humaneness, ecological awareness, and ethical responsibility.[12]

Children in child care centers enjoy stroking and watching baby animals or rabbits. A pet can offer children unequivocal companionship and love. Children can play imaginatively with animals. They enjoy picking them up and putting them in unusual places like cubbies, remote corners and in handmade cages. They enjoy getting into a monologue with a pet—a conversation that is something like role-playing. Animals will be asked questions and children will provide the answers. Animals will hide and children will seek. Animals listen to stories and are invited to tea parties. When properly cared for and respected, animals can become fully functioning members of a class. They can satisfy needs that humans cannot satisfy; they can become weekend visitors in children's homes.

CLASSROOM OBJECTIVES

In an affective environment teachers will:

- Be attentive to children's emotional and social needs;
- Provide space for personal interactions and reflection;
- Help children cope with adversity and stress by developing trusting and caring relationships;
- Provide an environment that cultivates individuality and self-worth;
- Help children deal with stress in ways that are personally and socially satisfying;
- Help children realize that failure is nothing more than a momentary setback;
- Help children distinguish reality from distortions that veil the truth;
- Let children know they are not alone and that they are loved;
- Facilitate friendships through open communication and positive, worthwhile experiences;
- Consult parents regularly regarding each child's progress;
- Provide a cooperative, nonstressful environment;
- Help children develop personal and social attitudes that are positive and growth-enhancing;
- Encourage children to accept and trust their environment;
- Encourage children to develop balanced and healthy personalities;
- Encourage children to acquire skills and values that will continue to enhance the quality of their lives;
- Encourage children to develop coping mechanisms and internal discipline;
- Encourage children to develop confidence in their ability to function as able and independent learners;
- Encourage children to become advocates for worthwhile causes that interest them;
- Encourage children to resist and redress injustices as paths cross and decisions are made.

INTEGRATING NURTURING INTO A CHILD-CENTERED CURRICULUM

Health and Nutrition

A comprehensive early childhood program will include health and nutrition as primary components in an integrated curriculum. To nurture a child's well-being is to provide basic information about physical and nutritional health and to become cognizant of the importance of mental health to child development. A healthy child is a child whose physical, nutritional, and mental needs are met and who is safe from environmental hazards.

Physical Health

The basic routines of a child care center such as dressing, hand-washing, eating, and resting are established early. Children learn self-management and body care through direct instruction and practice. They develop a greater awareness of their responsibility for self-care through vicarious classroom experiences. A nurturing curriculum, for example, may use a puppet to symbolically act out the habits and attitudes that adults are trying to reinforce in young children. One puppet may be a good rester, another a good cleaner, and another a good eater. Another puppet may have trouble following rules and be lax about self-care. The dialogue that ensues will make children think about the consequences of poor habits.

Each classroom can develop its own puppet theme to train children in health, safety, and nutrition. For example, a mother or father rabbit and seven bunnies can become active participants in a health curriculum. Each bunny can be good at some things but not good at others. The children themselves can become involved in training the bunnies. A bunny who hates to rest can become a resting friend for a child. A bunny who hates to clean up his mess can become an eating companion of another child. A bunny who never plays out-of-doors because it is too cold may get to wear a special coat and cap. A bunny who hates to wash his ears because they are too big, or who hates to wash her hands because she always plays in the dirt, will become a favorite buddy to a young child.

Professionals, like dentists and pediatricians, should be invited to a child care center to speak about self-care and hygiene. They may extend their services by inviting children to their office for a personal visit. A visit to a doctor or a dentist usually includes a treat: a paper mask or garment, some floss, or a toothbrush. Doctors who specialize in practices for children are usually people who care about children—people who will extend themselves to a child care center.

Body awareness and sex education are integral components of a nurturing curriculum. Children start asking questions at an early age and teachers are often reluctant to provide children accurate information. Teachers can use units or themes as a way of acquainting children with their bodies. Units such as "All About Me," "Me and My Family," or "Baby Animals" provide natural settings for sex education. There are many *natural opportunities* to increase children's aware-ness—through sensory and nurturing experiences, literature, weight and height charts, and body movement records.

Curiosity about genitals should be treated as a natural aspect of growth and development. It should be dealt with honestly but not elaborately—in ways that satisfy a child's questions and curiosity at the time. If a child wants to know the name of an organ, he doesn't need a dissertation on bodily functions; he only needs basic information. Unusual preoccupations with sex play or curiosity should be gently discouraged in social environments. A child who masturbates, for exam-ple, may need some additional attention from a teacher before he is ready to fall asleep. Children who are abruptly placed on cots after lunch and expected to sleep right away experience frustration that is expressed in self-satisfying ways. If chil-dren can play out-of-doors or listen to a story before resting, they will be ready to sleep at rest-time.

A wonderful way to satisfy children's curiosity about birth is to acquire classroom pets and offspring. Animals such as rabbits, mice, and guinea pigs make wonderful classroom pets. By observing and identifying with a birth experience, children learn about conception, prenatal development, and birth in natural, positive ways. Natural experiences are always preferable to instructional experiences at early childhood levels.

It is the responsibility of adults who work closely with children to alert them to a world that is not always nurturing—to people who harm and mistreat children and adults. This may best be accomplished by soliciting professional support from people who are trained and educated in the field of child safety and abuse. In addition, a teacher should have a selection of sex education books available for use with preschoolers and school-age children who have questions or needs that should be handled by a teacher. These books should be used with discretion. Ideally, they should be shared and discussed with parents who are primarily responsible for educating their children in areas of health and safety.

Mental Health

A wellness approach to child care education views stress reduction as a primary factor in curriculum planning. Stress in young children is one of the more serious consequences of disruptive, unbalanced living patterns. When children feel neglected, fatigued, or confused, they are limited in their coping, adjustment mechanisms. Children signal stress in many ways: irritability, sucking thumbs, deviant behavior, hostility, anger, poor concentration and short attention span, stuttering, eye blinking, preoccupation with body parts, poor eating and resting habits, withdrawal, complaints about not feeling well.

In designing a curriculum for children in child care, each content area should be examined from a perspective of mental health/stress reduction. Activities and room arrangements should be organized to *reduce competition,* to *enhance self-confidence,* and to *promote self-expression.* Teachers should become attentive to a child's internal environment, to what is producing unhappiness and stress. By reducing stress levels, a teacher is reducing conflict and accompanying misbehavior.

A mental health program should include time for: outdoor play, rest at intervals throughout the day, creative self-directed play, and recreation. On a regular basis, children should stop, rest, and breathe deeply. School-age children should be offered the opportunity to practice some form of meditation such as yoga. When children meditate, they reduce stress levels by integrating mind and body. They feel better inside and increase their energy level. They gradually learn to respond to stress by making the adjustments that make them feel better about themselves and happier inside.

Nutrition

Nutrition is a process by which children obtain food and nutrients. Children can become familiar with the basic food groups through cooking, shopping, and experiences such as going on fieldtrips to see how food is grown, processed, and distributed. They can help a teacher plan a nutritious meal by providing the foods that are essential to growth, energy, and health. Children can consult their classroom food chart as they plan a menu. They have learned from their chart that a nutritious lunch should include healthy amounts of the following food groups: milk and milk products, meat or meat alternatives, vegetables and fruits, breads and cereals, and limited amounts of fats and sugar. They have learned that raw vegetables are more nutritious than cooked vegetables and that water is essential to the digestive process and to general physical health. They have learned that salt and butter are not essential add-ons in nutritional planning. They also have learned about junk food!

With lots of information, children may plan a very appetizing and nutritious lunch or snack. A lunch might include macaroni and cheese, a fresh green salad, a piece of pita bread, milk, and homemade applesauce. Children may even get to sprinkle granola on their applesauce. A snack might include pineapple chunks with cottage cheese and bread sticks or a fresh fruit cup with half a bran muffin. Because many children bring lunch, snack options are important to planning. Morning snacks should be served at least one and one-half hours before lunchtime and be limited so as not to interfere with children's appetites and nutritional needs. Afternoon snacks are generally more substantial because many children do not eat dinner until seven o'clock or later. A snack list might include finger foods such as dried fruit; cut-up fresh vegetables; cheese cubes; fresh fruit or tomato wedges; or a combination of raisins, coconut, cereal, and pretzels. Children also enjoy snacking on crackers; yogurt; 100% fruit juice; milk; milk shakes; fruit shakes; oatmeal cookies; granola bars; peanut butter; or special bakery items like blueberry muffins and zucchini, cranberry, or pumpkin bread.

School-age children love pizza, vegetable dips, peanut butter, cheese combinations, interesting crackers, granola cookies, ice milk bars, fresh fruit, yogurt, soups, and pancakes or french toast. Children enjoy cooking and preparing foods that involve several steps. They are also big milk and juice drinkers and should not be unduly limited in the amount of beverage and food they select for snack. Ideally, children should be given choices (milk or juice, cheese and crackers, or a dried fruit mix). School-age children should understand what makes a meal or snack balanced and healthy and the vitamin content of various foods that are common to their diet. They should learn how to select and prepare balanced, healthy meals and be encouraged to drink lots of water. A center should always have low-fat milk, juices, and fresh fruits as staples for snacks.

An important part of children's nutritional training takes place when children observe and prepare food. Children need to make healthy choices of foods, and they need to learn how to handle and care for the foods they select. They need to practice personal hygiene and to perceive a cooking or food-preparation experience as an extension of themselves. Cooking, like many other aspects of development and personal expression, is an art that requires training and skill. Through selective experiences children will learn that some foods need refrigeration, all foods need careful storage, and some need considerable preparation before they are ready to add to recipes (washing, peeling, cutting, chopping, removing seeds). As children prepare and work with foods, they observe changes in texture, volume, and consistency. Because cooking is a hands-on experience, children will quickly become knowledgeable about the process. They will learn how to prepare fresh green beans, corn, melons, and strawberries. They will learn to approximate amounts and to select foods that are in season (and therefore less costly).

Equally important is serving food. Children can become culinary artists in the way they set a table and arrange food. Children should learn to pass food trays or plates and to show discretion in the amount they take at one time. They should learn to use their napkins and to practice good table manners (no thank you, please, would you care for . . .). Inappropriate table behavior should be dealt with quickly by a teacher. If a teacher is apathetic to table etiquette, children will not perceive eating as a pleasurable, social experience.

A nutrition curriculum should include problem solving and critical thinking as well as decision making. A teacher can help children plan by using problem-solving strategies: "I think we need a green vegetable today because yesterday we had a yellow vegetable—who can think of a green vegetable?" Children can identify all the green vegetables they can think of, the teacher can print the choices, and the children can vote on the selection. Children can think of interesting ways to prepare and serve snacks; they can make up their own recipes and keep a recipe book. School-age children can research and prepare dishes and snack foods that reflect the international ethnic backgrounds of classmates.

An important aspect of educating children in health, safety, and nutrition is that *practical life training* must begin during the formative years. Children learn to function as independent managers when they are informed and knowledgeable about health and hygiene. They learn to be self-sufficient, wise decision makers respecting the habits designed to promote and protect their well-being. They learn to distinguish between and choose behaviors that promote growth and those that inhibit growth (poor attitudes and judgment, alcohol abuse, smoking cigarettes, or neglect or abuse of one's body). For further information on health, safety, and nutrition, see Appendix A.

Social Studies

Children need access to materials and ideas that inculcate positive values. Social studies involves the study of human beings: how they live; where they live; their customs, traditions, history, religion, and interdependency. A child's universe begins with self and extends to family, to community, and to her surrounding world. When children are exposed to social studies, they begin to appreciate and acknowledge community helpers and leaders, they develop a crosscultural connection to other people on the planet, they become sensitive to people's needs and differences, and they begin to identify with a one-world concept.

Study Units

A good way to extend children's knowledge of people is to implement a study unit such as "My Community." Preschool children may learn about their immediate community by direct observation and experience. They can develop an image of what life is like beyond their classroom. They can take walks, talk to bankers and postal employees, mayors, and librarians. Children can make simple maps and charts to extend their understandings. They can become involved in a community project each semester. For example, they might enjoy a "Helping Hands" project that provides food or clothes to the needy, books and games for children who are less fortunate, and opportunities for direct and sustained interaction. Young children should collect, pack, wrap, and deliver their gifts with their teachers (and parents). When children participate, they identify with the meaning of a project or an experience.

School-age children might want to plan a unit around a more remote, graphically appealing area such as Alaska. They will learn that Alaska is a distinct and important part of the United States. They will learn about its diverse geography and climatic conditions, about its dependency on community life and animals for support and survival. They might make soap sculptures, construct paper igloos, make a walrus puzzle, an Alaskan flag, construct a trading post or a fishing village, and learn about volcanoes. The children may learn about oil and its uses, and they might develop pen pals among Eskimo children using their own writing skills to communicate and share worlds. Children may enjoy reading books about Alaska such as *Arctic Lands* by K. Petty, *The First Book of Eskimos* by B. Brewster, *Eskimos* by J. Hughes, *Chooki and the Ptarmigan* by C. Codd, and *In Two Worlds: A Yupik Eskimo Family* by J. Rivers.

Teachers may further raise consciousness about the planet and its growing interdependency by sharing such books as *Can the Whales Be Saved* by P. Whitfield, *Environmental Diseases* by Anderson, *Our World: Oceans and Seas* by D. Lambert, *Fifty Simple Things You Can Do to Save the Earth* by The Earth Works Group, *Solar Power* by R. McKie, *Wind Power* by M. Cross, *How to Save the Planet* by B. Goodman, *Toxic Waste and Recycling* by N. Hawkes, *Global Warming* by L. Pringle, *Garbage* by K. O'Conner, and *Let's Explore a River* by J. R. McCauley. A nurturing teacher might also subscribe to *National Geographic* and *Ranger Rick*.

The following are ideas for units on interesting topics for children to delve into:

1. All About Me (to include senses)
2. Me and My Family
3. Me and My Family and My Community
4. A Nearby Community
5. A Faraway Community (such as Paris, Taiwan, Senegal)
6. Transportation
7. A Make-believe Community (design, build, and describe it)
8. Homes (may be animal homes such as ants working together to build an ant colony or bees working on a hive; people's homes such as farms, apartments, trailers, huts, igloos, and streets)
9. Comparing and contrasting Native American lifestyles (e.g., the Hopi in Arizona and the Cherokee in North Carolina)
10. Pioneer Life (how did pioneers work together to survive?)
11. An Imaginary Space Station

12. A Circus Community
13. Caring for the Environment
14. Adopt a Friend (a senior citizen, a pet, an organization, a third-world child)

Literature

Literature can serve as a primary vehicle for nurturing children. Fictional characters can become very real to the child, particularly to one who can identify with their problems. *Literature facilitates problem solving* by indirect association and identification. It also serves as a catalyst for training in values and morals. When children solve their own problems, they become stronger, less vulnerable young persons. In a listening/sharing experience, children can gain insight about themselves by sharing someone else's perspective. In an article, "Learning to Share: How Literature Can Help," Suzanne Krogh and Linda Lamme describe the value of books in training for nurturing:

> Literature can help children learn about sharing, employing their budding ability in role-taking. Literature takes sharing, an essentially abstract concept, and places it inside a more concrete setting. It provides children with an opportunity to take, for a while, the role of a protagonist, to step inside the shoes of someone facing a dilemma or making a decision. Specifically, it offers children an opportunity to learn why people share.[13]

Literature can serve as an entrance to the inner self–to what motivates and validates one's personage.

Some Nurturing Books for Young Children[14]

1. *George & Martha* by J. Marshall. The message: friendship. Two hippopotamuses named George and Martha have a special friendship. They always look on the bright side, and they always know how to cheer one another up. And, they also tell the truth!

2. *We Are Best Friends* by Aliki. The message: adapting and adjusting to change. Robert's best friend, Peter, is moving away. Robert tells his friend not to move because "you will miss me too much." Peter does move and, for Robert, there was no fun anymore—until he meets Will.

3. *Tico and the Golden Wings* by A. Mosel. The message: the gifts of love transcend the ordinary. Tico is a little bird born without wings and dependent on friends for survival. The day comes when Tico magically grows golden wings, to the amazement and envy of other birds. Tico uses these wings as gifts for the poor and helpless until they are all gone and replaced by plain, black wings.

4. *Make Way for Ducklings* by R. McClosky. The messages: making good choices, responsibility. Mrs. Mallard is very particular about finding a suitable place to nest and raise her offspring and Mr. Mallard is very patient with her. They finally settle on a quiet spot on the Charles River in Boston; and just in time.

5. *Goodnight Moon* by M. Brown. The message: security.   A warm, cozy, and comforting story for the very young child; "Goodnight stars . . . Goodnight air . . . Goodnight noises everywhere."

6. *Tikki Tikki Tembo* by A. Mosel. The messages: cultural awareness, respect for adults.   This exquisite Chinese folktale comes to life through its adorable characters and rhythmic verse, "Oh, most honorable mother, Tikki tikki tembo-no sa rembo-chari bari ruchi-pip peri pembo has fallen into the well."

7. *Let's Be Enemies* by J. Udry. The message: friends can have disagreements and still remain friends.   John went to James's house to tell him he was his enemy, but he found that friends can be enemies but still remain friends—best friends.

8. *Daddy Makes the Best Spaghetti* by A. Hines. The message: pitching in and sharing responsibilities.   Corey is at a day care center and when Daddy picks him up, wonderful things happen. Corey helps with the shopping, setting the table, cooking, and then, the games begin.

9. *William's Doll* by C. Zolotov. The messages: overcoming stereotypical behavior, doing one's thing, what's wrong with being me?   William wants a doll of his very own, a wish that concerns his family. Grandmother understands the nature and importance of this need and buys William a doll.

10. *Ira Sleeps Over* by B. Waber. The message: anxiety (we all need teddy bears sometimes).   Ira is excited about sleeping over at his friend's house (he had never slept out before) but as the day progresses he develops anxieties about parting with Ta Ta his best bear. When his friend Reggie pulls out his bear during a ghost story, Ira rushes home to get Ta Ta.

11. *What Mary Jo Shared* by J. Udry. The messages: decision making, the need to feel special.   Mary Jo needed to share with her classmates during show-and-tell but everything she thought of someone else had already shared. One day she invited her daddy to school and shared him. Mary Joe and her friends delighted in the specialness of her first sharing.

12. *Nick Joins In* by J. Lasker. The message: being different—how children with special needs feel when they are mainstreamed.   Nick expresses his fears about being integrated into a new school and, at the same time, children at the school he is about to attend express their concerns, too. They quickly reconcile their differences and view Nick as a special friend.

13. *The Little Engine That Could* by W. Piper. The message: if you think you can, you probably can.   As the immortal little blue engine puffs over its final hill, the enraptured listener becomes a passenger. The train says, "I think I can," and the children say "I know you can."

14. *The Tenth Good Thing About Barney* by J. Viorst. The message: regeneration; renewal.   When a funeral is held for Barney, a cat, the family has difficulty thinking up a tenth good thing to say about their beloved cat. When the father covers the ground with seeds, the little boy finds one more good thing to say. Barney will help the flowers grow!

15. *Peter's Chair* by E. Keats. The message: sharing is not always easy.   Peter has to give his special things to a new baby in the house. His chair is a different matter.

16. *Timothy and Gramps* by R. Brooks. The message: everyone needs someone to love. This is a tender and beautifully illustrated story about a shy and lonely little boy whose greatest pleasure is being with his grandfather. One day grandfather comes to school to share a special story with Timothy's classmates and Timothy begins to feel special too.

17. *A Story, A Story* by G. Haley. The message: we can overcome obstacles. In this beautifully illustrated African tale, a defenseless man succeeds against great odds to obtain Sky God's stories. Children will enjoy Ananse's quests, feats, and identify with his fears.

18. *Mommies at Work* by E. Merriam. The messages: identification and understanding. Children will see mommies in a variety of roles—making cookies, kissing places that hurt and places that don't hurt, working on ranches, building bridges. But best of all, mommies come home to a lot of love at the end of the day.

19. *On Mother's Lap* by A. Scott. The message: there's always room when there is love. This wonderful and tender book about a little Eskimo boy who is sensitive to a new baby on his mother's lap, tests her love for him by loading more and more on her lap before placing himself there also. Mother lets Michael know there is plenty of room on mother's lap.

20. *The Birthday Wish* by I. Chihiro. The message: we all make mistakes; being thoughtful is what counts. Allison accidentally blew out the candles on her friend's birthday cake. Allison feels very upset, but the next day, on her fifth birthday, Allison lets Judy blow out her candles.

21. *Alexander and the Wind-up Mouse* by L. Lionni. The message: love makes it own magic. This is the story about a real mouse and a wind-up mouse and their special friendship. Alexander thought he wanted to be a wind-up mouse like Willy until the day came when Willy was put in a throwaway box with other old toys. Helped by a magical lizard and a purple pebble, Willy turns into a real mouse to live happily ever after with Alexander.

22. *Frederick* by L. Lionni. The message: we all have something special to give, even if it isn't always apparent to others. Frederick was not a worker like his mice family. Instead of gathering food for winter, he gathered sun rays, colors, and imagination. But it was Frederick who entertained his friends with poems during the long winter months when there wasn't much work to do.

23. *Annie and the Old One* by M. Miles. The message: a child experiences loss gently through the death of her grandmother. This sensitive book suggests that life and death are a part of a process. Annie is a little Navajo girl who learns that when her mother finishes weaving a rug, it will be time for her beloved grandmother to die and return to the earth. Annie resists the inevitable death of her grandmother and tries to prevent the completion of the rug. When the old one explains that it is time for her return to the earth, Annie understands and is filled with the wonder of it all.

24. *The Red Balloon* by A. Lamorisee. The message: life can be sad and cruel but often there are happy endings. This tender story about a lonely little boy's love for a red balloon generates tremendous feeling in children (and adults). At the end of the book, when bullies taunt Pascal and throw stones at his balloon, the sky is suddenly filled with balloons rising in freedom, carrying Pascal away from sadness and loneliness. This is a picture book that can be read with or without discussion.

A wonderful source of information about children's literature is the book review section in educational periodicals such as *Childhood Education*. The books listed below have been reviewed and recommended by Helen H. Shelton, editor of *Books for Children*.[15]

Examples of Nurturing Literature for School-age Children

1. *Benjamin's Book* by R. Baker. The message: you can't cover up mistakes. A little hamster mistakenly gets a small pawprint on a clean white page. He tries to cover his mess by painting the paper white and finally gives up, only to accidentally leave a pawprint on the next piece of clean, white paper. (Ages 3 to 7)

2. *Stina* by L. Anderson. The message: feeling sometimes lost and frightened. During a visit to her grandfather's fishing cottage, Stina slips away to observe a big storm. She is frightened until her grandfather finds her. Fear turns to fascination when Stina and her grandfather find treasures from the sea. (Ages 4 to 8)

3. *Song and Dance Man* by K. Ackerman. The message: intergenerational experiences. This Newbery Award Winning book sensitively describes an old man's continued love for vaudeville—a joy shared by his grandchildren when they accompany him to the attic, unpack his trunk, and watch him rediscover the old days. (Ages 4 to 8)

4. *Ira Says Goodbye* by B. Waber. The message: goodbyes are never easy. When Ira discovers that his best friend Reggie is moving, the two friends act like it doesn't matter. The friends are not being honest with one another, which they acknowledge when they eventually express their true feelings. (Ages 5 to 10)

5. *Once When I Was Scared* by H. C. Pittman. The message: overcoming fears with imagination and courage. Daniel has to borrow coals from a neighbor's house that is located over two hills. To test his endurance and to overcome fear, Daniel uses his imagination and becomes a fox, a bobcat, and an eagle. These images help Daniel find courage. (Ages 5 to 9)

6. *Tillie and the Wall* by L. Lionni. The message: taking down walls that prevent friendships. Tillie, a mouse, determined to get to the other side of a wall, discovers a passageway and eagerly digs her way through. Much to her surprise she finds more mice just like herself on the other side of the wall. (Ages 5 to 9)

7. *The Josefina Story Quilt* by E. Coerr. The messages: animal love, tenderness, courage. On a covered-wagon journey West, Josefina's pet hen becomes a nuisance to adults—until she saves them from robbers. For each adventure, Faith has created a block for her quilt. (Ages 5 to 9)

8. *Harry's Visit* by B. Porte. The message: sometimes we have to do things we don't want to do.   Harry has to visit friends of the family and endure things he dislikes—kisses, listening to records he doesn't like, and eating bean soup for lunch. Things begin to look up when Harry is invited to shoot baskets with Jonathan. (Ages 6 to 8)

9. *Island Winter* by C. Martin. The message: there is great value in simple pleasures.   When summer visitors leave a remote island, a little girl happily returns to old-fashioned, simple pleasures. (Ages 6 to 10)

10. *Pet Mice* by R. Wexler. The message: caring for pets.   This is an excellent how-to book that will inform children about caring for and nurturing pets. (Ages 7 to 13)

11. *Rosie and the Dance of the Dinosaurs* by B. R. Wright. The message: overcoming a handicap.   Rosie is under stress. Her father has been transferred, her mother refuses to join him, and Rosie has to play a difficult piano piece (with only four fingers on her right hand) for her school recital.

12. *Yours Truly, Shirley* by C. Martin. The message: being dishonest with one's self.   Shirley, a dyslexic child, covers up for her disability by being a class clown. Her feelings surface when an adopted sister from Vietnam becomes a competitor and Shirley resorts to a cruel joke. (Ages 9 to 12)

13. *P.J.* by J. Balis. The message: you can't be what you are not.   Jessica, a fifth grader changes her image as an act of resistance to being labeled a perfect child and a teacher's pet. She becomes a poor student, baffling her friends and her playmates, and has a miserable summer. (Ages 8 to 11)

14. *Sugaring Time* by K. Lasky. The message: hard work pays off, especially when it is sweet.   The Lacey family, who live in New England, enjoy the hard work involved in processing maple sugar. The outcome (maple sugar on pancakes) is well worth the effort! (Ages 8 to 11)

A SUMMARY FOR A "PLAN" CURRICULUM

A program that is designed for a child's total development must address the central issue of how children learn and develop according to their own unique potential. A *PLAN* approach supports a child-centered, homelike environment for *all* children raised in a child care community. It is premised on the belief that a child's emotional and social well-being plays a critical role in a child's ability to learn and to adapt within his or her immediate community and within the greater society. An *affective* environment provides opportunities for self-growth and social development, creative and cognitive development, moral and practical life-skills development. It views a child's world as unified, balanced, and challenging and endorses a *developmental interactional* (whole child) approach to learning and teaching. This approach requires a supportive and compatible relationship between a center and a child's primary home environment.

In a child-centered environment, children are not hurried into experiences that are not appropriate and do not serve the needs of childhood. Rather, they are given time and space to discover their world and themselves. A *guided discovery* approach recognizes the importance of self-initiated learning through choices, problem solving and positive reinforcement. It also recognizes the critical relationship between teaching and learning by acknowledging the importance of values, play, self-expression, and children's feelings. This approach encourages interests and talents and places the child at the center of his or her own learning experience.

An environment must be loving and supportive if children are to experience happiness and security. It must be sensitive to cultural differences, to learning rates and to backgrounds. The environment should discourage unhealthy competition that makes children feel inadequate. An individualized program acknowledges the specialness of each child. As children become confident, they reach out toward others. They perceive their child care center as something like a home—rich with possibilities, filled with friends, and ripe for learning.

NOTES

1. Judith Leipzig, "Helping Whole Children Grow: Non-Sexist Childrearing for Infants and Toddlers," in Bonnie Neugebauer, ed., *Alike and Different: Exploring Our Humanity with Children* (Washington, DC: Exchange Press, 1987), p. 43.

2. Louise Derman-Sparks and the A.B.C. Task Force, *Anti-Bias Curriculum: Tools for Empowering Young Children* (Washington, DC: NAEYC, 1989), p. 69.

3. Charles A. Smith, *The Social Development of Young Children: Strategies and Activities* (Palo Alto, CA: Mayfield), 1982; as cited in Mary Renck Jalongo, "Promoting Peer Acceptance of the Newly Immigrated Child," *Childhood Education* 60(2) (November/December, 1983): 123.

4. Derman-Sparks, *Anti-Bias Curriculum*, p. 4.

5. Ibid., p. 2.

6. Susan Wichert, *Keeping Peace: Practicing Cooperation and Conflict Resolution with Preschoolers* (Philadelphia, PA: New Society Publishers, 1989), p. 54.

7. Barbara J. Meddin, Anita L. Rosen, "Child Abuse and Neglect," in Janet B. McCracken, *Reducing Stress in Young Children's Lives* (Washington, DC: NAEYC, 1986), pp. 78, 80.

8. S. Wichert, *Keeping Peace*, p. 15.

9. Eric Fromm, *Man for Himself* (New York: Holt, Rinehart, & Winston, 1947); as cited in

Daniel A. Prescott, "The Role of Love in Preschool Education," in *Readings from Early Childhood Education*, ed. M. Rasmussen (Washington, DC: ACEI, 1966), p. 56.

10. Sue Spayth Riley, *How to Generate Values in Young Children* (Washington, DC: NAEYC, 1984), p. 8.

11. Jim Greenman, *Caring Spaces, Learning Places: Children's Environments That Work* (Washington, DC: Exchange Press, 1988), p. 74.

12. Gladys F. Blue, "The Value of Pets in Children's Lives," *Childhood Education* 63(2) (December 1986): 85.

13. Suzanne L. Krogh and Linda L. Lamme, "Learning to Share: How Literature Can Help," *Childhood Education* (January/February 1983): 189.

14. Reprinted by permission of Ellen Cromwell and Acropolis Books Ltd. from *Feathers in My Cap: Early Reading through Experience* (Washington, DC: Acropolis Books Ltd., 1980), pp. 197–204.

15. Reprinted by permission of Helen H. Shelton, ed., *Children's Books* (Wheaton, MD: Association for Childhood Education International, [11501 Georgia Avenue, Suite 200], copyright 1989, 1990 by the Association).

RESOURCES

Brown, Janet M., ed. *Reducing Stress in Young Children's Lives*. Washington, DC: NAEYC, 1986.

Cavin, Ruth. *Pinch of Sunshine, ½ Cup of Rain: National Food Recipes for Young People*. New York: Atheneum, 1973.

Cooper, Jane. *Love at First Bite*. New York: Knopf, 1977.

Goodwin, Marty T. *Creative Food Experiences for Children*. Washington, DC: Center for Science and Public Interest, 1980.

Hendrick, Joanne. *Why Teach?* Washington, DC: NAEYC, 1987.

Kendrick, Abby S., et al., eds. *Healthy Young Children: A Manual for Programs*. Washington, DC: NAEYC, 1988.

Kindersley, Dorling. *My First Cookbook*. New York: Knopf, 1990.

Lewin, Esther. *Growing Up—A Child's Natural Food Book*. Pasadena, CA: Ward Ritchie Press, 1977.

Luvmour, Sambhava and Josette. *Everyone Wins! Cooperative Games and Activities*. Philadelphia, PA: New Society Publishers, 1990.

Montessori, M. *Education and Peace*. Chicago: Henry Regnery Press, 1972.

McGinnis, Kathleen, and Barbara Oehlberg. *Starting Out Right: Nurturing Young Children as Peacemakers*. Yorktown Heights, NY: Meyer Stone Books, 1988.

Neugebauer, Bonnie, ed. *Alike and Different: Exploring Our Humanity with Young Children*. Washington, Exchange Press, 1987.

Prutzman, Priscilla, et al. *The Friendly Classroom for a Small Planet: A Handbook on Creative Approaches to Living and Problem Solving for Children*. Philadelphia, PA: New Society Publishers, 1988.

Riley, Sue Spayth. *How to Generate Values in Young Children*. Washington, DC: NAEYC, 1984.

Saifer, Steffen. *Practical Solutions to Practically Every Problem: The Early Childhood Teacher's Manual*. St. Paul, MN: Toys 'n Things Press, 1990.

Saracho, Olivia N., and Bernard Spodek, eds. *Understanding the Multicultural Experience in Early Childhood Education*. Washington, DC: NAEYC, 1983.

Satir, Virginia. *Peoplemaking*. Palo Alto, CA: Science and Behavior Books, 1972.

Simon, Sidney B., and Sally W. Olds. *Helping Your Child Learn Right from Wrong: A Guide to Values Clarification*. New York: Simon & Schuster, 1976.

Stone, Jeannette G. *A Guide to Discipline*. Washington, DC: NAEYC, 1987.

Surbeck, Elaine, and Michael F. Kelley, eds. *Personalizing Care with Infants, Toddlers and Families*. Wheaton, MD: ACEI, 1990.

U.S. Department of Agriculture, *A Planning Guide for Food Service in Child Care Centers*. Washington, DC: 1989.

Wanamaker, Nancy, et al. *More than Graham Crackers*. Washington, DC: NAEYC, 1979.

Warren, Rita M. *Caring*. Washington, DC: NAEYC, 1977.

Wichert, Susanne. *Keeping the Peace: Practicing Cooperation and Conflict Resolution with Preschoolers*. Philadelphia: New Society Publishers, 1989.

Wolf, Dennie P., ed. *Connecting: Friendship in the Lives of Young Children and Their Teachers*. Redmond, WA: Exchange Press, 1986.

Zavitkovsky, Docia. *Listen to the Children*. Washington, DC: NAEYC, 1986.

In a child care setting, an environment conveys a weblike
imagery that begins with the child and expands outward
creating a sense of harmony and order. Each center has
its unique features as well as common characteristics
that can be identified in all quality environments.

PART VI

A CHILD'S ENVIRONMENT

An environment is a living, changing system. More than the physical space, it includes the way time is structured and the roles we are expected to play. It conditions how we feel, think, and behave; and it dramatically affects the quality of our lives. The environment either works for us or against us as we conduct our lives.

— *Jim Greenman*

14

INDOOR ENVIRONMENTS

A CLASSROOM

Imagine a room that looks and feels and smells like little children; a room that is bristling with activities; a room that is a composite of distinct interests and dispositions; a room that, despite its individuality, is greater than its parts; a room that conveys feelings of harmony, of order, of completeness, of wholeness, of happiness; a room that welcomes all children and all adults; a room that is alive with growth and potential and possibility. Imagine a perfect environment—one that John Tessimond symbolically describes in his lovely poem, "Daydream":

One day people will touch and talk perhaps easily,
And loving be natural as breathing and warm as sunlight,
And people will untie themselves, as string is unknotted,
Unfold and yawn and stretch and spread their fingers,
Unfurl, uncurl like seaweed returning to the sea,
And work will be simple and swift as a seagull flying,
And play will be casual and quiet as a seagull settling,
And the clocks will stop, and no one will wonder or care or notice,
And people will smile without reason, even in the winter, even in the rain.[1]

In a child care setting, an environment conveys a *weblike* imagery that begins with the child and expands outward creating a sense of harmony and order. Each center has its unique features as well as characteristics common to all quality environments.

Caring

Evidence of caring permeates a child-centered room from pictures on the wall to an old rocking chair that is never stationary. There is an atmosphere of pleasing, unhurried movement. Many activities are taking place, and there are many choices within each activity. A teacher is writing a story with a child while another child sits on her lap quietly observing the activity. In another part of a room, an adult is patiently helping children assemble colors for a mural. Somewhere else children are playing in their own little play worlds, so absorbed in fantasy that they scarcely notice others in the room. One almost misses the little girl who is setting the table for a snack, carefully arranging napkins and cups near chairs that will soon be occupied by hungry little children. There is a rhythm and a naturalness to the way children are playing and working in this room. It is not by accident that the room appears remarkably complete; the room has been designed carefully and arranged by a creative and caring teacher who knows what children like.

Creativity

One is compelled to linger in this room. A huge stuffed bear named McGoo has quickly become an attention-getter and a classroom companion. Children are sitting in his lap and feeding him pretend food. He never seems to tire of the attention or affection he receives as children pass by. Nearby, one notices a mural of a snowy day, hastily painted by children. It is the first snowfall of the year. The picture, like the season, is still moist and fresh with whiteness. While some children paint, others are cutting up paper into tiny little pieces that will soon be added to the mural. Still others are listening to a scratchy, worn record; one child is avidly reading a book that contains no words, another is bargaining for a dress-up item that is on another child. Some children are chattering, smiling and some are arguing. Personalized touches are everywhere: soft pillows, a trunkful of costumes, child-sized furniture, a real telephone, mirrors, a rocker, and a wardrobe for McGoo!

Authenticity

Character permeates a room that is authentic and meaningful. Character has its unique markings: child-worn furniture; overfed pets; and scarred surfaces that have been played on, spilled on, and written on. It is unpretentious: windowboxes with bulbs announcing the arrival of spring, a large clean window surrounded by children's pictures, children's artwork with the remnants of glue still dripping down the wall, a fishbowl too small for a fish because of the rocks children keep adding to it, hairless dolls, and armless teddy bears. It is joyful—something to look forward to, something to feel good about, something that makes one feel warm and safe inside, even on snowy days. Character grows out of a room that has been truly lived in and enjoyed by children. A room with character allows children to become meaning makers, as poignantly described by V. Suransky in her book, *The Erosion of Childhood:*

> The child's mode of being in the world is such that the world becomes an invitation. It is the things in the beckoning world that invite the child, that awaken his curiosity, that invoke him . . . to make sense of that multitude of experiences lying beyond; in short to become, through his play, both an actor and a meaning maker.[2]

Playfulness

A special room has a feeling of playfulness; an environment that sustains interest and makes children want to return. There are activity centers for exploration, there are open play areas for children to move and dance in, and there are enclosed areas for imaginary play. There is quiet space to play with one's thoughts and space for small gatherings. Teresita E. Aguilar defines a playful atmosphere as one that:

- Increases the sense of freedom;
- Provides an outlet for self-expression;
- Encourages people to "play with" ideas rather than to "work for" solutions;
- Allows for manipulation; use "people-powered" devices;
- Provides risk/challenge in varying degrees;
- Encourages problem-solving activities;
- Incorporates the arts (music, dance, drama);
- Is flexible;
- Minimizes or eliminates negative consequences for playful behaviors;
- Allows for escapism, fantasy, and imagination;
- Encourages and demonstrates good humor;
- Allows for experimentation/exploration.[3]

WORKING WITH SPACE

Space communicates to children. It gives them information about what they can play with and where they can play. It makes them aware of dimensions. Children perceive space as both changing and unchanging. There are certain units in a room that are designated for a particular purpose, and although the parts may change, the structure remains fairly constant throughout a year. These units are called activity or interest centers and are designed for a specific kind of play or play/work. They are enclosed on two or three sides by frames or shelves, and they are organized in compatible patterns that reflect the purpose and use of a center.

Activity centers usually are connected by pathways that allow children to move freely from activity to activity in logical patterns. The number of centers in a room is determined by the space available and by the developmental levels of its occupants. A room for two-year-olds will have fewer centers and less equipment than one for four-year-olds. A room for eight-year-olds will have fewer play centers but more game and art centers than one for six-year-olds.

A good portion of children's play space should be left open for multipurpose use. Common space is needed for lunch, for group circles, and for cubbies. Large, open areas also may be used for a loft or to store a piece of equipment that does not fit into an activity center. A loft may become a reading area, a homework area, or a place to hang out until parents arrive. Common space is not only functional but promotes social development through natural interaction that takes place when children do not feel restricted by enclosed space.

In every classroom there is space that generally is not used; an oddly shaped corner or space between two shelves. Creative teachers can use little out-of-the-way nooks as personal spaces for children. A child may use such a space as a garage for small cars, a small fort, or a bedroom for dolls.

In child care environments, space is continuously adapting to the needs and interests of its occupants, to the creative influence of teachers, and to environmental exigencies. Throughout a year, a teacher may make several changes before she feels a room is working for a particular group of children. She examines space critically to determine if it is meeting her goals and objectives, if it is challenging, and if it is adding significantly to her environment. Sometimes only subtle changes are required: a small area rug and a soft cushion are added to a language center, a new theme is needed for a discovery center. Sometimes more dramatic changes are necessary: a heavily used block center needs a larger corner of a room, a library corner is too close to a common area. The more teachers experiment with space, the more adept they become in designing environments. Making changes is sometimes unsettling, often exhilarating, but in the long run, worthwhile. This poem from *Everychild's Everyday* aptly describes change:

> *If we change*
> *Time and space*
> *We can change*
> *Ourselves*
> *We can find new ways*
> *To communicate*
> *New words to say*
> *New topics to pursue*
> *We can find new ways*
> *To operate*
> *To invent*
> *To respond*
> *If I can change*
> *Time and space*
> *I can change habits too.*

DEFINING SPACE

Measuring for Children

From a child's vantage point, an environment that works is one that *offers* the possibility of *discovery and inventiveness*. For a young child, a child care room is like an oversized play room that has lots of parts, people, and hidden dimensions. Within this configuration, children begin to make mental maps. They find their way around a room by reading picture labels that describe activities and by learning the patterns and the pathways that lead to favorite toys and activities.

There are many choices to make and there are hidden dimensions as well. For a small resident, a classroom is a very big world to explore, even with a map. Each child reacts to an environment in his or her own way. Some children will plunge right into activities, others will move more cautiously, while some will stay near the door until they feel acclimated and assured that the new surroundings are safe to enter.

To a child, an environment is companionable and manageable when it is neither too cluttered nor too bland. A room is inviting when it is neither too structured nor too disorganized. Teachers, who tend to view an environment from the eyes of adults, are often insensitive to children's impressions of space. Rooms are too often set up for public viewing rather than for children's play. Teachers forget that children may not feel comfortable in a sanitized, perfectly arranged room that looks very much like the room down the hall. If children had to choose between a comfortable, lived-in environment and a manicured room that gives a hands-off impression, they would clearly choose the former. When a room in a child care center has its own aura, children look forward to each day and each year.

Children prefer a homelike setting. They immediately notice freestanding novelty items like cardboard-box houses or imaginative handmade props. They are attracted to soothing activities like modeling with clay, playing in water, and painting—activities that do not require a great deal of interaction. As they become familiar with a room, children react to warm, soft colors, to an interesting balance of activities, and to a creative distribution of space.

Their perception of space widens to accommodate all parts of their physical and human environment. Children identify playmates and favorite centers by name. They find hidden corners to explore. They absorb an atmosphere, identifying its play space, activity centers, common areas, space that is off-limits. Within these boundaries, they perceive a sense of order, routine, and harmony.

Measuring for Toys and Things

A child-centered environment requires a long measuring tape, one that goes around and through objects that take up play space. A preschool classroom must offer children a variety of toys and activities that generate learning and motor development. They need both nonrealistic (unstructured, imaginative) and realistic (structured, recognizable) toys. Structured toys are those that are easily recognized and identified: a bus, a drum, a doll, a long wooden train, or a riding truck. Young children are primarily at a level for structured, realistic toys, although novelty items (such as a feather, an animal scull, a snake skin, a wind machine, or a fossil) should always be slipped into an activity center for discovery learning.

Unstructured toys are items that may or may not be identified by name. They are less defined objects that are labeled by the child in the context of his immediate play needs (scarves, shawls, baskets, bags, zippered containers, items with unusual shapes). Indoor materials might include interesting props such as a wagon wheel, a lantern, an old weathered chest with an intriguing lock, and unusual stuffed animal, a surprise box; play items such as a cane, or a wand;

sensory pieces such as lace, streamers, net, fur, feathers, a fan, or a plastic horse with a long soft mane.

Outdoor materials might include gatherings from nature such as rocks, sticks, stones, bark, pinecones, nutmeats, and so on. During unstructured, outdoor play, sticks may be used as fishing poles, twigs as birthday candles, rocks as gold or silver, and little hills as miniature forts or underground tunnels for little action figures. Tactile experiences in sand, water, mud, and clay also lead to imaginative, open-ended play. These unstructured experiences are under a child's control from beginning to end. For most children, they are the best parts of a day.

A classroom also needs variety in the types of play units that are offered to children. In her excellent book, *Planning Environments for Young Children,* leading educator and writer Elizabeth Prescott classifies play units as:

1. *Simple:* A play unit that has one use and does not have subparts (swings, jungle gym, rocking horse, trike).
2. *Complex:* A play unit with subparts that can be manipulated or improvised by children (art activities, a table with books to look at, an area with pets).
3. *Super:* A complex unit that has one or more additional play materials (a sand box with play materials and water, dough table with tools, movable climbing boards and boxes, and large crates).[4]

Young children (ages two to three) generally are happy (and safe) with fewer parts to interact with. They enjoy the motion of getting on and off items that are relatively fixed and uncomplicated. As children become more physically adept and imaginative in their play (ages four to five), they increasingly look for units that offer more challenge. An independent, inventive four-year-old loves to move parts around to create new structures.

Measuring for Interests

The composition of a class affects space. If boys dominate a group of children, there will be a need for an expanded large-motor construction center. If girls dominate, there will likely be a need for an expanded drama and arts center. In traditional play patterns, boys gravitate toward large-motor, active play while girls prefer less active, more focused play. Boys like rough-and-tumble direct-contact play while girls prefer less physical outlets. Although all activities should be encouraged for both sexes, if given the choice, boys and girls will probably make the same choices.

Sex-role stereotyping in play begins early and continues throughout childhood according to a study of play activities conducted by Betty S. Beeson and R. Ann Williams (1979). The study found that preschool boys still prefer wheeled vehicles, blocks, sand, tractors and climbing frames, trains and kiddie-kars, while girls prefer art activities, dolls, formal games, and house play. In crossovers, house play (or dramatic play) was the one area that was not found to be sex stereotyped—

it was chosen by both boys and girls as a preferred activity. The research indicated that there may have been some changes in the sex stereotyping of play activities of young children but only in one direction. Boys' choices had expanded to include house play while girls' play choices had not expanded.[5]

Similarly, a study on toy preferences of preschool children conducted by Charles H. Wolfgang (1983) found that contemporary children attending child care do not differ from children of previous studies in their preferences for gender-specific toys: basically little had changed since studies that date as far back as 1934—one done by Vance. Results of a preschool Play Materials Preference Inventory (PMPI) indicate that boys preferred categories of structured materials, letters, numbers, carpentry, number shapes, number cards, and colored pegs while girls preferred the category of fluid constructional materials and the toy farm, doll play, housekeeping, symbolic activities as well as letter shapes and clay.[6] These natural, early preferences would suggest a disposition toward math (for boys) and language (for girls).

If early childhood is a time for making choices and expanding knowledge, children's environments should reflect their interests. If teachers take away toys that are identified with one sex, they deny children access to natural play preferences, i.e., boys tend toward blocks and girls tend toward housekeeping. The place to make changes in children's perceptions is not through contrived methods of social engineering that deny children access to the toys and experiences they enjoy but in home environments where identity begins.

One way to discourage gender stereotyping is to expand a dramatic play or block center to include themes and activities that appeal to both sexes—e.g., a barber shop, a bank, a shoe shop, a paint store, a post office—or by adding interesting accessories in a large-motor area. Another way might be to expand an arts section to include activities such as woodworking, clay modeling, models (rockets, boats, windmills, mobiles), and innovative assemblages (creating a small farm, a castle, or pond diorama). If an arts table is not inviting to little boys, chances are they will gravitate back to a block corner where they can create in more satisfying ways.

Measuring for a Total Environment

Children and their activities fill up a room. When setting up a classroom, teachers often forget to consider children as an integral and sizeable component of space. Children physically occupy space with form, shape, and backpacks. School-age children naturally take up more space than young children, yet these rooms are often the most crowded, e.g., a 26 to 2 student/teacher ratio for children older than five years of age. Licensing personnel, who establish school-age student/teacher ratios under the current allocation of 35 square feet per child, have not given much thought to movement or personal space.

Designing a classroom to *maximize the feeling of space* without limiting activities is a creative challenge for a teacher. Confined space restricts activities and choices of toys. Large-motor activities, such as tumbling or push toys that require room, are usually the first items to be removed from a crowded classroom. Many teachers are not opposed to giving up large-motor toys; which are identified with noise and movement. Unfortunately, in crowded centers, large-motor development is limited to outdoor time.

Play curriculums are forcing teachers to rethink and restructure their organizational patterns and use of space. With limited space, teachers find it necessary to eliminate some activity centers or find creative ways to integrate existing centers. For example, they might combine a language center with a discovery center, or a listening/language center (it can be closed during group time) might frame a circle area. They might change the dimensions of activity centers or place compatible centers, such as dramatic play and construction, back to back using long shelves as dividers. Another alternative is to reduce the number of tables and chairs in a room by storing them until lunch or by setting up a separate lunchroom for all children in a center. By eliminating tables, teachers are eliminating a structured, school-like appearance as well as opening space. By experimenting with patterns, and by increasing the space allotted to each child to a minimum of 50 square feet, a teacher will be better able to manage space. She may even have some left over for several pet homes.

Space includes not only cubbies and common space but also utility objects and units such as doors, windows, sinks, heating units, built-in storage areas, and bulletin boards. It includes office space, a food preparation area, storage areas, closets, bathrooms, personal shelves for children, file cabinets and personal space for teachers, and a staff lounge/resource room. These areas must be considered when designing and measuring a room. With space at a premium, teachers can use auxiliary space for a file cabinet, personal cubbies, or to store "space-heavy" items such as a television, props for a play, or a refrigerator. As much as possible, items that are not considered part of children's play should be moved to adjacent rooms. Clearly, the layout and management of space is an important factor in child care planning, influencing both child and staff behaviors.

ORGANIZING SPACE

Activity Centers

Most child care centers use interest centers to organize and define space and activities. These centers have boundaries to encourage privacy and to facilitate organized play. Boundaries reduce children's natural tendency to encroach on another's space. They help to hold children's attention and to reduce noise levels.

Shelves or screens that define the perimeters of an activity center are scaled in size to ensure safety and to provide visibility at all times. A standard size for shelves is 11½" deep by 28" high by 48" wide. When four-year-olds and school-age children share activity centers, a shelf height of 36" is preferable because it can provide children a greater sense of privacy. Locker cubbies, constructed with hooks and cubicles for storage, provide excellent boundaries for dramatic play centers.

Averaging 7 feet in height these units serve a dual purpose of enclosing space and providing a storage area for dress-up garments. Activity centers encourage personal quiet time as well as opportunities for cooperative play. Materials that identify and enhance a center should be organized and labeled in a systematic way that can be understood and respected by children.

Activity centers commonly include: a block area, a dramatic play area, a science center, a listening area, an arts and crafts area, and a book nook. An easel and a sand/water table usually are placed in separate sections of a room, away from areas of great activity. Carpeted space is set aside for circle, manipulative play, and other activities requiring floor time. Because activity centers accommodate play that ranges from active to less active, they must be planned carefully. Each play center must be considered from the vantage of: purpose, activity level (high or low), noise level (high or low), and its potential appeal to children (popular centers need more space to accommodate more children). Finding ways to enclose and define activity areas is always a creative challenge for a teacher with limited resources. Shelves, pegboard screens, props, and visuals are common ways to solve the problem.

School-age children also need activity centers that can be used for constructive and imaginative play, for quiet activities, and for group activities. A physical and human environment carefully tailored to ages and interests will communicate caring to children.

Pathways

Activity centers (or clusters) are joined by connecting pathways. These are open-space access routes that encircle and connect activity areas and common areas. They help to ensure safety and create a sense of openness and organization. Pathways should be kept free of clutter. Children naturally find pathways as they move from activity to activity. Pathways need not be marked or coded with colored tape.

Layout

There is no quick and easy method for setting up a classroom for large numbers of children throughout the day, especially when a room must be shared by several age levels. The existing shape and design of space automatically dictates certain placements. If there are few electrical outlets in a room, a teacher would naturally begin her classroom design with a listening center and put plug-in appliances near the existing outlets. An easel for painting would logically be placed near a sink, and if a teacher does a fair amount of cooking with children, she would probably want her food preparation table area near a sink and countertop. Doors, windows, storage closets and odd-shaped corners also will influence decision making. Windows are wonderful attributes but often hard to work with. Drafts, sunlight, and safety are always primary considerations when arranging activity centers near windows.

PLAY FEATURES

After practical considerations, a teacher will begin to think in terms of prominent centers of interest: a circle (carpeted) area, a dramatic play area, a construction area (block play), and a learning area (math and science). A carpeted circle area for group activities usually is placed away from distraction and noise in a section of a room that can accommodate bulletin boards, standing easels, visuals, charts, and other useful materials. Often a science or discovery center is in the group circle area. Block play also can be located in the circle area because of its size and because it is carpeted (essential to block play). If blocks are stored neatly in units that can be closed during group activities, this arrangement works very nicely. As favorite and well-populated centers, dramatic play and block play should not be too close together. An important objective in designing a child care room is to separate key activity areas so that children are not congregated in one section of a room and noise levels are not concentrated in one area.

AUXILIARY NEEDS AND CONSIDERATIONS

Large tables and chairs are necessary items that must be worked into a room design. Selecting and arranging tables and chairs so that they are not obtrusive and do not constrict space involves a great deal of trial and error until a workable pattern emerges. Tables often are set up in the center of a room so they can provide common space for lunch and other group activities such as art projects. By varying the shapes and arrangements of tables, rooms will appear less cluttered and more comfortable. An L-shaped arrangement (two rectangular tables) is more amenable to socializing than two parallel tables. One long table and a large oval table are compatible coordinates as are two square tables. To further reduce the number of tables in a common area, small activity center tables may be used for snacks or lunch for two children.

Standard chair and table heights are:

Age	Chair Height	Table Height
1½ to 2 years	9 inches	16 inches
3 to 5	10–12 inches	18–20 inches
5 to 7	14 inches	22 inches
Adult	17 inches	30 inches

Most tables are adjustable, from 18 to 24 inches high in 1 inch increments. If rooms are shared with school-age children, several larger tables can be positioned against walls while not in use. Extra tables will provide valuable space for drying paintings, temporary storage, notes, and so on.

Chairs should be purchased for stability as well as durability. Plastic chairs withstand hard use, are light and stackable, and do not tip easily. They come in bright colors that can enhance an otherwise bland room. Unfortunately, bright colors draw unnecessary attention to table areas. Colored furniture is not as authentic as natural wood and should be used sparingly in classrooms. Regardless of the selection, it is important to the harmony and decor of a room that tables and chairs match and that they be purchased carefully for long-term use. A teacher who orders bright royal blue rather than neutral chairs may regret her decision for years to come.

Cots

Cot rest is a necessary chore for child care providers. Cots take up a large amount of space and, over the years, become faded and uninviting. All children in licensed care centers through the age of four years, and five-year-olds who spend longer than 3.5 hours in a center, are required to rest on a cot for a period of time that typically falls between 12:30 and 2:30 p.m. Children in centers normally rest on canvas or vinyl stackable cots that are scaled to age. Toddler cots average approximately 24 by 42 inches and preschool cots are 24 by 52 inches. Most licensing agencies require that cots be placed at least 3 feet apart, wiped clean weekly with a safe solution such as clorox and water, labeled with each child's name, and outfitted with clean linens at least once a week. Most centers request parents to bring a pillow, tie-on sheets, a resting friend, and a light blanket.

Storage

Adequate storage space is an absolute imperative for child care centers. Directors will need to allocate space for centerwide storage of ongoing consumable items and bulk items that are bought for long-term storage. Examples of high-use consumables that require advance purchasing and storing are: paint, paper rolls, easel paper, language experience paper, markers and crayons, paper goods, glue, and other popular arts and crafts items as well as office supplies. Examples of food staples are: peanut butter, applesauce, canned fruit, 100% sugar-free juice, hot chocolate, cold cereal, pretzels, crackers, granola mixes, raisins, and other dried fruit snacks. Space also will be needed for sundry items such as first-aid kits, cleaning items, personal items, files, toys that are not used regularly, prop boxes for dramatic play, toys for rainy days and ongoing projects that require temporary storage. In addition, storage space will have to include materials for children's play and learning that takes place inside the classroom. Sectional shelves are customarily used as boundaries for activity centers and as open storage areas for materials and equipment.

Most group centers solve a portion of the problem by initially investing in sectional metal shelves. They are relatively inexpensive, functional, and easy to assemble. They can accommodate most consumables but should not be substitutes for classroom activity shelves or for personal space areas needed for children and staff. Open shelves that are centrally located and heavily used by staff tend to get untidy and unmanageable after a while. The best solution for storage is to have a central storage closet for centerwide use and individual storage shelves in each room to accommodate consumables, special materials, and personal needs.

A day care center never seems to have enough storage space. Storage facilities are costly to install or to purchase and are not usually at the top of a director's wish list. The common reaction to storage is that it can be improvised for now and dealt with later. As centers grow, their storage needs grow and, as is often the case, "later" never comes. Inadequate or poorly designed storage facilities can cause a creative, open program to quickly become chaotic and sloppy in appearance. Teachers who have no place for personal items or for ongoing projects quickly express irritation. They begin to fight with colleagues for space. Children who have no place for personal items can hardly be expected to settle into a center and treat it as a second home.

When storage is not given adequate attention, a lovely room can quickly become disorganized and unattractive. Children are not going to do their fair share of room maintenance if there is no place to put their toys. Conversely, when items are systematized and attractively arranged in a defined location, children will gladly pitch in.

There are several ways to address storage decisions in a center. First a director must decide what storage is needed based on her budget, her staff's needs, the number and ages of the children, her buying practices, and her program emphasis—a program that emphasizes the arts and large-motor indoor and outdoor play will need considerable space for large and small items. For storing and categorizing items that are used by all staff members, clear containers work nicely because they come in different sizes, are economical, and can be added to as the need arises.

Many storage bins have colored lids that can facilitate coding and labeling stored items. For storing items that are too large for shelves or that are used as props for routine play activities, hard plastic cubes (that resemble milk cartons) are functional and come in attractive colors that add a pleasant touch to a room. Records, tapes, puppets, dress-ups, collections of small cars, action figures, and sets of small blocks are examples of items that may require separate storage. Whatever the choice, it is important that storage containers be the right size, color coordinated, and match in style so that children see order and practice organizational skills during play and pick-up.

In addition to common storage space for consumable items and children's activities, personal space for children and teachers must be considered. Every teacher should have a storage unit (preferably with doors) for personal belongings—hot pots, tea, coffee, snacks, soups, and medicines as well as for classroom items that reinforce a program (visuals and items for special projects and individualized learning activities), hand-made games, or other items that are held in reserve.

Children, too, require personal space. Having a locker or a cubby makes a child feel important, and from a developmental perspective, *facilitates responsibility*. Cubbies are good friends to children. They accommodate a host of collectibles like lunch boxes, backpacks, coats, invitations, and leftover food. Personal space is a luxury in many centers. Storage units are costly, necessitating sharing. When two buddies have to share one cubby, they begin to become suspicious of one another's motives. In shared arrangements, one child begins to encroach on another, creating "wars" over space. When space is limited, children have difficulty manipulating and finding personal things, and they lose interest in managing their own space.

Hide-aways

Children seem to need little spaces tucked away from action areas to sit in, play in, and escape to. Suggestions for hide-aways are: a small playhouse, an indoor log cabin, a variplay gym that has an interior section to crawl into, a loft, large cardboard boxes, or an improvised fort set up between tables or chairs covered with sheets or blankets. Sometimes the sheet can be painted in a design that matches a play theme. An investment such as a log cabin or a play house is well worth the cost. Children feel like they are in a home within a home when they can isolate themselves in a framed play area. They can decorate and change items to suit their tastes and to accommodate their play themes.

Durable, Safe Equipment

When purchasing equipment for activity centers, it is important to look at every piece of equipment for durability and safety. The structure and quality of toys greatly affects the way a classroom functions. Therefore, a director/teacher should give thoughtful consideration to needs before purchasing a major item: What is its intended use? Is it really needed at this time? Is it the right size for its intended use? Will it be compatible with the rest of the furnishings? How difficult will it be to assemble?

When purchasing equipment for indoor use, a director should seek input from teachers as to how a room should be equipped. In addition, she should follow guidelines for safety and durability such as these:

- Fixed equipment should be purchased from a reputable toy distributing company that stands behind its products.
- Equipment should not have sharp edges.
- Shelves should be long and wide enough to place objects for children's continuous use.
- Paint should be nontoxic.
- Large pieces (such as cubbies) ideally should be secured to a wall or placed back to back to avoid tipping over.
- Structures for climbing should be securely assembled to withstand vigorous use and not be able to be moved around by children.
- Fixtures on shelves and storage units should be secure and positioned away from children's hands.
- Materials for young children should not contain small pieces that might be swallowed, should not be flammable, and should not contain sharp objects.

- Maintenance-free surfaces such as formica tops or treated wood surfaces clean easily and retain their appearance longer than untreated or poorly painted surfaces.
- Chairs should be light enough for children to manage and sturdily constructed to prevent tipping.
- Electric or battery-operated equipment should not be purchased.
- Audiovisual equipment should be strictly monitored and off-limits to young children.
- The dimensions and potential use of lofts should be carefully considered before an investment is made.

Equipment purchased through early childhood supply catalogs is designed for long, hard, and safe use by children. By reviewing catalogs, a consumer-conscious director can shop and select from attractive options that offer ranges of quality, design, functionality, and durability.

USING SPACE EFFICIENTLY AND EFFECTIVELY

When organizing space, a director/teacher should consider the total environment. The following guidelines are important:

- Carefully consider the placement of quiet, personal space, indoor climbing equipment, and, of course, common space that requires tables and chairs.
- Place activity centers back-to-back to conserve space.
- Consider storing some seasonal equipment in order to increase space when needed.
- Locate activity centers in areas that are play-safe, physically appropriate, and harmonious to a room.
- Position heavily used centers in areas of a room that can be seen and quickly accessed by adults.
- Scale activity centers to size, and design them for durability, safety, independent play, and group play.
- Equip centers with both realistic and imaginative toys, novelty items, and a variety of sensorimotor activities.
- Provide ample space for storage, for consumables, for large-motor items.
- Provide space for a media center where staff and children can check out items for enrichment and pleasure.
- Provide personal space for teachers and for children.
- Organize and label supplies so that a room connotes a feeling or orderliness.
- Train children to respect their activity centers.
- Train children to care for their activity centers.
- Consult children before selecting new toys, games, or play equipment.
- Pay attention to *safety* factors: electrical fixtures and outlets; heating, cooling and ventilation systems; plumbing and sanitary facilities; unsafe equipment;

high equipment that might not adequately protect children from falling such as lofts or nesting bridges; ground coverings and fences; entrances, exits, and corridors; fire prevention; child-safe kitchen equipment, placement and condition of doors, windows, and screens; storage and food areas; loose tiles; posting of rules, regulations, and emergency numbers, and procedures; updating records on children and staff; and the placement and height of water fountains and sinks.

- Pay attention to *health* factors: disposal of wastes and diapers; bathroom and handwashing routines; toxic materials; unsafe plants; food storage; fabrics and play materials; keeping a room sanitized, free of rodents and germs; keeping medical records updated; training teachers in first-aid; training teachers to recognize the signs and symptoms of contagious diseases or other illnesses and of child neglect or abuse; training staff to prepare nutritional meals and snacks; ensuring that children get rest and good care throughout the day; having procedures and policies for emergency care, sick care, and personal care such as brushing teeth and washing hands; maintaining adequate custodial services; and enclosing an area for emergency care of a sick child.
- Pay attention to *environmental* factors: harsh lights and colors, noise levels, the look and feel of a room, and stress factors.
- Recognize a child's human and physical environment as interconnected.

When a room begins to function as an interdependent unit, each section reinforces and complements the natural flow of space. At this point, a teacher can move into a creative mode to work with her remaining space, adding touches and novelties to heretofore empty, unused space. Colors and unique blendings of textures will work together to form a personality—a room becomes a harmonious and integrated whole.

ACTIVITY CENTERS FOR A "PLAN" CURRICULUM

Activity centers reflect a program's philosophy, objectives, and teaching methods. They inspire and promote learning through self-initiated play. They provide a system of play that is organized and readily understood by children. Activity centers are designed for a total child approach to teaching and learning. They are particularly important in an open, play-oriented environment because they provide balance, diversity, and organization to a child's day. Activity centers reflect a child's need for personal and social development and for physical, creative, and cognitive development. They enable children to fully express and experience themselves within a cooperative, child-centered environment. As children make choices, accept responsibility, and develop competencies, they feel a sense of security and belonging. They solve problems as they occur—if a center is too crowded, a child will voluntarily move or make a change. Children begin to take the perspective of others as they learn to share. Gradually, they discover that learning is an integral part of their play world.

"PLAN" activity centers are defined as:

1. Play Centers: for construction and for dramatic play
2. Discovery Centers: for language and for math/science
3. Art Centers: for arts and crafts and for woodworking
4. Nurturing Centers: for social, emotional, and personal development

Play Centers

Play centers are activity areas that encourage children to play independently and with peers with minimal supervision. When children play, they are challenged physically and mentally. They release tension as they express themselves in an unstructured, cooperative environment. As children explore and master their play environments, they shape and define their personalities, their interests, and their talents. Children's play centers are identified by their organization, purpose, materials, and potential for specific kinds of play. They have a defined location, a shape, and a distinctive personality. In most centers these areas are called Construction Centers and Dramatic Play Centers.

A Construction Center

A construction center is primarily a large-motor block area where children assemble and build constructs using a variety of blocks and interesting, imaginative accessories. It may also include small-motor toys as well as a variety of wooden trucks, planes, and cars. Some centers include a gym house or freestanding structure, such as a tent, to extend dramatic play. The area should be large enough for children to build horizontally as well as vertically. If the area is expanded to include a wooden train set or riding toys, it must be large enough for children to move freely as they play. Storage shelves that encourage organizing blocks by size and shape and accessories by sets are recommended. A block cart (on wheels) may also be used for storage. Equipment that does not fit on shelves can be stored in large plastic containers neatly positioned on the floor. Because noise levels tend to be high when children play with blocks, an area rug is recommended. Toys and materials need to be labeled, age-appropriate, and challenging.

Equipment and Materials.   Teachers select equipment and materials to correspond with the age and interest level of a particular group of children. An activity center may contain: a complete set of wooden blocks consisting of approximately 390 pieces and 28 shapes, cardboard blocks in rectangular shapes (these are preferred for the younger child), an interesting variety of plastic multishaped blocks or interlocking blocks such as waffle blocks, large hollow blocks consisting of approximately 12 pieces in 4 shapes (ramps, shortboards, longboards, squares), and appropriate wooden toys and accessories to enhance play themes.

Accessories.   Block accessories may include: small-scale airports, farms, villages, cities, garages, train sets, dollhouses, vinyl floor mats with play scenes that children can add objects to for pretend play, a variety of miniature transportation vehicles, small-scale animals, people or action figures for theme-building, odds and ends such as a variety of cardboard shapes from an arts and crafts center, cardboard boxes that may be painted or sat in, interesting styrofoam props, spools from thread or construction site spools (sanded and varnished). Manipulatives may include Bristle Blocks, Flexi Blocks, Snap blocks, Lego sets, Towerifics, Rig-A-Jigs, Bolt-A-Toys, Connectos, Sprocketeers, Constructo Straws, Lincoln Logs, Tinker-toys. Young children may also enjoy a rubber tire, a wooden boat, a small hose, traffic signs, and role-playing hats. Photographs of children at play, murals, and posters will increase motivation and imagination.

School-age children may enjoy more complex construction sets, particularly in the Lego family. They also love interesting action figures and challenging manipulatives such as Build-A-Raceway or Nuts and Bolts sets. In addition, pulleys and magnets, flags, a walkie talkie, a flashlight may be added to a construction center.

A Dramatic Play Center

A dramatic play center is an area that encourages children to play independently and imaginatively for extended periods of time. All children enjoy role-playing experiences that promote self-expression through creative activities and materials.

Equipment and Materials. Teachers select equipment and materials to correspond with the age and interest level of a particular group of children. An activity center may include basic role-playing equipment: a stove, a refrigerator, a sink, a cupboard, kitchen appliances, food, a small table and chairs, a dresser, a rack or storage unit for dress-ups, assorted dress-ups for boys and girls, a telephone, a mirror, doll beds and dolls, stuffed animals, an unbreakable metal mirror, a rocking chair.

Accessories may include a trunk for dress-ups, a small lamp, an area rug, a log cabin or another type of freestanding house, a dollhouse, various play kits and props, real-life uniforms, an attache case, a suitcase, a cash register and play money, books, games and puzzles that are theme-related, a small desk or writing area, a small chair or sofa, an iron and ironing board, a microwave oven.

School-age children may enjoy prop boxes containing imaginative play items such as a hospital, a construction site, a paint and wallpaper store, a beauty parlor, a florist, a theatre, a circus, a country fair, a zoo, a shoe store, a bank. They may enjoy making a puppet theatre; a vanity table with mirror and make-up, accessories from antique or second-hand stores; posters from theatres, museums, or travel bureaus; beanbag chairs; an old hutch or dresser; and musical instruments.

Learning Centers

A learning center is a quiet area designed for cognitive and personal development. It may include a language center and a math/science center. A quiet center should be away from large-motor, active play centers such as blocks or dramatic play. It should invite exploration and thinking through visuals, attractively arranged materials, and living things such as plants and animals. It should provide cozy areas that encourage children to investigate, to find out, and to quietly interact with friends. Learning centers might include plants, a large, low table (children sit on the floor), L-shaped shelves, an area rug, beanbag chairs, and a small round table with chairs.

A Language Center

This center contains a listening area, a reading area, and a writing area. Because these components are complementary and reinforcing, a language center can be designed to integrate the language arts.

Equipment and Materials.   Teachers select equipment and materials to correspond with the age and interest level of a particular group of children. A listening area may include a record player, head phones, a tape recorder, records and tapes. A reading area may include a small bookshelf with books openly displayed, small chairs, and a rug. A writing area may include a table, chairs, paper, markers, pencils, a typewriter, and a computer.

Accessories for Language.   Accessories may include teacher-made big books and games; several sets of beginning readers; paper and pencils; personal journals; tactile, magnetic, and flannel letters; a large blackboard and colored chalk; commercial games that encourage reading and memory such as Uncle Wiggly; materials for making original books; musical instruments; and video cassettes.

School-age children may enjoy commercial games that expand language and thinking such as Trivial Pursuit for Juniors, Life, Risk, Go to the Head of the Class, storytelling objects grouped and stored in small containers by theme (the zoo, the circus, the farm), a large blackboard and colored chalk, a set of encyclopedias, a dictionary, library books, and magazines. Children may also enjoy organizing a writer's center, a lending library, a current events club, or a debate club. They may enjoy learning a second language using books, tapes, and visuals.

A Math/Science Center

A shelf for science activities, a shelf for math activities, and a large display area (the top of a shelf) that integrates the two discovery areas make up this center. A science center is designed to develop study themes such as the water cycle, plants and animals, amphibians, animal homes, electricity, fossils, rocks, the solar system. A math center is designed to develop basic skills, reasoning, and conceptual development. A math/science center encourages hands-on learning, and problem-solving activities that promote critical thinking through the scientific method.

Equipment and Materials—for Math.   Teachers select equipment and materials to correspond with the age and interest level of a particular group of children. A math center may include magnetic numbers; an abacus; discrimination, grouping and classification, and pattern cards; counting bars and number boards; number puzzles and books; flannel board counters and cutouts; counting cubes; items for measuring and pouring; sorting trays, objects, and numbers; tactile numbers; pegboards; attribute blocks; charts and graphs; a wall measurement; play money; magnetic marbles; commercial games that encourage thinking such as Bingo, Memory, Rack-O, Uno, and Connect Four. Many of these items may be used for science projects and displays.

Equipment and Materials—for Science. Teachers select equipment and materials to correspond with the age and interest level of a particular group of children. A science center may include a magnifying glass, nails, magnets, paper clips, sorting items (buttons, shells, bottle caps, money), sorting trays, collections from nature, collections of cards such as a sea life collection, a "five senses" display, an aquarium, a terrarium, "let's find out" books and magazines, a thermometer, a balance scale, a flashlight, a ruler, chart paper, science posters, funnels, sifters, eye droppers, measuring cups and pitchers, a water table, floating and sinking items, real plants and animals, fossils and rocks, an old radio to take apart, journals for documentation and recordkeeping. Many of these items may be used for math projects and displays.

Accessories for a Math/Science Center. Accessories may include a discovery kit; a hiker's kit; a weather wheel or a weather station; a root vegetable garden; an ant colony; hamsters, gerbils, or a hermit crab; science puzzles and books; films; a sketchbook and markers; sensory discrimination games and activities; charts graphs, and posters; a telescope; binoculars; a compass; a prism.

School-age children may enjoy playing challenging strategy games such as Monopoly, Risk, Uno, Clue, Life, or Stratego. They may also enjoy environmental projects, scout projects, cooking projects, assembling models, woodworking, and computer games. They may want to subscribe to informative magazines such as *Science Digest, Your Big Back Yard,* or *Ranger Rick.*

Art Centers

An art center is an area that is designed for creative arts, crafts, and woodworking. An art center needs to be near a sink in a quiet area of the room. A woodworking table should be nearby but not so close as to disrupt a child who is painting at an easel.

Equipment and Materials
Teachers select equipment and materials to correspond with the age and interest level of a particular group of children. An art center may include an easel, paints, and brushes; smocks; a drying rack; an art table; and an art shelf. An art shelf contains a variety of craft and paper materials. In addition, it provides children with crayons, markers, and pencils; clay; play dough; watercolors; glue; and scissors. A woodworking table contains a variety of wood shapes, assorted nails

and screws, pliers, hammers, a small saw, screwdrivers, clamps, a vise, sandpaper, glue, string, a ruler, and a tape measure, paints and clay, and a display shelf.

Accessories

Accessories may include a box of odds and ends that is always full and always changing (flannel shapes, foil, doilies, cellophane, tissue paper, paper scraps, toilet paper rolls, waxpaper rolls), a craft box (pom poms, pipe cleaners, feathers, popsickle sticks, tongue depressors, yarn, glitter, spools, craft kits, ribbon, cotton balls, small wooden objects to paint), a sewing box (buttons, thread, yarn, needles, embroidery frames), a fabric box (assorted materials for puppets, dolls, and theme-related art projects), charcoal, chalk, pen and ink, watercolors and finger paints, textured paper, and a variety of construction paper.

School-age children may enjoy organizing an art or a photo gallery, making candles, working with ceramics, and sculpting. They may also enjoy creating crafts for senior citizens and sick children such as painting rocks and shells, making magnets or mosaics, making small dried arrangements or wall hangings, or doing pen and ink drawings.

A Nurturing Center

A nurturing center is a comfortable and restful area that encourages communication and companionship. It serves as a bridge between a child's center and home. Homelike in appearance, it encourages children, staff, and parents to visit, to interact, and to develop friendships. Most important, it encourages children to discuss feelings, concerns, and problems in ways that are growth-enhancing.

Play Equipment and Materials

Teachers select equipment and materials to correspond with the age and interest level of a particular group of children. A nurturing center may include a sofa, chairs, a rug, a lamp, bookshelves, plants, a hammock, an adjoining porch, a small activity center for clubs, writing projects, reading, homework, or a hobby, as well as photographs and posters that nurture and inspire children.

Accessories

Accessories may include books, magazines, videos, puzzles, games, a tape recorder, tapes, a radio, a television, a dollhouse or puppet theatre, hand-made paper dolls, writing and construction paper, pencils and markers, an arts and crafts kit, a snack tray, a small refrigerator, and a large terrarium that is decorated with seasonal themes.

School-age children should feel a sense of pride and privacy about their *den*. They should be able to decorate and care for it much as they might care for their own room at home. Ideally, centers for preschool and school-age children should not be shared. A modified version of this center is appropriate for young children.

SUMMARY

An indoor environment that reflects a center's philosophy and the principles of child development will create space that is both functional and meaningful to its occupants. A staff will feel positive about working in a well-designed, carefully organized environment that maximizes opportunities for creative, child-centered learning. Children will profit from a child-centered environment that is designed to challenge their imaginations and to extend their knowledge. Each room will be designed as a unique and special place for children. The total environment will truly reflect the sum of its parts.

NOTES

1. As cited in John Coe, "Children Come First," *Childhood Education* 64(2) (December 1987): p. 74.

2. V. Suransky, *The Erosion of Childhood* (Chicago: University of Chicago Press, 1982), p. 39.

3. Teresita E. Aguilar, "Social and Environmental Barriers to Playfulness." In *When Children Play*. eds. Joe L. Frost and Sylvia Sunderlin (Wheaton, MD: ACEI, 1985), p. 76.

4. S. Kritchevsky, and E. Prescott, *Planning Environments for Young Children: Physical Space* (Washington, DC: NAEYC, 1977), pp. 11, 12.

5. Betty Spillers Beeson and R. Ann Williams, "The Persistence of Sex Differences in the Play of Young Children." In *When Children Play*, 39.

6. Charles H. Wolfgang, "Preschool Children's Preferences for Gender-Stereotyped Play Materials." In *When Children Play*, 273–78.

RESOURCES

American Public Health and Safety Performance Standards: Guidelines for Out-of-Home Child Care Programs. *Caring for Our Children*. Elk Grove, IL: American Academy of Pediatrics, 1992.

Cherry, C. *Creative Play for the Developing Child*. Belmont, CA: Pitman Learning, 1976.

Gandini, L. "Not Just Anywhere: Making Child Care Centers into Popular Places." *Beginnings* (Summer 1984).

Greenman, J. "Babies Get Out." *Beginnings* (Summer 1985).

———. *Caring Spaces, Learning Places: Children's Environments that Work*. Redmond, WA: Exchange Press, 1988.

Hohmann, J., B. Banet, and D. Weikart. *Young Children in Action*. Ypsilanti, MI: High/Scope Press, 1979.

Prescott, E. "The Physical Environment—A Powerful Regulator of Experience." *Child Care Information Exchange* (April 1979).

Prescott, E., and E. Jones. *Day Care as a Child Rearing Environment*, vol 1. Washington, DC: NAEYC, 1972.

Prescott, E., and S. Kritchevsky. *Day Care as a Child Rearing Environment*, vol 2. Washington, DC: NAEYC, 1972.

Weber, L. *The English Infant School and Informal Education*. Englewood Cliffs, NJ: Prentice-Hall, 1971.

Yamamoto, K. *Children in Time and Space*. New York: Teachers College Press, 1979.

As the playground movement grows, school designers will give greater attention to the preservation of the natural landscape immediately surrounding schools as the first, essential step in creating high-quality integrated indoor–outdoor learning environments. . . . The citizens of more and more communities in the near future will realize that playgrounds are a viable alternative for TV and boredom and a major vehicle for learning. They will construct exciting, functional play environments and seek facilitative play leaders as they grow to understand that the cost in human effort and material resources is a wise investment in children.

— Joe L. Frost

15

OUTDOOR ENVIRONMENTS

THE IMPORTANCE OF OUTDOOR PLAY

An outdoor environment is integral to curriculum development. It is an enlarged activity center providing an educational, developmental, and recreational environment that is equal in importance to an indoor environment. It should be considered one of the primary objectives in child care planning because it:

- Sharpens senses and stimulates awareness;
- Enables children to conceptualize their world as less circumscribed and bounded;
- Brings children into intimate contact with nature;
- Nurtures curiosity and divergent thinking;
- Deepens and challenges learning;
- Encourages cooperative play;
- Encourages problem solving and teamwork;
- Promotes children's interaction with natural and man-made resources;
- Challenges and welcomes children's need for physical activity;
- Gives children a strong sense of mastery and control over their environment;
- Reduces stress by eliminating adult/child barriers;
- Promotes and encourages physical education and gymnastic talents that may be unique to a child.

For many teachers, outdoor time is considered free, unstructured time that is conditional, in part, on the weather and, in part, on indoor priorities—"We must finish our projects before we can go outdoors." On intemperate days, teachers find a reason not to take children outdoors even though the weather is acceptable for children's play. Such attitudes reveal what little emphasis teachers place on out-door play and on its importance to growth and development.

Teachers should not minimize their role and responsibility for a child's total development, which includes ample outdoor play during various times of the day, e.g. morning, afternoon, and, if appropriate, during transitions as well. Outdoor play should be given as much attention as indoor play. It should not be considered bench time for staff to converse with one another or to rest. It is a time for teachers to observe children in unstructured social interaction, to inter-act with children in sensitive and meaningful ways, and to share children's experiences with the natural world. It is a time to complement children for reaching new heights in physical development and to encourage children to go higher.

Teachers, therefore, will perceive their role as primarily that of observer and partner. At times, when children are engaged in group games, however, a teacher will become an initiator: "Would you like to play Duck, Duck, Goose?" or "Would you like to play basketball with me?" Teachers and children tend naturally to complement one another during outdoor time—the sense of freedom and space brings out the best in both ages. Outdoor time enables adults and children to know one another in a different setting and context. When teachers relax, children relax. Conversely, when teachers define their outside role as supervisory, they are unable to share special moments with children and unable to appreciate the treasures and pleasures of outdoor play.

Outdoor time provides children a sense of renewal from the programmed activities that consume so many of their waking hours. When children play outdoors, they often free themselves from expectations and uncertainties. There is no classroom that can quite capture the harvest of a natural landscape. Wherever there is dirt, there is something growing: a weed, a wild flower, a little bug that will have to hurry to escape a child's curious hands. Wherever there is open space, there is something to look at, something to listen to, something to wonder about: the passing clouds, the darkness before a storm, birds, planes, and distant trains. And wherever there are children, there is some new creation somewhere in nature that is waiting to be noticed.

Children's outdoor behavior is influenced by the quality and style of their play equipment, the organization of space, the degree of freedom they have to make choices, social skills, adult/child interaction, rules and regulations, the weather, physical factors, the period of time scheduled for outside play, and the general feeling of safety and security that prevails. In a child centered environment, children are given freedom to play with minimal supervision unless there is reason for an adult to intervene. Sometimes children enjoy an adult's compan-ionship or prolonged peer play, but more often than not, children prefer proxi-mal play (making contact with friends but not being dependent on them for sustained interaction). Most children prefer independence and autonomy during outdoor play, which may or may not include friends. Outdoor play may be likened to dramatic play. When children get into a pretend play world they need little encouragement or support.

A VARIETY OF PLAY MODES

Children need a variety of experiences during outdoor playtime. They need to exercise their bodies, their minds, their creativity, and their social skills. Outdoor activities might include:

- Circle games (Duck, Duck, Goose, Here We Go Loopty Loo, What Can You Do Punchinello Funny Fellow) and organized sports (Dodge Ball; Four Square; Red Rover, Red Rover);
- Independent play (swinging, climbing, rollerskating);
- Small group cluster play (play in sandbox, playing in water, playing house, or making a fort under a tree);
- Large-motor physical play (on equipment);
- Productive play (making gardens, picking up litter);
- Sidewalk and blacktop play (riding trikes, rollerskating, basketball, making chalk drawings);
- Rainy-day play (a canopied or protected area for marching or riding trikes);
- Dramatic play (a log cabin or an enclosed section of a climber);
- Sand and water play (sandbox, water table or mudpile)
- Construction play (blocks and things to haul around and build with).

Children need to *manipulate* and *investigate* when they are outdoors. They need to carry, to construct, and to take things apart. Therefore, an outdoor environment must provide things that are portable (that can be taken apart and moved around by children) as well as stationary (fixed) equipment. If children do not have enough to play with out-of-doors they will complain about having nothing to do.

Children who are unaccustomed to vigorous outdoor play feel uncomfortable out-of-doors. They often stand near a teacher and avoid making play choices or contacts with peers. These children especially need encouragement if they are to overcome inhibitions and fears. They need to develop healthy attitudes about playing outdoors and about their ability to manage themselves in a less structured, free-choice environment.

TYPES OF PLAYGROUNDS

Contemporary Playgrounds

As more and more children spend a majority of their outdoor time in playgrounds contiguous to schools or child care centers, there is growing interest in the quality and types of playgrounds available to children within a defined area. Gradually, traditional, ad hoc type playgrounds are being replaced by play environments that are meeting the total needs of children—a playscape concept that is developmentally appropriate. In this setting, stationary equipment is seen as only one element in a total environmental design. New designs and new concepts are blending traditional with contemporary needs. Conventional fixed playgrounds (climbing bars, a merry-go-round, a see-saw, and a set of swings) are being replaced or used in combination with more innovative contemporary playgrounds.

The premise is that children will become enthusiastic participants in a playground that is both familiar and challenging—a playground that promotes physical development as well as curiosity and creativity. By using a natural landscape to its maximum advantage, children can enjoy an infinite number of interactional possibilities for both independent and cooperative play. They can ride on a traditional whirlybird, or they can move things around and control their environment in more exciting ways. In both experiences, children become masters of their environments and feel very fulfilled when they come indoors.

A suitable, creative play space for children, therefore, will include:

- A mixture of wood and metal climbing structures with platforms, wheels, ropes, and other features;
- Age-appropriate swings;
- A contour slide;
- Barrels, bridges, and balance beams;
- Ride-on items;
- Playhouses, cabins, and hide-aways that invite entrance;
- Assorted railroad ties, cable spools, and tires;
- A fort or interesting structure to crawl in or crawl up;
- Hollow blocks, logs or, large pieces of treated wood;
- Wagons, wheelbarrows, trikes, doll carriages, scooters;
- Plastic crates, tires, rocking boats, or items to sit in;
- Large sand pits and digging equipment in all sizes, shapes, and forms.

Make-Your-Own Playgrounds

Many child care centers are not in a financial position to design the perfect playground to meet a child's total needs. Director's have to look not at what they want to do but at what they can afford to do.

Jay Beckwith, author of *Build Your Own Playgrounds,* has designed playgrounds that produce environments in which children play longer, show less aggressive and more cooperative behavior, have improved self-concepts, develop better language skills, and engage in more novel and physically demanding motor activity than on traditional playgrounds.[1] The essential components are:

> *Complex:* The environment should contain as many different types of experiences as possible.
>
> *Linked:* Play events should be connected to create a natural "flow" of play activity.
>
> *Social:* The total environment should foster interaction between children and play events should be designed for group use.

Flexible: Playground flexibility can be both mechanical, i.e., equipment mounted on springs, or functional, i.e., events that can be used in many different ways.

Challenging: Creative playgrounds contain events that require motor coordination, balance ability, flexibility, and strength.

Development: Playgrounds should offer events that will challenge a wide range of skills and ages.

Safe: Modern playgrounds must conform to the Consumer Product Safety Commission's guidelines. The safe playground not only has fewer accidents, but also encourages more inventive and creative play because the children are able to take greater risks with less fear of injury.

Often directors have limited funds and are unable to create a satisfactory play space for children. They may need to ask parents for assistance. Parents can build forts, playhouses, and storage sheds, design and landscape an environment for children's play, make sandboxes, construct trike paths and balance beams, locate cable spools and truck tires, and provide picnic tables. If parents are less than amenable to helping create a playground, there are always fund-raisers—events that are, for the most part, worth the effort.

Creating Adventure Playgrounds

The adventure playground originated in Denmark in the 1930s. Over the years, these playgrounds have been implemented in England, Sweden, Japan, and more recently in the United States. The adventure playground has been seen by the Danes as an aid to socialization:

The adventure playground is one of the means by which we transfer the child from the role of observer to that of actor, the role where the child is allowed to do something and see the results of efforts. The adventure playground not only teaches the child some elementary things about the nature of culture and the "answer to challenges," but it goes beyond this. The child can also meet with challenges when busy doing something on his or her own.[2]

The premise is that children love to interact with materials, shapes, smells, and other physical phenomena in their natural environment. An outdoor play environment that maximizes space for movement and exploration will encourage children's natural curiosity. When children are not limited to defined equipment, they become inventive. They look for objects to play with: a piece of bark, twigs, berries, rocks, trenches, and small hills. Unstructured outdoor play promotes resourcefulness and inventiveness.

There is little doubt that playgrounds are becoming important dimensions of planning in child development centers. As child care centers begin to recognize the value of outdoor play to child development, play yards are becoming playscapes that are linked to the greater world. Eventually, a child in the United States or

Canada will be playing in the same way as a child in Israel, Italy, France, Denmark, or England. They will be moving objects that are designed for creative play; objects that meet the objectives of child development; objects that meet the universal needs of childhood. The irrepressible, joyful engagement that a child experiences as she interacts with her natural environment connects her to the greater world—to all children everywhere. When a child care center identifies itself as a *part of the larger world,* children become citizens of the world.

PLANNING AND SAFETY GUIDELINES

The following guidelines should be considered when planning play environments in child care centers:

- Is the equipment durable and relatively safe?
- Is it properly installed and maintained?
- Is it of appropriate size for the age group?
- Does the playground provide for work/play activities such as art, gardening, and science projects?
- Are a variety of loose parts available for sand and water play, wheeled vehicle play, dramatic play, building?
- Is the playground designed to involve large groups of children simultaneously?
- Is the playground aesthetically pleasing?
- Is it economically feasible?[3]

It is important to remember that careful attention to equipment and to its use will significantly reduce accidents. (See Appendix C, Safety Guidelines.)

For guidelines on playground safety, write to the Consumer Product Safety Commission, 5401 Westbard Ave, Bethesda, Md. 20816. For guidelines on the environment in the area, write to the Environmental Protection Agency, 401 M Street, SW, Washington, DC 20460.

SUMMARY

An outdoor environment is an extension of an indoor environment. It is a place where children can take pleasure in the arts and nature, where children can communicate feelings and ideas, where children can experience human individuality and human sociality. It is a place where children can make choices and take responsibility for their play experience and its outcome. Sometimes outdoor play is all consuming and sometimes it is less than perfect. In child care centers there are never enough balls or swings to play with. Often the toys that are left to play with are the ones nobody wants. On some days, nobody wants to be a friend, but, more often than not, children find companionship and happiness when they are engaged in outdoor play.

The full dimensions of being a child are operative in outdoor play. If play holds such potential for growth and development, why don't we give it more space and attention on calendars and in budgets?

Often, a playground holds little appeal because it is uncreative and uninviting. Safe and challenging equipment and attractive landscaping are costly items for most budget-conscious directors. A play-conscious director, however, will find a way to create and fund a landscape. She realizes that outdoor play is as fundamental and important to a little child's mental and physical health as any indoor activity. She may need to fence a play yard for security, but the director will select a fence that is high enough, but not too high, to restrict a child's view beyond the immediate playscape to the larger community.

NOTES

1. Jay Beckwith, "Equipment Selection Criteria for Modern Playgrounds." In *When Children Play,* eds. Joe L. Frost, and Ann R. Williams (Wheaton, MD: ACEI, 1985), pp. 209–10.

2. Jens Pedersen, "The Adventure Playgrounds in Denmark," in Joe L. Frost, "The American Playground Movement," in *When Children Play,* p. 207.

3. Frost, "The American Playground Movement," p. 168.

RESOURCES

Aronson, Susan S. *Health Safety in Child Care.* New York: HarperCollins, 1991.

Caring for Our Children. National Health and Safety Performance Standards: Guidelines for Out-of-Home Child Care Programs. Washington, DC: American Public Health Association, 1992.

Esbensen, S. *The Early Childhood Playground: An Outdoor Classroom.* Ypsilanti, MI: High Scope Press, 1987.

Frost, Joe L., and Ann R. Williams, eds. *When Children Play.* Wheaton, MD: ACEI, 1985.

Greenman, Jim. *Caring Spaces, Learning Places: Children's Environments that Work.* Redmond, WA: Exchange Press 1988.

Hatcher, Barbara, ed. *Learning Opportunities Beyond the School.* Wheaton, MD: ACEI, 1987.

Kritchevsky, Sybil, and Elizabeth Prescott. *Planning Environments for Young Children's Physical Space.* Washington, DC: NAEYC, 1990.

Lovell, P., and T. Harms. "How Can Playgrounds Be Improved?" *Young Children* 40(3), 1985.

Miller, Karen. *The Outside Play and Learning Book.* Mt. Rainier, MD: Gryphon House, 1989.

Redleaf, Rhoda. *Open the Door Let's Explore: Neighborhood Field Trips for Young Children.* Mt. Rainier, MD: Gryphon House, 1983.

Rockwell, Robert E., Elizabeth Sherwood, and Robert A. Williams. *Hug a Tree and Other Things to Do Outdoors with Young Children.* Mt. Rainier, MD: Gryphon House, 1986.

Tilgner, Linda, *Let's Grow!: 72 Gardening Adventures with Children.* Pownal, VT: Storey Communications, Inc., 1989.

My everyday
Is my identity.
It is my now.
It is my moment
My new start
My chance to create
A new vision
For myself
For my child
What I make of this moment
Will determine
The story of us.
    — *From* Everychild's Everyday

CONCLUSION

Children are strongly influenced by the quality of their human and physical environment during the formative years of development. When children are respected and valued as unique and special human beings, they will feel secure about themselves and they will begin to experience their potential. Through sustained interaction with caring and competent adults in child-appropriate environments, there is every reason to expect that every child can lead a quality life. By believing in children, by challenging children, and by providing a beacon for children to follow, adults can guide children toward tomorrow's world. In the continuum of growth and development, some things, like childhood, do not change. Eugene Ionesco put it this way:

> Childhood is the world of miracle and wonder: as if creation rose and bathed in light, out of the darkness, utterly new and fresh and astonishing. The end of childhood is when things cease to astonish us. When the world seems familiar when we have gotten used to existence, one has become an adult.

Childhood is a time of sprouting and nurturing. It is a passageway to adulthood that is filled with the promise and potential of a spring garden. Each day and each moment is important.

APPENDIX A

LEGAL OPERATIONAL MATERIALS

This appendix contains examples and outlines that will be useful to anyone planning to establish a child care facility. The forms should be used for guidance and adapted as necessary to a center's specific requirements—not all centers will need to use all of these forms.

1. A Contract for Employment

2. An Enrollment Agreement

3. An Outline for a Parent Handbook

4. An Outline for a Staff Handbook

5. A Job Description for a Director

6. A Job Description for Teachers

7. A Job Description for Assistants

8. An Organizational Health Checklist

9. An Informal Evaluation

Contract for Employment

Received:
Medical form ❑
Tine test ❑
College transcript ❑
Fingerprint check
and approval ❑
Date _____

Name of employee: _____

Address: _____

Phone: _____

Marital status: S ❑   M ❑

Social security number: _____

Withholding status: _____

Person(s) to contact in case of emergency: _____

     Phone number: _____

Schedule: _____

_____

Salary: Employee will receive salary of $_____ per month/ per day/ per hour, payable the fifth day of each month. If the fifth day of the month is a Saturday, a Sunday, or a holiday, checks will be dated on the following schoolday.

Benefits: Employee will receive _____ personal/sick leave days from the period _____ to _____. Personal/sick leave may not be carried over to the following schoolyear.

     Employee will receive contributions to social security (FICA), unemployment insurance, worker's compensation coverage, and the following benefits:

_____

Terms of Employment: Employees salaried under a monthly contract are paid for all holidays listed on the Center's calendar with the exception of winter break. On inclement days when the Center is closed, employees are paid for no more than 2 days in a row.

     Employees, substitute teachers, and specialized teachers who are paid on a daily or hourly basis are not paid for holidays, winter or spring break, or inclement days when the Center is closed.

Substitute head teachers receive $_____ per hour; substitute assistants receive $_____ per hour. Additional time accrued is paid by the fifth day of the following month.

Reasons for warning, probation, or dismissal include but are not limited to: a breach of confidentiality; a failure to carry out assigned duties as defined by the Center's **Job Description**; inappropriate conduct toward children or staff; unprofessional or irresponsible behavior; distorting or falsifying information; evidence of alcohol, drugs, or threatening behavior while on the premises; evidence of physical or mental illness that interferes with performance; repeated absenteeism; failure to attend the Center's staff meetings; failure to maintain personal and student records; negligent conduct; inattentiveness to the Center's policies; failure to implement the Center's program and objectives; an inability to work harmoniously with staff members; talking in a disparaging way or spreading rumors about children, families, or employees of the Center; disseminating materials written or developed for this Center without permission from the Director.

An employee may contest or appeal a disciplinary action by submitting a letter of grievance to the Center's board of directors. Members of the board will review the grievance and report back to the employee within thirty (30) days.

Either party may nullify this contract, with cause, by submitting a minimum of thirty (30) days written notice.

Contracts are contingent on sufficient enrollment in every class and on securing space.

It is understood that employees will conform to all policies and regulations herein stipulated; that at all times the safety and well-being of children will be given absolute attention; that employees will maintain the confidentiality of the Director and the Center; that employees will work together to provide a positive and secure environment for staff and children.

The Center maintains a nondiscriminatory, open hiring and employment policy with regard to race, color, religion, age, sex, and national origin. Your signature below constitutes the acceptance of this contract and its terms as set forth herein.

Director _____

Date _____

_____

I agree to respect and abide by the policies and responsibilities stated in this Contract for Employment and its terms as set forth herein. Please retain one copy and return the original signed copy to _____ by _____.

Employee _____

Date _____

Enrollment Agreement

For the Period _____

Date _____

Name of child: _____   Preferred name (if nickname): _____

Age: _____   Birthday: _____   Grade next year: _____

Public school child currently attends: _____

Center or school child attended last year: _____

Address: _____

Home phone number: _____   Business phone (mother) _____

(father) _____

Mother's place of employment: _____

Father's place of employment: _____

Name(s) of legal guardian(s): _____   Phone number _____

Nearest relative: _____   Phone number _____

Persons to notify in case of emergency or sickness:

1. _____   Phone number _____

2. _____   Phone number _____

3. _____   Phone number _____

Family doctor: _____   Phone number _____

Family dentist: _____   Phone number _____

Allergies and/or other specific concerns: _____

_____

Are there any known developmental delays or concerns?

Please describe: _____

_____

Language(s) spoken at home: _____

Is the child adopted? _____   Does the child know? _____

Number of siblings under 18 years of age: _____

Name(s): _____   _____   _____

_____   _____   _____

Special instructions: _____

_____

Any other information that might be helpful to know about your child, e.g., sleeping patterns, eating patterns, anxieties?

Please describe: _____

_____

I agree to enroll my child in the following program(s): _____

_____

at a monthly tuition rate of $_____, to be paid (check one):

❑ in nine equal payments

❑ by the semester

❑ by the year

With this Enrollment Agreement, I am submitting a nonrefundable Registration/ Insurance fee of $_____ and a nonrefundable Advance Tuition of $_____ to cover the month of September, _____.

I understand that:

• Tuition is due by the fifth day of each month and subject to a 7% late fee thereafter;

• Tuition is mailed to: _____

• A State Medical and Emergency Information Form must be completed and on file by August 15th;

• No adjustment is made in tuition for sickness or vacations;

• This contract is contingent upon enrollment requirements and space available;

• Written permission is required for all fieldtrips.

The Center may terminate this Enrollment Agreement with two (2) weeks written notice if:

• The parent fails to abide by the terms of this Enrollment Agreement;

• The parent fails to abide by the Center's administrative policies as defined in the Parent Handbook.

• The program does not meet the developmental or special needs of a child.

The Center has the right to request the immediate withdrawal of a child for health or behavioral reasons that threaten the safety and well-being of the child or others.

Parents may terminate this Enrollment Agreement with thirty (30) days written notice.

_____

I give the Center permission to use my child's name, address, and phone number for a class directory.   ❏ Yes   ❏ No

The following person(s) are authorized to pick up my child:

    Name, address, and phone numbers: _____

    _____

    _____

The following person(s) are not authorized to pick up my child: _____

_____

In case of emergency the following person(s) should be contacted:

    Name, address, and phone numbers: _____

    _____

    _____

In the event of an accident, I give the teacher in charge permission to either administer first-aid or to obtain immediate medical attention at a hospital or clinic.   ❏ Yes   ❏ No

_____

The Center does not discriminate on the basis of race, color, or national origin in the admission of students, the employment of staff, and in its administrative policies and practices.

_____   _____

Director   Parent/Legal Guardian

Date: _____   Date: _____

Outline for a Parent Handbook

Contents

1. A Welcoming Statement from the Director
2. A Center's Philosophy
3. Registration and Admissions Policies
4. Programs Offered
5. The Calendar Year
6. Policies and Procedures
7. A Center's Sick Policy
8. A Center's Discipline Policy
9. A Center's Health, Nutrition, and Safety Policy
10. A Center's Fieldtrip Policy
11. A Center's Transportation Policy
12. Celebrating Holidays and Birthdays
13. Conferences
14. Parent Visits
15. A Parent Volunteer Program

Explanation

1. This section promotes confidence, trust, and friendship.

2. This section provides a foundational premise for a center. It includes goals and objectives.

3. This section provides information about an open hiring and admissions policy, a registration contract, the method of paying tuition, late fee charges, late pick-up charges, additional hours charges, and parents' responsibilities.

4. This section describes the programs offered at varying age levels, the hours a center is open, and unique features about a center's enrollment policy.

5. This section defines the calendar year, half-days, holidays, inclement days, and emergency closing days.

6. This section provides information about the policies and procedures that govern a center—i.e., parents must submit a medical form and an emergency card; parents must provide a center with children's records, custody agreements, and the names of persons authorized to pick up a child; parents must provide extra clothes and bedding for cot rest; parents must read a child's calendar to keep informed about classroom activities and needs; parents must be informed about a center's policies for reporting accidents, for handling sick children, for informing parents about emergency closings; parents are expected to participate in their child's center life as often as possible.

7. This section provides information about sick policies such as a child cannot be admitted to a center with a communicable or contagious illness or with a temperature of 100°F. It explains that a child must be symptom-free for 24 hours before returning to class and requests that parents call a center if a child has a communicable disease or has been absent from a center more than two days. It provides resources on health-related matters, i.e., how to recognize the signs of communicable diseases and other common childhood infections, caring for sick children, preventing illnesses, following a sound nutritional diet and health plan.

8. This section informs parents about the importance of nurturing children toward positive, cooperative behavior and about a center's procedures for handling a crisis or upset at the time of occurrence.

9. This section provides information about snacks, meals, and suggestions for lunch. It provides information about a center's attentiveness to sanitation, general safety, and specific policies pertaining to children's safety.

10. This section provides information about fieldtrips, transportation, and parent consent forms.

11. This section informs parents about bus transportation and fees between a public or private school and a center.

12. This section provides information about how birthdays and holidays are celebrated.

13. This section provides information about parent/teacher conferences and periodic progress reports.

14. This section establishes a visitation policy between a center and parents of enrolled children.

15. This section encourages parents to participate in a center's programs, activities, and leadership.

Outline for a Staff Handbook

Contents

1. A Welcoming Statement from the Director
2. A Center's Philosophy
3. The Calendar Year
4. The Role of Staff
5. The Responsibilities of Staff
6. Terms of Employment
7. Staff Qualifications
8. Staff Training Requirements
9. Curriculum Requirements
10. Policies and Procedures
11. Grievance Procedures
12. Evaluation Procedures
13. Parent's Rights and Responsibilities

Explanation

1. This section welcomes new staff members.

2. This section emphasizes a center's belief in, and support of, the principles of child development.

3. This section provides information about half-days, holidays, inclement days, and emergency closing days.

4. This section emphasizes the important role staff members play in meeting the social, personal, and developmental needs of each child in their care.

5. This section refers to an employee's job description.

6. This section describes an employee's legal contract with a center and benefits offered.

7. This section defines the qualifications for various positions, i.e., a head teacher, an associate teacher, an assistant, and specialized teachers.

8. This section informs staff about their training obligations requisite to continued employment. It covers in-service and out-of-center training requirements.

9. This section provides information about a center's curriculum and programmatic requirements, i.e., a monthly calendar, a weekly activity plan, a newsletter, and parent/teacher conferences.

10. This section provides information and resources for policy implementation; for health, safety, and nutrition requirements; and for general management procedures.

11. This section provides information about the manner in which concerns or complaints are communicated and reviewed for follow-up action.

12. This section describes evaluation methods and procedures.

13. This section provides a list of rights and responsibilities designed to encourage positive and supportive relationships between parents and a center.

A Job Description for a Director

Qualifications

A director must have a bachelor's degree in early childhood education or a related field plus at least two (2) years experience in teaching and/or directing a licensed child care center. In addition, a director must agree to earn one certificate per semester for attending an accredited workshop or a national conference.

Responsibilities

1. *Personnel Management and Supervision*
   - Hire, supervise, monitor, and train staff;
   - Provide a job description, an employee contract, and a handbook;
   - Provide opportunities for continued professional development;
   - Maintain a level of high performance and morale;
   - Examine ways to increase benefits and incentives;
   - Provide a written curriculum guideline;
   - Provide checklists for student evaluation;
   - Provide opportunities for developing interpersonal relations;
   - Encourage staff to work as a team and to share ideas;
   - Require a monthly calendar and a unit or project plan;
   - Share materials, articles, and personal resources with staff;
   - Contribute ideas for special events, fieldtrips, projects;
   - Visit classrooms at least once a week; ask questions, show interest, know what is going on; evaluate informally;
   - Communicate observations and concerns in appropriate ways;
   - Formally evaluate staff once a semester;
   - Require an annual conference between parents and staff;
   - Require that children's records be reviewed and kept up-to-date;
   - Require that all accidents be recorded at the time of occurrence;
   - Require that daily attendance be taken and that children be checked out at the end of the day;
   - Alert staff to risks or potential accidents;
   - Inform staff of improper language or conduct;
   - Inform staff when there is an indication of negligence;
   - Require all teachers to have a first-aid course;
   - Be available to discuss concerns openly and objectively;
   - Bring teachers into leadership positions whenever possible;
   - Inform staff about trends in the field;
   - Expect staff to maintain creative, neat, and clean rooms;

- Impress staff with the importance of confidentiality and professionalism at all times;
- Impress staff with the importance of developing a partnership with parents.

2. *Administrative Responsibilities*

- Maintain an efficient, well-managed organization;
- Assure that licensing standards are maintained;
- Develop written policies and procedures for parents and staff;
- Maintain student and personnel records;
- Ensure that the environment is healthy;
- Ensure that nutritional needs are met;
- Inspect indoor and outdoor play areas periodically for safety;
- Submit all reports in a timely, concise manner;
- Maintain a comprehensive recordkeeping system;
- Monitor enrollment—advertise when necessary;
- Order consumables—paper, art supplies, and so on;
- Purchase consumable and nonconsumable items as needed;
- Seek approval from the board of directors for any item that costs more than $100;
- Plan a Parent/Teacher meeting once a year;
- Maintain resource and referral services;
- Schedule annual screenings of vision and hearing;
- Provide staff with a substitute help list;
- Be alert to staffing needs at all times, particularly on atypical days such as half-days, inclement days;
- Communicate effectively with support personnel;
- Review and evaluate a center from a total administrator/teacher perspective.

3. *Bookkeeping Responsibilities*

- Prepare an annual budget for approval by the board of directors;
- Keep a balanced checkbook;
- Record and deposit tuition payments when received;
- Keep a monthly ledger that records amounts receivable and accounts payable;
- Pay bills on time;
- Approve petty cash disbursements;
- Monitor the cash flow; keep informed about the center's financial status;
- Be prepared to call emergency or unscheduled meetings with the board of directors;

- Solicit help from the center's accountant as needed;
- Be certain that financial information is always ready for auditing, that tax forms are filed on time, and that the center has an annual review by an accountant.

4. *Interpersonal Relations*

- Plan a minimum of two (2) meetings per year with the board of directors;
- Maintain close contact with board members and consult them when there are serious concerns or impending changes;
- Invite members of the board to special events and activities;
- Recognize the board's service at an annual dinner or special event;
- Maintain a friendly, empathetic manner;
- Interact with children on a personal basis;
- Visit and participate in classroom activities whenever possible;
- Attend parties, special events, and other activities;
- Accompany children on fieldtrips on occasion;
- Plan special events and workshops to maximize opportunities for parent/center interaction and friendships;
- Become recognized in a community as a "quality" director and as a leader in the field;
- Plan and budget quality time "outside" a center—national/international conferences/seminars.

A Job Description for Teachers

Purpose

A job description details the duties of an employee, the expectations of an employer, and the requirements of an organization.

Qualifications

A teacher of preschool children must have a bachelor's degree in the field of early childhood education from an accredited college or university. If a degree is in a related field, an employee must have earned, or be in the process of earning, at least 12 credit hours in early childhood coursework that includes a course in curriculum and a course in the foundations of education. Teachers are required to show evidence of continued training in the field by attending at least one workshop per semester. The workshop is to be approved by the director. Teachers are required to attend all staff meetings. Teachers are required to take a first-aid course every three years.

A teacher of school-age children must have at least two years of college, two years experience working with children, and specialized skills in areas that include recreation and the arts. He or she is required to take a three-credit-hour curriculum course and to show evidence of continued training in the field by attending at least one workshop per semester. Teachers are required to attend all staff meetings. Teachers are required to take a first-aid course every three years.

Benefits

An employee is entitled to 10 sick and personal leave days per year. Personal leave days should not exceed two days per month. Employee receives a contract for the period September 1 through June 30. Employee is paid for all national holidays and inclement weather days that fall within the calendar year. Employee is expected to work on all days that a center is open during the period September 1 through June 30. (See calendar in the Employee Handbook.) In addition, employee may participate in the center's health insurance program. Employee is entitled to enroll her child in this program at half tuition. Employee automatically receives the following fringe benefits: social security contributions (FICA), worker's compensation and unemployment insurance coverage. Employee is reimbursed by the center for one workshop or conference per year. In addition, the center will reimburse an employee for a first-aid course.

Responsibilities

Head teachers are responsible for:

1. Reading and reviewing the Staff Handbook;
2. Reading and reviewing the Curriculum Guide;
3. Establishing learning objectives that are consistent with the center's philosophy;
4. Planning and executing a program that reflects the center's philosophy and program;
5. Including play, learning, the arts, and nurturing as primary components in a curriculum;
6. Arranging an attractive bulletin board;
7. Preparing a monthly calendar of activities and events for distribution to parents;
8. Preparing a written unit plan or project plan for review by the director;
9. Preparing projects and activities that reinforce themes and extend learning;
10. Taking daily attendance: call parents or public schools immediately when school-age children fail to arrive at their scheduled time;
11. Working cooperatively with an assistant in developing and implementing a program;
12. Attending all staff meetings and in-service workshops;
13. Meeting on occasion with the director to review objectives, plans, and evaluations;
14. Planning an annual conference with a parent and filing a developmental checklist on children's progress;
15. Planning at least one classroom event per semester for parents to share with their children;
16. Reviewing children's records periodically; update as needed;
17. Being attentive to health, sanitation, nutrition, and safety at all times;
18. Having materials in on time;
19. Dressing and conducting one's self in a professional manner;
20. Recording information pertinent to a child's development;
21. Recording accidents in an accident log;
22. Planning at least two field-trip events per semester;
23. Taking children to the library and the park as often as possible;
24. Attending one workshop per semester;
25. Maintaining a neat, orderly, and attractive classroom;
26. Reviewing and contributing to the center's media center;
27. Requiring parents to sign children in and out of a center;
28. Reporting any unusual occurrences or behavioral changes in children;
29. Providing substitute teachers with activity plans and instructions;

30. Obtaining approval from the director for extended personal leave days;
31. Obtaining a physical examination, a tine test and completing first-aid course within a designated period of time;
32. Maintaining the confidentiality of student records, conferences, and family matters at all times;
33. Valuing and supporting each child and staff member without regard to race, religion, or national origin.

A Job Description for Assistants

Purpose

A job description details the duties of an employee, the expectations of an employer, and the requirements of an organization.

Qualifications

Assistants must be twenty-one years of age or older and must have at least one year's experience working with children under supervised conditions, i.e., volunteering in a camp, coaching, interning in a child care center, participating in a child development class, lifeguarding, babysitting on a regular basis. An assistant must demonstrate skills and talents in areas that interest young children or be willing to develop appropriate skills and talents. Examples of areas that can enhance a program are: sports, the arts, storytelling, music, dance, photography, embroidery, tutoring, cooking, sculpturing. An assistant is required to attend one workshop per semester and all teachers' meetings. An assistant working in a preschool program on a full-time basis must complete an accredited course in early childhood curriculum by the end of the first working year and a certified first-aid course by the end of the first semester.

Benefits

Said employee receives five sick and personal leave days per year. Personal leave days must be approved by the director. Employee receives a contract for the period September 1 through June 30. Employee is paid for all holidays and inclement weather days that fall within the calendar year. Employee is scheduled to work on all days that a center is open from the period September 1 through June 30. (See calendar in the Staff Handbook.) In addition, employee may participate in the center's health insurance plan. Employee is entitled to enroll her child in this program at half tuition. Employee automatically receives the following fringe benefits: social security contributions (FICA), worker's compensation and unemployment insurance coverage. The center will reimburse employee for half the cost of a required curriculum course.

Responsibilities

Assistants are responsible for:

1. Reading and reviewing the Staff Handbook;
2. Reading and reviewing the Curriculum Guide;

3. Maintaining clean and orderly rooms;
4. Setting up activities for table and art activities;
5. Cleaning up after activities have been completed;
6. Preparing children for snack, lunch, and other transitions;
7. Assisting a head teacher as needed: replacing name tags; ordering equipment; discarding, sorting, and replacing equipment; making special notations on children's progress reports; phoning parents with routine messages; making suggestions that are helpful and supportive to a teacher; decorating bulletin boards; returning films; going to the library; purchasing food for snacks or cooking projects;
8. Interacting and communicating with children in positive, and reinforcing ways;
9. Being role models for children;
10. Contributing to a program by telling or reading stories; planning group experiences, projects, or fieldtrips;
11. Participating in parent conferences on request;
12. Participating in planning units and special events;
13. Attending general staff meetings and one workshop per year;
14. Maintaining positive relationships with parents and with staff;
15. Demonstrating leadership in training children to be respectful, responsible, kind, and well-mannered;
16. Demonstrating leadership in encouraging children toward appropriate behavior;
17. Demonstrating leadership in training children in areas of health, nutrition, and safety;
18. Becoming motivated toward advancing in the field—becoming a team teacher, a workshop leader, a head teacher, a specialized teacher;
19. Being attentive to and reporting to the classroom teacher and the director unusual changes in children's appearance or behavior;
20. Being on time;
21. Getting a physical examination, a tine test, and, in some cases, completing a first-aid course within a designated period of time;
22. Maintaining confidentiality in areas that pertain to children's records, conferences, staff-related matters, and center-related matters;
23. Valuing and supporting each child and staff member without regard to race, religion, or national origin.

Organizational Health Checklist

Planning and Evaluation

1. The organization has identified what it is in business for—it has developed a manageable list of specific goals for the curriculum and for the organization as a whole.

2. Members of the organization helped shape these goals, are well aware of them, and are motivated to achieve them.

3. Strategies for accomplishing these goals have been implemented. The organization pays more than lip service to the goals—its daily activities are directed toward achieving them.

4. The organization has developed an ongoing process for evaluating progress toward achieving the goals.

5. The evaluation process is taken seriously at all levels in the organization. Staff members are continuously searching for ways to improve the organization's performance.

6. Evaluation findings are acted on—strengths identified are supported and weaknesses are remedied. The organization does not shy away from abandoning unsuccessful activities and unachieveable goals.

Motivation and Control

7. All staff members take the quality of the organization's services seriously.

8. All staff members know their roles in the organization as well as the specific tasks they are to perform.

9. Staff members exercise self-control over their own performance—they are motivated to perform well out of their commitment to achieving the organization's goals, not out of fear of punishment or desire for financial rewards.

10. Staff burnout is minimized by giving staff members considerable responsibility for managing their own work, by providing variety in their work assignments and training opportunities, and by offering whatever support they need to perform well.

11. Staff members accept the value of constructive conformity to necessary organizational rules and procedures.

12. Staff members perceive salaries and fringe benefits as being administered equitably and fairly.

Group Functioning

13. Staff members feel they are a part of a group and have a sense of loyalty to the organization.

14. Staff members freely cooperate. They share resources, ideas, and experiences.

15. Staff members feel comfortable enough in the group to openly express their feelings. The exchange of negative, as well as positive, feedback is accepted and encouraged.

16. Disagreement about ideas—goals, philosophies, methods, or results—is fostered by the organization.

17. Conflict over personal issues is dealt with directly through confrontation or negotiation rather than by smoothing it over or ignoring it.

18. Communication flows freely and accurately in all directions—plans, problems, decisions, and developments are shared freely by the director; and problems, suggestions, and criticisms are routinely brought to the director's attention by subordinates.

Staff Development

19. The organization assigns high priority to the staff recruitment and selection process to assure that the staff has sufficient skills to accomplish the organization's goals.

20. The organization's leadership has complete confidence in the skills of staff members and makes every effort to tap these skills to the fullest extent.

21. Staff members set their own training objectives and strategies and assume responsibility for carrying them out. The organization's leadership supports their efforts by providing, whenever possible, the resources they require for self-development.

22. Staff members assume responsibility for supporting each other in their efforts to develop to their full potential.

23. Staff members continually provide each other with objective feedback on the effects of their performance and behavior. Performance appraisal is a daily, not yearly, occurrence.

24. Staff creativity is encouraged by providing an idea-rich environment and by fostering a permissive atmosphere for brainstorming and experimentation.

Decision Making and Problem Solving

25. Problems are identified and addressed early—before they get out of hand.

26. Problems are solved and decisions are made in a timely, effective manner.

27. Staff members most directly affected by, or involved with, a decision either have responsibility for making the decision on their own or have major input before a decision is made.

28. Parents' opinions are solicited regarding decisions affecting their children.
29. Decisions, once made, are communicated to all affected members of the organization and are implemented in full.

Financial Management

30. The organization develops a formal annual budget. The budget is viewed as a means of accomplishing the organization's goals for the year. It is based on a realistic projection of the expenditures required to achieve the goals and the revenues likely to be generated.
31. The organization has a sound accounting system that incorporates adequate safeguards against mismanagement and theft and that generates required reports on a timely basis.
32. Monthly financial status reports are utilized to monitor the actual implementation of the budget.
33. Cash flow is projected at least 12 months in advance.
34. The organization carries out a routine schedule for property and equipment inspection and maintenance.

Environmental Interaction

35. The organization is effective in collecting information on new ideas and new resources, as well as in processing this information for use in developing the organization.
36. The organization has an ongoing plan for marketing its services throughout the community.
37. Members of the organization actively participate in efforts to influence public policy decisions that impact the organization.
38. The organization is effective in securing adequate financial and in-kind resources from public and/or private sources.
39. The organization maintains its autonomy by drawing resources from a wide range of external sources, thus not becoming overly dependent on any one source.
40. The organization is alert to changes in consumer needs, political moods, and economic conditions so that strategies can be developed in time for reacting to these changes.

Source: From *Child Care Information Exchange,* "Do You Have a Healthy Organization," by Roger Neugebauer, April 1990. Reprinted with permission from Child Care Information Exchange, PO Box 2890, Redmond, WA 98073, (800) 221-2864.

APPENDIX B

STAFF MATERIALS

This appendix provides forms, ideas, and resources that may be used as guidelines by administrators and teachers.

1. A Developmental Checklist: Ages Two to Three

2. A Developmental Checklist: Ages Four to Five

3. A Developmental Checklist: School-Age Children

4. A Sample Science Unit for a Class of Four to Five-year-olds

5. A Sample Literature Theme for a Class of Five-year-olds

6. A Sample Discovery Theme for a Class of Four-year-olds

7. A Sample of a Project for School-Age Children

8. A Sample of Clustering

9. A Self-evaluation Form for Teachers

10. An Informal Evaluation

11. A Formal Evaluation

12. Resources: Professional Organizations

13. Resources: Books/Journals/Guidelines

A Developmental Checklist:
Ages Two to Three

Play—Independent and Group Play

_____ Child is beginning to play imaginatively and creatively.

_____ Child can play independently for a reasonable period of time.

_____ Child is learning to play cooperatively with peers.

_____ Child is beginning to make choices and solve problems during peer play.

_____ Child initiates and expands play opportunities.

_____ Child is demonstrating thinking and logic during play.

_____ Child is developing small-motor skills (e.g., cutting, pasting, assembling manipulatives, organizing constructs).

_____ Child is developing large-motor skills (e.g., jumping in place, climbing on jungle gym, catching a ball, balancing on one foot, coordinating body movements during creative activities, riding a trike, performing simple gymnastic exercises).

Learning—Listening, Oral Language, Basic Skills, Thinking and Conceptual Development, Following Simple Directions, Comprehension, Recall, Imitating, Attending to a Task, Problem Solving, Self-management, Social Skills

_____ Child can manage personal needs.

_____ Child is demonstrating independence and initiative.

_____ Child can listen without much distraction.

_____ Child can focus on an idea, a story, or an activity.

_____ Child demonstrates self-control.

_____ Child is developing a good attention span during circle-time.

_____ Child can follow directions.

_____ Child demonstrates reasoning.

_____ Child is beginning to discriminate like and unlike objects.

_____ Child is beginning to understand concepts.

_____ Child can understand one-to-one correspondence.

_____ Child can recognize numbers one through five or more.

_____ Child is beginning to understand some spatial concepts (e.g., over/under, in front of/behind/between, far/near, full/empty).

_____ Child demonstrates curiosity.

_____ Child can complete a simple task.

_____ Child demonstrates perceptual/motor skills.

_____ Child demonstrates sensory awareness and discrimination.

_____ Child is developing recall.

_____ Child is beginning to count.

_____ Child can recognize basic shapes.

_____ Child can assemble simple puzzles.
_____ Child is acquiring basic language skills.
_____ Child can recognize some letters.
_____ Child can repeat rhyming words and simple verses.
_____ Child can recognize own name.
_____ Child can identify familiar words.
_____ Child is developing an awareness of sounds (phonics).
_____ Child can comprehend stories.
_____ Child can remember "What comes next?"

The Arts—Painting, Arts and Crafts, Making Wood Constructs with glue and paint, Music, Movement, and Dramatic Play
_____ Child enjoys painting at an easel.
_____ Child applies himself/herself to project-at-hand.
_____ Child demonstrates creative thinking in artwork.
_____ Child enjoys dramatic play with peers.
_____ Child is demonstrating imagination.
_____ Child uses language to express himself/herself.
_____ Child can focus on dramatic play for a reasonable period of time.
_____ Child is learning to cooperate and to take the position of a friend in order to sustain a play experience.
_____ Child is demonstrating body coordination in creative movement activities.
_____ Child can recall simple verses and nursery rhymes.
_____ Child can coordinate movement and language in finger plays.
_____ Child is demonstrating recall.
_____ Child is developing an attention span during group activities that focus on the arts.

Nurturing—Self-development and Social Development
_____ Child is developing a good self-concept.
_____ Child is showing independence and initiative.
_____ Child is beginning to demonstrate self-control and patience.
_____ Child respects and cares for equipment.
_____ Child has a good attitude most of the time.
_____ Child can perform simple tasks (washing hands, putting a chair under a table, putting shoes on, getting a jacket for outdoor play or an apron for artwork).
_____ Child is learning to wait his/her turn.
_____ Child is interested in peers.
_____ Child is developing affection.
_____ Child can play cooperatively.

_____ Child is developing good manners.
_____ Child is cooperative during pick-up and transitions.
_____ Child is a good eater.
_____ Child appears to be healthy and active most of the time.
_____ Child sleeps during naptime.
_____ Child is happy.
_____ Child is beginning to self-manage.
_____ Child is beginning to express feelings in positive ways.
_____ Child is making a good adjustment to his/her environment.

Special qualities: _____

Things that child enjoys doing: _____

Things that are still difficult: _____

Ways that parents can assist in child's development: _____

_____

_____

_____

Special friends: _____

Concerns: _____

_____

_____

Recommendations: _____

_____

_____

Name of child: _____   Evaluation code:

Teacher: _____   Use check or check minus

Date: _____   Date of parent conference: _____

A Developmental Checklist: Ages Four to Five

Play—Independent and Group Play

_____ Child plays imaginatively and creatively.

_____ Child displays initiative and independence.

_____ Child is able to make choices.

_____ Child is able to solve problems.

_____ Child can play cooperatively with friends.

_____ Child demonstrates self-control most of the time.

_____ Child is able to share and take turns.

_____ Child demonstrates patience toward peers and projects.

_____ Child demonstrates responsibility in the care and handling of materials.

_____ Child communicates needs.

_____ Child shows an interest in completing tasks.

_____ Child can play for reasonable periods of time without adult intervention.

_____ Child is developing social skills.

_____ Child is developing interests and competency in play tasks.

_____ Child is developing large-motor skills.

_____ Child is developing fine-motor skills.

Child is particularly interested in: _____

Child is particularly good at: _____

Learning—Language, Math/Science, and Thinking

_____ Child is developing sensory awareness.

_____ Child can discriminate, sort, and classify materials.

_____ Child is demonstrating organization.

_____ Child can group numbers, match numbers, and work with simple sets.

_____ Child can identify numbers 1 to _____.

_____ Child can identify shapes.

_____ Child can understand a one-to-one correspondence.

_____ Child can see likenesses and differences among objects.

_____ Child enjoys table games and activities.

_____ Child can assemble puzzles with little difficulty.

_____ Child is beginning to understand qualitative terms such as equal/unequal, long/short, empty/full.

_____ Child is developing concepts.

_____ Child enjoys hands-on experiences in a discovery center.

_____ Child is developing language fluency.

_____ Child communicates needs and ideas appropriate to his or her age.

_____ Child demonstrates comprehension and recall.
_____ Child reasons and asks questions.
_____ Child demonstrates problem solving and flexible thinking.
_____ Child can recognize few, some, most, all letters.
_____ Child can identify beginning and ending consonant sounds.
_____ Child can recognize and use vowel sounds (a, e, i, o, u).
_____ Child can read familiar words.
_____ Child is developing an interest in books.
_____ Child can read simple sentences.
_____ Child enjoys language experience activities.
_____ Child enjoys writing in a personal journal.
_____ Child is beginning to write inventively.
_____ Child enjoys listening to records and storybook tapes.
_____ Child can follow directions.
_____ Child uses his/her time constructively.
_____ Child is motivated to learn.

Child is particularly interested in: _____

Child is particularly good at: _____

The Arts—Drama, Painting, Arts and Crafts, Music, Movement, Woodworking
_____ Child demonstrates originality and creativity.
_____ Child stays on task and shows pride in work.
_____ Child can cut, paste, and assemble materials.
_____ Child is interested in expressing himself/herself through many mediums of art.
_____ Child demonstrates patterning and symmetry in artwork.
_____ Child demonstrates spatial organization and perspective.
_____ Child demonstrates a good concept of self in artwork.
_____ Child demonstrates confidence and resourcefulness.
_____ Child cleans up after activities with little need for teacher intervention.

Child is particularly interested in: _____

Child is particularly good at: _____

Nurturing—Self-development, Social Development
_____ Child is developing a good self-concept.
_____ Child is developing a sense of responsibility.
_____ Child is developing values and good social conduct.
_____ Child is patient and caring toward peers most of the time.
_____ Child demonstrates affection and love.
_____ Child expresses feelings.
_____ Child is developing emotional control.

_____ Child has a positive attitude most of the time.
_____ Child is a helper in the classroom.
_____ Child is cooperative in peer play.
_____ Child is conscientious in his/her attitude toward tasks.
_____ Child is developing a sense of community.
_____ Child is developing life skills.
_____ Child is becoming an independent thinker.
_____ Child has good manners.
_____ Child appears to be happy and well-adjusted.

Special qualities: _____
_____
_____

Areas of concern: _____
_____
_____

Recommendations: _____
_____
_____

Name of child: _____   Evaluation code:
Teacher: _____   Use check or check minus
Date: _____   Date of parent conference: _____

A Developmental Checklist: School-Age Children

Play—Independent and Group Play

_____ Child enjoys independent play.

_____ Child enjoys group play.

_____ Child enjoys sociodramatic play.

_____ Child can follow the rules of a game.

_____ Child can play cooperatively with peers.

_____ Child demonstrates problem-solving skills.

_____ Child communicates effectively.

_____ Child demonstrates good perceptual-motor skills.

_____ Child can play constructively for reasonable periods of time.

Child is particularly interested in: _____

Child is particularly good at: _____

Learning—Thinking, Problem Solving, Initiative, Motivation, Organizational Skills, Staying on Task, Competency, Social Skills

_____ Child applies himself/herself to a task with a good attitude and a sense of determination.

_____ Child is developing skills in strategy games.

_____ Child uses language effectively.

_____ Child is developing interests and talents.

_____ Child enjoys challenging games with peers.

_____ Child can think and solve problems.

_____ Child makes good use of time.

_____ Child is motivated to learn.

_____ Child is organized and a good self-manager.

_____ Child shows initiative and independence.

_____ Child interacts effectively with peers most of the time.

_____ Child shows interest in projects and classroom activities.

Child is particularly interested in: _____

Child is particularly good at: _____

The Arts—Drama, Painting, Arts and Crafts, Music, Movement, Woodworking, Creative Writing, and Arts Classes

_____ Child enjoys expressing himself/herself in the arts.

_____ Child demonstrates creative thinking.

_____ Child has a good attitude toward activities in self-expression.

_____ Child makes choices and selects activities that are interesting and challenging.

_____ Child demonstrates leadership in coordinating group projects that involve the dramatic arts and writing.

_____ Child is resourceful and imaginative.

_____ Child is acquiring knowledge about his/her artistic heritage.

Nurturing—Self-development, Social Development

_____ Child is developing a sense of identity.

_____ Child demonstrates confidence and self-esteem.

_____ Child is developing a sense of autonomy.

_____ Child expresses empathy and kindness toward others.

_____ Child has friends and appears to be well-adjusted.

_____ Child demonstrates patience and self-control.

_____ Child has a good attitude.

_____ Child uses judgment in decision making; understands consequences.

_____ Child is motivated and challenged by his/her environment.

_____ Child demonstrates responsibility toward homework and classroom chores.

_____ Child can cope with problems and handle stress most of the time.

_____ Child is interested in community projects.

_____ Child demonstrates leadership in organizing and implementing nurturing projects.

_____ Child can take the position of another.

_____ Child expresses feelings and emotions in healthy ways.

_____ Child is trustworthy.

_____ Child has a sense of community and the greater world.

Special qualities: _____

_____

Areas of general concern: _____

_____

Areas of specific concern: _____

_____

Recommendations: _____

_____

Name of child: _____   Evaluation code:

Teacher: _____   Use check or check minus

Date: _____   Date of parent conference: _____

A Science Unit for a Class of Four- or Five-year-olds

1. *A Brief Description of the Unit:* A teacher plans to present a science unit that will integrate learning and the arts through hand-on activities. She wants children to learn to identify and appreciate nature from first-hand experience in their own backyard, and she wants children to become aware of how seasons and nature interact.

2. *Main Objectives:* To identify, compare, and contrast items in nature; to develop sensitivity toward living things; to develop understandings about changes—falling leaves, migration, and preparation for winter.

3. *Procedures and Materials:* Teacher will have children collect leaves, materials for nests, feathers, and nutmeats. As they gather items, children are encouraged to use their senses, to discriminate, and to make observations. Children's findings are sorted, labeled, and stored for placement in a discovery center. During the following days, the teacher plans to extend children's learning about leaves and related subjects such as a life cycle, self-preservation, and ways that children can help nature during the winter months. To develop her three themes she will use objects from nature, literature, films, projects, and language experience activities. She also will plan fieldtrips and special events.

4. *New Words:* The teacher makes a chart of the words that children have selected, e.g., leaf, tree, fall, winter, migration, hibernation, nest, food, snow, sleep. Next to each word, a child is asked to draw a corresponding picture.

5. *Integrated Activities:*

For leaves—Children will identify and sort leaves by shapes and names. They discover that some leaves are smooth, some have prickly points, others are lobed. Some leaves are green, some turning colors, and some are brown. The teacher points out that some trees hold onto their leaves (evergreens) while others drop their leaves (deciduous). The latter are leaves that can no longer make food for plants; they are tired leaves that can no longer give off oxygen (photosynthesis). The teacher will read A. R. Tresselt's "Johnny Mapleleaf," a sensitive story about a leaf that finally decides it's time to let go. Additional activities include leaf rubbings (place a leaf between two pieces of paper and rub the surface with the flat side of a crayon); stained glass leaves to hang in a window (shave pieces of multicolored crayons, put shaving on a real leaf placed between two pieces of wax paper, press lightly with a warm iron until the wax has melted and blended); and leaf people that will become the focus of an original language experience story (paste a leaf on paper, add personality with markers and create an illusion of dancing or falling leaves). Children also may enjoy leaf imprints (painting a leaf and pressing it onto plain paper), leaf play (raking and jumping in leaves), and making their own fall tree. The children may enjoy being falling leaves:

> *The red leaves are falling, are falling, are falling,*
> *The red leaves are falling all over the town,*
> *And winter is coming, is coming, is coming,*
> *And winter is coming, when the leaves are all down.*
> *The squirrel will sleep, will sleep, will sleep,*
> *The squirrel will sleep, curled up in a tree,*
> *And snow falls so gently, so gently, so gently,*
> *And snow falls so gently, on you and on me.*

For migration—A teacher may introduce the concept by reading Eric Carle's *Very Hungry Caterpillar* and Charlotte Zolotow's *Something Is Going to Happen* to stimulate children's senses about forthcoming changes. She may direct attention to birds by pointing out the concept of migration for some animals, hibernation for others, and winter survival for those that neither migrate nor hibernate. She may expand understandings by asking about ways that grown-ups and children prepare for winter. Activities will include: finger-print drawings that depict birds in flight, making bird stations, recording bird sounds, identifying birds that stay behind, making birdfeeders and reading "The First Snowfall," by Anne and Harlow Rockwell. Depending on children's interest, the unit can be expanded to how animals adapt to winter, the squirrel gathering and storing acorns, the rabbit nesting, the bear seeking a quiet place to sleep.

For people—This unit provides an opportunity for teachers to discuss seasonal changes and their impact on people, animals, and plant life. Children might discuss seasonal activities such as raking, cleaning furnaces, and canning. Discussions might include how people interact with nature in positive ways such as feeding animals, mulching plants, and protecting vulnerable plants from winter's cold. Discussions also might include how people can help one another through seasonal changes by focusing on people who have special needs or who are deprived of necessities.

6. *Complementary Literature:* In addition to the above activities, teachers may plan to read favorite stories that depict seasonal changes and a need for adaptation, "The Sleepy Bear" by Lydia Dabcovich, "The Snow Day" by Ezra Keats, "Frederick" by Leo Lionni, "Sylvester and the Magic Pebble" by William Steig, *The Ugly Duckling*, by Hans Christian Andersen, "Annie and the Old One" by Miska Miles, "Katie and the Big Snow" by Virginia Lee Burton, "Goodnight Moon" by Margaret Wise Brown, "The Caterpillar and the Polliwog" by Jack Kent, "Animals Sleeping" by Masayauki Yabuchi.

7. *Special Events and Culminating Experiences:* Teachers may take children to visit nature centers, invite park rangers and scouts to speak to children, show educational films such as "Winter Comes to the Forest," and plant bulbs for spring blooming. Children may enjoy raking leaves, making jam, making feeding stations, and planning winter projects for people in their environment with special needs (visitations, letter writing, and ongoing group projects). They may shop for favorite consumables like hot chocolate, pancake mix, and lots of peanut butter for long winter days in child care.

A Literature Theme for a Class of Five-year-olds

1. *Name and Author:* "The Red Balloon" by Albert Lamorisee.

2. *Focus:* This tender and symbolic story about a lonely little boy's love for a red balloon is a cherished contribution to children's literature. When neighborhood bullies taunt Pascal and throw stones at his beloved balloon, the sky is suddenly filled with balloons rising in freedom, carrying Pascal away from sadness and loneliness. The interpretive focus is on creative movement.

3. *Main Objectives:* The teacher shares the book with her children to prepare them for interpreting the moods and feelings that are generated. The story is extremely symbolic—the balloon is real to Pascal who is a very lonely little boy. The balloon symbolizes to Pascal and to the reader freedom, hope, and companionship. The teacher wants to generate awareness and identification in children so that they can experience empathy. She wants them to express themselves symbolically through creative movement by "becoming" balloons.

4. *Procedure and Materials:* There is one red balloon used as a prop near a circle area that will be used for dramatic improvisation (the children "become" balloons). The teacher creates a mood of sensual identification between a child and a balloon fantasy. She tells a story:

> Oh wouldn't it be fun to be a balloon for just a little while; to pick a favorite color, curl up tight, and slowly move through space? Would you like to be a balloon for just a little while? Just close your eyes and imagine yourself a balloon. Gradually unfold—open your arms and expand your bodies into space. You are swaying back and forth until you feel at one with your world. The gentle wind is your friend, guiding you through your journey into space. Soft raindrops will fall on you. Soft clouds will be there for rest. Balloon friends will pass, nodding and bobbing about, happy to be free and open to whatever comes next. . . . Stop for a moment and pretend you are looking at haystacks, hills and mountains, grazing cattle, rushing streams, and old sleepy houses . . . flashing lights, bustling cities, and the organ-grinder man! Fly high, little friends, until you are at your journey's end. . . . Then, fall gently back to earth and be with your friends—red, yellow, blue, green, and deep purple; and all the colors of the world.

5. *New Words:* The children follow up the experience with an original book about balloons; the children select the key words to print in their book: balloon, boy, fly, clouds, red, yellow, green.

6. *Outcome:* Teachers will want to evaluate each experience in terms of objectives achieved and staff development.

A Discovery Theme for a Class
of Four-year-olds

1. *An Idea:* The teacher would like children to understand the practical uses for beans as well as their creative potential. In the course of a day, she will provide many opportunities for children to discover beans.

2. *Main Objectives:* The teacher would like children to understand the food value of beans, how they grow, different ways they can be eaten, and their creative potential. She would like children to take a concrete object and expand their thinking toward conceptual awareness.

3. *Procedures and Materials:* The teacher shares various kinds of beans with children during a group circle, identifying them by name, comparing them, and discussing how they are eaten or used. The children get to open up beans and to examine the interior. Children may compare moistened beans to packaged beans to demonstrate expansion or growth (the wet beans swell). Each child then gets to plant a bean in a styrofoam cup filled with dirt. The teacher talks about how beans grow and their environmental needs. She points out that bean plants, if taken care of, can grow very, very tall—like Jack's beanstalk. The teacher will complete her circle by reading, "Jack and the Beanstalk."

4. *Extended Activities:* Children may make a bean collage on a paper plate (arts and crafts), play beanbag games (movement and listening skills), make baked beans for lunch, and sort and count beans (science and math). At the end of the day children can play a bean game. A child sits in a chair, hides her eyes, and a classmate takes a bean that had been placed under her chair. All children put their hands behind their backs. The child says, "Bean, bean, who took my bean, someone who is VERY mean." The player gets three turns to pick the mean friend who has taken her bean.

5. *New Words:* The teacher can have children add their favorite words to a word bank in the science center: beans, dirt, sun, water, germinate, grow, food.

6. *Evaluation:* It may be a good idea for teachers to note how a lesson went—what worked well, what needs to be changed, or any other observations that could help with a different group.

A Project for School-Age Children

1. *Project Design:* The children will design a format for a center newspaper to be published monthly.

2. *Estimated Time Frame:* They anticipate publishing their first newspaper within the month.

3. *Materials Needed:* A typewriter, paper, and a copying machine.

4. *Main Objectives:* A cooperative project such as publishing a monthly newspaper encourages:

- Skill development;
- Cooperative interaction;
- An interest in reading a real newspaper;
- A greater awareness of one's community and world;
- Incentive and interest in a school-age program;
- A sense of pride and accomplishment;
- Continuity and mastery.

5. *Classroom Activities:* Children elect editors, select a name (*The Express*) and make decisions regarding: the length of the paper, its readership, how many copies will be needed, the cost of producing a paper, and the subjects that will be included in their newspaper. They decide to have a sports section, a fashion section, a "what's going on" section, a "getting to know our center" section, a free-writing section, a comic section, and a crossword puzzle on the last page. They weigh the advantages and disadvantages of having a short paper each month or a long paper every two months. Because the cost of printing the paper is a consideration, the children give some thought to selling copies. They decide to distribute the paper free to students in their center but to sell copies to parents or friends of the center for $.15 per copy. It is hoped that, in time, they will be able to buy a computer. The teacher suggests the possibility of a spring fund-raiser for this purpose.

6. *Community Activities:* The children visit the offices of a local paper to learn more about the publishing field. They meet several writers and visit with editors. A follow-up visit to observe how a paper is printed is planned for the following week. The children ask their new friends to evaluate their first newspaper.

7. *A Culminating Activity:* A "staff" party is planned to celebrate the center's first newspaper.

8. *Resources:* The teacher brings in several newspapers to share with the children and to stimulate ideas. She invites a parent "writer" to speak to children about publishing a real book.

9. *Evaluation:* The children are enthusiastic about their newspaper to the extent that they are working on articles at home. They especially enjoy interviewing peers, parents, and staff members for their "getting to know our center" section. Coordinating pictures and writing is difficult for children of this age and requires teacher assistance. Because the teacher is a fairly good typist, she decides to help with typing and layout. The children decide to extend their project in the near future to interviewing famous people in the community. A child photographer suggests taking pictures and the project continues to grow.

An example of a child's writing:

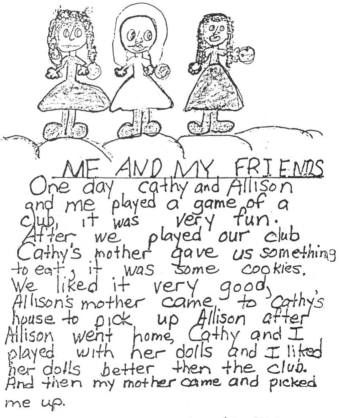

ME AND MY FRIENDS
One day, Cathy and Allison and me played a game of a club, it was very fun. After we played our club Cathy's mother gave us something to eat, it was some cookies. We liked it very good. Allison's mother came to Cathy's house to pick up Allison after Allison went home, Cathy and I played with her dolls and I liked her dolls better then the club. And then my mother came and picked me up.

BY: JULIE
GRADE 3

A Sample of Clustering

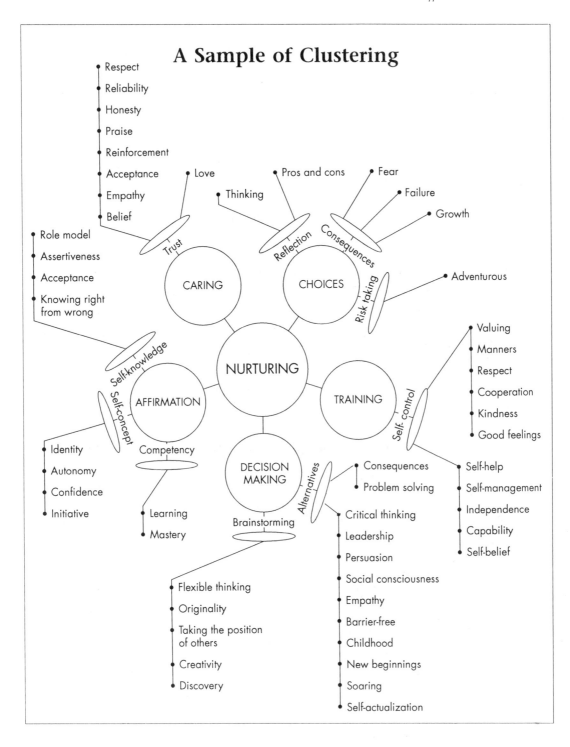

A Self-evaluation Form for Teachers

Name: _____   *Code:* Teachers may rank their responses from
Session: _____   1 (excellent) to 3 (needs improvement).
Date: _____

Controls children in directed activities by using positive role-modeling to encourage participation and enthusiasm.

     1   2   3

Permits children an appropriate degree of freedom and choice during open activity periods.

     1   2   3

Presents materials and ideas that are interesting and innovative to children.

     1   2   3

Is prepared and organized before coming to class.

     1   2   3

Arranges and sets up table activities in an attractive, inviting manner.

     1   2   3

Has a good command of basic content areas: language, math, science, social studies.

     1   2   3

Has a basic understanding how how children learn: by active, independent exploration, by playing, by cooperative experiences, by interacting with teachers, by self-initiated experiences, by solving problems and making choices.

     1   2   3

Provides many opportunities for hands-on discovery learning and creative expression.

     1   2   3

Manifests a knowledge of child development in handling emotional problems or disruptive behavior.

     1   2   3

Prepares and presents units creatively and effectively.

     1   2   3

Understands the importance of nurturing by cultivating values and developing theme-related activities.

     1   2   3

Values individuality in children's choice of activities, manner of play, expression, modes of learning, and levels of interests.

      1   2   3

Is tolerant and sensitive to children's differences and preferences.

      1   2   3

Encourages children to do their best in a noncompetitive and positive atmosphere.

      1   2   3

Provides opportunities for children to develop competencies in practical life activites such as cooking, gardening, cleaning.

      1   2   3

Reads in the field, attends workshops, and visits other schools for the prupose of obtaining new ideas about teaching, equipping, managing, and enjoying a child care environment.

      1   2   3

Praises children honestly without inhibitions, predispositions, or unrealistic expectations.

      1   2   3

Welcomes new ideas and is willing to share with others.

      1   2   3

Is effective in observing and documenting children's progress and/or problems as they occur.

      1   2   3

Is conscientious in attending to the duties and responsibilities required of staff in this center.

      1   2   3

Is tuned in to children's needs by showing caring and patience to children in stresss or who are unable to cope with their environment.

      1   2   3

Understands the importance of communicating effectively with parents so that children can fully benefit from their child care experiences.

      1   2   3

Appreciates the importance of reinforcing appropriate values, morals, and positive lifestyles.

      1   2   3

Contributes to a child's lifelong learning by opening doors of understanding to the immediate community and the larger world.

      1   2   3

An Informal Evaluation

Evaluator: _____

Date: _____

Class: _____

Teacher: _____

Things I liked: _____

_____

_____

Comments on the program: _____

_____

_____

Comments on the environment: _____

_____

Comments on interactions: _____

_____

Evidence of creativity: _____

_____

Ideas to think about: _____

_____

Center resources you may enjoy using: _____

_____

_____

A Formal Evaluation

Code: Check + = excellent
      Check   = satisfactory
      Check − = not satisfactory

Evaluator: _____

Teacher: _____

Class: _____

Date: _____

Child Development—The teacher is effective in developing or promoting:

_____ Practical life readiness skills;

_____ Foundational skills;

_____ Self-management;

_____ Language skills;

_____ Reasoning and thinking skills;

_____ Problem-solving skills;

_____ Fine- and large-motor skills;

_____ Creative expression;

_____ Social skills;

_____ Self-awareness and self-concept;

_____ Responsibility and initiative;

_____ Healthy attitudes toward self and others;

_____ Self-control;

_____ Independence and decision making;

_____ Valuing and moral development;

_____ Good work habits;

_____ Cooperative learning;

_____ Self-esteem and confidence;

_____ An awareness of health and nutrition.

The Environment—The teacher is organized so that the environment:

_____ Reflects orderliness and creativity;

_____ Offers children many choices and opportunities for hands-on discovery learning;

_____ Offers many opportunities for self-expression and imagination;

_____ Provides interesting materials that are age-appropriate;

_____ Does not appear overcrowded or overstimulating;

_____ Reflects children's interests and abilities;

_____ Provides a healthy balance between active and quiet play;

_____ Offers many opportunities for children to play independently;

_____ Offers many opportunities for children to play with peers;

_____ Provides personal space for children's belongings;

_____ Provides storage space that is neat and uncluttered;

_____ Is defined by activity centers;

_____ Provides a place for communicating with parents;

_____ Is language-rich offering a wide variety of activities and resources;

_____ Promotes creative thinking and independent learning;

_____ Is soft and cozy with special places for children to enjoy;

_____ Provides many opportunities for large-motor play;

_____ Provides areas for specialized instruction in movement and the creative arts.

Personal Attributes—The teacher reflects:

_____ Friendliness and empathy;

_____ Patience and love;

_____ Organization and competency;

_____ Responsibility and reliability;

_____ Good teaching skills;

_____ Good classroom management skills;

_____ An understanding of the center's philosophy and objectives;

_____ Encouragement and cooperation;

_____ High professional standards;

_____ Creative thinking and originality;

_____ Unbiased, objective teaching qualities;

_____ An ability to communicate;

_____ An ability to motivate and inspire children;

_____ A respect for cultural diversity;

_____ Good feelings among staff and parents;

_____ An interest in learning and growing in her field;

_____ The potential for leadership.

Parent Relationships—The teacher demonstrates an ability to work with parents in partnership:

_____ Parents are pleased with their child's program;

_____ Parents are involved in classroom activities and special events;

_____ There is an effective system of communication between the teacher and parents;

_____ Parents found their conference informative, objective, and well prepared;

_____ Parents are fully informed about fieldtrips, special events, activities, and monthly plans.

Resources:
Professional Organizations

Organizations that provide useful research reports, information, advice, and conferences on all aspects of child care are:

American Child Care Foundation,
  Inc.
1801 Robert Fulton Drive, Suite 400
Reston, VA 22091

Association for the Care
  of Children's Health
3615 Wisconsin Avenue, NW
25 E Stree, NW
Washington, DC 20016

Association for Childhood Education
  International
11411 Georgia Avenue, Suite 200
Wheaton, MD 20902

California Child Care Resource
  and Referral Network
320 Judah Street, Suite 2
San Francisco, CA 94122

Child Care Information Exchange
P.O. Box 2890
Redmond, WA 98073

The Child Care Law Center
625 Market Street, Suite 815
San Francisco, CA 94105

The Children's Defense Fund
25 E Street, NW
Washington, DC 20001

The Children's Foundation
1420 New York Avenue, NW
Suite 800
Washington, DC 20005

The Southeastern Pennsylvania
  School-Age Child Care Project
601 Knight Road
Ambler, PA 19002

High/Scope Educational Research
  Foundation
600 North River Street
Ypsilanti, MI 48198-2898

The National Association
  for Child Care Management
1800 M Street, NW
Washington, DC 20036

National Association for the
  Education of Young Children
  (NAEYC)
1834 Connecticut Avenue, NW
Washington, DC 20009-5786

National Commission on Children
1111 18th Street, NW, Suite 810
Washington, DC 20036

Save the Children, Inc.
Southern States Office
1182 West Peachtree Street, NW
Suite 209
Atlanta, GA 30309

Society for Research in Child
  Development
5720 South Woodlawn Avenue
Chicago, IL 60637

Wellesley School-Age Child Care
  Project
Center for Research on Women
Cheever House
Wellesley, MA 02181

RESOURCES:
BOOKS/JOURNALS/GUIDELINES

For Early Childhood Programs

Bredekamp, Sue, ed. *Developmentally Appropriate Practice in Early Childhood Programs Serving Children from Birth through Age Eight.* Washington, DC: NAEYC, 1987.

Brown, Janet F., ed. *Curriculum Planning for Young Children.* Washington, DC: NAEYC, 1982.

Cook, Annette Tessier, and Virginia Ambruster. *Adapting Early Childhood Curricula for Children with Special Needs.* St. Paul, MN: Toys 'n Things Press, 1987.

Derman-Sparks, L. *Anti-Bias Curriculum: Tools for Empowering Young Children.* Washington, DC: NAEYC, 1989.

Dodge, Diane Trister. *The Creative Curriculum for Early Childhood.* Washington, DC: Teaching Strategies, Inc., 1989 (distributed by Gryphon House, Inc., P.O. Box 275, Mt. Rainier, MD 20712).

———. *A Guide for Supervisors and Trainers on Implementing the Creative Curriculum for Early Childhood.* Washington, DC: Teaching Strategies, Inc., 1988.

Hamilton, Darlene S., and Bonnie M. Flemming. *Resources for Creative Teaching in Early Childhood Education,* 2d ed. Washington, DC: Harcourt Brace Jovanovich, 1977.

Hohmann, B. Banet, and D. P. Weikart. *Young Children in Action.* Ypsilanti, MI: High/Scope Press, 1979.

Hohmann, B. Banet. *Study Guide to Young Children in Action.* Ypsilanti, MI: High/Scope Press, 1983.

James, Jeanne C., ed. *A Planning Guide to Preschool Curriculum.* Winston-Salem, NC: Kaplan Press, 1976.

Katz, L., and S. Chard. *Engaging Young Children's Minds: The Project Approach.* Norwood, NJ: Ablex, 1989.

Mitchell, G., and H. Chmela. *I Am! I Can!: A Preschool Curriculum.* Marshfield, MA: Telshare Publishing Co., Inc., 1987.

Segal, M., and D. Adcock. *Play and Learning.* Fort Lauderdale, FL: Nova University Series,

1979. (Available from: B. L. Winch & Associates, 45 Hitching Post Drive, Bldg. 2, Rolling Hills Estates, CA 90274.)

Segal, M., and A. Manburg, eds. *All About Child Care: Books 1, 2 and 3.* Fort Lauderdale, FL: Nova University, 1981.

Staifer, Steffen. *Practical Solutions to Practically Every Problem: The Early Childhood Teacher's Manual.* St. Paul, MN: Toys 'n Things Press, 1990.

For School-Age Programs

Baden, R. K., A. Genser, J. A. Levine, and M. Seligson. *School-Age Child Care: An Action Manual.* Dover, MA: Auburn House, 1982.

Bender, J., C. H. Flatter, and B. E. Schuyler-Hass. *Half a Childhood: Time for School-Age Child Care.* Nashville, TN: School-Age NOTES, 1984.

Bergstrom, Joan M. *School's Out—Now What?* Berkeley, CA: Ten Speed Press, 1984.

Blau, R., E. H. Brady, I. Bucher, et al. *Activities for School-Age Care.* Washington, DC: NAEYC, 1989.

Dorman, Gayle. *Programs for Young Adolescents: Planning Programs for Young Adolescents.* Chapel Hill, NC: Center for Early Adolescence, 1985.

Fink, Dale. *School-Age Children with Special Needs: What Do They Do When School's Out?* Boston, MA: School-Age Child Care Project, 1988. (Available from School-Age Child Care Project, Center for Research on Women, Wellesley, MA 02181.)

Lefstein, L., W. Kerewsky, E. A. Medrish, and C. Frank. *Young Adolescents at Home and in the Community.* Chapel Hill, NC: Center for Early Adolescence, 1982.

The Multicultural Project for Communication and Education. *Caring for Children in a Social Context.* Cambridge, MA: The Multicultural Project for Communication and Education (71 Cherry Street, Cambridge, MA 02139).

Neugebauer, Roger, ed. "School-Age Child Care," Reprint #101 *Child Care Information Exchange.*

Newman, Roberta L. (President). "Indicators of Quality in School-Age Child Care." In *American Child Care Foundation, Inc.* presented at conference "Perspectives on School-Age Child Care," 1991. (Available from: ACCF, 1801 Robert Fulton Drive, Suite 400, Reston, VA 22091.)

Scofield, Richard T., ed. *School-Age NOTES.* (Available from: School-Age NOTES, P.O. Box 120674, Nashville, TN 37212.)

Tiedt, Pamela L., and M. Iris. *Multi-Cultural Teaching: A Handbook of Activities, Information and Resources.* Boston: Allyn and Bacon, 1979.

For the Arts

Arnosky, Jim. *Sketching Outdoors in Autumn.* New York: Lothrop, 1988.

Bjork, Christina. *Linnea in Monet's Garden.* New York: Metropolitan Museum of Art, 1989.

Cromwell, Liz, and Dixie Hibner. *Finger Frolics.* Livonia, MN: Partner Press, 1976.

Egan, K., and D. Nadaner, eds. *Imagination and Education.* New York: Teacher's College Press, 1988.

Eisner, Elliot W. *Educating Artistic Vision.* New York: Macmillan, 1972.

Feldman, Edmund B. *Becoming Human Through Art.* Englewood Cliffs, NJ: Prentice-Hall, 1970.

Frank, Marjorie. *I Can Make a Rainbow.* Nashville, TN: Incentive Publications, 1976.

Froman, R. *Street Poems.* New York: Dutton, 1971.

Hopkins, L. B. *Pass the Poetry, Please.* New York: Citation Press, 1972.

Laughlin, Mildred. *Readers Theatre for Children: Scripts and Script Development.* Denver, CO: Teacher Ideas Press (Libraries Unlimited Inc.), 1990.

Lessac, Frane. *Caribbean Canvas.* New York: J. B. Lippincott, 1987.

McCaslin, Nellie. *Creative Dramatics in the Classroom,* 2d ed. NY: David McKay Co., 1974.

Mayesky, Mary. *Creative Activities for Young Children.* Albany, New York: Delmar, 1985.

Moore, L. (compiler) *Go With the Poem.* New York: McGraw-Hill, 1979.

———. *Something New Begins.* New York: Atheneum, 1982.

Morrison, L. *The Sidewalk Racer and Other Poems of Sports and Motion.* New York: Lothrop, 1977.

Nelson, Esther L. *Musical Games for Children of All Ages.* New York: Sterling Publishing, 1976.

Petrich, Patricia, and Rosemary Dalton. *The Kids' Arts and Crafts Book.* Concord, CA: Nitty Gritty Books, 1975.

Redleaf, Rhoda. *Teachables II: Homemade Toys That Teach.* St. Paul, MN: Toys 'n Things Press, 1987.

Richards, Emil and Celeste. *Making Music Around the Home and Yard.* New York: Award Music Co., 1974.

Romberg, Jenean, and Miriam Rutz. *Art Today and Every Day.* New York: Parker Publishing Company, 1972.

Ryder, Joanne. *Under Your Feet: A Book of Poems.* New York: Four Winds Press, 1990.

Siks, G. B. *Creative Dramatics, An Art of Children.* New York: Harper & Row, 1960.

Spolin, Vila. *Improvisation for the Theatre.* Evanston, IL: Northwestern University Press, 1963.

Ward, W. *Playmaking for Children.* New York: Appleton-Century-Crofts, 1957.

Weske, E. B. *Exploring Music: Kindergarten.* New York: Holt, Rinehart and Winston, 1969.

Worth, V. *Small Poems.* New York: Farrar, 1972.

———. *More Small Poems.* New York: Farrar, 1976, 1978, 1984.

For Child Health Information

Aronson, S. S. "Health Update: Health Concerns for Caregivers." *Child Care Information Exchange* 54 (March 1987): 33–37.

———. "Care of Ill Children in Child Care Programs." *Child Care Information Exchange* (July, 1987): 34–38.

————. "What to Do About Rashes." *Child Care Information Exchange* (May 1985): 26–28.

————. "Prevention and Management of Infectious Diseases in Child Care." *Child Care Information Exchange* (December 1984): 8–10.

————. "Child Care for Children with Chronic Illness." *Child Care Information Exchange* (January 1986): 14–16.

Harrison, D. D. *Health and Safety for Young Children: Child Involvement in Personal Health.* New York: Macmillan, 1974.

Kendrick, A. S., R. Kaufmann, and K. P. Messenger, eds. *Healthy Young Children: A Manual for Programs.* Washington, DC: NAEYC, 1988.

Kerr, A. *Health, Safety, and Nutrition Early Childhood Curriculum.* Carson City, CA: Lakeshore Curriculum, 1985.

Marotz, L., J. Rush, and M. Cross. *Health, Safety, and Nutrition for the Young Child.* Albany, NY: Delmar, 1985.

Peterson, P. *Ready . . . Set . . . Grow!! A Comprehensive Health Education Curriculum for 3–5 Year Olds.* St. Paul, MN: Peterson Publishing, 1984.

Reinish, E. H., and R. E. Minear, Jr. *Health of the Preschool Child.* New York: Wiley, 1978.

For Child Safety Information

American Red Cross. *Standard First-Aid and Personal Safety,* 2d ed. New York: Doubleday, 1979.

Aronson, S. *First Aid in Child Care Settings.* Washington, DC: American Red Cross, 1988.

————. "Aids and Child Care Programs." *Child Care Information Exchange* (November 1987): 35–39.

Green, M. *A Sigh of Relief—The First-Aid Handbook for Childhood Emergencies,* 2d ed. New York: Bantam, 1984.

National Highway Traffic Safety Administration. *We Love You—Buckle-Up!.* Washington, DC: (distributed by) NAEYC, 1984.

Rovertson, A. A. *Health, Safety & First Aid: A Guide for Training Child Care Workers.* Bear Lake, MN: Toys 'n Things Press, 1980.

U.S. Consumer Product Safety Commission. *A Handbook for Public Playground Safety,* vols. 1 and 2. Washington, DC: 1981.

For Child Nutrition Information

Bershad, C., and D. Bernick. *Bodyworks: The Kid's Guide to Food and Physical Fitness.* New York: Random House, 1981.

Brody, J. *Jane Brody's Nutrition Book.* New York: W. W. Norton, 1981.

Goodwin, M. T., and G. Pollen. *Creative Food Experiences for Children.* Washington, DC: Center for Service in the Public Interest, 1980.

National Dairy Council. *Chef Columbo.* Rosemont, IL: National Dairy Council, 1979.

Natow, A., and J. A. Hesline. *No-Nonsense Nutrition for Kids.* New York: McGraw-Hill, 1984.

Strickland, J., and S. Reynolds. "The New Untouchables: Risk Managment for Child Abuse in Child Care—Policies and Procedures." *Child Care Information Exchange* 64 (December 1988): 33–36.

————. "The New Untouchables: Risk Management for Child Abuse in Child Care—New Laws and Trends." *Child Care Information Exchange* 66 (April 1989): 51–55.

U.S. Department of Agriculture, Food and Nutrition Service. *A Planning Guide for Food Service in Child Care Centers.* Washington, DC: U.S. Government Printing Office, 1985.

Vonde, D., and J. Beck. *Food Adventures for Children.* Redondo Beach, CA: Plycon Press, 1980.

Wanamaker, N., K. Hearn, and S. Richarz. *More Than Graham Crackers: Nutrition Education and Food Preparation with Young Children.* Washington, DC: NAEYC, 1979.

APPENDIX C

HEALTH, MEDICAL, NUTRITION AND SAFETY GUIDELINES

The material and forms in this appendix can be used as guidelines to ensure that basic requirements and most state regulations are followed. As necessary, forms can be adapted and/or expanded.

1. Health and Emergency Guidelines

When a Child Becomes Sick at the Center
Temperature and Thermometer Tips
Signs and Symptoms of Illness
General Guidelines for Preventing the Spread of Disease
Cleaning and Disinfecting
   Cleaning Hints
   Sanitizing a Center
Outdoor Play
Naptime
Brushing Teeth
Handwashing
A First-Aid Kit
Disaster Planning
Poison Prevention
Guidelines for Pets
Recognizing Child Abuse and Neglect
Appropriate Discipline Can Prevent Child Abuse

2. Medical Guidelines

Medication Administration
A Physician's Medication Order Form
An Emergency Information Form
A Sample Questionnaire for Special Needs Child
An Accident Log
An Accident Report Form

3. Nutrition Guidelines

USDA Child Care Food Program Requirements
Sample Breakfast and Lunch Menus
Snacks
Choking

4. Safety Guidelines

Playground Safety Checklist
Site Safety Checklist

The source for health, emergency, medical, and nutrition guidelines is:

Health Guidelines for Child Care Providers, June 1990
Montgomery County Department of Health
Child Care Consultation Services
Montgomery County, MD 20852

The source for safety guidelines is:

Statewide Comprehensive Injury Prevention Program
Massachusetts Department of Public Health
150 Tremont Street
Boston, MA 02111

Health and Emergency Guidelines

WHEN A CHILD BECOMES SICK AT THE CENTER

The center policy should list the diseases that require exclusion. Diarrhea, vomiting, undiagnosed rashes, fever, pallor, irritability, excessive sleepiness, and change of behavior are signs of illness that must be noted. If a child has any of these signs, the parent should be notified and the provider must make the decision whether to exclude or further observe the child. When a child is sent home, he should remain at home for at least 24 hours or submit a written statement, from the physician, approving the return to the center. Advise parents to arrange a plan for backup care in case a child becomes ill.

When a child becomes ill while in your care, every attempt must be made to keep him comfortable until the parent arrives. Have a cot and blanket available. The bedding must be washed after each use. Separate the ill child from the other children, but keep her within sight and hearing of an adult. Notify the parents to pick up the child from the center. If parents cannot be reached, notify the person designated on the emergency card. If neither parents nor persons designated on the emergency cards can be reached, or if parents are delayed in picking up the child and the child's condition warrants immediate medical attention (i.e., bleeding, breathing problems, very high fever—105°F), call 911.

TEMPERATURE AND THERMOMETER TIPS

Fever can be a sign of illness, but a child also can be sick and not have a fever. The recommended method for taking a preschooler's temperature is under the armpit. The child's arm should be held securely against his body for four minutes. The normal armpit temperature is 97.6°F, one degree lower than oral temperature.

A school-age child can use an oral thermometer. Keep the thermometer in the child's mouth for three minutes. The normal oral temperature is 98.6°F. Any child with a temperature of 100°F or above is considered to have a fever and should be sent home.

To clean the thermometer: wash it with soap and cold water, rinse in water, soak in chlorine solution, air dry. Use the same strength solution you use to wash toys and dishes. Wash the thermometer even when a plastic sheath is used. Store in a clean, dry container.

SIGNS AND SYMPTOMS OF ILLNESS

Appearance/Behavior: Child looks or acts differently than usual: unusually tired, pale, lacking appetite, confused, irritable, difficult to awaken, has a fever of 100°F or above.

Source: Pages 431–457 adapted from *Health Guidelines for Child Care Providers,* June 1990, Montgomery County Department of Health, Child Care Consultation Services. Used with permission.

Breathing and Coughing: See respiratory symptoms.

Diarrhea: An increased number of and/or abnormally loose stool in the previous 24 hours.

Eye/Nose Drainage: Thick mucous or pus draining from the eye or nose.

Fever: Remember that temperatures taken under the arm are one degree lower than oral temperatures. Therefore, one degree Fahrenheit should be added to the armpit reading. Any child with a temperature of 100°F or above is considered to have a fever.

Respiratory Symptoms: Difficult or rapid breathing, severe cough, high-pitched croupy or whooping sound after cough.

Skin Problems: Skin rashes, undiagnosed or contagious.

Infected Sores: Sores with crusy, yellow or green drainage.

Sore Throat: Sore throat and/or difficulty swallowing, especially when fever or swollen glands in the neck are present.

Unusual colors: Eyes or skin is yellow (jaundice); stool is grey or white; urine is dark, tea colored. These symptoms can be found in hepatitis and should be evaluated by the family health-care provider.

Vomiting: Two or more episodes of vomiting within the previous 24 hours.

GENERAL GUIDELINES FOR PREVENTING THE SPREAD OF DISEASE

Children should be observed daily for changes in their health and behavior. Concerns should be shared with parents and appropriate referrals for health and developmental evaluations should be made.

Diseases Spread Through the Intestinal Tract

Child care facilities that accept diapered children are at the greatest risk for the spread of diseases such as infectious diarrhea. Diseases that spread through contact with stool are among the most common in child-care facilities.

Because intestinal tract illnesses spread so easily, good handwashing is especially important. Children and staff members should be taught to consider all stool to be infectious.

Thorough handwashing alone can reduce the incidence of diarrhea in day care centers by as much as 50 percent.

Some simple rules to prevent the spread of all intestinal tract diseases are:

- Encourage frequent and thorough handwashing for all staff and children.
- Consider using disposable gloves when changing diapers.
- Preparation of food should not be done by the same staff member who changes diapers.
- Try to have each staff member work with only one group of children.
- Disinfect diaper-changing areas after every diaper change.
- Change diapers only in diapering area. Separate diaper area from food storage, preparation, and eating areas.
- Wash hands after diapering, helping a child in the bathroom, and before preparing or eating food.
- Have child wash hands after using bathroom.
- Clean and disinfect potty seats, toilets, and toys daily or when soiled.
- Store soiled diapers in covered containers, away from food and other items used by children and staff. Empty as needed, and at least daily.
- The use of cloth diapers should be discouraged.
- Sinks used for handwashing should not be used for food preparation.

Diseases Spread Through the Respiratory System

Another group of diseases common in child-care groups are respiratory infections. These diseases are spread through droplets from nose, eye, or throat secretions. Respiratory-tract illnesses range from the common cold to more serious illnesses such as whooping cough or bacterial meningitis.

Respiratory diseases can spread through the air when a person coughs, sneezes, speaks, or blows his or her nose. They also can be spread by objects contaminated with saliva or nasal secretions. In fact, an infected person often spreads the disease before coming down with symptoms. The spread of many of these diseases can be avoided by thorough handwashing after coming in contact with secretions and potentially contaminated objects. Proper disposal of infected tissues also is important.

Some simple rules to stop the spread of all respiratory system diseases are:

- Wash hands thoroughly after contact with nose, throat, and eye secretions and before preparing and eating food.
- Do not allow food to be shared.
- Air out center every day.
- Use disposable towels and tissues.
- Dispose of tissues in a covered container.

Diseases Spread by Direct Contact (Touching)

Direct contact is another common cause of infections in day-care settings. A child or staff member can get these diseases simply by touching the infected area of another person's body, secretions, or personal objects. These infections spread easily in a day-care setting.

Some simple rules to stop the spread of diseases by direct contact are:

- Wash hands thoroughly after contact with possible infectious secretions.
- Use disposable tissues and towels.
- Dispose of tissues properly.
- Have a bin handy for collecting mouthed toys after a child uses them. Clean and disinfect these toys before another child plays with them.
- Provide each child with individual cots and sheets.
- Do not allow children to share personal items such as brushes, combs, blankets, hats, or clothing.
- Store each child's dirty clothes separately in plastic bags. Do not launder children's clothing at the center.
- Wash and cover all sores, cuts, or scrapes promptly.

Diseases Spread Through Blood

Some very serious illnesses are spread through contact with infected blood. These diseases are not common in day care. They are so serious that staff members should be acquainted with them and ways to prevent them.

The viruses that cause these illnesses can be spread when blood containing the virus enters the blood stream of another person. This can happen when infected blood comes in contact with a broken surface of the mucosa (such as inside lining of the mouth, eyes, nose, or rectum). An infected mother also can transmit these infections to her newborn infant. Once these viruses enter a person's body, they may stay for months or years. This person may appear healthy, but can spread the virus.

Some simple rules to help prevent the spread of diseases due to blood contact:

- Wash hands thoroughly after handling any secretions, even when gloves are worn.
- Use disposable gloves when handling blood or items soiled by blood.
- Clean all blood spills promptly and then disinfect the area with a bleach solution. (See the following guidelines for Disinfecting.)

CLEANING AND DISINFECTING

General Information

Child-care settings bring children together for long periods of time, where they may be exposed to many different germs. Although the environment cannot be made germ-free, the harmful effects of germs can be lessened by keeping their numbers at low levels. Germs can most effectively be controlled by: 1) handwashing by children and staff, 2) frequent, thorough cleaning and disinfection of objects that come into contact with children and staff. In addition, proper handling and disposal of contaminated items are necessary to prevent the spread of infections.

Definitions

Cleaning: A mechanical process (scrubbing), using soap or detergent and water, that removes dirt, debris, and large numbers of germs. It also removes invisible debris that interferes with disinfection. Disease-causing germs grow best in warm, moist debris, but they may be found even on objects that are not visibly soiled.

Disinfecting: A process that destroys specific, harmful germs outside the body with chemicals (bleach, alcohol, etc.) or physical agents (heat, for example).

Sanitizing: A process that reduces the amount of germs to a "safe" public health level.

Cleaning Hints

Plan and post a cleaning schedule. Encourage staff to share the responsibility and make sure that all assignments are completed and performed at regular intervals.

Cribs, Cots, Linens:
- Cots that are used by more than one child should be cleaned and sanitized after each use. (See next section for solutions to use.)
- If used for the same child continually, cots and linens should be cleaned and sanitized weekly or more often if soiled. An additional supply of clean linens should be available.
- Sheets and blankets may remain folded on the child's own cot or in the child's cubby. Be careful that each child's bedding is kept separate.

Toys:
- All toys should be capable of being routinely and effectively cleaned.
- Baby toys (such as rattles) that frequently enter the child's mouth should be removed and placed in a basket or box for cleaning and sanitizing before they are reused.
- All other toys should be washed monthly or more often if necessary. Many stuffed toys can be washed in a washing machine. Some plastic toys can be washed in a dishwasher. Other toys need to be washed with soap and water, rinsed with water, and either sprayed or submerged in a sanitizing solution of chlorine and water.

Food Surfaces:
- Equipment surfaces used for feeding such as high-chairs, trays, infant seats, and feeding tables should be cleaned off immediately after each use. High-chair trays and other eating surfaces should be sanitized after each use, and before reuse, if used for purposes other than eating.

- Use disposable placemats and dishes to decrease the spread of germs. **Be sure the food preparation sink is separate from the handwashing sink.**
- Serving area—counters, tables, chairs, and so on, should be scrubbed and sanitized weekly.
- Floor of feeding area should be cleaned after each use. Eating areas should not be carpeted to simplify the cleanup of spills.
- Soak soiled mops and nondisposable cleaning equipment in a sanitizing solution for 10–30 minutes immediately after use.

Sanitizing a Center

The following are suggested strengths for sanitizing solutions of bleach (sodium hypochlorite) based on 5.25% available chlorine.

¼ cup bleach to 1 gallon water	Disinfect potty seats, diaper area, and toilet
1½ teaspoons bleach to 1 gallon water	Sanitize general surfaces such as equipment, floors, and walls
¾ teaspoon bleach to 1 gallon water	Sanitize mouthed toys, eating utensils, and surfaces that come in contact with food/tables, refrigerators

Bleach solutions must be made fresh daily because bleach loses its ability to kill germs with time.

Important: Objects and surfaces contaminated with blood should be disinfected immediately after cleaning procedure. Use a 1:10 solution of bleach and water (2 tablespoons of bleach to 1 cup of water) that is freshly made up for any object or surface contaminated with blood.

Procedures

Cleaning:
- Clean objects and surfaces by scrubbing with detergent and fresh water to remove debris. Do not reuse water that has been standing in pails, basins, or sinks.
- Use disposable towels and discard.
- Rinse objects (under running water when possible).
- Follow cleaning with disinfection of the area/objects.
- **Clean objects and surfaces contaminated with blood and body fluids immediately.**
- Wear disposable gloves when:
  - Handling blood (nosebleeds, cuts) or blood/body fluid-soiled items, surfaces, or clothing, especially if you have open cuts or sores on your hands.
  - Cleaning bathrooms.

Wash hands **immediately** after contact with any body fluids, even if gloves have been worn. Wash thoroughly and vigorously with soap and water, under warm running water, for at least 20 seconds. Discard disposable gloves after use.

Disinfecting and Sanitizing: A recommended disinfectant for child-care settings is a solution of household bleach and water. A bleach solution is recommended because it is effective, inexpensive, readily available, and not harmful to humans, surfaces, and objects when used as recommended.

Recommended bleach solutions: First, clean the surface with detergent and water, rinse with water, then saturate the area with the bleach solution, and allow to air dry. Always use a single-service, disposable towel and discard in a plastic-lined container.

OUTDOOR PLAY

Children thrive outdoors. They eat better, sleep better, play better, learn better, and look better. Outdoor time should be scheduled for both morning and afternoon. Even a few minutes of fresh air is beneficial. While the children are outside, open the windows in the classroom. The fresh air will decrease the bacteria count in the room. In cold weather, plan outdoor playtime in the late morning and early afternoon, and keep the children indoors during the coldest period of the day. During the summer, the time can be changed to early morning and late afternoon in order to keep children indoors during the hottest time of the day. Because the location of each playground differs, the amount of sun, shade, wind, or ice should be considered when planning outdoor activities. In hot weather, water activities are fun; take a water table outside. Have children wash their hands before they play in it. Never use a wading pool; it is not sanitary. Use a sprinkler. Make sure the towels are dried and stored separately.

How cold is cold? Temperature and wind both affect the heat lost from the body. The effect of these two factors is the wind chill index. If the wind chill index is zero degrees (0°F) or below, keep the children indoors. Make sure children and staff are dressed appropriately for the weather.

NAPTIME

Naptime is an important part of all preschool programs. Tired children tend to be irritable, uncooperative, and more likely to succumb to the spread of disease. Rest time should be planned to provide each child with a cot and bedding in a quiet, semi-dark area. Post a cot chart designating where each child will sleep.

Adjust the transition time to suit the needs of the group. Some children will have trouble settling down after active play; others can go to sleep right after running around outdoors. Staff should be available to comfort and reassure children who are having difficulty settling down. Soft music, a story, a favorite toy, or a backrub will encourage a child to make the transition from active play to rest.

All preschool children need a rest on a cot. At the discretion of the director, older children who need less rest time should be permitted quiet play on or off their cots. Their cots can be placed away from the sleepers in an area that is not so dark.

Rest time is a good time for staff to relax. However, it must be remembered that staff will be needed to help evacuate sleepy children in case of an emergency. Therefore, it is important that the staff-child ratio be maintained at naptime.

BRUSHING TEETH

Start a good health habit. Children can be taught to brush their teeth at an early age. Toothpaste is good, but if you feel it is too messy, don't use it. Water and friction will dislodge most of the food particles.

Store the brushes in an open rack on the wall or use a plastic ice cube tray turned upside down with a hole punched into the bottom of each compartment. Use your imagination, but make sure the brushes are stored separately, so they don't touch. Each brush and storage slot should be labeled with the child's name. Do not use egg cartons—germs from the eggs could get on the brushes.

When two-year-olds are enrolled in a child-care program, parents should be advised to wean them off the bottle and pacifier. If the pacifier is needed to help with transition from home to center, we suggest using it only at naptime. This will prevent the pacifier from being dropped on the floor and picked up by another child. Pacifiers should never been worn on a string around the neck. Bottles should be discouraged; two-year-olds are able to drink from a cup.

HANDWASHING

Handwashing is the most effective way to stop the spread of disease. Germs are transmitted by hand contact from person to person. Children and staff should wash hands:

- When arriving at the center;
- Before preparing food or eating;
- After toileting and diapering;
- After handling body fluids (i.e., blood, vomit, urine, stool, mucous);
- After touching pets;
- Before starting water play.

Both staff and children should be made aware of the following effective handwashing method. Children need supervision when washing hands. Twenty seconds is a good amount of time to wash. Using a timer will show the children how long a period of time twenty seconds is.

- Use soap and *running* water.
- Rub hands vigorously.
- Wash all surfaces, including: backs of hands, wrists, between fingers, and under fingernails.
- Rinse well.
- Dry hands with a paper towel.
- Turn off the water using a paper towel instead of bare hands.

Children like using liquid soap. Wash the container and pump before refilling it. Bar soap can be a media for bacteria. If it is used, be sure to keep the soapdish free of the "jelly-like residue."

Children should not sit on the floor after washing hands before mealtime. Guide them to the table and have them play a finger game or sing a song while they wait for the meal. Keep the waiting time short because the children will get restless and start fighting or playing with the dishes on the table.

FIRST-AID KIT

The following list of first-aid equipment is recommended. Please note that these recommendations do not take the place of state regulations (available from most city or state public health departments).

A quick-reference first-aid manual
Note cards and pen
Thermometer
Flashlight
Blunt-tip scissors
Tweezers
10 4" × 4" gauze pads
10 2" × 2" gauze pads
1 roll 4" flexible gauze bandage ("Kling")
1 roll 2" flexible gauze bandage ("Kling")
25 1" and 25 assorted small Band-Aids
1 roll 1" bandage tape
2 triangular muslin bandages
Syrup of Ipecac (give only when ordered by a Poison Control agent)

In addition, we suggest a fieldtrip first-aid kit that includes: coins for use in pay phones, soap for washing wounds, cleaning pads, and a list of emergency phone numbers.

DISASTER PLANNING

Planning for evacuation in the event of fire, flood, sudden loss of heat, water, air conditioning failure, or other disaster is essential. Fire emergency plans should include use of direct and alternative exit routes and evacuation drills at different times of the day, including naptime. Drills should be held at least once a month. The chain of command and duties of each staff member in the event of an emergency should be worked out in advance and staff should be aware of the plan.

Arrangements should be made for a temporary shelter that can be used if children are evacuated. Parents should be informed of the location of this temporary shelter. When the children are moved to other space, the emergency cards should be taken so that parents can be notified quickly.

POISON PREVENTION

Each year at least 600,000 children are treated for accidental poisonings. Sixty percent of cases involve children younger than five years of age, with young children between the ages of one and three at the highest risk for poisoning.

Children put anything and everything into their mouths, even if it doesn't taste very good. This is why a center must make sure that all poisonous substances are out of the reach of children. Even if teachers don't think children can reach that far, they might find a way. Do not underestimate a young child. Where there's a will, there's a way.

Almost all household products and medications can be poisonous if swallowed in sufficient quantity. Even some art supplies can cause accidental poisonings.

- Be sure to store all art and cleaning supplies out of reach of the children.
- Keep all cleaning fluids, drain openers, and so on, in their original bottles with labels intact.
- Make sure that plants are nonpoisonous and hung out of the reach of children. Label the plants with their names for easy identification.
- Don't use diaper pail deodorants, stickers, or disks.
- Use only lead-free paint on equipment and walls. Buy toys painted with non-toxic paint.
- Use of aerosol sprays is discouraged.

GUIDELINES FOR PETS IN CHILD CARE FACILITIES

When an animal bite occurs in a center be sure to wash the area of the bite with soap and water, notify the parent and advise him to contact the child's physician. Be aware that there may be children in the center with animal allergies.

Kinds of Pets: Domestic, small, easy to maintain and keep in a small, covered cage.

- Recommended: Hamsters, gerbils, fish.
- Not recommended: Turtles, rabbits, poultry, cats, dogs, birds, snakes, lizards, salamanders, toads, frogs, and crabs. These are wild by nature, often found with disease, or hard to maintain in a classroom.

Where to Keep:
- Remove from food area—not in kitchen, food storage room, dining area, or other food service area.
- Caged—easily cleanable, covered cage.

Care:
- Clean cage daily or as necessary.
- Children should not assist with pet care or maintenance.
- Separate facilities are required for cleaning of cages and food service.
- Handwashing is mandatory after handling pets or pet waste.

Storage of Supplies: All pet food and cleaning supplies should be separate from food service supplies.

Pet Health: All pets should be in healthy condition; pets that appear ill should be isolated and brought to veterinarian.

Sources of Pets: Licensed pet shops or other sources approved by the local heath department.

Waste Disposal: Waste must be disposed of away from the food service area and away from children.

RECOGNIZING CHILD ABUSE AND NEGLECT

Child abuse and neglect is a serious problem that requires the involvement of all private citizens and professionals in the community for the purposes of prevention, identification, and treatment. In most states, the child abuse and neglect law requires that anyone who **suspects** a child has been or is being mistreated must report the matter to the Department of Social Services. (In cases of child abuse, a report may be made to Social Services or the Police.) Any professional who knowingly fails to make a required report of child abuse may be subjected to certain professional sanctions. The professionals identified in most states include: health practitioners, police officers, educators, and social workers. And, any person who, in good faith, makes a report of abuse or neglect is immune from any civil liability or criminal penalty.

The following information is provided so that child-care providers will be familiar with the physical and behavioral indicators of child abuse and neglect. Please note that the presence of any of these indicators does not necessarily mean a child is being abused or neglected. They may, however, lead one to suspect abuse or neglect and therefore to report it.

Physical Abuse

Physical Indicators

Bruises: on any infant; facial bruises; in unusual patterns; clustered in one area of the body; in various stages of healing; both eyes "blackened" with no injury to the nose.

Burns: caused by immersion in hot liquid; cigarette burns usually on palms of hands (leaving crater-shaped burns); caused by a hot implement, such as an electric curling iron (leaving burn marks in the shape of the implement); or caused by ropes that indicate confinement.

Welts, cuts, abrasions, fractures, and internal injuries: Because these injuries may occur through normal childhood experiences, they should only cause concern when coupled with some other physical or behavioral indicator. Child-care providers also should be concerned if the injury does not seem likely to have resulted from normal activity, given the child's age and physical development.

Behavioral Indicators

Child: overly compliant, shy, or aggressive behavior; avoids parents; inhibited crying; hyperactive; avoids physical contact; low tolerance for frustration; distrustful.

Parent: holds unrealistic expectations for the child's physical or emotional development, "immature", dependent; aggressive; low sense of self-esteem; sees the child as "bad," "different," or "evil," low tolerance for frustration; inappropriate coping skills.

Protective service agencies will investigate reports of physical abuse where there is suspicion of **all** of the following:

- The child is younger than 18 years of age.
- There is a current, nonaccidental injury to the child.
- The alleged abuser is a parent or someone in a temporary caretaker role at the time of the injury.

Sexual Abuse

Physical Indicators

Child: difficulty in sitting or walking; repeated symptoms of medical problems with the genitals or digestive system; venereal disease; pregnancy.

Behavioral Indicators

Child: unusual sexual behavior or knowledge; nightmares; poor peer relationships; few social skills, extremely isolated; repeated "runaways."

Parent: extremely overprotective; overly interested in child's social and sexual life; sees child as highly sexualized; jealous.

Protective service agencies will investigate reports of sexual abuse ranging from allegations of suspected sexual fondling or child pornography, to allegations of sexual intercourse with a child. The child must be younger than 18 years of age and the alleged abuser must be a parent or someone in a temporary caretaker role at the time of the incident.

Suspected abuse by a stranger should be reported to the police.

Concern about child abuse or neglect is often based on a series of observations or events that form a pattern. To effectively convey that pattern of information to the child protective agency, it is helpful, but not necessarily essential to reporting, that child-care providers document their observations.

Reporting cases of suspected child abuse and neglect is difficult. There often seems to be more good reasons not to report than to report. The child-care program must look at what is in the best interest of the child.

The law provides immunity from any civil liability or criminal penalty when a report is made in good faith. If a child-care provider suspects or knows of any type of child abuse, it is a center's responsibility to report it to the appropriate agency. If a center makes a legitimate report and the social worker indicates she or he is not going to investigate, ask to speak to a supervisor.

Neglect

Physical Indicators

Child: extremely dirty and unkempt; clothes inadequate for the weather; medical problems left untreated; inadequately supervised; undernourished.

Behavioral Indicators

Child: withdrawn, shy; passive; always tired; developmentally slow.

Parent: apathetic; shows little concern or awareness of the child's needs; shows anger when questioned about child's care; impulsive in making decisions; inconsistent disciplinary practices; overwhelming personal needs.

Protective service agencies will investigate reports of neglect that indicate a suspicion that a child younger than 18 is suffering some harm because of some action or omission on the part of a parent or caretaker.

Generally, categories of physical, medical, educational, moral, and emotional aspects of a child's care are considered when assessing reports of neglect.

APPROPRIATE DISCIPLINE CAN PREVENT CHILD ABUSE

All licensees or directors are encouraged to develop written policies for staff to use when establishing behavioral limits and controls and to distribute these policies to staff and parents. The recommendations of the American Academy of Pediatrics may be one source of information on developing a policy. "A Guide to Discipline" by Jeanette G. Stone, an NAEYC publication, is another source with many helpful ideas. In writing a discipline policy, a center may wish to include the following:

A General Statement that describes the center's understanding of how children develop, their maturity levels, and how staff members relate to children.

Specific Statements regarding positive approaches to discipline such as:

- Discipline is teaching and guiding, not punishment.
- Staff goal is the development of each child's internal controls leading to socially acceptable behavior.
- Reinforcement of positive behaviors is encouraged.
- Respect for children and their feelings is important.
- Director informs staff of the center's discipline policy, supervises staff, plans with them, and evaluates their performance.

Prohibitions: What center staff may **not** do:

- No physical/corporal punishment, or threats of such punishment.
- No verbal abuse; no belittling or demeaning children.
- No use of food as rewards or punishments.
- No isolating children out of sight or hearing of the staff.

Strategies the center uses for children who misbehave such as:

- Redirect young children; offer alternatives.
- Communicate with children in language they understand.
- Let children express their feelings and ideas.
- Set clear limits; establish and use rules consistently.

- Examine center's program to see if program or the room arrangement can be modified to better assist children and avoid conflicts.
- Staff models acceptable behavior, using polite, not authoritarian, language and quiet voices.

Parent–Center Relations

- Center works cooperatively with parents.
- Conferences with parents are encouraged.
- Center may suggest evaluation of a child and/or suggest resources or referrals.
- Center has a termination policy and parents have withdrawal rights when problems cannot be resolved. These policies are clearly communicated to parents, in writing, at enrollment time.

What About "Time Out"?

- It should *not* be the only strategy used by a center.
- If used, it should have clear age restriction: i.e., it should not be used with young children (under four years old). When used with children four years old and older, it should be for short periods of time (two to three minutes). If used, it must be clear that there is an adult close by.
- The purpose of "time out" should be explained to the child in a positive way, with the child given an opportunity to discuss what happened.

Medical Guidelines

MEDICATION ADMINISTRATION

Staff and parents should be informed of the center's policy for the administration of medication. The American Academy of Pediatrics advises that prescription and over-the-counter medication be given only on written authorization from a licensed health provider (i.e., physician or nurse practitioner) as well as from the child's parent. Have the parent obtain a signed Physician's Medication Order Form (see sample).

The following suggestions will help staff prevent errors in the administration of medication:

- The first dose of any medication should be given at home.
- Medications may be given only as prescribed and should be in the professionally labeled container.
- Read the label carefully. Make sure the person dispensing the medicine has the right child and the right medication and that all the instructions match.
- Question the parent if there are any concerns about the medication.
- Store medications as instructed on the label. All medications should be locked up at all times.
- Be alert to any side effects that may be developing as a result of the medication.
- Keep a record of when medication is given. If medication is not given when ordered, record reason for not giving it.
- If medication is found in a child's lunch box remove it, lock it up, call the parent and tell them that the medication was removed and why.
- Orders that medication is to be given "in case of" (i.e., asthma or bee stings) should state at whose discretion the drug is to be dispensed. This type of medication order should be renewed once a year by the physician. Be sure that a staff member has been trained by the parent or a physician on how to administer any medication that needs to be injected or inhaled.
- Children who need diaper rash medication (i.e., Desitin) need a physician's written order.
- Containers or bottles of over-the-counter drugs must be labeled with the child's name.

Useful Forms

Licensing agencies generally require day care centers to have completed forms, such as those shown on the following pages, on file for each child. If specific forms are not provided, use or adapt these as necessary in order to keep adequate information readily available.

PHYSICIAN'S MEDICATION ORDER FORM

To be filled out by physician ordering medication and returned to parent for delivery to center.

NOTE: A non-medical and non-nursing person will administer medication(s). If possible arrange time of dosage so that medication(s) will not have to be given while the child is in the center.

Name of patient: _____ Telephone: _____

Address of patient: _____

The following medication is to administered only until the following date: _____

The following medication(s) must be given during care hours:

Medication	Dosage	Hour Given

Administration (specify water, milk, food, etc.): _____

List any reasons for not giving medication at the prescribed time (vomiting, fever, drowsiness, convulsion): _____

The following medication is to administered only until the following date: _____

The following medication(s) are administered only at home:

Medication	Dosage	Hour Given

For all MEDICATIONS, including those given at home, list all side effects which should be observed by center personnel.

This form must be kept current. Whenever there is a change in the medication, the parents must have a new form completed by the physician.

Physician's Signature: _____ Date: _____

Address: _____ Telephone: _____

TO PARENTS: Before a day care center, its agents, employees or representatives, can administer any medication to your child, you are required to sign this authorization form which signifies your desire to have the medication(s) administered, as well as your agreement to relieve the center, its agents, employees or representatives of any responsibility for ill effects resulting from the administering of said prescribed medication as set forth herein.

We therefore authorize and request _____ to administer the medication(s) prescribed by our physician, and in so doing relieve the center, its agents, employees or representatives, of any responsibility for ill effects which may result from the administering of said prescribed medication.

Signature of Parent: _____

Witness: _____ Date: _____

EMERGENCY INFORMATION

For Day Care Centers, Day Nurseries, Family Day Care Homes,
Non-Public Nursery Schools and Kindergartens

Child's Name _____ Birthdate _____

Enrollment Date _____

Hrs. and Days of Expected Attendance _____

Child's Home Address _____

Mother's Name _____

Mother's Employer or School _____

Business Address _____

Business Telephone _____ Hrs. of Work _____ Days Off _____

Father's Name _____

Father's Employer or School _____

Business Address _____

Business Telephone _____ Hrs. of Work _____ Days Off _____

Name of Person Authorized to Pick-up Child (daily) _____

Address _____ Telephone _____

When parents cannot be reached: List at least one person who may be contacted in an emergency.

1. Name _____ Telephone _____
   Address _____

2. Name _____ Telephone _____
   Address _____

3. Name _____ Telephone _____
   Address _____

Child's Physician _____ Telephone _____

Address _____

Preferred Hospital for Emergency Care (if any) _____

Child's Dentist _____ Telephone _____

Address _____

In EMERGENCIES requiring immediate medical attention, your child will be taken to the NEAREST HOSPITAL EMERGENCY ROOM. Your signature authorizes the responsible person at the center to have your child transported to that hospital.

Signature of Parent or Guardian _____ Date _____

SAMPLE QUESTIONNAIRE FOR SPECIAL NEEDS CHILD

When writing a plan of care for a child with special needs who attends a child care center, the parent may wish to address the following:

1. Name of child: _____

2. Date of birth: _____

3. Name and phone number of physician/therapist: _____
   _____

4. Diagnosis or nature of special need: _____

5. Medications taken and possible side effects: _____

6. Special instructions for emergency situations: _____
   _____

7. Special treatments or procedures: _____
   _____

8. Self care needs:
   A. Toileting: What assistance, if any, is needed? _____
                   How will the child communicate toileting needs? _____
   B. Eating: What assistance, if any, is needed? _____
                   Are certain foods difficult to eat? _____
                   Are certain utensils easier to use than others? _____
                   Food likes and dislikes. _____
   C. Dressing: Is assistance needed with tying shoelaces, putting on hats, gloves, coats, etc? _____
   D. Sleeping: Does the child have difficulty in falling or staying asleep? _____
                   If so, what methods have been used to induce sleep? _____
   E. Locomotion: What are the child's limitations, if any? _____
                   Is a device, such as a wheelchair or crutches used to assist the child? _____

9. Socialization: How does the child interact with other children? _____
                   How does the child interact with adults? _____
                   How does the child feel about his special needs? _____

10. Language: What are the verbal skills of the child? _____
                   Are there any special words/signals that may be used to indicate wants? _____

11. Programming: Are there activities that the child especially enjoys? _____

_____

Are there any activities the parent or teachers/therapist
would like encouraged? _____

12. Behavior: What is the child's temperament? _____
What is the child's activity level? _____
Does she/he tire easily? _____
What kind of discipline has been found effective? _____

_____

13. Additional comments: _____

_____

_____

ACCIDENT LOG

Month _____ Year _____

Name	Age	Date	Time	Teacher	Place	Details	Follow-up

*ACCIDENT REPORT FORM**

DESCRIPTION

Name of injured _____

School/Center _____

Date of accident: _____ 19 ___ Time: _____

Describe how and where accident occurred _____

Describe injury _____

_____

_____

_____

MANAGEMENT

1. Describe first aid given and by whom _____

_____

_____

2. Did child continue activities? _____

3. Child transported by whom? _____

   Where? Home _____ Which Hospital _____

   Which clinic _____

   Physician's name and address: _____

   _____

   How were parents notified? _____

   Date _____ Time _____

LEGAL FOLLOW-UP

Report submitted by _____ Position _____

Date of report _____

*This report is to be made out for each injury a child receives. Completed forms are to be in-cluded in child's case record.

Nutrition Guidelines

USDA CHILD CARE FOOD PROGRAM REQUIREMENTS

		Age		
		1–2	**3–5**	**6–12**
BREAKFAST	Fluid milk	½ cup	¾ cup	1 cup
	Juice or Fruit or Vegetable	¼ cup	½ cup	½ cup
	Bread or Bread Alternate	½ slice*	½ slice*	1 slice*
SNACK (Supplement) select 2 out of 4 components	Fluid Milk	½ cup	½ cup	1 cup
	Juice or Fruit or Vegetable	¼ cup	½ cup	¾ cup
	Meat or Meat Alternate	½ ounce	½ ounce	1 ounce
	Bread or Bread Alternate	½ slice*	½ slice*	1 slice*
LUNCH/ SUPPER	Fluid Milk	½ cup	¾ cup	1 cup
	Meat or Poultry or Fish or	1 ounce	1½ ounces	2 ounces
	Cheese or	1 ounce	1½ ounces	2 ounces
	Egg or	1	1	1
	Cooked Dry Beans and Peas or	¼ cup	⅜ cup	½ cup
	Peanut Butter	2 tablespoons	3 tablespoons	4 tablespoons
	Vegetables and/or Fruits (2 or more) Bread or Bread Alternate	¼ cup total ½ slice*	½ cup total ½ slice*	¾ cup total 1 slice*

*or an equivalent serving of an acceptable bread alternate such as cornbread, biscuits, rolls, muffins, etc., made of whole-grain or enriched meal or flour, or a serving of cooked or enriched whole grain rice or macaroni or other pasta product

Source: From U.S. Department of Agriculture Food and Nutrition Service, Washington, DC: July 1989. For specific menu planning, see *A Planning Guide for Food Service in Child Care Centers,* revised July 1989. USDA Publication No FNS-64 (pp. 16–17). Available at most state child care agencies.

The sample menus that follow meet USDA requirements. Centers should serve milk to all children even those who bring their own lunch. This encourages parents not to send fruit drinks.

Sample Breakfast Menus

MONDAY	TUESDAY	WEDNESDAY	THURSDAY	FRIDAY
Orange Juice Wheatena Milk	Blueberries Wheaties Milk	Pineapple Chunks Oatmeal Milk	Orange Juice Cheerios Milk	Grapefruit Juice Scrambled Eggs Whole Wheat Toast with Butter Milk
Banana Wheaties Milk	Orange Juice Cream of Wheat with wheat germ Milk	Oatmeal Strawberries Milk	Grapefruit Juice Raisin Bran Milk	Sliced Oranges Cheerios Milk
Orange Juice Oatmeal with Milk Cinnamon Toast Milk	Pineapple Juice Raisin Bran Milk	Orange slices Cream of Wheat with wheat germ Milk	Peaches, sliced Wheaties Milk	Banana Peanut Butter on Whole Wheat Milk
Apple Juice Zucchini Bread Milk	Orange Juice Bagels with Cream Cheese Milk	Grapefruit Whole Wheat Toast with Cinnamon Milk	Peaches Oatmeal Milk	Stewed Fruit Cold Cereal Milk

Sample Lunch Menus

MONDAY	TUESDAY	WEDNESDAY	THURSDAY	FRIDAY
Meat Loaf Stewed Tomatoes Corn Whole Wheat Bread with Butter Pear Slices Milk	Spaghetti and Meat Sauce Green Salad Orange Sesame Muffin Watermelon Chunks Milk	Chicken Salad with Pineapple Chunks Green Pepper Sticks Summer Squash Whole Wheat Bread Rice Pudding Milk	Grilled Cheese Sandwich on Whole Wheat Toast Tomato Slices Sliced Peaches Oatmeal Cookies Milk	Tuna-Vegetable Salad Whole Wheat Bread with Butter Banana Milk
Baked Chicken Green Beans Bulghur (cracked wheat) Watermelon Chunks Milk	Hamburger- Tomato- Macaroni Casserole Green Salad Sliced Pears Milk	Grilled Cheese Sandwich Broccoli Carrot Sticks Apricot Halves Oatmeal Cookie Milk	Turkey Salad Sandwich on Whole Wheat 4 Bean Salad Cherries or Grapes Milk	Baked Stuffed Fish Fillets Spinach Broiled Tomato Halves Whole Wheat Bread Ice Cream Milk
Vegetable Soup Egg Salad on Whole Wheat Cucumbers Peaches Fig Newtons Milk	Hamburger Patty on roll Tomato Slices Cole Slaw Applesauce Milk	Cottage Cheese Corn bread Turnip, Celery, green pepper sticks Sliced Pears Milk	Roast Turkey String Beans Mashed Yellow Squash Whole Wheat Bread Orange gelatin Milk	Breaded Fish Potato Salad Broccoli Sliced Tomato Vanilla Pudding Milk
Fillet of Haddock Rice Mixed Veg. Bread Sticks Bananas Milk	Baked Chicken Baked Potatoes Carrots Rye Bread Fruit gelatin Milk	Lasagna Tossed Salad Roll Orange slices Milk	Chef's Salad w/egg, ham and cheese Bran muffin Baked apple Milk	Vegetable Soup Tuna Sandwich Celery sticks Frozen yogurt Milk

SNACKS

Snacks should be simple, easy to prepare, nutritious, and appealing to the children. School-age children would rather play than eat. Therefore, snacks must be planned to entice them. After sitting in class all day, some groups may need a short outdoor activity before snack. This age group can help plan the snack, prepare and serve the foods, set and clear the table. Try a buffet table to give the children a chance to choose their own snack. "Host" or "hostess" for the day is another way of involving a child in the food program.

Preschoolers also can help with meal preparation. A food project such as cutting and pasting pictures of nutritious foods can be fun. Young children also can help to wash and cut vegetables and fruits (use a small, dull knife). Children can measure, pour, and mix ingredients. Keep the activity simple to suit the child's age. Work with a few at a time and make sure everyone washed their hands before handling the food.

When planning menus both USDA-required food amounts, according to age, and food groups should be considered. A beverage should be served with each snack. Milk should be served at one snack and a serving of 100% fruit juice, fruit, or vegetable should be served at least once a day. If the requirement for two food groups has been fulfilled, water may be served. Cream cheese, butter, and jam are spreads and are not to be counted as a food group. Be sure to read food labels; the grain products must be prepared with enriched flour in order to be counted.

Sample Snack Menus

	MONDAY	TUESDAY	WEDNESDAY	THURSDAY	FRIDAY
AM	Oatmeal with Cinnamon and Raisins Milk	Bran Muffin Apple Juice	Dry Cereal Milk	Peanut Butter on Whole Wheat Orange Juice	Bagel Orange Wedge Water
PM	Hot Cider Bread Sticks	Fruit Kabobs Milk	Fresh Vegetables Cottage Cheese Water	Frozen Banana Pops Milk	Pita Bread Hummus Milk
AM	Scrambled Egg Juice	Raisin Bread Toast Milk	Hot Cereal with Bananas Milk	French Toast Applesauce Water	Boston Brown Bread Milk
PM	Whole Wheat Muffin Milk	Scones with Apple Butter Tomato Juice	Spinach Salad with Egg Milk	Macaroni & Cheese V-8 Juice	Fruit Cup Cottage Cheese Water

CHOKING

Many childhood deaths are the result of choking on solid foods. Children, younger than four, make up the highest risk group. Round, firm foods commonly cause children to choke and should be avoided. If a center chooses to serve them, be sure to take these precautions:

- Hot dogs—cut lengthwise into 4 sections
- Grapes—cut into fourths
- Peanut butter—serve on a hard surface such as a crisp cracker
- Raw carrots—cut in strips

Safety Guidelines

The checklists that follow have been adapted with permission from The National Association for the Education of Young Children and The Statewide Comprehensive Injury Prevention Program (SCIPP) in Massachusetts (Department of Public Health, 150 Tremont Street, Boston, MA 02111). They were originally printed in *Healthy Young Children: A Manual for Programs* (pp. 66–81, figures 6-6 and 6-7), eds. A. Kendrick, R. Kaufmann, and K. P. Messenger. Washington, DC: NAEYC, 1988.

PLAYGROUND SAFETY CHECKLIST

Checked by: _____

Item	Checked (yes/no)	Date	Corrections Made/Comments
All equipment Nuts, bolts, and screws are recessed, covered, or sanded smooth and level.			
Nuts and bolts are tight.			
Metal equipment is free of rust and chipping paint.			
Wooden equipment is free of splinters and rough surfaces.			
Equipment is free of sharp edges.			
Ropes, chains, and cables have not frayed or worn out.			
Equipment has not shifted or become bent.			
There are no "V" entrapment angles on any part of the equipment.			
There are no open holes in the equipment forming finger traps (e.g., at the ends of tubes).			
There is no corrosion at points where equipment comes into contact with ground surface.			
All parts of the equipment are present.			
Anchors for equipment are stable and buried below ground level.			
Children who use equipment are of the age/developmental level for which the equipment was designed.			
Slide ladders have handrails on both sides, and flat steps.			

Item	Checked (yes/no)	Date	Corrections Made/Comments
All equipment *(cont'd)* There is a flat surface at the bottom of the slide (if the slide is more than 4 feet high, the flat surface should be 16 inches in length).			
The bottom of the sliding surface is no more than 15 inches above the ground.			
There are no "tube" slides.			
There are no circular slides in the pre-school area.			
The sliding surface is not made of wood or fiberglass.			
If the slide is made in several pieces, there are no gaps or rough edges on the sliding surface.			
The sliding surface faces away from the sun or is located in the shade.			
The steps or rungs on the slide are slip-resistant.			
Steps and rungs are regularly spaced, 7 to 10 inches apart, from top to bottom.			
Rungs are between ¾ and 1½ inches in diameter.			
Climbing equipment An adequate impact-absorbing surface under the structure extends 6 feet beyond the sides of the apparatus.			
Handholds stay in place when grasped.			
Equipment height does not exceed 6 feet height.			
Climbers have regularly spaced footholds (7 to 10 inches apart) from top to bottom.			
There is an easy, safe way out for children when they reach the top.			
Rungs are painted in bright or contrasting colors so children will see them.			
Rungs, climbing bars, and handrails are between ¾ and ½ inch in diameter.			

Item	Checked (yes/no)	Date	Corrections Made/Comments

Climbing equipment *(cont'd)*
There is a 28 to 32 inch (or higher) barrier around preschool equipment that is more than 30 inches above the ground.

The space between slats of barriers does not exceed 4 inches.

There is no head entrapment area on the apparatus.

Ground surface
All elevated play equipment (slides, swings, bridges, seesaws, climbing apparatus) has 8 to 12 inches of impact-absorbing material underneath, such as sand, pea gravel, or wood chips. (Pea gravel and wood chips should be avoided in the infant/toddler areas.)

Surfaces are raked weekly to prevent them from becoming packed down and to remove hidden hazards (e.g., litter, sharp objects, animal feces).

Standing water is not found on the surface or inside equipment.

Spacing
Swings have adequate clearance in both directions (14 feet beyond the farthest extension of the swing: 8 feet of impact-absorbing surface, plus a 6 foot safety zone).

Swings are at least 18 inches from each other and 28 inches away from the frame.

Slides have 2½ to 3 yards of space at the bottom.

There is at least 8 feet between all equipment.

Boundaries between equipment are visible to children (for instance, painted lines or low bushes).

Play areas for active play (e.g., bike riding, running games) are located away from areas for quiet activities (e.g., sandbox, outdoor tables).

Slides
An adequate impact-absorbing surface under structure extends 5 feet beyond the sides of the apparatus.

Item	Checked (yes/no)	Date	Corrections Made/Comments
Slides *(cont'd)* Slides are 6 feet in height or less.			
Side rims are at least 2½ inches high (5 inches for circular or wave slides).			
Slides have a flat surface at the top (with safety barriers).			
Swings Swing seats with back supports and safety bars are available for toddlers and children with disabilities.			
All swing seats are made of canvas, rubber, or other pliable material.			
There are no "S" or open-ended hooks.			
Hanging rings are less than 5 inches, or more than 10 inches, in diameter (smaller or larger than child's head).			
The point at which the chain/rope and the seat meet is designed to prevent entrapment.			
Chain link openings do not exceed ¼ inch in diameter. When stationary, all seats are level.			
There are no more than two swings on any one apparatus.			
Preschool swing seats are at a maximum height of 18 inches.			
The swing seat cannot be rised more than 6 feet above the surface.			
For the tire swings, there is at least a 19 foot safety zone between the support structure and the farthest extensions of the swing.			
Tire swings have drainage openings.			
Plane swings (gliders) have stable handholds, footholds, and seats.			
Seesaws There is an adequate impact-absorbing surface under the structure and beyond the sides of the apparatus.			
The seating does not reach more than 5 feet above the ground.			
The fulcrum is enclosed or designed to prevent pinching.			
Handholds stay in place when grasped, without turning or wobbling.			

Item	Checked (yes/no)	Date	Corrections Made/Comments

Seesaws *(cont'd)*
A wooden block is on the underside of the seats **or** a rubber tire segment is buried in the surface under the seats.

Sandboxes
Sandboxes are located in a shaded spot.

The sand is raked at least every week to check for debris and to provide exposure to air and sun.

The box is covered at night to protect from moisture and animal excrement.

The sandbox has proper drainage.

Rocking equipment
There is an adequate impact-absorbing surface under the structure and extending 6 feet beyond the sides of the apparatus.

Seating surfaces are less than 39 inches about the ground.

There are no parts that could cause a pinching or crushing injury.

Handholds stay in place when grasped.

Footrests stay in place.

Tunnels
The internal diameter of the tunnel is at least 2 feet 6 inches.

There are two exits from the tunnel.

The tunnel is designed to drain freely.

General environment
The playground can be reached safely by children (on foot or bicycle).

The playground is accessible to people with disabilities.

If needed, a suitable perimeter fence is provided (e.g., if the playground is near a road, pool, or pond). Seating (benches, outdoor tables) is in good condition.

Item	Checked (yes/no)	Date	Corrections Made/Comments
General environment *(cont'd)* Signs give information about: • where to seek help in case of an emergency; • restrictions on the use of playground (hours, pets); • name and address of playground operator (to report hazards).			
A road sign advises motorists that a playgound is nearby.			
Trash receptacles are provided and located away from the play areas.			
Poisonous plants are removed from play area.			
There is a sources of clean drinking water available in the play area.			
There is shade.			
The entire play area can be seen easily for good supervision.			

SITE SAFETY CHECKLIST

Checked by: _____

Item	Checked (yes/no)	Date	Corrections Made/Comments
General environment There is a floormat or other nonskid surface at each entrance to the facility.			
Floors are smooth and have a nonskid surface.			
Pipes and radiators are not accessible to children or are covered to prevent contact.			
Hot tap water temperature for handwashing is 115°F or lower.			
All equipment with motor or an electrical connection is grounded.			
Electrical cords are out of children's reach and are kept out of doorways and traffic paths.			
Unused electrical outlets are covered by furniture, outlet covers, or shock stops			

Item	Checked (yes/no)	Date	Corrections Made/Comments
General environment *(cont'd)* Medicines, cleansers and aerosols are stored in their original containers and kept in a locked place where children are unable to see and reach them.			
Matches and lighters always are kept out of sight and reach of children.			
All windows have screens that stay in place when used; expandable screens are not used.			
Windows can be opened 6 inches or less from the bottom.			
All storage units are stable and secured against sliding and collapsing.			
Drawers are kept closed to prevent tripping or bumps.			
Trash is covered at all times.			
Walls and ceilings are free of peeling paint and cracked or falling plaster. Facility has been inspected for, and is free of, lead paint.			
There are no disease-bearing animals such as turtles, parrots, or cats.			
Children are always supervised.			
There is no asbestos.			
Equipment and toys Desks and chairs are in good repair and free of splinters and sharp edges.			
Toys and play equipment are checked often for sharp edges, small parts, and sharp points.			
Lead-free paint is used on all painted toys.			
Toys are put away when not in use. Whenever possible, open shelves are used.			
There are no toy boxes at the facility.			
Toys are appropriate for the age and abilities of the children who use them.			
Art materials are nontoxic and have either the AP or CP label.			
Art materials are stored in their original containers in a locked place.			

Item	Checked (yes/no)	Date	Corrections Made/Comments
Equipment and toys *(cont'd)* Audio-visual equipment (VCR, television, computer, film projector) is secured on stands in a way that prevents tipping.			
Teaching aids (e.g., projectors) are put away when not in use.			
Curtains, pillows, blankets, and cloth toys are made of flame-resistant materials and laundered regularly.			
Hallways and stairs Stairs and stairways are free of boxes, toys, and other clutter.			
Stairways are well lit.			
The right-hand railing on the stairs is at child height and does not wobble when held. There is a railing or wall on both sides of the stairway.			
Stairway gates are in place when appropriate.			
Doors to unsupervised or unsafe areas are always locked unless this prevents emergency evacuation.			
Staff is able to monitor strangers entering the building.			
Kitchen Trash is kept away from areas where food is prepared or stored.			
Trash is stored away from the furnace and hot water heater.			
No-Pest Strips are **not** used. Pesticides for crawling insects are applied by a certified pest-control operator.			
Cleansers and other poisonous products are stored in their original containers away from food and out of children's reach.			
Nonperishable food is stored in labeled, insect-resistant containers. Perishable food is stored in covered containers in the refrigerator.			
Food preparation surfaces are clean and free of cracks and chips.			
Eating utensils are free of cracks and chips.			

Item	Checked (yes/no)	Date	Corrections Made/Comments
Kitchen *(cont'd)*			
Electrical cords are placed where people will not trip over them or pull them.			
There are no sharp or hazardous cooking utensils within children's reach (e.g., knives, glass).			
Pot handles are always turned toward the back of the stove.			
The fire extinguisher can be reached easily.			
All staff members know how to use the fire extinguisher correctly.			
Bathrooms			
Stable step stools are available when needed.			
Cleaning products, soap, and disinfectant are stored in a locked place out of children's reach.			
Floors are smooth and have a nonskid surface.			
The trash container is emptied daily and kept clean.			
Water for handwashing is no hotter than 115°F.			
Emergency preparedness			
All staff members understand their roles and responsibilities in case of an emergency.			
At least one staff person is always present who is certified in first-aid and CPR for infants and children.			
The first-aid kit is checked at least monthly for supplies and kept where it can be reached easily by each staff member.			
Smoke detectors and other alarms are checked regularly to make sure they work (e.g., batteries replaced regularly).			
Each room and hallway has two fire escape routes posted in clear view.			
Emergency procedures, telephone numbers, and the address and directions to the facility are posted in clear view near all phones.			

Item	Checked (yes/no)	Date	Corrections Made/Comments
Emergency preparedness *(cont'd)* Children's emergency phone numbers are kept near a phone.			
All exits are clearly marked and free of clutter.			
Doors open in the direction of exit travel.			
Cots are placed so that walkways are clear for evacuation in an emergency.			
Traffic and pedestrian safety There is a safe drop-off and pick-up location for children arriving in motor vehicles.			
There is a clearly posted, one-way traffic pattern in the loading zone.			
Bus parking is isolated from the flow of automobile traffic and parking.			
Bus drop-off and pick-up times are supervised by a staff member each morning and afternoon.			
Signs are posted to warn motorists they are approaching a school zone.			

Source: Adapted from Statewide Comprehensive Injury Prevention Program (SCIPP), Department of Public Health, 150 Tremont Street, Boston, MA 02111.

Index